An Introduction to Human Movement
The Sciences of Physical Education

Charles H. Shea
Texas A&M University

David L. Wright
Texas A&M University

Allyn and Bacon

Boston   London   Toronto   Sydney   Tokyo   Singapore

Senior Series Editor: Suzy Spivey
Vice President, Editor-in-Chief, Social Sciences: Sean W. Wakely
Editorial Assistant: Amy P. Braddock
Marketing Manager: Quinn Perkson
Editorial-Production Administrator: Joe Sweeney
Editorial-Production Service: Walsh & Associates, Inc.
Composition Buyer: Linda Cox
Manufacturing Buyer: Megan Cochran
Cover Administrator: Suzanne Harbison
Photo Researcher: Sue C. Howard

Library of Congress Cataloging-in-Publication Data
Shea, Charles H., 1948–
    An introduction to human movement: the sciences of physical
education / Charles H. Shea, David L. Wright
        p.   cm.
    Includes bibliographical references and index.
    ISBN 0-13-795113-2
    1. Exercise—Physiological aspects.   2. Sports—Physiological
aspects.   3. Human mechanics.   4. Motor learning.   I. Wright,
David L.   II. Title.
    QP301.S466   1997
    612'.044—dc21   96-47288
                                                                CIP

Printed in the United States of America
10 9 8 7 6 5 4 3 2 1   00 99 98 97 96

Contents

Preface

The last twenty years have seen widespread curricular and research changes in physical education. These changes are reflected in the name changes that have occurred in academic units concerned with human movement in colleges and universities throughout the United States and Canada. Just a few years ago a department, school, or college of physical education could be found at most universities. Today, departments of kinesiology, human movement science, or exercise science (see list in Chapter 1) are more commonplace. The trend is toward using a name that reflects a multidisciplinary, scientific approach to understanding human movement, as well as recognition that many students are interested in careers beyond the traditional boundaries of physical education.

Students in these redesigned curricula are aiming for careers not only in teaching and coaching, but also in a variety of emerging professions that deal with rehabilitation, fitness and health, and the promotion of sports and sport skills. In addition, students increasingly view these science-based programs as a viable preparation for professional schools of physical therapy, occupational therapy, medicine, or even dentistry.

These trends provided the impetus to write this text. This text is designed to provide students with an overview of the scientific approaches used to study human movement and a working knowledge of the terminology that is used in each discipline. We believe that knowledge of the research and theoretical perspectives in these disciplines will provide students with the foundation on which a broad-based knowledge of the science of human movement can be built. Each chapter is designed to describe research findings as well as highlight "hot and interesting" topics in each of the disciplines, facilitated by the inclusion of short anecdotes and stories dispersed within the chapters designed to enhance understanding and increase readability. While each chapter provides a wealth of information and is designed to be both informative and interesting, our aim is not to provide comprehensive coverage of each area. The text is intended to whet the student's appetite. Hopefully, as a result of using the text, the student will be primed and motivated to take a number of in-depth courses in the human movement family of disciplines and will develop a better appreciation for the contribution of each area to our understanding of human movement.

The text can be divided into four sections. The first section is composed of two chapters that provide an introduction to the disciplines that engage in the scientific study of human movement and an introduction to the scientific process. The second section introduces the student to the scientific study of the biological foundations of human movement. This section includes four chapters that describe research on human movement from anatomical, biomechanical, physiological, and health/fitness perspectives. The third section provides an introduction to the behavioral foundations of human movement and includes three chapters. In this section the student is exposed to the fields of motor development, motor learning and control, and sport psychology. The final section acquaints the reader with the teaching of human movement skills by examining the field of sport pedagogy.

FEATURES OF THE TEXT

The text offers a fresh, new perspective consistent with the current changes in the field of kinesiology, human movement science, and exercise science. Each chapter begins with **Chapter Objectives** and an **Introduction** that provides an interesting, practical frame of reference for the discussions that follow. Each chapter ends with a **Final Comment** that summarizes the material presented in the chapter. In addition, **Highlight** boxes are integrated into each chapter to feature new, historical, or interesting topics that are designed to pique the interest of the student.

Each chapter also includes **Questions for Thought** and **Resources** sections. The Questions for Thought are designed to promote discussion and integration of the concepts that span disciplines. The Resources section provides an extensive listing of textbooks, journals, professional organizations, and **internet sites** for each of the disciplines addressed in the textbook. An **appendix** provides detailed information on accessing the internet, internet resources, and terminology. In essence, this appendix is a guide on how to begin to use the internet.

We have taken great care to write with the student in mind—to make the text contemporary, inviting, and relevant to students. This is facilitated by the inclusion of **short anecdotes and stories** dispersed within the chapters designed to enhance understanding and increase readability. Nevertheless, we have made a great effort not to sacrifice the content and rigor that this new perspective requires and deserves. While we have liberally used figures and pictures to heighten visual appeal, many of the figures are data-oriented to capture the research emphasis that his new perspective embodies.

For the instructor we have written a comprehensive instruction manual, including teaching suggestions, topics for class discussion, figures that can be used as overheads or slides, a test item bank, and a listing of additional supplementary readings. The teaching suggestions include interesting analogies and practical examples that are useful in supplementing the text material; also included are suggestions for outside class activities and hints on using the class discussion figures to stimulate discussion. The test item bank includes multiple choice, fill-in-the-blank, short answer, and discussion questions for each chapter.

ACKNOWLEDGMENTS

First and foremost, we wish to acknowledge the support we received from our wives, Kirstin and Natalie. Without their willingness to accept greater responsibility for supervising our little ones (Brek, Grace, Kacy, and William) and to endure our mood swings throughout this process, the book would not have been possible. For this, we dedicate this text to them. A special thanks to William, Kathleen, Paul, and Caroline for a lifetime of support and encouragement.

We would also like to thank our graduate students; Maarten, Chad, Qin, and Yuhua who had to pick up the slack in the laboratory while we devoted our attention to the writing of this text.

In addition, we would like to thank our mentors, Craig Wrisberg and John Shea for instilling in us a deeply felt appreciation for the science of human movement. They provided us with the understanding that human movement could only be truly understood through a multidisciplinary approach.

We owe a debt of gratitude to the publishing team at Allyn and Bacon for their collaborative efforts in the careful review, editing, and production of the text. Suzie Spivey, physical education editor, and her editorial assistant Amy Braddock, provided generous help and encouragement.

We are also most grateful for the thoughtful criticism and helpful suggestions of the following outside reviewers: Stephen A. Ames, Radford University; Paul Bishop, University of Nebraska at Kearney; Janet S. Dufek, University of Oregon; Gale Gehlsen, Ball State University; Stephen J. Langendorfer, Bowling Green State University; Richard A. Magill, Louisiana State University; G. Wayne Marino, University of Windsor; Michael W. Metzler, Georgia State University; David C. Nieman, Appalachian State University; Robert Rothstein, Miami-Dade Community College; Paul G. Schempp, University of Georgia; Mary Slaughter, University of Illinois; J. Frank Smith, St. Edward's University; Steven Snowden, Eastern New Mexico University; Richard K. Stratton, Virginia Polytechnical University; and Donald H. Sussman, Bemidji State University. We are also deeply indebted to our colleagues at Texas A&M University: Bob Armstrong, Bill Barnes, Kevin Davis, Carl Gabbard, John Lawler, and Ron McBride for their many readings of earlier drafts and constructive suggestions that helped improve each chapter.

CHAPTER 1

Introduction to the Sciences of Human Movement

CHAPTER OBJECTIVES

- To examine the study of human movement from a historical perspective
- To introduce the sciences of human movement

INTRODUCTION

The emphasis in this text will be on growth, health, training, learning, and performance as they impact an individual's capacity to move. We will be interested in the fluid and powerful movements of a dancer, a basketball player, and a diver; the precise finger-arm movements of an artist, a typist, and a pianist; the capacity of a distance runner, a sprinter, and a shot-putter; and the movements of a pilot, machinist, and laborer. This text will introduce to the reader the scientific study of the everyday movements of everyday people and the wondrous actions of the highly trained. Our understanding is important because movements are our link with the environment around us. We can explore, interact with, and change our environment through movement. The ability to move allows us to eat, work, and play. Movement influences our mental and physical health, which in turn increases our capacity to move.

The text focuses on the scientific study of a broad range of movement capabilities, not just those related to sport or work. The text concentrates on the development of the capacity to perform movements and work, the factors that facilitate or inhibit this capacity, and the approaches to analyze movement and work. The focus is not on the aesthetic qualities of movements, but rather on the processes and mechanisms that allow movement to be accomplished. Thus, the focus is more with the processes leading to the movements of an artist, a pianist, and a dancer rather than with the processes leading to an appreciation of art, music, or dance.

In addressing the capacity to move, we will be concerned with the interrelated ways in which the capacity to move is studied. This chapter presents a brief introduction to the disciplines of human movement; a more in-depth discussion of the disciplines will be presented in Chapters 3 through 10. The disciplines to be discussed are anatomical kinesiology, biomechanics, exercise physiology, fitness and health, motor development, motor learning and control, sport psychology, and sport pedagogy. Research in each of these disciplines can be considered the scientific foundation of human movement.

The introductions to the disciplines concerned with human movement presented in this text are not meant to take the place of a more complete coverage of these fields such as would occur if you were to take a class in one of the disciplines. Rather, the purpose is to introduce you to the type of research and the approaches used in each of the disciplines. Thus, the coverage of each discipline should be considered a sample of the concerns facing researchers and practitioners in the area, not a complete inventory.

HISTORICAL PERSPECTIVE

Humankind's recorded history is full of accounts highlighting the importance placed on movement. The ability to plan and execute quick and powerful movements was the most basic survival skill for early humans. Early civilizations in China, Egypt, and southeastern Europe (e.g., Mesopotamia, Babylonia, and Assyria) heralded training and competition in foot races, boxing, wrestling, and swimming as well as competition in throwing, archery, and batting. Movement skill, competition, and dance played a central role in nearly all early civilizations. In fact, records from this early period reveal that humans began to speculate on the health and medical benefits of exercise. Early Chinese history noted a series of medical exercises called Cong Fu (Rice, Hutchinson, & Lee, 1958). The Chinese thought that diseases were the result of inactivity. Movement combined with breathing exercises were intended to keep the internal organs functioning and to prolong life. However, it was not until the time of the Greek and Roman empires that understanding of movement was well documented.

Avenues Beyond Teaching

Traditional physical education programs have focused on the preparation of teachers for elementary, middle, and secondary school settings. Recently this conventional perspective has been replaced with an approach that relies on a more in-depth scientific study of human movement. This approach, in addition to the resurgence of public awareness of the importance of exercise and physical activity for the health and well-being of the population at large, has now opened a wide variety of professional opportunities previously unavailable to students interested in physical activity. For example, many students are using their academic preparation in kinesiology as a springboard to professional careers in clinical settings such as occupational therapy, physical therapy, or medicine. Cardiac rehabilitation is another allied health field in which knowledge of exercise testing and fitness is used to organize and supervise programs for individuals with cardiovascular ailments. The clinical setting is not the only environment in which physical training and fitness programs have become an integral component. In many industrial or corporate settings exercise facilities and equipment are being installed for use by business employees. Corporate executives are beginning to realize that a happy and healthy workforce is also a more productive workforce. Not only that, but a healthy employee is less likely to need sick days, which cost the company money.

Students of human movement can also make invaluable contributions to a growing field called ergonomics or human factors. Work in this area focuses on optimizing the interaction of human performers with their work environment, such as in assessing the mechanical, physiological, and psychological demands placed on the performer while driving a car, flying a fighter jet, or typing at a computer terminal. Since we all want to perform these tasks effectively, appropriate design of equipment to accommodate the human performer is crucial.

It is clear even from these brief examples that the common perception of the physical educator "rolling out the balls" on the playing field is far from an accurate description of the present-day movement scientist. These are exciting times for those interested in this emerging field. Hopefully reading this book can contribute to this excitement.

Early Contributions

Two Greek scholars played an important role in the early understanding of animal and human movement. Aristotle (384–322 B.C.) might be deemed the founder of anatomical kinesiology (see Chapter 3). His treatises *Parts of Animals, Movement of Animals,* and *Progression of Animals* are considered by many to be the first major scholarly account delving into how movements are accomplished. The treatises described the actions of muscles on bones, the role of the center of gravity and mechanics, and the precursors to what later would be considered the laws of motion. A few generations later Archimedes (287–212 B.C.) devised accounts of the principles of levers as they are involved in movement; these accounts have been considered the foundation of theoretical mechanics. Chapter 6, which addresses health and fitness, will discuss what has come to be known as Archimedes' principle as it applies to hydrostatic weighing.

About 300 years later Galen (129–199 A.D.) produced the essay *De Motu Musculorum,* which distinguished motor and sensory nerves and is considered the first textbook on kinesiology. Galen noted that muscles act in opposition and described agonist and antagonist muscles. Because Galen served as a trainer and physician for gladiators, he is considered to be the founder of sports medicine. After the decline of the Roman Empire, nearly 1000 years passed before the study of human movement reemerged.

Age of Enlightenment

In the fifteenth century Leonardo da Vinci (1452–1519) studied the human body and human motion in great detail. He described the origins and insertions of muscles by detailing the motion of a joint. His paintings attest to his knowledge of human anatomy and the physics of motion. Galileo Galilei (1564–1642) used mathematics to discover the laws governing physical phenomena. Although Galileo was not particularly concerned with human movement, his use of mathematics and experimental methodology in the study of mechanics was a strong impetus for the scientific study of human movement.

Alfonso Borelli (1608–1679) applied the techniques of Galileo to animal and human movement. He described bones as levers, muscles in mathematical terms, and nerves as conducting vesicles. The treatise *De Motu Animalium* (1630) described animals in machine terms. Borelli is considered by some to be the father of biomechanics because he first related muscular movements to mechanical principles (see Chapter 4). About the same time Francis Glisson (1597–1677) proposed that muscle fibers produce force only through contraction (shortening of the muscle). Until this time it was generally thought that muscles contracted and expanded to produce movement. He first suggested that muscles respond to stimuli, a capacity that he termed irritability. About this time Neils Stensen (1648–1686) proposed the radical notion that the heart was merely a muscle. Until then it was commonly believed that the heart possessed spiritual qualities. Stensen asserted that the muscle is a collection of individual fibers that can shorten and that the individual fibers are connected at the ends to a tendon.

Eighteenth and Nineteenth Centuries

One of the most important scientific discourses of all time appeared in *Principia Mathematica Philosphiae Naturalis* by Sir Isaac Newton (1642–1727) in 1668. Newton's three laws of motion proposed relationships between forces and their effects. Newton viewed changes in motion as a measure of the forces that produced the changes. His proposals are perhaps the most important formulations upon which modern biomechanics is founded.

By the mid-eighteenth century specific exercises were viewed as therapeutic. In 1741 Nicolas Andry (1658–1742) coined the term *orthopedics* to indicate a physician who prescribes corrective exercise. This view is thought to have influenced Per Henrik Ling (1776–1839) in the development of the Swedish system of gymnastics, which was characterized by a formal progression of exercises from easy to difficult. The advocates of this system claimed that the heart and lungs were fundamental to good health. The development of muscle strength and speed were simply a by-product of developing the heart and lungs. In contrast to the Swedish system, Frederick Ludwig Jahn (1778–1852) and Guts Muths developed the German system of gymnastics, which trained both the muscles and the mind. Marching; exercises of alertness and attention; free exercises with wands, dumbbells, rings, and clubs; and apparatus work were designed to train the whole person.

About this same time the study of electrical stimulation of muscles was occupying the attention of a number of physiologists. Luigi Galvani (1737–1798) observed that on occasion the muscle of a frog contracted when touched with a scalpel during dissection. Because Galvani noted the electrical potentials in nerve and muscle tissue, he is considered the father of experimental neurology. Guillaume Benjamin Amand Duchenne (1806–1875) attempted to classify the functions of individual muscles by using electrical stimulation. His book *Physiologie des Mouvements* (1865) has been acclaimed as one of the greatest books of all times (Jokl & Reich, 1956).

In 1814 the Royal Central Institute of Gymnastics offered three- and four-year courses of study that stressed both the theory and practice of physical education. By the mid- to late-1800s physical education was becoming a part of many seminary and college curriculums. In the United States many gymnasiums were erected after the Civil War to accommodate the increased interest in physical education. In 1867 Dartmouth built a gymnasium cost-

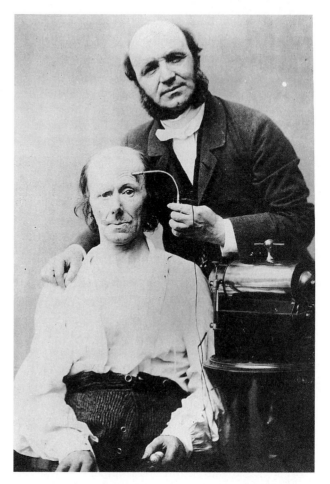

PICTURE 1.1   *Guillaume Benjamin Amand Duchenne de Boulogne investigated the effect of electrical stimulation on the facial muscle.* (Photo Credit: Corbis-Bettmann)

ing $24,000 and a few years later a $38,000 gymnasium at Princeton was her-alded as the best of its day. Dudley Sargent established a physical education program at Bowdoin College and later at Yale University. In 1879 Heming-way Gymnasium was built at Harvard University at a cost of $110,000, and Sargent became the director of physical training. The interest in both the art and science of human movement was growing at a steady rate.

Twentieth Century

The advances in the scientific study of human movement in the twentieth century are difficult to chronicle in a brief history like this. Important events that ultimately influenced the scientific study of human movement as we know it today occurred in so many different disciplines that it is not possible to mention all of them. Therefore, only a few important people and events from the disciplines of physiology, engineering, psychology, and education are discussed. You might say that these disciplines are the parents or grandparents of the disciplines that are involved in the scientific study of human movement today. Scientists and practitioners in each of these disciplines conceived experiments and theories that formed the foundation of the current field. The following sections will briefly highlight the work of a few scientists in each of the disciplines. It is important to note that many other individuals and groups from each discipline have made important contributions to our understanding of human movement. Our attempt is only to characterize the types of contributions made and emphasize the importance of our closest scientific relations.

Physiology.   Early work in this area made significant contributions to many areas concerned with the scientific study of human movement today. Work by an English physiologist, Sir C. S. Sherrington (1857–1952) and his colleagues on the role of reflexes in the control of voluntary movements is still important in our thinking today. A number of his important papers were included in his book *The Integrative Action of the Nervous System* (1956). He is credited with the creation of a number of classical concepts of motor control, including reciprocal innervation and the final common pathway. Reciprocal innervation refers to the idea that when one muscle group is activated (turned on), the opposing muscle group is deactivated (turned off). The notion of a final common pathway suggests that the neural commands from the brain, sensory receptors, and reflexes converge at the spinal level to produce the set of commands elicited to the muscle. Sherrington also coined the term *proprioception* as a result of his work on the sensory receptors that detect body position and orientation. Proprioception is the sensation of body part position and status from sensory receptors in the muscle, tendons, and tissue.

Sherrington concentrated on understanding the nerve–muscle interaction. He was concerned not with the movement per se but rather with the neurophysiological processes that result in the movement. A Russian physiologist, N. A. Bernstein (1897–1966), blended behavioral and neurological theory and techniques in his study of complex movements such as locomotion. This work described coordinated movement in terms of both neurophysiological processes and biomechanical characteristics. Bernstein is especially noted for the formulation of general laws relating to the organization of human movement, self-regulation, and the role of feedback in motor control. Unfortunately, Bernstein's 40 years of research was not known in the United States until the late 1960s because his works were not translated into English until after his death.

In 1927 the Harvard Fatigue Laboratory was opened in the Harvard Business School to conduct physiological research on industrial hazards. Dr. David Dill was appointed the director. His text *Life, Heat, and Altitude* (1938) is now considered a classic.

PICTURE 1.2   *Early method used by exercise physiologists to measure oxygen consumption and carbon dioxide production during exercise.* (Photo credit: Corbis-Bettmann)

Engineering.　In the late 1940s it became obvious that engineers, who were designing increasingly complex machinery, needed to consult with psychologists and other training/learning experts. Technology was being developed without consideration for the capabilities of the human operator. This resulted in the emergence of the field of industrial engineering in which human factors engineering is a subfield. A. T. Welford, an Englishman trained in psychology, viewed humans as active processors of information. He proposed the notions of central intermittency and the single-channel hypothesis. The notion of central intermittency holds that humans process information in discrete bursts rather than continuously. The single-channel hypothesis maintains that while one set of information is being processed (a decision is being made), the processing of a new set of information is delayed. These concepts have played an important role in terms of the design of complex machines, particularly aircraft. Clearly the operators' processing abilities could be overloaded, and the engineers needed to consider this in their system designs.

About the same time, P. M. Fitts (1912–1965) applied mathematical and information processing principles to hand-arm movements. In what has come to be known as Fitts' Law (Fitts, 1954), he derived an index of difficulty for aiming tasks that considered both movement extent and target size. Decreases in target size and increases in movement distance increased the index of difficulty and movement time. This work paved the way for many more researchers' attempts to apply mathematical, engineering, and psychological principles to the understanding of human movement.

Psychology.　Psychology is close kin to disciplines of motor development, motor learning and control, and sport psychology. Psychology can be defined as the scientific study of human behavior, which includes motor behavior. Wilhelm Wundt (1832–1920) is credited with both establishing the first research laboratory in psychology in 1879 and writing the first book on psychology in 1862. Thus, he is considered by many scholars to be the father of modern scientific psychology. His work in sensation, perception, and attention and his use of reaction time to assess the speed of mental processes has direct application to the study of human movement today.

Toward the end of Wundt's academic career, a number of psychologists adopted an approach termed behaviorism, which maintains that scientists must concern themselves with observable events. The functioning of the mind, such as thinking or feeling, cannot be observed directly but rather must be inferred from observable events. One of the well-known advocates of this approach was B. F. Skinner (1904–1990). His most widely known work concerns operant conditioning, a type of learning in which an animal or person learns to make responses to get a reward or avoid punishment. He was concerned with the strength of the relationship between stimuli and motor responses.

Education.   Education has a very long history, but as a distinct scientific discipline the roots are much shorter. Educators for many generations were concerned primarily with the practice of teaching, leaving the study of principles of learning to the psychologists. In 1900 John Dewey delivered the presidential address to the American Psychological Association, emphasizing the need for formal programs of research on the education of children. John Dewey was a proponent of an approach to psychology termed functionalism, which stressed the function of thought. The functionalist asked: How do mental processes (thought) function to fufill our needs? How do our mental abilities enable us to adapt to our environment? As a result of his work in this area, John Dewey is considered the founder of educational psychology.

Franklin Henry (1904–1994), who was trained in psychology but worked in physical education, is considered by many to be the founder of motor learning and control. Henry influenced many faculty and doctoral students who subscribed to his general method and point of view. Many of those directly or indirectly influenced by him held academic positions in physical education departments during the college growth boom of the 1960s. These leaders created Ph.D programs and trained more students in the scientific tradition. Henry, whose influence was pervasive by the 1970s, is probably best known for his work with reaction time, which resulted in a memory drum theory of neuromotor reaction in 1960.

In 1944 the Illinois Research Laboratory, which was associated with the physical education program at the University of Illinois, focused attention on exercise physiology as it related to physical fitness. The work arising from this laboratory under the direction of Thomas K. Cureton, Jr., resulted in volumes of published papers and books on physical fitness. However, as with Franklin Henry, Cureton's greatest legacy was the many students he directly or indirectly influenced.

Today and Tomorrow

At least since World War II there has been a trend for those concerned with movement to find academic homes in departments of physical education. University programs at the undergraduate and graduate level have flourished. In 1950 only 16 colleges or universities had research laboratories housed in departments of physical education (Hunsicker, 1950). The number of laboratories had grown to 151 by 1966 (Van Dalen & Bennett, 1971). Physical education faculty like C. H. McCloy (tests and measurement) at the University of Iowa, Elsworth Buskirk (physiology) at Pennsylvania State University, Thomas Cureton (sports medicine) at the University of Illinois, Lolas Halverson (motor development) at the University of Wisconsin, Franklin Henry (motor learning and control) at the University of California–Berkley, Dorothy Harris (sport psychology) at Pennsylvania State University, and John Nixon (pedagogy) at Stanford University influenced physical education curricula and, perhaps most importantly, trained graduate students in the scientific disciplines of human performance.

Today there is a renewed dedication to the scientific study of human movement. This is reflected in the trend for physical education programs to change their names to departments of kinesiology, exercise and sport sciences, or human movement studies (Figure 1.1). This name change, at least to some extent, reflects the faculties' and administrations' interest not only in preparing teachers of physical education but in conducting basic and theoretical research on human movement.

The name changes have not occurred without a great deal of discussion and debate. There was a time when most programs in higher education concerned with human movement were labeled physical education, a title almost universally recognized within higher education, school systems, and society as programs focusing on the education of and through the physical. However, the use of this title appears to be on the decrease. Several articles by Karl Newell and reactions by leaders in the field of human movement on

Health and Physical Education	Physical Education, Sport and Leisure Studies	Exercise and Sport Studies
Physical Education and Health Fitness	Sport and Movement Studies	Human Kinetics and Leisure Studies
Physical Education and Fitness	Health, Sport, and Leisure Studies	Human Performance
Physical Education and Dance	Health and Sport Sciences	Health Promotion and Human Performance
Physical Education and Sports Medicine	Sport Medicine and Management	Human Development Studies
Physical Education and Health Sciences	Sport and Health Sciences	Movement Sciences and Leisure Studies
Physical Education and Exercise Science	Sport Sciences	Human Kinetics
	Sport Fitness and Leisure Studies	Kinesiological Studies
		Human Movement Studies

FIGURE 1.1 A partial listing of academic department labels from the *Physical Education Gold Book 1987–1989,* as reported by Newell (1990).

 **HIGHLIGHT**

Outsmarting the Future

Physical education has not merely changed its name to kinesiology. More importantly the name change reflects a move toward adopting a more scientific perspective to the study of human movement. With this change in emphasis comes a need to change the mode of operation or approach in order to attack the critical questions. Such a change can often lead to interesting outcomes. Take Joel Arthur Baker, for example, a futurist with a rather interesting philosophy that he uses to help corporations anticipate changes in their marketplace. He provides methods that can help these corporations develop new ideas and stay current in a rapidly changing world. His lectures have helped corporations all over the world become more innovative, competitive, and successful.

What does this have to do with the scientific study of human performance? One of the basic premises he operates on is that of the paradigm. Paradigm is defined in *Webster's New Collegiate Dictionary* as "an example or pattern, especially an outstandingly clear or typical example or archetype." The philosopher Thomas Kuhn (1970) simplified this definition and referred to paradigm as a set of rules and regulations that (1) set boundaries and (2) provide rules for success within these boundaries.

Paradigms are not as abstract as they might sound and are actually found everywhere. The way your mom taught you to fold clothes, the coach's approach to sliding into home plate, Apple's method for learning Macintosh, all of these are paradigms. A paradigm can be very helpful when you are learning something new, but it can be a detriment as well. Often people think that because there is an established paradigm, nothing else will work. Following are a few outstanding examples that Mr. Baker uses in his presentations.

In sixteenth-century Italy, as in the rest of the world, people presumed that the earth was the center of the universe. The astronomer Galileo studied the heavens extensively with a newly perfected telescope and discovered that the earth revolved around the sun and that the sun was actually the center of our universe.

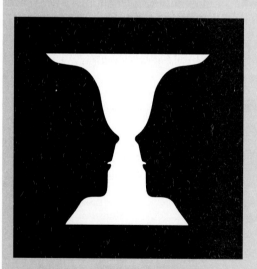

HIGHLIGHT 1.2   *What do you see first—a vase or two faces? The "reversible" picture reminds us that the way we look at the world determines the way we perceive it.*

When he presented this astounding discovery to his intellectual peers and the city leaders, they were so shocked that they threatened him with torture if he did not retract his abominable statement.

In 1938 a man named Chester Carlson presented a new idea to several photographic research corporations. His combinations of metal plates, powdered ink, and a light bulb seemed ludicrous to them all, but Chester had faith in his new invention and gained a patent, even though no one was interested in it. Today this invention, electrostatic copy, is considered by many to be the most popular one in history. Copy machines are now a multibillion-dollar business that saves countless working hours for almost every profession.

For over a hundred years, Switzerland made 65 percent of the entire world market share of watches and was renowned as the home of the world's finest clockworks. In 1968, however, a group of Swiss researchers invented a new concept. Their quartz movement watch was totally electronic, battery-powered, and much more reliable than the original spring and bear-

ing watch. Enthusiastically they approached one Swiss watch manufacturer after another, only to be turned down by everyone. Later that year two small electronics companies, one Japanese (Seiko) and one American (Texas Instruments), bought the Swiss researchers' idea. One decade later, the Swiss only produced 10 percent of the world market share of watches and over 90 percent of the employees of this trade had been laid off.

The sixteenth-century Italians, the photographic researchers of the 1930s, and the Swiss watch manufacturers all had one thing in common—their fear of new ideas, their fear of going beyond an existing paradigm. Established patterns can be very comfortable and easy to continue, but they can also cause people to not be receptive to concepts that may be more effective. This is where paradigms can work to your detriment or benefit. None of us would choose to be blind to good ideas, but we are just the same. Open your eyes and look beyond the edges as you begin your examination of the sciences of human movement.

this topic appeared in *Quest* in the early 1990s. The articles described the chaos surrounding the label for the discipline. Newell (1990) argued:

> Kinesiology is the study of movement or, more generally, the study of physical activity. The term kinesiology meets all the criteria for labeling the academic physical activity domain and has the useful advantage of being neutral in many of the current debates regarding emphasis on the disciplinary, professional, or activity dimensions and subsets thereof. The

study of physical activity in higher education should uniformly be called kinesiology at the levels of programmatic core, degree title, field of study, and department title.

As you might guess, the proposal by Newell was not uniformly agreed upon. For a very interesting dialogue, you are encouraged to read Newell's complete proposal and reactions in *Quest* (1990–91).

A FAMILY OF SCIENTIFIC DISCIPLINES

It should be apparent from the previous discussion that the scientific study of human movement is conducted within a family of related disciplines. Each discipline is concerned with the human capacity to perform movements and each discipline employs similar scientific methods in the study and measurement of movement, yet each is unique in the aspect of movement production on which it chooses to focus. Figure 1.2 depicts the various disciplines concerned with developing the scientific foundations of

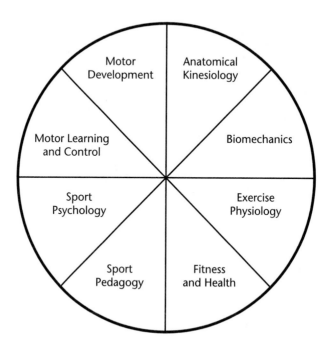

FIGURE 1.2 The family of disciplines that participate in the scientific study of human movement.

human movement. It is not uncommon for these disciplines to overlap, and in a number of cases the line between disciplines is relatively hazy. Each of the disciplines is briefly introduced below and a chapter is devoted to a more in-depth examination of each discipline.

Anatomical Kinesiology

Anatomical kinesiology is at the heart of any description of the science of human movement because this discipline provides an examination of the anatomical structures that contribute to producing the diverse but proficient movements we are all capable of executing. Central to any investigation of anatomical kinesiology is a thorough knowledge of skeletal, neural, and muscular structures and their movement functions. This is important to the kinesiologist because it is the interaction among these structures that shape the type and extent of movement that can be produced at each joint in the body. Furthermore, much of this information provides the foundation for many of the commonly used principles of training.

Concerns of the Anatomical Kinesiologist. Anatomical kinesiologists have as their central focus the interaction of the various components of the human system as they relate to producing movement. Kreighbaum & Barthels (1990) point out that a number of independent areas of study impact the anatomical kinesiologist, including osteology (study of the skeletal system), neurology (study of the nervous system), and myology (study of muscles). While our understanding of these areas can progress in isolation, it is the way in which these factors work together to provide the opportunity for efficient and economical movement that is of greatest interest to the scientist and practitioner alike.

For example, one can examine the human system from the standpoint of the skeletal component. The human skeleton is essential for providing a rigid internal framework, protection for important internal organs such as the heart and lungs (see Chapter 5), and acting as a machine using muscle torques to produce movement. However, one cannot overlook another important interaction between the human skeleton and the musculature. That is, the skeleton provides the areas of attachment for muscles. The locations of these attachments exert a critical influence on the way we move.

Similarly there is an essential interplay between the muscles and the nervous system. Obviously the muscle could not contract without being innervated by the appropriate efferent or motor nerves (see discussion of the motor unit in Chapter 3). In turn, the activity taking place in the muscles is relayed to the central nervous system via afferent nerves. This allows the system to respond continually to the needs the environment places on it. The nervous system then is a means of communication, carrying information back and forth to the muscles.

One final example further highlights how different components of the human body complement other components. In order for the muscles to contract, blood must deliver a variety of "supplies." One of the essential supplies, oxygen, is transported by the red blood cells, which are produced in the bones of the skeleton. The skeletal system is also responsible for providing the body with essential minerals such as calcium and phosphates. The importance of such minerals for human performance will become clear as you progress through subsequent chapters of this text.

Scientific Study in Anatomical Kinesiology.   Anatomical kinesiology is probably the oldest area of scientific study concerned with human movement, rivaled only by exercise physiology. Students studying physical education, physical therapy, or other movement science programs will typically be introduced to anatomical kinesiology early in their studies. This discipline provides the foundation required for advanced study of the human's capacity to move. Classes in anatomical kinesiology may include dissection of a small animal (or in special preparations like medicine or physical therapy the dissection may be on a human cadaver), which provides a "hands-on" exposure to the organization of bones, nerves, and muscles. It is especially important that introductory courses in anatomical kinesiology provide a language in which the structure and function of the human body can be discussed. This language will facilitate the more precise communication required in the study of human movement.

Anatomical kinesiologists typically publish research articles in *Research Quarterly for Exercise and Sport* and *Journal of Anatomy*. However, in the last 20 years some of the scientific research in anatomical kinesiology has focused on rehabilitation questions especially related to surgical intervention and the use of prostheses. For these reasons anatomical research can also be found in *Journal of Bone and Joint Surgery, Muscle and Nerve,* and *Physical Therapy*. An in-depth discussion of anatomical kinesiology will be provided in Chapter 3.

Biomechanics

Biomechanics is the discipline that applies mechanical laws to the musculoskeletal system of the human body and the implements (e.g., tennis

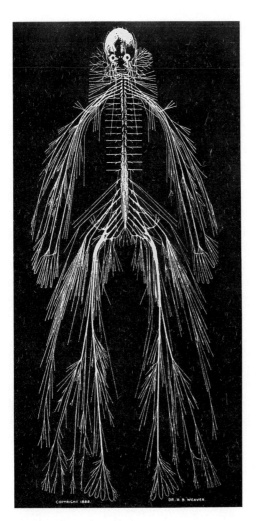

PICTURE 1.3 *Cerebrospinal nervous system. Harriet Cole, a scrubwoman at Hahnemann Medical College, willed her body to anatomy professor Rufus B. Weaver. The doctor used it for what is probably the only preserved dissection of the human nervous system. The brain was removed, but the spinal cord and the peripheral nervous system are shown.* (Courtesy of Hahnemann University Archives, Allegheny University of the Health Sciences, Philadelphia, Pennsylvania)

racket, socket wrench) used in sport and work. Mechanical laws describe how forces, both internal and external, affect the motion of bodies. In particular, biomechanists examine how forces act on the human body and provide a description of the resultant effects. Research in biomechanics often uses high-speed cameras or video, force platforms, and electromyography to describe the dynamics of a movement. Moreover, measurements of force are determined in order to assess the impact of the resulting forces on the movement sequence. An understanding of biomechanical principles can contribute to the identification of methods to improve both movement efficiency, as well as prevent, control, or reduce the possibility of injury.

Concerns of the Biomechanist

On many occasions the questions asked by the athlete, coach, or researcher center not on whether the athlete makes the basket, cleared the bar, or hit the ball. The concern represents a focus on the efficiency or effectiveness of the movement itself, not the outcome. Was the movement correct? Was it fluent? Was it efficient? These questions, and many more, require information about the movement of the limb segments though space and time as well as the forces that act on the limbs.

To achieve this type of description the biomechanist attempts to delineate both the kinematics and the kinetics of motion. Kinematics is concerned with providing an appropriate description of a movement with respect to time and space. A number of instruments are available that will locate special markers or sensors placed at the critical locations on the body and display the kinematic analysis of a movement in a matter of seconds. The relative ease with which these analyses can be conducted, along with the need to ask important questions concerning the kinematic qualities of movement, seem to account for the increasing utilization of these techniques. In Figure 1.3, the position of critical locations on the shoulder, arm, hip, and leg were plotted at intervals of time during the execution of a jumping motion from a squat position.

While a kinematic description of movement disregards the forces that are either produced or result from the movement, kinetics specifically focuses on this aspect of action. For example, rather than describing the displacement of the hand holding the tennis racket during different tennis strokes, an evaluation of movement kinetics might address the force produced by the hitting arm during forehand topspin and slice tennis strokes.

Movements are generally a combination of two "building block" categories of motion termed linear and angular motion. Linear motion occurs when the body moves in such a way that all parts travel the same distance, in the same time, following the same path. In contrast, during angular motion the body undergoes a circular motion in which all parts travel through the same angle, in the same direction, within the same time frame. A gymnast performing giant swings on the high bar is a good example of this type of motion. Biomechanists examine both linear and angular motion by evaluating similar kinematic and kinetic variables. For example, one can consider linear or angular acceleration or the conservation of linear and angular momentum. The link between linear and angular motion will become clear in Chapter 4 and will provide an important study framework to aid your understanding of this information.

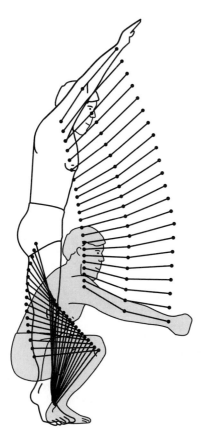

FIGURE 1.3 Example of a person jumping from a squatting position. Position of various landmarks are plotted as a function of time. These positions are the basis for kinematic analysis.

Scientific Study in Biomechanics. Biomechanics research requires some additional technical and quantitative skills that are not necessarily required in other disciplines in the movement domain. In particular, students specializing in this area are often exposed to advanced mathematics, mechanics, and physics courses. Since research in this area is used to contribute to the identification of methods both to improve movement efficiency and to prevent, control, or reduce the possibility of injury, there are numerous possibilities for employment. For example, large sport-footwear companies, transportation institutes, and athletic teams use biomechanists to provide crucial information.

The International Society of Biomechanics and the American Society of Biomechanics provide a forum for the exchange of ideas and research in biomechanics. Scientific research in biomechanics can be found in a number of journals, including *Research Quarterly for Exercise and Sport, International Journal of Sport Biomechanics,* and *Journal of Biomechanics,* as well as journals devoted to specific sports especially swimming/diving, gymnastics, and track and field. Chapter 4 will focus on biomechanics.

Exercise Physiology

Exercise physiology is the discipline concerned with the study of the physiological processes that provide the basis for our capacity to move. In an attempt to better understand the human capacity to move, exercise physiologists study the neuromuscular (nerve–muscle), cardiovascular (heart and arteries/veins), and respiratory (lungs) systems. How these systems respond to increased physical demands causes the physiologist to study how the body produces and expends energy, supplies nutrients, eliminates waste products, dissipates heat, and adapts as a result of training or detraining (cessation of training). Of practical concern to the exercise physiologist is the translation of research findings into better methods of training and factors that affect health as well as a better understanding of physiological and biochemical mechanisms related to strength, power, and endurance.

Concerns of the Exercise Physiologists.   All muscle activity requires fuel. The exercise physiologist is concerned with the processes that provide the fuel for movement. In high-intensity activities of a short duration, fuel is provide by anaerobic metabolism, which supplies fuel very quickly but not in large quantities and often with unwanted side effects. A by-product of one type of anaerobic metabolism is lactic acid, which causes a burning sensation when it builds up in the muscle. Alternately, activities of lower intensity can be fueled by aerobic metabolism. This system can provide very large quantities of energy but the conversion process is relatively slow. What happens if you pick up the pace during a relatively long run? You quickly become fatigued because you have increased demand for fuel to a point that aerobic metabolism cannot supply.

Exercise physiologists recognize the role the cardiovascular system plays in the delivery of nutrients and oxygen to the living tissue, in the dissipation of heat, and in the removal of waste products. For this reason they are concerned with the changes that occur during exercise and training to the lungs, heart, blood, and circulatory system. Clearly, training results in the increased capacity to perform. What changes occur in this system to support this increased ability?

The exercise physiologist is also concerned with factors that will increase or decrease your capacity to perform. What factors or environments can you

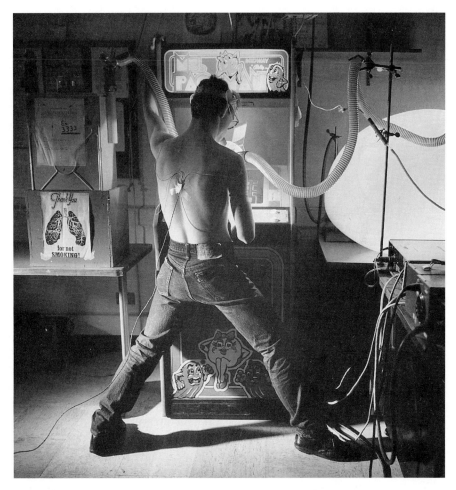

PICTURE 1.4   *Have you ever wondered how your heart rate is affected by playing an exciting video game? How much energy do you use? These and many more questions are being answered by researchers in exercise physiology.* (Photo credit: Nathan Benn/ National Geographic Image Collection)

name that will increase or decrease this capacity? For example, what happens to your ability to do aerobic exercise when you are at relatively high altitude? Why can't you perform at the same levels as you can at sea level? Answering this and related questions is the concern of the exercise physiologist.

Scientific Study in Exercise Physiology.   Exercise physiology is perhaps the oldest and most recognized field of scientific study concerned with human movement. Students studying exercise physiology quickly realize that this field of study relies on basic knowledge in physics, chemistry, biochemistry, anatomy, and biology. Indeed, students, particularly graduate students studying exercise physiology, will typically take course work in these allied areas. Many universities have undergraduate programs with concentrations in exercise physiology that prepare students to be exercise specialists in hospital and corporate fitness programs.

The American College of Sports Medicine (ACSM) is a professional organization that brings together physicians and those concerned with exercise physiology. In fact, ACSM offers certification programs and lecture tours for eminent scholars. Scientific research in exercise physiology can be found in a wide variety of journals, including *Research Quarterly for Exercise and Sport, The Physician and Sports Medicine,* and *Medicine and Science in Sport and Exercise,* as well as more general physiology journals like *Journal of Physiology* (London) and *Journal of Applied Physiology.* Exercise physiology will be discussed in detail in Chapter 5.

Fitness and Health

Fitness and health is a discipline concerned with the interaction of exercise, nutrition, and health. Research evidence has suggested that a number of diseases such as cancer and atherosclerosis are associated with our lifestyle. Clinical programs in this discipline provide facilities and personnel trained to evaluate health risk factors and recommend lifestyle changes that will reduce an individual's risk of disease. Research in fitness and health as well as in exercise physiology has indicated that proper exercise, nutrition, and stress control can contribute to one's health. Beginning in the 1980s, there has been a rapid growth in hospital, corporate, and private fitness facilities designed to promote exercise as key to overall health, rehabilitation, and productivity. The discipline of fitness and health is sometimes considered the clinical or applied arm of exercise physiology.

Concerns in Fitness and Health.   One of the primary goals of clinicians and researchers in fitness and health is to increase both longevity and quality of life. Numerous research studies have found that moderate exercise does a great deal to increase these factors. These studies note that a lifestyle that includes moderate regular exercise tends to reduce an individual's risk of cardiovascular disease by 25 percent or more and may add a number of years to his or her life. Can you name other factors that will increase or decrease your risk of cardiovascular disease?

Clinicians are also concerned with the early detection of disease that affects the cardiorespiratory system. For this reason an evaluation of fitness and health typically includes measurements of the functioning of the heart, blood vessels, and lungs during rest and exercise. In addition, a number of analyses are usually performed on a blood sample taken prior to exercise testing. This sample is analyzed for a number of factors that will tell the clinician or physician the current state of the cardiovascular system. For example, high concentrations of low-density lipoproteins in the blood are associated with cardiovascular risk and are implicated in the hardening of the arteries called atherosclerosis.

Another goal of clinicians in the area of fitness and health is to prescribe safe and effective exercise programs. They recognize that the frequency, duration, and intensity of exercise must be carefully manipulated to produce the desired results. These professionals also realize that a training effect only occurs when the system is stressed to an unaccustomed level but that severe stress is both dangerous and unproductive. In aerobic activities, healthy individuals should train at between 70 and 90 percent of their age-predicted maximum heart rate (220 – age). Note that as individuals become more fit they will have to exercise at a higher absolute intensity to achieve this level because their heart-rate response to exercise becomes lower as they become more fit.

The clinicians and exercise specialists concerned with fitness and health typically make recommendations concerning a healthy lifestyle that includes a reasonable exercise and nutrition program. Nutrition is included because sound nutritional practices and a relatively lean body profile are correlated with freedom from cardiovascular disease. Body weight can be conceived of as a sum of lean body weight and fat. Lean body weight consists of muscle, bone, organs, and connective tissue, while fat consists only of adipose tissue. In the past ideal body weight has been determined by age-height-weight charts that have been based on relatively large samples of subjects. These charts provide a quick and easy way of assigning an ideal body weight to an individual but do not recognize individual differences other than gender, height, and weight. For example, many football players or other athletes that incorporate weight training into their overall training program are judged by these charts to be overweight but clearly they are not fat.

Commonly used individual methods of determining body composition include skinfold methods, underwater weighing, and bioelectrical impedance methods. Skinfold methods involve using calipers to measure the thickness of skin-adipose tissue at various sites on the body surface. Research has indicated that some sites are better predictors of overall body fat than other sites and that the best sites are different for men and women. Underwater weighing is based on Archimedes' principle that an object submersed in water is buoyant to the extent that the volume of water displaced weights

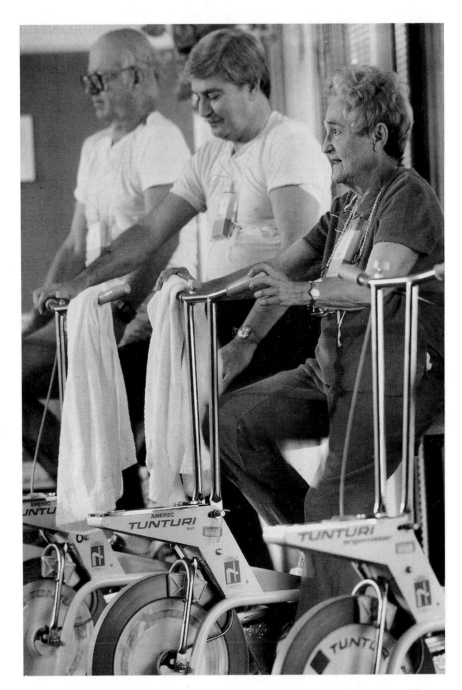

PICTURE 1.5   *Research indicates that people of all ages can benefit from sensible regular exercise. Individuals with cardiovascular risk factors are encouraged to consult a physician before embarking on an exercise program.* (Photo credit: Nathan Benn/ National Geographic Image Collection)

more than the object. Because fat is less dense than water (floats) and lean body weight is denser than water (sinks), a relatively lean person weighs more underwater than a relatively fat person of the same body size (volume). The bioelectrical impedance method is based on the fact that the transmission of an electrical signal in fat-free tissue is better than in fatty tissue. Thus a small electrical signal passed from the electrodes placed on one body site will be received better at another site in a leaner individual.

Scientific Study in Fitness and Health.   Scientists and clinicians in the discipline of fitness and health are concerned with exercise as a method of preventing cardiovascular disease and as a method of rehabilitation for those with cardiovascular disease. Because these practitioners are often dealing with sedentary individuals, athletes, and patient population, their preparation not only includes an in-depth study of exercise physiology but also includes class work related to psychology and sociology. These practitioners recognize that one of the most important challenges they face is convincing individuals of the short- and long-term benefits of exercise. They understand that individuals are more likely to adhere to exercise programs when they both understand the potential benefits of exercise and enjoy the activity.

The American College of Sports Medicine is a professional organization not only for exercise physiologists but for a wide variety of clinical practitioners (including physicians) concerned with health via exercise. In addition, practitioners and clinicians interested in corporate fitness programs participate in the Association for Worksite Health Promotion. Formerly known as the Association for Fitness and Business, this organization is a forum for scholarly and practical presentations related to fitness programs in the workplace, as well as the management and promotion of such programs. Scientific research in fitness and health can be found in the following journals: *Research Quarterly for Exercise and Sport, Medicine and Science in Sport and Exercise, Sports Medicine and Physical Fitness,* and *Exercise and Nutrition.* Fitness and health will be highlighted in Chapter 6.

Motor Development

The discipline of **motor development** provides information about the changes in human movement behavior across the lifespan and the influence of these changes on motor performance. The lifespan is often categorized as infancy, childhood, adolescence, and adulthood. This perspective goes beyond the traditional belief that motor development examines the changes in a child's motor behavior. The lifespan perspective assumes development progresses beyond the time that growth and maturational processes being to slow down. In examining motor behaviors that emerge throughout the lifespan it

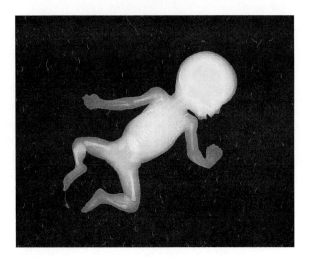

PICTURE 1.6   *The skeleton of a healthy newborn girl. Researchers in motor development are interested in changes from conception to old age.* (Photo credit: © LunaGrafix/Science Source/Photo Researchers)

is useful to consider some of the factors that mediate development, including biological, perceptual, memory, and movement-related influences. Each of these influences is scrutinized very carefully by the motor developmentalist.

Concerns of the Motor Developmentalist.   Of current concern for the motor developmentalist are four broad categories of issues. First, an issue that has long interested motor developmentalists is the role played by nature versus nurture during the developmental process. Put more simply, is it the genetic make-up of the individual that dictates the subsequent movement repertoire, or do the environment and other learning factors mediate the movement capability of the individual? Obtaining insight into this issue may be particularly useful to those interested in child development because it would indicate whether early movement experiences through specialized training programs can shape one's movement capacity. Alternatively, if genetics is the primary factor driving motor development there would be little reason for designing early childhood movement classes since they would provide little benefit to the individual.

A related issue that has also captured the attention of researchers in the area of motor development is the identification of sensitive or critical periods. A sensitive period is defined as a time span during which an individual is most susceptible to the influence of a particular factor or event (Haywood, 1993). In contrast, a critical period is a time frame in which a movement must be acquired if it is to achieve optimal performance. Clearly, if such time frames exist, this issue would have dramatic implications for training during the developmental process.

A third issue falls under the rubric of discontinuity versus continuity of development. More specifically, it does not necessarily require a trained eye to notice that improvements seem to continue to occur as development progresses. It is almost as if we gradually but systematically display improvements in motor performance. However, it is also quite bewildering to watch the sometimes dramatic qualitative changes in movement patterns that occur during the course of this continuous improvement in performance. Motor developmentalists attempt to describe the processes underlying these movement discontinuities.

Finally, the role of individual differences has reemerged as a factor on which motor developmentalists are currently focusing. As Thelen (1989) points out, variability in the developmental process may be just as informative as the most frequent behavior that is often described when delineating the developmental process. Thelen stresses that looking at how individuals achieve movement goals differently should not be overlooked as just an artifact but as a part of the plan of how movement behaviors emerge.

In addition to the examination of the aforementioned questions, there also seems to be a shift in theoretical perspective that is currently entertained by motor developmentalists. While a maturational approach was initially instrumental in delineating the occurrence of motor milestones (e.g., crawling, walking, and so on), more contemporary perspectives attempt to describe the underlying processes that can account for the emergence of the behaviors typically observed during particular periods during the lifespan. Both information processing and dynamical system positions appear to dominate recent work addressing this issue.

Scientific Study in Motor Development.   Specialists in motor development meet to discuss the current topics and research in the field at the annual meeting of the Motor Development Academy, which is a part of the American Association of Health, Physical Education, Recreation, and Dance. In addition, many of the researchers in motor development also attend the North American Society for the Psychology of Sport and Physical Activity, the Society for Research in Child Development, and the International Society for the Study of Behavioral Development. Research in motor development is published in a number of journals, including *Research Quarterly for Exercise and Sport, Child Development, Journal of Motor Behavior,* and *Journal of Applied Developmental Psychology.* An overview of motor development will be provided in Chapter 7.

Motor Learning and Control

Motor learning and control is defined as the scientific discipline concerned with the study of the processes that lead to skilled movement. Scientists in motor learning and control believe that by understanding the processes leading to skilled movement and the factors that facilitate and inhibit those processes, better learning environments can ultimately be devised. Environments and training techniques are desired in which students, athletes, and workers can efficiently learn motor skills that are accurate, consistent, and appropriate. Those in motor learning and control are concerned with determining the factors that result in learning that is adaptable to changing conditions, resistant to forgetting, and efficient in terms of physiological and cognitive demands.

Concerns in Motor Learning and Control.   In the discipline of motor learning and control scientists are concerned with the processing of information that occurs before the movement begins, during the movement, and after the movement is completed. Scientists in motor learning and control feel that humans do not passively act on environmental information, but rather they seek out information and actively process that information. These processes can be classified as relating to sensation/perception, response selection, and/or response execution. Sensation/perception processing occurs when an individual processes sensory information in such a way as to interpret the sensations. Response selection processing is concerned with deciding on a course of action based upon our perception of the demands of the environment. Response execution processing concerns the way in which we structure and control our movements after a decision to move has been made. Many researchers in motor learning and control do not believe that movements arise from a series of information processing steps. These scientists reject the view that humans process information in much the same way as a computer processes data. Rather they note that muscle and tendon groups and the neural circuits that innervate them are functionally linked together in a way that reduces the amount of processing that must take place. This view of motor learning and control has been called the dynamical systems approach.

PICTURE 1.7 *Researchers in motor learning and control are interested in understanding the processes that are involved in the performance and learning of motor skills.* (Photo credit: Nathan Benn/National Geographic Image Collection)

Researchers in motor learning and control study the impact of various conditions on our ability to perceive information accurately, process correct decisions, and produce appropriate responses. Their understanding of the factors that inhibit or facilitate this processing can be used to plan more effective practices that result in consistent, accurate, and flexible performance under a wide variety of conditions.

For example, researchers have been concerned with the role feedback plays in the planning, execution, and evaluation of movement. It is thought that some movements like threading a needle are dependent on feedback during the movement. Could you thread a needle in the dark? Alternately, a complex movement like writing your name may not require feedback during the movement. Could you write your name in the dark? This difference in the feedback requirement clearly indicated that these movements are controlled differently. This is of interest to the scientists in motor learning and control.

What about the need for feedback before the movement or after the movement is over? Researchers have found that feedback about the success of the movement after the completion of the movement is very important for learning. In fact, researchers are currently studying the most effective ways to present feedback. Likewise, motor learning and control researchers are concerned with all factors that influence the ability to perform and learn motor skills.

Scientific Study in Motor Learning and Control.   Specialization in motor learning and control is typically found only at the graduate level. These students take course work in psychology including industrial psychology, perception, and human memory to enhance their understanding of the factors that influence the performance and learning of motor skills. In addition, course work in physiology related to the function and control processes of the brain, spinal cord, and the neuromuscular systems is important to understand the processes involved in motor control.

Scientists in motor learning and control exchange research ideas at the annual meetings of the American Association of Health, Physical Education, Recreation, and Dance, the North American Society for Sports Psychology and Physical Activity, Neuroscience, and the Psychonomics Society. Motor learning and control research is published in a wide variety of journals, including *Research Quarterly for Exercise and Sport, Journal of Motor Behavior,* and *Human Movement Science,* as well as a number of psychology journals. Motor learning and control will be discussed in more detail in Chapter 8.

Sport Psychology

The discipline of **sport psychology** might be considered to have two thrusts. The first goal is to understand the effect of psychological factors on behavior in sport. In order to understand this relationship, the sport psychology researcher examines the influence of personality, self-efficacy, motivation, and anxiety and their effects on adherence to or attrition from particular physical endeavors. Second, the sport psychologist is interested in

PICTURE 1.8   *Sport psychology research has indicated relaxation techniques can reduce stress and improve performance.* (Photo credit: © Dan McCoy/Rainbow)

the enhancement of psychological well-being through participation in sport or exercise programs. This approach considers the positive changes that can occur in an individual's psychological make-up, such as reduced anxiety and aggressive tendencies, positive self-esteem, and personality development that might occur as a function of regular participation in physical activity or sport.

Concerns of the Sport Psychologist.   In addition to examining the physiological benefits of participating in regular exercise it is important not to overlook potential psychological gains. Some evidence indicates that improvements in self-esteem and self-concept can result from taking part in regular exercise programs. For this reason, it is not surprising that many sport psychologists spend a great deal of time seeking methods for improving entrance into and adherence to exercise programs and sporting activities as well as the use of exposure to competition for facilitating moral development. The introduction of Title IX of the Higher Education Act of 1972 also provided a major impetus for research efforts in the area of sport psychology. More specifically, this legislation revitalized sport psychologists' interest in gender issues. Recent research efforts have focused on the female athlete's tendency to display an androgenous psychological make-up. This occurrence has been associated with the role conflict some female athletes experience as they are socialized into the sport or exercise setting.

While specific theoretical issues consume much of the time of many researchers in sport psychology, there is a great deal of controversy about the training of a sport psychologist who will actually work with athletes. Up until the early 1980s programs in sport psychology did not have rigid guidelines as to what the needs of a sport psychologist were. In 1983 the U.S. Olympic Committee published a report in the *Journal of Sport Psychology*. Entitled "USOC establishes guidelines for sport psychology services," this document has served as a reference for the development of new programs as well as modifications to programs that existed before the document was prepared. Essentially the guidelines differentiate between three different routes a sport psychologist can take: clinical, educational, and research tracks. The guidelines suggest that sport psychologists have doctoral degrees in psychology, psychiatry, or a related area. Moreover, the sport psychologist should have experience working with athletes and coaches in an applied setting.

The sport psychologist is exposed to a variety of different areas during educational preparation. Relevant coursework might address group dynamics, developmental psychology, educational psychology, performance psychology, measurement and assessment, counseling psychology, and health psychology.

Scientific Study in Sport Psychology.   Sport psychology is now recognized as an official subdiscipline in psychology since its inception as Division 47 of the American Psychology Association. The two primary professional organizations for sport psychologists are the North American Society for the Psychology of Sport and Physical Activity (NASPSPA) and the Association for the Advancement of Applied Sport Psychology (AAASP). To complement the work presented at the annual meetings of these associations, new research findings are often published in *The Journal of Exercise and Sport Psychology, The Sport Psychologist,* and *Research Quarterly for Exercise and Sport.* Chapter 9 will discuss sport psychology in greater detail.

Sport Pedagogy

The discipline of **sport pedagogy** revolves around two very broad categories of research: research in teacher education (RTE-PE) and research on teaching in physical education (RT-PE). RTE-PE concentrates on examining three key ingredients of preparing individuals to teach motor skills: the student, the teacher, and the process the student and teacher engage in during the student's training. In contrast, work in RT-PE looks specifically at the elements involved in the teaching of movement. Siedentop (1991) has provided a thorough overview of these elements, which involve class management, instruction, and supervision.

Concerns of the Sport Pedagogist.   Currently the area of sport pedagogy is flourishing, as clearly indicated by the array of topics that have been addressed in recent volumes in the *Journal of Teaching in Physical Education*, including such areas as teacher preparation, teacher and student time management, socialization, student engagement and success rates, teacher supervision, and class planning.

Currently much of the research conducted in the sport pedagogy arena centers on teacher education issues and on the actual process of teaching motor skills. With respect to teacher education, most work has traditionally focused on the actual process that is used to educate future teachers. More specifically, the preservice, induction, and inservice phases are common themes that emerge from the work addressing the teacher education process. Probably the most documented component is that of student teaching, which typically occurs toward the end of a student's preservice activities. While most people assume that this component of a teacher's training is critical and highly informative, there appears to be some difference of opinion with regard to the usefulness of this dimension of teacher education. In fact, a growing number of sport pegagogists are seriously beginning to question the role of student teaching.

The induction phase, which is the period in which the new teacher is incorporated into the new teaching environment, has to date received very little research attention. However, it is becoming apparent that many students experience a number of frustrations as they are socialized into this new setting. This issue will very likely be examined quite closely in the coming years, with particular focus on identifying methods to ease the teacher into the real world.

Alternatively, sport pedagogists have the teaching of motor skills per se as their primary focus as opposed to the teacher education component.

Silverman (1991) identified three primary streams of interest to pedagogists with respect to RT-PE: teaching effectiveness, classroom ecology, and student-teaching cognitions. While the role of classroom ecology and cognitions are relatively new areas of study for the sport pedagogist, the examination of teaching effectiveness has consumed research efforts for some time. Recent issues such as teacher behaviors and the associated student outcomes as well as student engagement have become popular research topics.

Scientific Study of Sport Pedagogy.   Studying a complex issue such as optimizing teaching performance obviously necessitates an extensive period of training. This is reflected in the curriculum of most programs available for training sport pedagogists. Most programs reflect not only a concern with teaching "movement" but also a concern with developing an understanding of general teaching and learning principles. It is therefore not surprising that the more global literature on education has exerted a large impact on the structure of programs in sport pedagogy. Central to most programs in sport pedagogy is a thorough preparation in measurement and assessment. In addition, courses in supervision in physical education, instructional strategies, learning theories, creative thinking, and curriculum development and theory are not uncommon.

Sport pedagogy is a central element of the parent body of physical education—the American Alliance for Health, Physical Education, Recreation, and Dance. However, in keeping with the ties to general education, many sport pedagogists also have close links with the American Education Research Association (AERA). Much of the work referring to movement pedagogy can be found in *Research Quarterly for Exercise and Sport, Journal of Teaching in Physical Education,* and *Quest.* Some of this work reaches a broader audience in journals such as *Elementary School Journal* and the *American Educational Research Journal.* Chapter 10 will focus on sport pedagogy.

FINAL COMMENT

The scientific study of human movement has a long history. Advances in physiology, engineering, psychology, and education have provided the foundation for the field as we know it today. Eight disciplines that focus on the scientific study of human movement were briefly discussed and will be presented in more detail in Chapters 3 through 10. In general, these disciplines are concerned with the biological or behavioral foundation of human movement. More specifically, anatomical kinesiology, biomechanics, exercise

HIGHLIGHT

Surfing the Net

Throughout this textbook we will introduce new technologies that have resulted in improvements in movement acquisition, teaching, or assessment. Few people would question that these processes have been facilitated by continuing innovations in the computer industry. One particular advance in computer technology continues to impact many walks of society including the movement sciences—the internet. The internet is a worldwide system that links smaller computer networks together. This complex array of interlinked computers provides each of us with fast and efficient access to a wealth of information. The internet can be a valuable resource for obtaining information on diverse topics, from keeping tropical fish to monitoring the financial markets to checking the basketball scores from the Italian Basketball League. In order to use the internet one must have access to a computer and a modem or be lucky enough to attend a college or university that has computers connected to the internet. Once on the "net" the movement scientist can choose from many forms of communication, including using using e-mail, subscribing to listservers, contributing to newsgroups,

or surfing the Wide World Web with its "glitzy" graphics. (See Appendix A for a detailed overview of many of these communication modalities.)

These tools are not only valuable to the movement scientist, they can become part of a resource regularly utilized by the student just beginning to develop an interest in movement. To try to encourage you to venture onto the net, the "Resources" section at the end of each chapter provides the "addresses" of some interesting sites that pertain to the chapter. Appendix A offers step-by-step instructions on how to access these sites. You might be surprised about the wealth of information about movement that is floating around in cyberspace. To begin your search try finding information about the authors of this textbook, located at http://hlknweb.tamu.edu.

TEXAS A&M UNIVERSITY

HIGHLIGHT 1.3 *Texas A&M University's Department of Health and Kinesiology's homepage on the world wide web. You can access this page by going to the site at http://hlknweb.tamu.edu.*

physiology, and fitness and health are disciplines concerned with the biological foundations of human movement. Alternatively, motor development, motor learning and control, sport psychology, and sport pedagogy are concerned more with the behavioral foundations of human movement. While it is important to note that there is much overlap between the disciplines we will explore, it is equally critical to appreciate the unique contributions of each discipline to our understanding of human movement.

QUESTIONS FOR THOUGHT

- How is physical education different from kinesiology?
- Identify a current research concern that would interest a researcher in each of the disciplines discussed during the course of this textbook.
- Find the AAHPERD homepage on the World Wide Web (WWW).

KEY TERMS

anatomical kinesiology	motor development
biomechanics	motor learning and control
exercise physiology	sport pedagogy
fitness	sport psychology
health	

RESOURCES

Textbooks

Siedentop, D. (1990). *Introduction to Physical Education, Fitness, and Sport.* Mountain View, CA: Mayfield Publishing Co.

Thomas, J. R., & Nelson, J. K. (1990). *Research Methods in Physical Activity* (2nd ed.). Champaign, IL: Human Kinetics.

Journals

Journal of Human Movement Studies
Journal of Physical Education, Recreation, and Dance
Research Quarterly for Exercise and Sport
Quest

Professional Organizations

American Association for Health, Physical Education, Recreation, and Dance
National Association for Sport and Physical Education

Internet

World Wide Web
http://www.tahperd.sfasu.edu/aahperd/aahperd.html
http://www.tahperd.sfasu.edu/TAHPERD.html
http://www.tahperd.sfasu.edu/aahperd/naspe.html

Listservers
Sport Science
send: subscribe sportsci <your name>
to: majordomo@stonebow.otago.ac.nz

Fitness and Wellness
send: subscribe fit-L <your name>
to: listserv@etsuadmn.bitnet

Women in Sport
send: subscribe wishperd
to: listserv@sjuvm1.bitnet

Usenet
usenet: misc.fitness
usenet: misc.fitness.aerobic
usenet: misc.fitness.misc

REFERENCES

Aristotle: *Progression of Animals.* English translation by E. S. Forster. Cambridge, MA: Harvard University Press.

Dill, D. B. (1938). *Life, Heat, and Attitude.* Cambridge, MA: Harvard University Press.

Fitts, P. M. (1954). The information capacity of the human motor system in controlling the amplitude of movement. *Journal of Experimental Psychology, 47,* 381–391.

Haywood, K. M. (1993). *Life Span Motor Development* (2nd ed.). Champaign, IL: Human Kinetics.

Hunsicker, P. A. (1950). A survey of laboratory facilities in college physical education departments. *Research Quarterly, 21,* 420–423.

Jokl, E., & Reich, J. (1956). Guillaume Benjamin Amand Duchene de Boulogne. *Journal of the Association of Physical and Mental Rehabilitation, 10,* 154–159.

Kreighbaum, E., & Barthels, K. M. (1990). *Biomechanics* (3rd ed.). New York: Macmillan.

Kuhn, T. S. (1970). The structure of scientific revolutions (2nd ed.). Chicago: University Press.

National Geographic Book Service. (1986). *The Incredible Machine.* Washington, DC: National Geographic Society.

Newell, K. (1990). Kinesiology: The label for the study of physical activity in higher education. *Quest, 42*(3), 269–278.

Newton, Sir Isaac. *Sir Isaac Newton's Mathematical Principles of Natural Philosophy and His System of the World,* July 5, 1668. English translation by Andrew Motte, 1729; revision by Florian Cajori. Berkeley, University of California Press, 1946.

Rasch, P. J. (1989). *Kinesiology and Applied Anatomy* (7th ed.). Philadelphia: Lea & Febiger.

Rice, E. A., Hutchinson, J. L., & Lee, M. (1958). *A Brief History of Physical Education.* New York: Ronald Press.

Sherrington, C. S. (1956). *The Integrative Action of the Nervous System.* New Haven: Yale University Press.

Siedentop, D. (1991). *Developing Teaching Skills in Physical Education* (3rd ed.) Mountain View, CA: Mayfield Publishing Co.

Silverman, S. (1991). Research on teaching in physical education. *Research Quarterly for Exercise and Sport, 62,* 352–364.

Thelen, E. (1989). The (Re)Discovery of motor development: Learning new things from an old field. *Developmental Psychology, 25,* 946–949.

Van Dalen, D. B., & Bennett, B. L. (1971). *A World History of Physical Education: Cultural, Philosophical Comparative.* Englewood Cliffs, NJ: Prentice Hall.

CHAPTER 2

The Scientific Study of Human Movement

CHAPTER OBJECTIVES

- To develop an appreciation of the scientific process
- To understand the experimental tools available to researchers in human movement
- To examine the various facets of experimental validity
- To consider the importance of translating basic research and theory into practice

INTRODUCTION

Most undergraduate and even some graduate students find science a mysterious enterprise. Yet, the workings of science are not difficult to understand once you are familiar with the process and rules. Just as American football is very difficult to follow if you are not familiar with the object of the game and the rules, science is difficult to understand only until you understand the way in which scientists think and the manner in which they conduct experiments. In order to truly understand science you must understand the terms, processes, and rules governing it. In essence, the rules of science are set up to answer mysteries.

We are all aroused by mystery. We are curious creatures. When we observe ourselves, others, and the world around us, we continuously question. What? When? Where? How? Why? Sound like questions that only a detective or newspaper reporter would ask? No! These are the questions we all ask.

We are curious to know the answers, to solve the mystery. In the study of human movement, we ask questions about the processes that lead to learning and teaching of movement, health, and an increased capacity to perform.

- *What?* What limits my range of motion? What minerals should be contained in my diet? What can I do about controlling my anxiety prior to performance?
- *When?* When are gender differences the greatest during development? When do muscles generate greatest tension during an isometric contraction? When should a student be exposed to student teaching?
- *Where?* Where in the system (mechanical, physiological, psychological) do we falter when we become fatigued?
- *How?* How does an individual plan a movement? How does a performer adapt to performing at high altitude? How can an individual improve fitness?
- *Why?* Why is one person more coordinated than another? Why is this individual so aggressive? Why do adults' movement capabilities become limited?

The answer to these and many more questions enter our minds almost continuously, leading us to observe, to speculate, to observe again, to speculate further. On some occasions we even experiment. That is, we purposely try something new or manipulate some condition because our observations and speculations have resulted in a tentative understanding of the question. So we test our idea, our understanding.

THE SCIENTIFIC PROCESS

We all conduct experiments. When we take a new route home from school and measure how much time we save or lose compared to our normal route, we are conducting an experiment. When we apply fertilizer to only one part of our garden and observe the change in the growth of the plants, we are conducting an experiment. Even a trip to the grocery store can result in an experiment if we taste test two ice creams and judge one to be richer than the other.

Bottom-Up Thinking: Observation to Theory

One way our everyday thinking and experiments are different from those of a scientist is the manner in which the scientist is trained to think when posing scientific questions. Figures 2.1 and 2.2 depict the basic structure of scientific thinking and experimentation that plays a role in determining what questions the scientist will ask.

The process begins at the bottom of Figure 2.1 with observations. That is, information at this stage arises from observations or literature. When speculation leads to questions, formal and informal hypotheses are developed. A **hypothesis** is a tentative prediction of behavior under a set of conditions. To test hypotheses, experiments are devised. An **experiment** is an investigation in which a researcher manipulates one variable while measuring its effect on some other variable. Experiments are the most common method used to test hypotheses. Experiments provide evidence on which a hypothesis is rejected or held tenable. Note that science does not accept a hypothesis. Even repeated demonstrations do not prove a hypothesis true. This is the point that Polya (1954) made when he wrote, "Nature may answer yes or no, but it whispers one answer and thunders the other; its yes is provisional, its no is definitive" (p. 10). One demonstration that a hypothesis is not true is sufficient for the scientist to reject the hypothesis. However, many demonstrations that are consistent with a hypothesis only serve to keep the hypothesis viable. This is an important point and will be emphasized throughout the chapters of this text.

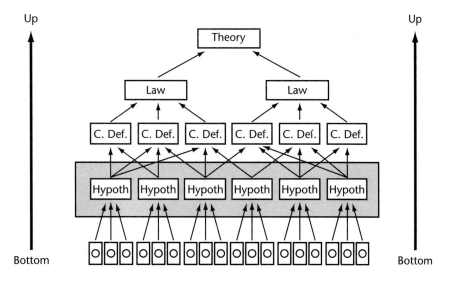

FIGURE 2.1   Bottom-up (empirical) research process. (From Shea, Shebilske, & Worchel, *Motor Learning and Control,* Copyright © 1993 by Allyn & Bacon. Reprinted by permission.)

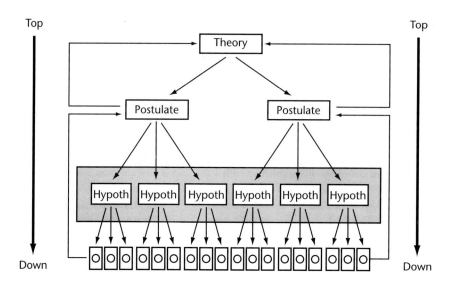

FIGURE 2.2   Top-down (theoretical) research process. (From Shea, Shebilske, & Worchel, *Motor Learning and Control,* Copyright © 1993 by Allyn & Bacon. Reprinted by permission.)

At this stage, experiments are termed empirical experiments. **Empirical** means based on observation and/or literature rather than theory. Facts are generated for facts' sake. This is the most inefficient level of scientific inquiry, but much important information is generated this way. These facts may appear to be isolated and of little use at the time yet are the very foundation of science (see Figure 2.1).

Science advances more quickly when the findings of individual experiments are linked. Coordinating definitions are used to tie together isolated facts. The logical reasoning from isolated facts to a more general description is termed **induction.**

A hypothesis or group of related hypotheses that continue to be held tenable after being subjected to repeated experimentation become law. More specifically, a **law** is a statement describing a sequence of events in nature or human activities that has been observed to occur with unvarying uniformity under the same conditions. Similarly, associated laws are linked by tentative explanations for the laws and, thus, the observation on which the laws were based. This explanation or **theory** is a statement of the processes that account for the lawful phenomenon. The term *theory* implies that there is considerable evidence in support of the explanation. In contrast, a hypothesis is a much more tentative prediction of behavior and does not necessarily consider explanations for that behavior.

The process to this point can be termed "bottom up" because the observations (facts) at the bottom, in conjunction with inductive reasoning, have driven the development of theory. The theory falls (is rejected) as its bases of support (hypotheses, coordinating definitions, and laws) are rejected. For young fields, the scientific process is largely bottom up.

Top-Down Thinking: Theory and Deduction

For more mature fields the scientific process also progresses in a "top-down" fashion (see Figure 2.2). This means that theories suggest new postulates and these postulates suggest testable hypotheses. A **postulate** is an assumption based on theory and not grounded in fact. Experiments of this kind are termed theoretical experiments. **Theoretical** means derived from theory. The top-down process involves deductive reasoning. **Deduction** is the process of reasoning from a general principle or theory to an unknown, from general to specific, or from postulate to testable hypotheses. A "postulate" is a basic principle derived without proof. Note that the top-down process, just like the bottom-up process, is self-correcting. Hypotheses that are rejected make suspect the postulate, and postulates that fail to be sustained can fell the theory. Through this top-down process, many scientists (e.g., Platt, 1964) feel they can most efficiently advance their science.

Scientists like to ask critical questions and then very carefully plan and carry out critical experiments. Critical, in this context, refers to those questions and experiments that have the potential to reject one hypothesis, law, postulate, or theory in favor of another. This makes efficient use of the scientists' resources since the experimental process is often very costly in terms of time and other resources. The identification of a critical question is very difficult and requires a great deal of insight into and/or knowledge of the phenomenon at hand. Empty experiments are to science what empty calories (calories from candy, potato chips, and the like) are to our health and that of our children. They are often costly and though they may provide some immediate satisfaction, they do little for our growth and development. The intent of the scientific community is to advance the understanding of the phenomenon to be studied in an orderly and most direct way.

Is Theory Necessary?

Throughout the later chapters you will be exposed to a number of theories. In fact the current trend appears to be to value theory development and theoretical research more highly than applied research. However, there are two sides to this story.

Theory: The Positive Viewpoint.   Theories are hypothetical statements of explanations for behavior under a specific set of circumstances. A theory, therefore, spells out in precise and potentially testable terms the current thinking of the scientist. A theory puts the scientist's understanding of the phenomenon and logic on stage to be viewed by the scientific community. This community is not a passive audience but critical and astute. The scientific community is trained to critically evaluate theory and devise experiments to test the critical features of the theory. A theory remains intact only as long as its assumptions and predictions are not shown to be wrong by experiment. Many tests that confirm the assumptions or predictions of a theory do not prove a theory correct, but a single demonstration of disproof causes the theory to become suspect.

In "Strong Inference" in *Science* (1964), John Platt argued that rapid advances come in science not by the process of confirmation but by disproof. Platt suggests that crucial experiments pit one hypothesis or theory against other hypotheses or theories. The result is that the experiment has the potential to exclude one or more of the alternatives. Platt states that all scientists should ask the following question of their theories and experiments as well as of those of their fellow scientists:

> "But sir, what experiment could disprove your hypothesis?"; or, on hearing
> a scientific experiment described, "But sir, what hypothesis does your experiment disprove?" (p. 146).

Platt was trying to make the point that many experiments are not very productive. Only those experiments that truly test our understanding (theories) result in substantial scientific progress.

Theory: The Negative Viewpoint.   Since theories are stated precisely and logically, a theory can appear very convincing even when it is not correct. In devising the theory, the scientist takes great care to present the evidence that has prompted him or her to propose the theory. Upon reading this evidence, it may be easy to interpret the evidence in support of the theory. Why not? The evidence was presented for just that purpose. The important question is whether your knowledge of the theory and evidence that has been presented in its support will cloud your ability to see alternatives.

Having been exposed to one way of thinking may cause other ideas or data to be essentially "invisible" to you. Greenwald, Pratkanis, Leippe, and Baumgardner (1986) present a number of examples in experimental psychology of what they call **confirmation bias,** which is the tendency for judgments based on new ideas to be overly consistent with preliminary hypotheses. This is in strict opposition to the "familiar stereotype of the scientist as an impartial observer whose hypotheses stand or fall according to the blind justice of objective data." The authors state:

> Perhaps the most generally admired research strategy in any scientific discipline is that of testing theories. However, this admirable strategy is easily misused to produce nearly useless research conclusions. To appreciate this, consider the enterprise of testing theory. The theory-testing approach runs smoothly enough when theoretically predicted results are obtained. However, when predictions are not confirmed, the researcher faces a predicament that is called the disconfirmation dilemma. The dilemma is resolved by the researcher choosing between proceeding (a) as if the theory being tested is incorrect . . . or (b) as if the theory is still likely to be correct (p. 219).

In either case, the researcher is in a difficult position. Continue to support the theory with contradictory data, discount the data, and try again until the data supports the theory or rejects the theory. In the latter case, the researcher is left with data without an explanation.

SCIENTIFIC TOOLS

Note the etched area of Figures 2.1 and 2.2. These are the points in the scientific process where experiments play their most important role. A general schematic of the experimental process is illustrated in Figure 2.3.

An experiment begins with a question. The question may arise from deductive or inductive reasoning. Questions that are generated from observation are termed empirical and those motivated by theory are termed theoretical. In either case, the experimenter must phrase the question or hypothesis so that it is testable. A hypothesis that cannot be tested is of little use to the scientist. Perhaps one of the most difficult jobs of the scientist is posing testable hypotheses. Next the experimenter must use the hypothesis to decide who to test, what measurements to take, and under what conditions. The following sections will discuss measurement, the selection of subjects (sampling), the experimental plan (termed paradigm), methods of analyzing the data (statistics), and the problem of experimental validity.

Measurement

Before embarking on a project that requires you to take measurements or administer a test, it is important to consider carefully the purposes for the mea-

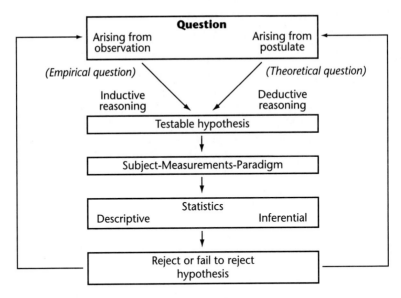

FIGURE 2.3   Schematic of the research process. (From Shea, Shebilske, & Worchel, *Motor Learning and Control,* Copyright © 1993 by Allyn & Bacon. Reprinted by permission.)

surements and to evaluate the characteristics of the measurements to be taken. These evaluations will hopefully result in the selection and utilization of the most appropriate measurement tool or tools. It would be unfortunate to use a poor measurement tool or to use a good measurement tool in an inappropriate situation. It would be a shame to measure the length of muscle fibers with a yardstick, and it would be overkill to time sprint events in track to .00001 seconds. What is needed is an appropriate measurement tool that is valid, reliable, objective, and economic.

Purposes of Measurement.   Measurements may be taken for a wide variety of purposes. A measurement is a value that is taken to represent a quality or quantity of a person, place, event, or thing. These measurements can be further classified as placement/diagnostic, formative, or summative measurements. **Placement and diagnostic measurements** are typically taken before a research project begins so that the approach can be altered to best suit the research purposes and the individuals involved. A scientist may also use placement/diagnostic measurements to place subjects into various treatment groups. For example, an experimenter may wish to evaluate the effect of an ergogenic aid on the performance of low-, moderate-, and high-fit individuals. The measurements of fitness level required to assign subjects to groups would be considered placement/diagnostic measurements. These measurements can also be used to group individuals with similar fitness interests or skill levels. Tests that might be administered before entering college, applying for a job, or entering the military are also examples of placement tests. The tests are designed to determine the program for which you are best suited. Similarly, diagnostic tests are used to determine areas of weakness and strength. An athlete might be given a diagnostic test called an electrocardiogram to determine if he or she has normal blood flow to the heart.

Formative measurements are used to track changes in measures that are taken during a particular time period, such as an experimental training period. These measures can be used to track change. Formative measures can also provide insight into the success or failure of the protocol or program. For example, a researcher and/or coach may monitor the times of a swim team each day. These formative measurements can be used by the swimmers to set goals and increase motivation as well as by the researcher and coach to monitor the effectiveness of the training program. Indeed, the coach may be able to adjust the intensity of the program based on the performances of the team as a whole. Alternatively, the researcher can determine the comparative effectiveness of the program compared with others being monitored.

After the research or training sequence is completed, the measurements are termed **summative measurements** because they represent the "sum effect" of the program. These can be utilized in assessing the instruction or training program that was used, or used to predict future success. In addition, measurements may be grouped together to produce norms for future evaluation procedures.

Summative measurements are especially important in experiments where a number of experimental conditions are being evaluated. In this type of experiment it is important to make summative measurements under the same conditions, not under the experimental conditions in which the subjects were trained (see the transfer paradigm in the section on experimental paradigms).

Desired Characteristics of Measurements.   Before using a measurement tool, it is important to determine the measurement quality of the tool. Measurement quality will be discussed under the headings of validity, reliability, objectivity, and economy. Measurement tools without these qualities may yield data that are not suited to the application.

HIGHLIGHT

Computers—A Historical Perspective

Being able to measure aspects of human movement is crucial to the movement scientist. The capacity to obtain many of the measures that we will discuss throughout this textbook was aided enormously by the advent of the computer. Today computers are not just the tools of mathematicians, engineers, and techno nerds. Computers are found almost everywhere: homes, workplace, schools, and businesses. They are no longer big, difficult to use, or expensive. Many of us who grew up with a slide rule strapped to our belt have to ask our children how to use the home computer. They grow up with the technology and learn at a very young age how to make the thing work. But remember just a few years ago no one even knew the terms RAM, ROM, megabytes, or megahertz, much less how to discuss the advantages of a 200 megahertz Pentium processor, flat-screen technology, 8X sampling, multimedia computing, surfing the internet, or 28.8 fax modems. Where and how did computers get their start?

Charles Babbage is considered by many as the father of the computer. In the early 1800s Babbage was a staunch critic of the errors that were contained in the mathematical tables used by scientists, bankers, actuaries, navigators, and engineers to perform relatively complex calculations. Extremely tedious and difficult to produce, the tables were prone to error. Babbage had traced clusters of errors to the transcription from one edition to another and he deduced that other errors were the result of loose type being

replaced after falling out. Babbage thought that mechanical computers should offer a means to eliminate computational errors. He dreamed of a machine that would not only perform calculation flawlessly but would transcribe the results.

In 1822 Babbage designed a mechanical computer that he called a "difference engine" because it was designed to use the method of finite differences to perform calculations. Each digit in a number was represented by a tooth on a gear wheel. A control mechanism ensured that a number was represented by a discrete

HIGHLIGHT 2.1   *A part of Difference Engine No. 1 designed by Babbage in 1822 and assembled in 1832.* (Photo credit: Corbis-Bettmann)

position on the gears. Babbage claimed that though the engine might jam, it could never perform a calculation incorrectly. The production of a full-size difference engine was started but was never completed because of the great expense associated with machining the gears and because of a dispute between Babbage and his chief engineer. Only about 12,000 of the 25,000 gears were completed when the project came to an end. However, in the late 1980s a team of engineers from the Science Museum of London constructed the Difference Engine #2 using Babbage's design with some modification and some of the original parts. At a cost of about $500,000 the engine was completed in 1991 (Babbage's 200th birthday). It performed flawlessly!

From Doron D. Swade, Redeeming Charles Babbage's Mechanical Computer. Scientific American *(February 1993).*

Validity. The extent to which a measurement tool measures what it was intended to measure is termed **validity.** Validity can be assessed mathematically or determined on logical grounds. At one time or another, all of us have questioned the validity of a test we have taken. For example, we could compare the cholesterol measurements that we received during an annual physical in a hospital with a measurement taken during a health fair in a local mall. If the measurement taken in the mall differs from that taken in the hospital, we may conclude that the measurement taken in the mall was not valid. What we were doing was comparing one measurement that we felt was valid with another measurement. Presumably the procedures and equipment used in the hospital were more accurate than the portable machine used in the mall.

Alternatively, we can question a measurement tool on logical grounds. Consider, for example, a hypothetical test battery for football players. Imagine that this hypothetical test was designed by a professional football team to test college players. The results will be used to make decisions about which players to draft. The test includes a timed 40-yard dash, the bench press, leg squats, and a 600-yard run. We could question the validity of the test on the grounds that it does not measure what we believe to be the behaviors important for playing football. We do not need to compare any numbers or even administer the test battery to come to this conclusion.

It is easy to see that validity can be assessed in a number of ways. Generally, measurement experts recognize two logical and two mathematical validation procedures. **Content validity** is a logical validation procedure

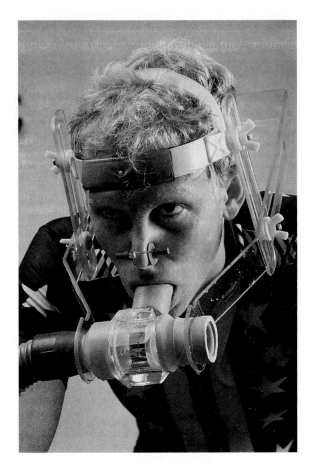

PICTURE 2.1   *When an exercise physiologist is collecting data for an experiment, he or she is very careful to make reliable, valid, and objective measurements.* (Photo credit: Will Hart)

that assesses the extent to which the measurements consider the content or behavior under consideration. This method implies a close relationship between the task or content under scrutiny and the measurements. A measurement that does not appear to represent the important components of the task under consideration or does not appear to be related to the content that was presented lacks content validity. For this reason content validity is sometimes called face validity or representative validity.

A second but closely related form of logical validity relates to attempts to measure constructs. A **construct** is a concept or characteristic that is difficult to define without first clarifying how the concept or characteristic is measured. Fitness, health, and intelligence are examples of constructs. In order to define these constructs carefully, it is necessary to clarify how we measure them. **Construct validity** is defined as the extent to which performance can be partitioned into constructs. If the performance under consideration can be partitioned into a clearly defined set of constructs, then the measurement scheme is said to have construct validity. Consider the hypothetical football test battery described earlier. The test battery is composed of the following constructs: speed (40-yard dash), upper-body strength (bench press), lower-body strength (leg press), and cardiovascular endurance (600-yard run). The battery would have construct validity if these constructs captured the essential elements for which the test battery was designed. What do you think? Are other constructs required to assess football skill? If other constructs need to be included, such as football knowledge, agility, and/or mental toughness, then the test lacks construct validity.

Mathematical procedures for assessing validity utilize statistical techniques to quantify the extent to which a measurement or test is valid. **Predictive validity** is defined as the extent to which a measurement or test is capable of predicting performance on another measurement or test. Entrance exams like the SAT (college), MCAT (medical), GMAT (business), or GRE (graduate) are said to have high predictive validity if high scores on the exam are related to future success in the program. The football test would have high predictive validity if players with high scores performed well in professional football. However, since predictive validity is a mathematical technique, a coefficient is calculated that expresses the extent to which the measurement or test is valid.

To determine the validity coefficient, it is necessary to have data on both the predictor measure and a criterion measure. For example, we could determine the validity of the SAT test if we had SAT scores from a group of students and their grade point average in college. The SAT is the predictor measure and the grade point average is the criterion. In essence, we are asking if the scores on the SAT test are correlated with grade point average. A coefficient of 1 would indicate "perfect" validity because the scores on the predictor test were indicative of scores on the criterion test. A coefficient of 0 would indicate that the test was not valid because scores on the predictor test were not related to scores on the criterion test. Of course most estimates of predictive validity do not yield coefficients of 1 or 0; rather validity is somewhere in between.

Another mathematical procedure for assessing validity also uses a correlation coefficient to quantify the extent to which a measure is valid. **Concurrent validity** is the extent to which a measurement or test is related to a criterion measure or test. In this case the criterion measure is determined at about the same time as the measure under evaluation. For example, we could assess the concurrent validity of a skinfold method of determining body fat. This method is accomplished by "pinching" a fold of skin and using a special caliper to determine the thickness of the fold. Typically, a number of sites are combined to determine body fat. The determination of concurrent validity would require that we assess body fat by the method under evaluation and by a criterion method. The criterion method in an idealistic sense should produce true measures of body fat. This is rarely possible, so we are left with using the best method available even though this method might not yield true measurements. Measurement experts have typically used a hydrostatic method of determining body fat (see Chapter 6) as a criterion measurement.

Reliability.   Any measurement scheme we use should produce the same measurement under the same condition. **Reliability** is concerned with how consistently a measure is recorded under a specific measurement scheme. This is important because in many instances only one measurement is taken, and we must have confidence that the measurement is stable. We would not be confident of the measurement of our weight on a bathroom scale if the scale recorded a different weight each time we stepped on it. The scale would be said to be unreliable. This is different from a set of scales that record a consistent but wrong weight; in this case the measurement recorded from the scales is not valid.

Objectivity.   The extent to which personal or situational factors influence measurements is termed **objectivity.** A good measurement scheme should not be greatly influenced by individuals or testing context. That is, the scheme should not be affected by either the individual taking the measurement, characteristics (other than the characteristic of interest) of the individual on which the measurement is being taken, or the situation in which the testing occurs. Only the quality or quantity of the factor being measured should influence the measurement. For example, researchers have found evidence that the handwriting used in answering a test question tends to influence teachers' grading of the question. This is a question of objectivity. Similarly, students' scores on standardized tests may be influenced by their cultural background, gender, or even their motor skill. An ideal measurement scheme should not allow personal or extraneous factors to impact the measurement. Note that objectivity and reliability have much in common.

Economy.   We are often forced to consider the economy of a measurement scheme. **Economy** is the cost of utilizing a particular measurement scheme. This cost must be considered in terms of time, money, and risk. Some measurement schemes may require a great deal of time to construct, administer, and interpret the measurements. Likewise, a measurement scheme may require expensive equipment or place the subjects at some risk. Often we substitute field tests for laboratory tests because it is felt that the additional costs are not offset by the increase in precision of measurements. These are the same problems faced by a physician in deciding on an appropriate measurement.

Sampling

An important question in every experiment centers on the selection and number of subjects to be tested. In an attempt to increase external validity, the scientist selects subjects for an experiment very carefully. The experimenter selects a sample of subjects from a population of subjects. A subject

PICTURE 2.2 *Random assignment is similar to a game of chance. Through random assignment, the experimenter ensures that each subject has an equal opportunity of being in each experimental condition.* (Photo credit: Brian Smith)

HIGHLIGHT

Ethical Treatment of Human Subjects

As a college student, you may be asked to be a subject in an experiment. This can be a very interesting and valuable experience. This is your chance to play a role in the progress of science but the experience may produce some anxiety. Anytime we enter into an unknown situation some degree of anxiety is normal. What is anxiety-producing about being a subject in an experiment? We have all heard of experiments in which the subject was exposed to something uncomfortable or even dangerous, tricked in some way, or simply made to look silly. Could I unknowingly appear on the scientific version of Candid Camera? What could happen to me?

Today many safeguards are in place to assure that you, as a subject, are protected from unnecessary risks. Professional organizations as well as agencies of the federal government have adopted and published guidelines for the handling of both human and animal subjects. Primary among the considerations for the ethical treatment of human subjects are issues related to informed consent, risk, privacy, deception, and debriefing.

Informed Consent. It is the experimenter's duty to inform subjects in writing of the pertinent aspects of the study they are requested to participate in and obtain written consent. This consent must clearly indicate the nature of the study and that the subject is free to withdraw consent without penalty at any time.

Risks and Benefits. Experimenters are charged with the safety and well-

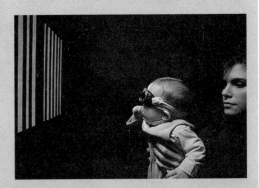

HIGHLIGHT 2.2   *The parent or guardian must provide an informed consent before a child is used in an experiment.* (Photo credits: left, Richard Howard; right, Lee Lockwood)

being of the subjects involved in their study. Likewise, subjects should be informed of potential physical and psychological risk and/or benefit that may arise from the conduct of the study. The experimenter, subject, and perhaps even an outside review board must weigh the potential benefits versus the potential risks.

Privacy. Unless the subjects specifically release their data or other material related to the experiment (e.g., videotape), the experimenter is charged with confidentially. The individual or group data can be presented as long as the individual's identity is withheld.

Deception and Debriefing. Whenever possible, an experimenter should avoid deceiving subjects. However, it is sometimes not possible to tell the subject the whole truth in advance. Prior knowledge may influence or bias the manner in which the subject responds. If it is necessary to deceive or simply withhold information from the subject, it is required that the experimenter conduct a debriefing session as soon as possible after the experiment. The subjects should be told what information was withheld and the reasons for doing so.

population is comprised of all persons that meet a particular set of conditions (e.g., gender, handedness, age, eye color). A **sample** is a subset of a population. The experimenter desires to use a sample that is representative of the population since it is rarely feasible to test an entire population.

Often, a process called randomization is used to help ensure that each person in the population under study has an opportunity to participate in the experiment. This procedure makes it more probable that subject differences in the population will be distributed throughout the sample. When possible, scientists randomly select subjects and then randomly assign them to groups.

A second problem related to sampling concerns the size of the sample needed for a particular experiment. Too few subjects limit chances of the sample being truly representative of the population and also limit the statistical tools that can be used to analyze the data. Increasing the sample size, however, may be costly in terms of time and in many cases money. Ideally, the scientist hopes to select a sample size that is large enough to permit a representative sample to be chosen and appropriate statistical analysis to be conducted, but small enough to be reasonably tested. Methods are available to estimate the sample size necessary to utilize certain statistical techniques, but the questions related to the representativeness of the sample are much more difficult to answer.

Experimental Paradigms

Of the many scientific methods available to those studying human movement, the experiment is by far the most common. The scientist begins by formulating a hypothesis that serves as a prediction of the change in a measured variable given a specific manipulation of another variable. A **paradigm** is a plan for an experiment that includes the variables to be measured and the variables to be manipulated. The manipulated variable is called an **independent variable;** the measured variable is termed a **dependent variable.** The change in the dependent variable is assumed to be a result of the manipulation of the independent variable.

An example of a simple experimental paradigm and hypothetical results is given in Figure 2.4. Two groups of subjects are tested. Subjects are randomly assigned to groups. One group is randomly assigned to be tested under Condition A and the other group under the experimental manipulation in which Condition B is added to (Sternberg, 1969) or subtracted from (Donders, 1969) Condition A. The group of subjects tested only under Condition A is called a **control group** because their performance is used as a baseline to determine the influence of the experimental variable B. The subjects who receive Condition A+B or A–B are termed the **experimental group.** The control and the experimental groups must be treated in exactly

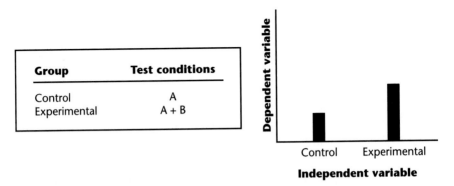

FIGURE 2.4 Simple two-group paradigm (left) and hypothetical data (right). (From Shea, Shebilske, & Worchel, *Motor Learning and Control,* Copyright © 1993 by Allyn & Bacon. Reprinted by permission.)

the same way except for the one variable under study, in this case Condition B. The hypothesis is that the introduction of Condition B influences (positively or negatively) the performance on the task of interest.

In the experiment described above, the scientist will have a difficult time convincing the scientific community that the manipulation of the independent variable (Condition B) caused, directly or indirectly, the change in the dependent variable. It is often not a very convincing experiment simply to manipulate a variable and observe the change. Who is to say that the manipulation of the independent variable was responsible for the change in the dependent variable?

The difference in the dependent variable may have occurred for the experimental group even if we had not introduced Condition B, or the groups may have been different in the beginning. These criticisms may be partially satisfied by including a baseline test in the experiment (see Figure 2.5). Baseline testing permits the comparison of the groups under the same conditions.

The control group and baseline testing serve two purposes: They provide a basis for the comparison of results with the experimental group, and they offer a means of eliminating some of the alternative explanations of the results. With the inclusion of the control group and the baseline test, the scientist is more assured that the changes in the dependent variable can be attributed to the independent variable. Since both groups were tested under the same conditions except for the condition of interest and since both groups were similar to each other at baseline testing, any difference between the groups at the end of the experiment can be argued to be a result of the experimental condition that was not shared (Condition B). Remember, conditions shared by both groups are controlled.

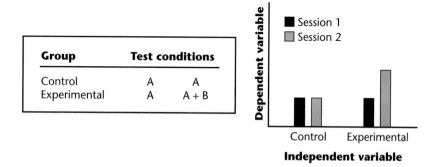

FIGURE 2.5 Two-group/pre-post paradigm (left) and hypothetical data (right). (From Shea, Shebilske, & Worchel, *Motor Learning and Control,* Copyright © 1993 by Allyn & Bacon. Reprinted by permission.)

A transfer paradigm is used when the experimenter is interested in the long-term impact of an independent variable (see Salmoni, Schmidt, & Walters, 1984). In the example (see Figure 2.6), one group of subjects is given practice on a task under Condition A and another group under Condition A + B. From the hypothetical results, it is clear that the addition of Condition B retards performance. However, these results may not accurately reveal how well the experimental group could perform when Condition B is removed. The hypothetical results illustrate a rather dramatic reversal from acquisition to transfer. The experimental group, whose performance had been inferior to that of the control group throughout acquisition, now "outperforms" the control when Condition B is no longer present.

A number of chapters later in this textbook will discuss this very important concept in detail and describe a number of independent variables that appear to influence training, adaptation, and/or the acquisition of skill in either a positive or negative way. To briefly illustrate this concept now, we will borrow an example from exercise physiology:

> Two groups of students with similar psychological and physical makeup are put on a running program for 16 weeks that will end in a 10-kilometer race. The students run the same workout each day but the members of one group are required to wear weighted vests. Times for the workouts are

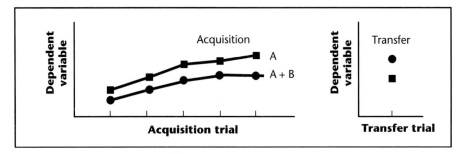

FIGURE 2.6   Transfer paradigm. The effects of Factor B on the learning of A can be determined in a transfer paradigm. (From Shea, Shebilske, & Worchel, *Motor Learning and Control,* Copyright © 1993 by Allyn & Bacon. Reprinted by permission.)

recorded each day and the group wearing the weighted vests makes progress over the 16 weeks but never is able to record times that are as good as the group without the vest. How will the two groups do on race day if they are tested under equal conditions (either with or without the vests)? We must run the race to find out.

It is easy to predict why the students running with the weighted vests recorded poorer workout times. How well will they do in the race without the vest? Did the extra weight they had to carry influence their fitness level or just their performance? Each of us can guess the results of the experiment just described, but we must collect and analyze the data to be sure. However, it should be apparent that it would be unfair to test the two groups under different conditions (one with vests and one without). The test must be completed under common conditions. Next, we must consider ways to analyze data from the experiment we are about to undertake.

Statistics

Raw data can appear overwhelming. Even the simplest of experiments often results in a great deal of data. The scientist uses various tools to organize and summarize data, graphically display the summarized data in such a way as to best illustrate the results, and then determine whether relationships, trends, or differences exist in the data.

In this section, we will discuss the dreaded concept of statistics. Scientists view statistics as a friendly tool, one of many available to help them understand and make decisions about data. It is not, however, the purpose of this chapter to dedicate much attention to statistics. Therefore we will only introduce from a conceptual standpoint the general classes of statistics that provide a framework upon which the reader can begin to build an understanding of the analysis of the experiments. Computational techniques to calculate the statistics discussed in this section are beyond the scope of this text.

Descriptive Statistics.   Many techniques are available to help reduce large amounts of data into understandable terms. **Descriptive statistics** are statistical tools used to organize and summarize raw data in order to communicate the important features more effectively. The first step is to organize the data. Suppose we have the scores from a fitness test administered to three groups of 60 students. The scores are organized from lowest to highest in a frequency distribution. The number of students receiving the lowest score (55) is entered first, then the number of students with the next lowest

score (60), and so on. Figure 2.7 presents a bar graph or histogram of hypothetical distributions for the three groups. This kind of display, is easier for
most people to understand than raw numerical data. From the histogram it
is easy to determine that the three groups did not perform equally well on
the test. Group C seemed to perform best, Group B performed worst, and the
scores for Group A were in between the other two groups.

Something else is apparent about the distributions. Only the scores for
Group A appear to be symmetrical; that is, if cut in half, the two sides are
identical. The other distributions are skewed. Group B is positively skewed

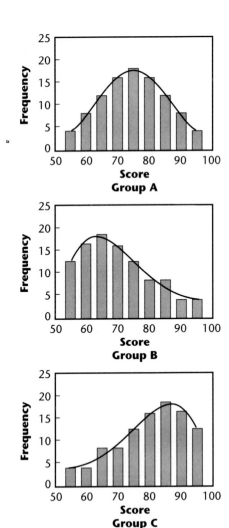

FIGURE 2.7   Examples of bar graphs
for three groups. The data from
Group A results in a symmetrical
distribution while Group B results in a
positively skewed distribution and
Group C a negatively skewed
distribution.

because the scores "trail off" toward the high end. That is, there are more scores at the lower end (50s, 60s, and 70s) than at the higher end (80s, 90s, and 100s). Group C is negatively skewed because the scores trail off at the low end.

Central Tendency. The histogram is useful in depicting the general characteristics of distributions but often it is important to determine one measure that best describes the distribution. **Central tendency** refers to measures that characterize the average, middle, or "typical" score of the distribution. There are three measures of central tendency: mean, median, and mode. The **mean** is the arithmetic average and is obtained by adding up all the scores in the distribution and dividing that sum by the total number of scores. The **median** is the exact middle of the distribution. Half the scores fall on one side and half on the other. The **mode** is the most frequently occurring score.

These measures are provided for the three groups in Figure 2.8. Note that the three measures are identical for Group A. This is always the case for symmetrical distributions. However, when the distributions are skewed, the mean and the median shift apart. The mean is by far the most often used measure of central tendency but when the distribution is skewed the median is the preferred measure. When the distribution is skewed, the median is preferred because it is not affected much by a few extreme scores. The mode is a crude measure of central tendency that is not often used to describe a distribution of scores or in statistical analysis. Note that in Figure 2.8 the medians and modes for the three groups are identical. This is not always the case for skewed distributions.

Variability. Measures of central tendency do not always tell us all we need to know about the distribution. It is also important to determine the extent to which the scores are spread out or variable. **Variability** refers to the dispersion or scatter of the scores. Distributions with low variability have scores that are tightly clustered while high variability indicates a large spread between scores. Figure 2.9 (top) illustrates two symmetrical distributions that have the same mean, median, and mode but that are quite different in terms

	Group A	Group B	Group C
Mean	75	70	80
Median	75	65	85
Mode	75	65	85

FIGURE 2.8 Mean, median, and mode for data displayed in Figure 2.7.

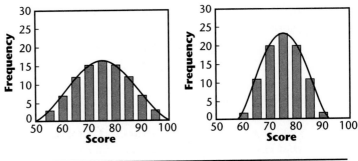

	Group A	Group B
Range	40	30
Variance	100	25
Standard deviation	10	5

FIGURE 2.9   Examples of two symmetrical distributions with the same measures of central tendency but different measures of variability.

of variability. Common measures of variability include range, variance, and standard deviation. These measures are provided for the two groups at the bottom of the figure. Note that the range, variance, and standard deviation are larger for the distribution (Group A) that is more spread out or variable.

The **range** is calculated by subtracting the lowest from the highest score. With only two scores considered in the calculation, it is easy to see that the range is a crude measure of variability and that it can be greatly influenced by a single score. The other two measures of variability consider all the scores and therefore are preferred. The **variance** is the average of the squared deviations from the mean; the sum of the squared differences from the mean divided by the number of squared deviations. It is important to know that the variance increases as the scores become more variable and decreases as the scores become less variable. The problem with using the variance is that in the calculation it is necessary to square all the deviations from the mean. Thus the variance is not in the same units of measurement as the raw scores. To solve this problem we turn to the most often preferred measure of variability. The **standard deviation** is the square root of the variance. Therefore, the standard deviation is expressed in the same units of measurement as the raw scores. As we will see in the next section, the standard deviation for many distributions can provide us with information about more than just variability.

The Normal Curve.   For many variables, the distribution of scores has a number of characteristics that are similar to a hypothetical distribution described by the mathematician Quetelet. This distribution, termed a **normal curve,** is symmetrical (the left half is a mirror image of the right half) so that the mean, median, and mode are identical and the scores cluster about the mean in a very special way. A normal distribution is illustrated in Figure 2.10. There are an infinite number of normal distributions but, by definition, all have the same bell shape, hence a normal distribution is often called the bell curve. A normal distribution is important because the approximate number of scores falling in each section of the distribution is known. For example in a normal distribution, 34.13 percent of the scores fall between the mean and 1 standard deviation above the mean. Because the distribution is symmetrical 68.26 percent of the scores fall between ± 1 standard deviation. Similarly, approximately 95 percent fall between ± 2 standard deviations and approximately 99 percent between ± 3 standard deviation units.

Suppose that the scores on a fitness test were distributed normally with a mean of 60 and a standard deviation of 10. How could you interpret a score of 90? This would mean the score was 3 standard deviations above the mean and that you would expect 99 percent of the scores in the population to fall below the score of 90. This kind of information is quite useful. In the next section, we will see that this information is helpful in determining whether or not one set of scores is statistically different from another set of scores.

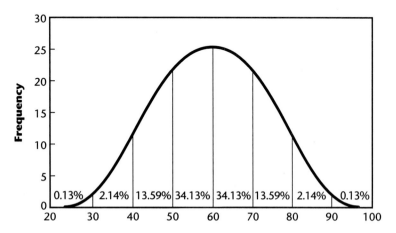

FIGURE 2.10   Normal distribution. Note that the density of the distribution is provided.

Inferential Statistics.   In most cases, it is impossible to test all the subjects in a population, and yet the researcher is often interested in generalizing to the entire population. For example, the researcher uses the sample mean and standard deviation as estimates of the population mean and standard deviation. Because the descriptive statistics are only estimates of the population values, it is sometimes difficult to determine if two means are the same or different. **Inferential statistics** are a set of procedures that can be used to make statistical judgments about population characteristics based on the characteristics of the sample. Many techniques are available, but we will only briefly review two general classes of inferential statistics. The first is used to test for differences in population means and the second is used to determine if relationships exist between variables in the population.

T-Tests and Analysis of Variance.   When the means for two populations are not equal, it is easy to judge that they are different. But when using sample means on which to base your judgment about the population means, the problem becomes somewhat more difficult. Since the sample mean may not be exactly the population mean, two sample means can be different but still come from the same population. How different must two means be before we have confidence that they come from different populations? That is the pertinent question. Note the distributions illustrated in Figure 2.11. In Figure 2.11A, the means are 20 points apart and in Figure 2.11B, the means are 30 points apart. Is it possible that the difference in the means for Figure

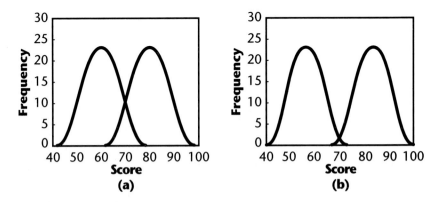

FIGURE 2.11   Comparison of distributions for two sets of data. In Example A the distributions are 20 units apart, and in Example B the distributions are 25 units apart.

2.11A is simply due to the sample that we selected? How about the difference in Figure 2.11B? As the means are farther apart, we become more confident that the difference is real and not due to chance.

A procedure called a **T-test** can used to determine if two means are significantly different from each other, and a set of procedures termed **analysis of variance** (ANOVA) can be used to test for differences in two or more means. Both procedures consider not only how far apart the means are but how variable the scores are about the mean. Consider the distribution illustrated in Figure 2.12. Both the T-test and analysis of variance procedures would determine that the means in Figure 2.12B are significantly different but that there is not enough evidence to conclude that the means in Figure 2.12A are significantly different. Note that in both cases the means are 20 points apart but in Figure 2.12A, the distributions are more variable. Relatively speaking, increases in variability decrease our confidence. That is, the differences in the means must be larger to be judged significantly different when the variability of the distributions are larger.

Correlation and Regression.   In many experiments, the researcher attempts to determine if a relationship exists between two or more variables. A **correlation** is a statistical technique that quantifies the extent to which two variables are interrelated. Variables are said to be correlated when they vary together such that a change in one variable is paralleled by a uniform, predictable change in the other. The correlation coefficient can range from +1,

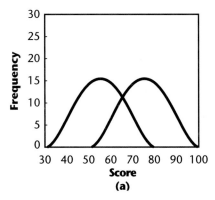
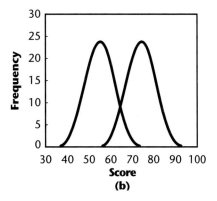

FIGURE 2.12   Comparison of distributions for two pairs of data. In both pairs the distribution on the left has a mean of 55 and the distributions on the right a mean of 75. Notice, however, the distributions in Example A overlap more than the distributions in Example B.

meaning that as one variable increases the other increases in a predictable, uniform way, to 0, where the change in one variable does not indicate any predictable change in the other, to –1 such that the increase in one variable indicates a predictable, uniform decrease in the other variable. Figure 2.13 illustrates five hypothetical relationships between two variables. Note that as the correlation increases, either positively or negatively, the points more closely approximate a straight line. When the correlation is +1 or –1 the points actually do form a straight line.

Regression is a set of statistical procedures that use, in a mathematical sense, the correlation between two or more variables to construct an equation that best summarizes the relationship. In many cases the relationship is linear (straight line) but this is not always the case. Figure 2.14 illustrates the correlation between two variables. Note the line superimposed on the figure. This regression line best summarizes the correlation. That is, the regression line is placed in a position that minimizes the distances between the actual points and the corresponding points on the regression line. In fact, the sum of the distance deviations above the regression line is equal to the sum of the deviations below the regression line. This procedure assures us that no other straight line "fits" the data better.

Under special circumstances, the regression procedure can be used to predict the scores of an individual, from the same population, who has been tested on only one of the variables. Remember, the correlation and regression procedures use the sample data to estimate the relationship in the population. Therefore, the regression equation shown in Figure 2.14 can be used to predict the performance of other members of the same population. If we select a new individual from the same population and measure performance on Variable A but not on Variable B, the regression equation can be used to predict or estimate performance on Variable B.

How much confidence do we have in the predicted value? Our confidence depends on how strong the relationship is between the two variables.

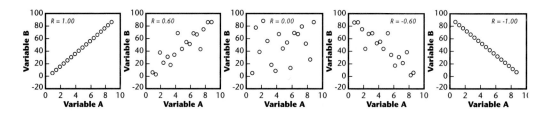

FIGURE 2.13   Five scatter plots illustrating correlations ranging from +1 (left) to –1 (right).

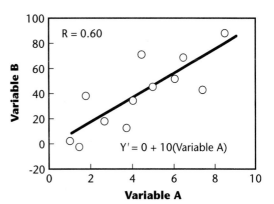

FIGURE 2.14 Scatter plot with regression line. Y′ represents the predicted value of B for any value of A that is "plugged" into the regression equation.

If the relationship or correlation is very high, we have more confidence than if the correlation is low. Still, our prediction is just that—a prediction. If the correlation is high, we would expect on the average that our prediction would be pretty good.

EXPERIMENTAL VALIDITY

Other ways our everyday experiments are different from those of the human movement scientists are that scientists take care in controlling the environment in which the experiments are conducted and in designing the testing methods, and that scientists exhibit concern for the generalizability of the results. Scientists are concerned with the internal, external, and ecological validity of their experiments, as demonstrated by the great care they use in planning, conducting, analyzing, and interpreting experiments.

Internal Validity: Cause of the Results

Control is necessary to ensure the internal validity of the experimental results. **Internal validity** refers to the degree to which the manipulation of an independent variable in an experiment truly accounts for the changes observed by the experimenter. Internal validity increases because the experiment provides a more convincing demonstration that the observed change was a result of the experimental manipulation. Consider the everyday experiments discussed earlier in this chapter. Was the change in driving time a predictable result of the new route or did a car wreck or other irregular event influence driving time? Did the fertilizer cause the increase in plant size or was it that the plot had better drainage and more sun? Could it be that the second brand of ice cream sampled tasted richer because it was chocolate and not because it was truly richer? By more carefully controlling our experiment, we would increase internal validity and be better able to attribute the change to the variable under consideration.

This is not to say that a carefully controlled experiment proves that a manipulation causes a specific change. The cause of an event is often very difficult to establish. By conducting experiments, scientists can find evidence that is consistent with a cause-and-effect relationship. It is possible to find evidence that disproves causality, but it is not possible to prove directly that a manipulation of one variable causes the change in another.

External Validity: Generalizability

A second type of validity is termed external validity. **External validity** refers to the extent to which the results of the experiment are generalizable. Scientists are concerned with the generalizability of the results. Would the shortcut save time for other drivers, at different times of day or in different weather conditions? Would the fertilizer produce similar results for different types of plants, or soil conditions, or at different times of the year? Can we expect other customers who sample the ice creams to choose as we did if they prefer a different flavor, if the time of the day was different, if the outside temperature was very cold, or if they had just come from the dentist? Generalizations are important to scientific study. A goal of research is to make statements that extend beyond the specific experiment and that can be applied to a range of situations involving similar variables.

Ecological Validity: The Real World

A third type of validity that is closely related to external validity is termed ecological validity. **Ecological validity** refers to the degree to which the conditions of the experiments are representative of conditions encountered in the real world. This term was popularized by Niesser (1967) because of a concern that laboratory research was becoming more and more distant from real life. Ecological validity increases when the experiment involves performances in real, everyday, and culturally significant situations. The ecological concern is that as the experimenter more carefully controls the experimental conditions and tasks, the results tell us less about how a person performs in everyday situations. This does not mean that all laboratory experiments are ecologically invalid but rather that laboratory experiments should be concerned with capturing the fundamental principles existing in more natural environments.

The reader should be aware that the controls used by human movement scientists to increase internal validity often decrease external and ecological validity. This causes scientists a great deal of concern because they would like to generalize from their research to other situations, especially real-life situations, and to a wide range of subjects. However, questions of internal validity require very careful control of the subjects and the environment in which the tests are conducted. The scientist wishes to conduct an experiment in which the results are clearly attributable to the experimental manipulation. This requires a great deal of control. Thus, the scientist is left with questions of trading off internal validity for external and ecological validity or vice versa.

This trade-off often causes scientists to include more groups or more testing conditions in order to clearly demonstrate the influence of an independent variable and still be able to generalize the results to more than the specific testing conditions and subjects. But proof in a mathematics or logic sense is not necessary for scientific inquiry to advance. The scientist cannot prove that the sun will come up tomorrow but we all have confidence that it will. Scientists have not been able to prove a link between smoking and lung cancer but their experiments have left little doubt in our minds.

RESEARCH AND THEORY INTO PRACTICE

The general aim of this section is to describe a research and communication model that has the potential to efficiently accomplish the translation of basic/theoretical human movement research into practice. This thesis is based on three assumptions. The first assumption is that principles derived from basic/theoretical research in human movement often have potential to increase productivity and/or efficiency in field settings. The second assumption is that basic research findings result in principles that have not yet been communicated to practitioners and thus have not been implemented in applied settings. Finally, it is assumed that many basic researchers are not in a position to maintain a direct link with the practitioners in the field, and therefore applied and operations researchers are responsible for at least part of the communication process. The research and communication model presented in Figure 2.15 links basic, applied, and operations research together by formal lines of communication between the research levels.

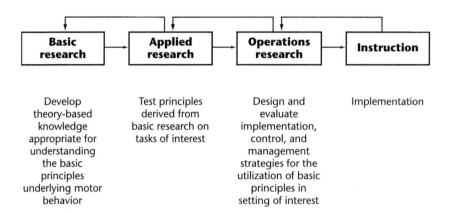

FIGURE 2.15   Proposed model of research communications that links basic research with instruction. Note that it is equally important to have communication move from basic research to instruction as from instruction to basic research. (From Shea, Shebilske, & Worchel, *Motor Learning and Control,* Copyright © 1993 by Allyn & Bacon. Reprinted by permission.)

Research Classifications

Basic research in human movement is concerned with the development of hypotheses, principles, laws, and theories pertaining to the processes that account for human movement and behavior. Typically, basic research is involved in testing hypotheses in laboratory and field settings using tasks specifically designed to involve/isolate the process(es) and/or environmental demand(s) under study. These tasks tend to be relatively simple so that experimental process can progress quickly, novel so the influence of past experiences is minimized, and artificial so that the process or environmental condition of interest can be isolated. Thus many of the tasks used in basic research appear to have little direct relevance to the field settings. The laboratory environment in which the tasks are observed during a basic experiment tends to be quite different from the teaching, coaching, work, or play environments.

Applied research is typically defined as research aimed at testing potential solutions (hypotheses) to problems that present themselves in real-world settings. Applied research should be concerned with determining via controlled experiments the potential application of findings derived from basic research. The tasks utilized are typically real-world tasks and the testing occurs in real world environments. This research may, however, require some control, modification, and/or restriction of the task(s) and environment(s) found in typical real-world settings. These modifications may occur because the applied researcher is concerned that the results achieved can be attributed to the manipulation under consideration. The applied researcher is concerned with whether or not the principles derived from basic research are valid for the task and in the environment of interest. Usually applied researchers do not deal directly with implementation strategies.

Operations research involves the testing of the impact, control, and management strategies required to optimize the implementation of new findings, information, laws, or principles derived from applied research into real world settings. The operations researcher wishes to modify real-world tasks and environments only to the extent that is required for implementation. This represents the final stage prior to implementation. At this level, principles discovered in the laboratory and confirmed in applied experiments may still be found impractical or too costly for implementation. Many techniques tested in basic and applied experiments could be beneficial in instructional, training, or work environments but simply require expensive equipment, specialized space, too much time, or private instruction. Added expense sometimes limits the development and utilization of new and potentially effective concepts.

Communication

It is important that the basic and applied researcher communicate directly with each other. The basic researcher must carefully distill stable findings from the laboratory into principles, laws, and theories. This information must be communicated effectively to the applied researcher, who must determine via experiment the extent to which these findings can be applied to nonlaboratory tasks and environments. Consistent results that indicate principles derived in the laboratory do not result in the predicted outcomes in applied settings must be communicated back to the basic researchers. This may indicate boundary conditions for the principle that were not considered in the laboratory setting but represent important mediating factors. This information may be important to the basic researcher because it may lead to important experiments that may better delineate the principle under consideration.

When the applied researcher finds that the results from laboratory experiments are reproducible with real-world tasks and conditions, the results should be communicated directly to operational researchers. It is the operational researcher's responsibility to test the various strategies of implementing and integrating the instructional concept into the classroom or onto the playing field. Given that the concept can be effectively translated to field settings, it is the mission of the operational researcher to communicate these strategies to the practitioners. If not feasible, the applied research should be informed so that the applicability of the principle can be reevaluated. The practitioner, in turn, must provide feedback to the operations researcher regarding the success or failure of the implementation strategy.

It is important to note that direct lines of communication that skip a level of research may not be as effective as the lines of communication outlined. Large volumes of basic research are collected each year. Only a small percentage of this research subsequently develops to a point that would warrant examination at the applied level. In addition, it would be inefficient for the operational researcher to evaluate implementation strategies for a principle that has not been subjected to scrutiny at the applied level. Likewise teachers and coaches could waste a great deal of time attempting to evaluate the efficacy of principles established in basic and applied research settings. Thus the communication model serves to systematically "cull" the number of notions derived from basic research that are prematurely translated into practice and, thus, the number of unnecessary intrusions into real-world settings. At the same time researchers at all levels are provided feedback relevant to their level of study.

Two major additional comments relating to the research and communication model presented in this section need to be expressed. First, will communication of why a method is effective be lost as operations researchers determine how a method can be implemented? In any multilevel communication model great care must be taken so that information is not distorted or lost in the translation from level to level. A great tragedy would exist if teachers were taught how to teach utilizing a technique derived from basic research but did not understand the principle upon which the technique was founded. In our opinion, the current communication system has failed in this regard. A significant number of current training, teaching, and coaching practices have their roots in basic research. It is our opinion, however, that a relatively large percentage of the practitioners that utilize these techniques do not understand how or why they are effective.

Second, it is important to note that the principles discovered in one discipline or field of study potentially can be utilized in other application domains. Figure 2.16 attempts to illustrate that basic research can lead to applications in many domains. A motor learning and control example is used but the notion applies to all areas of study in human movement. Because basic research may be utilized across application domains, it may be inefficient for the basic researcher to become too occupied with specific applications.

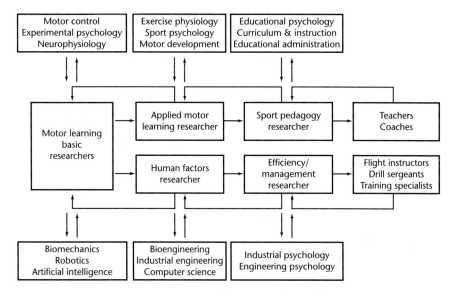

FIGURE 2.16   Example of a model for motor learning and control. Note that research may have application in a number of performance domains. Note also that different areas of research may draw upon basic and applied research from an allied area.

FINAL COMMENT

Each of the related disciplines discussed in Chapter 1 is concerned with the science of human movement. These disciplines are unique in many aspects but similar in their reliance on scientific methods to advance the understanding of their area. The scientists in these areas form hypotheses and conduct carefully controlled experiments to test their hypotheses. Sometimes the scientist formulates hypotheses by using inductive reasoning and the experiment is termed empirical. That is, the hypotheses are based on observation, isolated facts, or literature, not theory. Other times, the hypothesis is formed on the basis of a theory of human movement. In this case, the reasoning of the scientist is termed deductive and the experiment is referred to as theoretical. Theoretical experiments are thought by many scientists to be an efficient method of advancing the knowledge in a discipline but other scientists feel that theoretical experiments tend to blind the experimenter to findings that are not consistent with the particular theory being tested.

One fact shared by all scientists is that our understanding is only truly advanced when science is grounded in the careful selection of reliable, valid, and objective measurements, careful sampling of subjects, appropriate

Chaos in the Brickyard

The following is a short story by Bernard K. Forscher, Mayo Clinic, Rochester, Minnesota.

Once upon a time, among the activities and occupations of man there was an activity called scientific research and the performers of this activity were called scientists. In reality, however, these men were builders who constructed edifices, called explanations or laws, by assembling bricks called facts. When the bricks were sound and were assembled properly, the edifice was useful and durable and brought pleasure, and sometimes reward, to the builder. If the bricks were faulty, or if they were assembled badly, the edifice would crumble, and this kind of disaster could be very dangerous to innocent users of the edifice as well as to the builder who sometimes was destroyed by the collapse. Because the quality of the bricks was so important to the success of the edifice, and because bricks were so scarce in those days, the builders made their own bricks. The making of bricks was a difficult and expensive undertaking and the wise builder avoided waste by making only bricks of the shape and size necessary for the enterprise at hand. The builder was guided in this manufacture by a blueprint, called a theory or hypothesis.

It came to pass that builders realized that they were sorely hampered in their efforts by delays in obtaining bricks. Thus there arose a new skilled trade known as brickmaking. These brickmakers were called junior scientists to give the artisan proper pride in his work. This new arrangement was very efficient and the construction of edifices proceeded with great vigor. Sometimes brickmakers became inspired and progressed to the status of builders. In spite of the separation of duties, bricks still were made with care and usually were produced only on order. Now and then an enterprising brickmaker was able to foresee a demand and would prepare a stock of bricks ahead of time, but in general, brickmaking was done on a custom basis because it still was a difficult and expensive process.

It came to pass that a misunderstanding spread among the brickmakers (there are some who say that this misunderstanding developed as a result of careless training of a new generation of brickmakers). The brickmakers became obsessed with the making of bricks. When reminded that the ultimate goal was edifices, not bricks, they replied that if enough bricks were available, the builders would be able to select what was necessary and still continue to construct edifices. The flaws in this argument were not readily apparent, and so, with the help of the citizens who were waiting to use the edifices yet to be built, amazing things happened. The expense of brickmaking became a minor factor because large sums of money were made available, the time and effort involved in brickmaking was reduced by ingenious automatic machinery, and the ranks of brickmakers swelled with augmented training programs and intensive recruitment. It even was suggested that the production of a suitable number of bricks was equivalent to building an edifice and, therefore, should entitle the industrious brickmaker to assume the title of builder and with the title, the authority.

And so it happened that the land became flooded with bricks. It became necessary to organize more and more storage places, called journals, and more and more elaborate systems of bookkeeping to record the inventory. In all of this the brickmakers retained their pride and skill and the bricks were of the very best quality. But production was ahead of demand and bricks no longer were made to order. The size and shape were now dictated by changing trends in fashion. In order to compete successfully with other brickmakers, production emphasized those types of brick that were easy to make and only rarely did an adventuresome brickmaker attempt a difficult or unusual design. The influence of tradition in production methods and in types of product became a dominating factor.

Unfortunately, the builders were almost destroyed. It became difficult to find the proper bricks for a task because one had to hunt among so many. It became difficult to complete a useful edifice because as soon as the foundations were discernible they were buried under an avalanche of random bricks. And saddest of all, sometimes no effort was made even to maintain the distinction between a pile of bricks and a true edifice.

selection and execution of experimental paradigms, and careful utilization of statistical tools. This leads the scientist to take great care is selecting and utilizing measurements. Measurement protocols and measurement instruments should yield the same value each time the measurement is taken under the same circumstance (reliability). The scheme must yield measurements that measure the specific quality or quantity that the scientist is intending to measure (validity). Moreover, the measurement must not be influenced by the individual taking the measurement or the specific context in which the measurement is taken (objectivity).

The scientist is also careful to select representative samples and randomly assign them to groups, when possible, in an appropriate experimental paradigm. A representative sample and random assignment to groups tend to increases the external validity of the experiment. That is, the results can be generalized to the population from which the sample was drawn. An appropriate experimental paradigm and good measurements tend to increase the internal validity of the experiments.

An important part of the scientific process comes after the experiment is conducted. The scientist's job is not complete until the results of an experiment are carefully summarized, analyzed, and communicated to the scientific community. In this process the scientist uses both descriptive and inferential statistics. Descriptive statistics allow the scientist to summarize the data from an experiment. The summarized data is generally easier to comprehend than the raw data. Inferential statistics are used to make inferences from the sample upon which the experiment was based to the population from which the sample was drawn. Just because differences are found between treatments or groups in an experiment, the scientist can not be sure the differences would be found if the entire population was tested. Inferential statistics are tools that will assist in making this judgment without having to include the entire population in the experiment.

In the end, however, research results are only valuable when they are communicated to others in an understandable way. It is a real challenge to find ways to translate appropriate research results from the scientists to the ultimate users of the information, the practitioners in the field. This chapter summarized a model that could be used to facilitate this communication process.

QUESTIONS FOR THOUGHT

- In the stories and movies about Sherlock Holmes, he was known for the way he approached a mystery. Explain how you could solve a mystery using bottom-up thinking (induction) and top-down thinking (deduction). Discuss the differences in the methods.
- Before taking measurements scientists often test their measurement instruments by measuring items of known value. Why would the scientist take the time to do this?
- In a simple experiment, an individual wanted to know if a low-fat diet resulted in weight loss. To do this she weighed her four children (two boys and two girls, ages 1 to 8 years). After two months on a low-fat diet, she found the children actually gained an average of 1.5 pounds. She concluded that low-fat diets result in weight gain, not weight loss. Discuss this experiment in terms of internal, external, and ecological validity. How could the experiment be improved?
- What are basic research and applied research? How are they different? Is one more important than the other?
- At the conclusion of this chapter Figure 2.16 was presented to illustrate the interaction between motor learning and other performance and research domains. Take any one of the other movement sciences discussed in this textbook and construct a diagram similar to Figure 2.16.

KEY TERMS

analysis of variance (ANOVA)

applied research

basic research

bottom-up reasoning

central tendency

concurrent validity

confirmation bias

construct

construct validity

content validity

control group

correlation

deduction

dependent variable

descriptive statistics

ecological validity

economy

empirical

experiment

experimental group

external validity

formative measurements

hypothesis

independent variable

induction

inferential statistics

internal validity

law

mean

median

mode

normal distribution

objectivity

operations research

paradigm

placement and diagnostic
     measurements

population

postulate

predictive validity

range

regression

reliability

sample

standard deviation

summative measurements

theoretical

theory

top-down reasoning

T-test

validity

variability

variance

RESOURCES

Textbooks

Thomas, J. R., & Nelson, J. K. (1990). *Research Methods in Physical Activity* (2nd ed.).
    Champaign, IL: Human Kinetics.

Journals

Research Quarterly for Exercise and Sport

Professional Organizations

American Association for Health, Physical Education, Recreation and Dance

Internet

World Wide Web (WWW)
  http://alep.unibase.com

Listservers
Computer in Sport
  send: subscribe sportpc <your name>
  to: listserv@unbvm1.bitnet

Sport Science
  send: subscribe sportsci <your name>
  to: majordomo@stonebow.otago.ac.nz

REFERENCES

Donders, F. C. (1969). On the speed of mental processes. *Acta Psychologica* 30, 412–431.

Greenwald, A. G., Pratkanis, A. R., Leippe, M. R., & Baumgardner, M. H. (1986). Under what conditions does theory obstruct research progress? *Psychological Review* 93, 216–229.

Neisser, U. (1967). *Cognitive Psychology.* New York: Appleton-Century-Crofts.

Newton, Isaac. (July 5, 1668). Sir Isaac Newton's Mathematical Principles of Natural Philosophy and His System of the World. English translation by Andrew Matte, 1729; revision by Florian Cajori. Berkeley: University of California Press, 1946.

Platt, J. R. (1964). Strong inference. *Science* 146, 347–353.

Polya, G. (1954). *Mathematics and Plausible Reasoning.* Princeton, NJ: Princeton University Press.

Salmoni, A. W., Schmidt, R. A., & Walters, C. B. (1984). Knowledge of results and motor learning: A review and critical appraisal. *Psychological Bulletin* 95, 355–386.

Shea, C. H., Shebilske, W. L., & Worchel, S. (1993). *Motor Learning and Control.* Englewood Cliffs, NJ: Prentice-Hall.

Sternberg, S. (1969). The discovery of processing stages: Extensions of Donder's method. *Acta Psychologica* 30, 276–315.

Swade, D. D. (February 1993). Redeeming Charles Babbage's mechanical computer. *Scientific American,* 86–91.

CHAPTER **3**

Anatomical Kinesiology

CHAPTER OBJECTIVES

- To provide a basic introduction to human anatomy
- To describe the structure and function of the human skeletal system
- To describe the structure and function of the human central nervous system
- To describe the structure and function of the human peripheral nervous system
- To examine the role of the human muscular system

INTRODUCTION

In order to understand some of the limitations of the human, it is critical to examine the fundamental parts of the system, which in this case is the human body. The human body is a highly complex but organized system. The organization of the parts of the body contributes greatly to the incredible flexibility of human movement. In the subsequent sections we will explore the body's key components. We will begin this "anatomical tour" with the skeletal system, including examinations of the different types of bones that make up the human skeleton as well as distinct articulatory capabilities. Next, we will inspect the anatomy of the central nervous system, which is made up of the brain and the spinal cord, which might be thought of as the primary "control center" for human movement. The peripheral nervous system will be evaluated next, paying close attention to the means by which the human interacts with the environment. Of course, no examination of the human's movement architecture would be complete without a visit to the site of movement—the muscles. While this approach investigates the movement anatomy in isolation, the student of movement science should not forget that it is the interplay between these elements that allows the human system to perform such extraordinary movement feats.

THE SKELETAL SYSTEM

An important component of the structure of the human body is the **skeleton.** The skeleton consists of a number of different bony structures and can be divided into two separate subsections called the axial and appendicular skeletons (see Figure 3.1). The **axial skeleton** consists of the skull, thorax, pelvis, and the vertebral column. The **appendicular skeleton** contains all the other bones: the upper and lower, right and left extremities. The first important question is: What is the purpose of the skeleton? Probably the three most obvious roles of the skeleton are to provide a rigid internal framework, to provide an area of attachment for the muscles, and to produce movement using muscle torques, functioning much like a machine in this capacity (see Chapter 4 on biomechanics for a more complete description of torque).

The skeleton also provides other critical functions that bear some relation to subsequent chapters in the book. For example, the skeletal system provides protection for vital organs in the body. Many of these organs (heart, lungs, and so on) are central to any discussion of exercise physiology and health/fitness. Another role of the skeleton also impacts these areas: the bones in the human body serve as production units for red blood cells, which are essential for transporting oxygen around the body. The availability of oxygen is, of course, a vital ingredient for optimum human movement when it is performed aerobically. Finally, the skeletal system also supplies the body with important minerals such as calcium and phosphates, which are important to ensure adequate development and maintenance of the human body throughout the lifespan. This obviously impacts physical growth, which is a particular concern of those interested in motor development.

In the following section, the central element of the skeletal system— bone—begins our discussion, followed by a discussion of how bones are linked together throughout the human body. This section is complemented by a more global discussion of how the skeletal system moves. This section focuses on the different planes in which the segments of the body can move. The examination of the skeletal system concludes with a look at how the

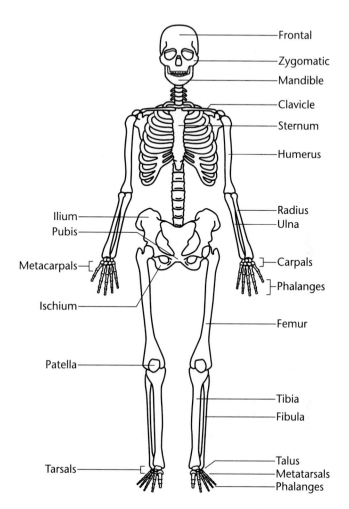

FIGURE 3.1   The human skeleton.

principles of levers can be applied to the human body. First, let's get at the "heart" of the skeletal system by examining bones.

Bones

The most common type of bone in the extremities (arms and legs) of the human body is called a long bone. The shape of this bone is just as you might expect it to be, given its name. A long bone in the leg is usually stronger and larger than those in the arms because of its weight-bearing requirement. Furthermore, the long bones in the upper extremities are lighter because of their use in more "fine control" movements.

It is no surprise, since there are long bones in the body, that there are also short bones. Short bones account for most of the bones in the hands and feet. There are also flat bones that are ideal for protective purposes and as locations for important muscle attachments. For example, the scapula in the shoulder complex is a flat bone. Finally, there are a number of irregular bones that have a specific role, such as the vertebrae, which surround the spinal cord.

It is clear just from this brief classification of bones that there are numerous types of bone in the human body. However, our understanding of bone is made considerably easier if we identify some landmarks that are present in most classes of bone. Indeed, there are quite a number of similarities between the distinct bone types. A **tuberosity** is a raised section of a bone that provides an ideal location for tendon, ligament, or muscle to attach. A shallow, dishlike area on a bone is called a **fossa.** A fossa is often a space where an articulation with another bone occurs or a muscle attaches. Nerves that must pass through bone do so through a hole in the bone called a **foramen.** Finally, a part of the bone that is an important part of an articulation with another bone is called a **condyle,** which is a rounded prominence of the bone.

A particular interest of the developmental scientist (e.g., motor developmentalist) is the study of changes that occur in bone across the lifespan. One method to obtain some insight into this process is to examine the type of injuries that occur to bone at different stages of development. A frequent problem seen in teenage males is Osgood-Schlatter disease, in which the material that connects muscle to the bone (the tendon) begins to develop small tears. Osgood-Schlatter disease can occur if the young athlete is exposed to stressful, abrupt stopping motions. This is commonplace in many athletic activities such as basketball, volleyball, and gymnastics.

Many parents are concerned about how soon a child may begin a structured training program without causing any lasting harm to the body. This question directly impacts the current discussion about the bony structures in the body. One concern is rigorous training at too early an age can reduce the relative strength of the muscle tissue and the strength of the connective tissue (i.e., tendon) between the bone and the muscle. Extensive training at an early age can, in some cases, cause the muscle to tear from the bone.

With the advent of little league and peewee football, it is not unusual to see young children participating in competitive activities as early as 6 and 7 years old. Wood, Tullos, & King (1973) have revealed some severe bone-

PICTURE 3.1 *Children begin participating in gymnastics at a very early age when their bodies are not fully developed.* (Photo credit: Will Hart)

related injuries to children who are little league pitchers. In some cases, the stress that results from pitching in baseball or repeatedly hitting a tennis ball can lead to small parts of the joint cartilage chipping away or parts of the actual bone "breaking down."

A number of different activities can exert great stress on the skeletal system. Probably the most prevalent activity is gymnastics. Even at elite levels such as the Olympics, competitors are often as young as 12–17 years old, particularly in the women's competition. Activities on the balance beam and floor exercise exert massive stress for the immature bones. Caine & Lindler (1985) reported that overuse injuries of the hand and wrist complex are quite common in gymnastics.

Articulations and Joints

While it is important to understand the specific components that make up the human skeleton, to understand movement we must also consider how these smaller parts are put together to make up the whole. The junction between two bones is called an **articulation.** The type of articulation dictates the type of joint that exists in an anatomical unit. A joint is defined by the type of movement it can support. Let's look at some different articulations.

Sutures between the bones in the skull allow a minute amount of movement to occur, merely enough to allow for some shock absorption. This type of articulation that minimizes movement is called **synarthrodial articulation.** In contrast, **amphiarthrodial articulation** contains fibrocartilaginous discs that allow some movement between the bones contained in the joint. An example of this type of articulation is the vertebrae in the spinal cord. The most interesting articulations to movement scientists, however, are ones that support free movement. This involves a **diarthrodial articulation.** This type of articulation has particular characteristics that need to be examined.

A diarthrodial articulation includes a number of elements that are important to its function. At the surface of each bone included in the articulation is hyaline cartilage, which provides a relatively friction-free environment in which bones can move against one another. It is essential to keep the cartilage in good working order to ensure that actual bone does not rub against bone. To aid the maintenance of the cartilage, the joint cavity (see Figure 3.2) is filled with synovial fluid, which lubricates the cartilage so it does not crack or wear away. The synovial fluid is encapsulated in the joint cavity by means of the synovial membrane. On the outside of the joint capsule the bones are held together by **ligaments. Tendons,** which have already been mentioned, attach muscle to bone outside the joint capsule.

Many forms of joints involve diarthrodial articulations. A **nonaxial joint** is one that does not exhibit angular movement. The movement that this type of joint supports is a gliding motion. Nonaxial joints are found between the carpal bones in the hand. A **uniaxial joint,** often referred to as a hinge or pivot joint, allows movement around a single axis. The most commonly cited example of a uniaxial joint is the elbow. When a joint allows movement around two perpendicular axes it is considered a **biaxial joint.**

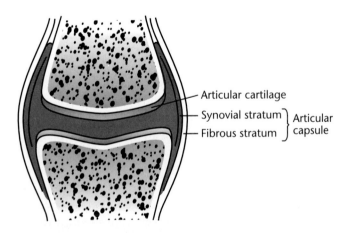

FIGURE 3.2   A synovial joint has synovial fluid to help maintain the cartilage, which in turn reduces the friction that exists between the bones making up the joint.

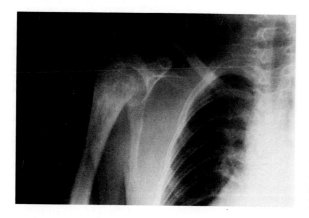

PICTURE 3.2 *The shoulder complex is one of the most commonly cited examples for a ball and socket joint.* (Photo credit: Susan Leavines/Photo Researchers)

Typical movements entertained by this joint type are flexion-extension and adduction-abduction. Biaxial joints also support circumduction, which is a combination of the aforementioned movements. Examples of this type of joint include the wrist and thumb. Finally, the human body also has triaxial joints, more commonly known as ball and socket joints. A **triaxial joint** permits movement in three planes; in other words, it allows the same type of movements found in biaxial joints with the addition of rotary motion. The best examples of triaxial joints are the shoulder and the hip joints.

This brief discussion of diarthrodial articulation gives the impression that there is a lot of material contained in any one joint. In fact the amount of movement that can occur before being restricted by surrounding tissue is known as the joint's **mobility.** The degree of mobility exhibited by any joint is determined by its **range of motion,** the total amount of movement through which the components of the joint can pass. We also refer to a joint's range of motion as **flexibility.**

Range of motion is limited by the tightness of the ligaments and the muscles surrounding the joint. The bony projections that exist in certain joints can also limit the range of motion. Can an individual's range of motion be changed? Yes! Most of us are familiar with a variety of exercises that are designed to increase our range of motion. Such exercises are part of routines usually performed before a bout of rigorous activity. These exercises are designed to try to "squeeze out" every last bit of stretch in the muscle and tendon material to allow the joint to move through a greater range of motion. Gymnasts and ballerinas are known for their incredible flexibility. They have no problem reaching down and touching their toes without bending their knees.

PICTURE 3.3   *Ballerinas exhibit extraordinary flexibility.* (Photo credit: ©Ray Massey/Tony Stone Images)

Muscle Attachments

The range of motion that can be exhibited at a particular joint also depends on how the muscle fibers are attached to the skeleton. In the simplest situation, there are two muscle attachments with bony structures with the muscle crossing one joint. One attachment is usually referred to as the origin of the muscle and the other attachment is referred to as the insertion. In many cases throughout the human anatomy, the origin and insertion of a muscle is not quite as simple as just described. For example, the biceps brachii is a fusiform (cigar-shaped) muscle that has two heads or points of origin, at the upper rim of the glenoid fossa and at the coracoid process of the scapula. The muscle traverses the elbow joint and inserts on the tuberosity of the radius. It is essential to consider the origins and insertions of muscles because they not only influence the range of the motion of the joint but also the efficiency of movement (i.e., mechanically and physiologically) that occurs about that joint. Obviously there is not sufficient space in this chapter to examine the origin and insertion of each and every muscle. However, the student of human movement would be well served by having a complete understanding of the diversity of muscle attachments distributed throughout the human body and the impact these attachments have on movement behavior.

Anatomical Planes and Axes

In order that each person studying human movement "speaks the same language," an anatomical reference system has been adopted that focuses on the cardinal planes of motion. The anatomical planes of motion are the sagittal, frontal, and transverse planes. The **midsagittal plane** extends from the top of the head to the feet splitting the body into right and left sides (Figure 3.3). Movements that can occur in the midsagittal plane are flexion, extension, and hyperextension.

The second plane of motion, the **frontal plane,** slices the body to create a front and back side. The common warm-up exercise of jumping jacks is a very good example of movement in the frontal plane. Sideward movement of the arms in the manner used during jumping jacks is called adduction and abduction.

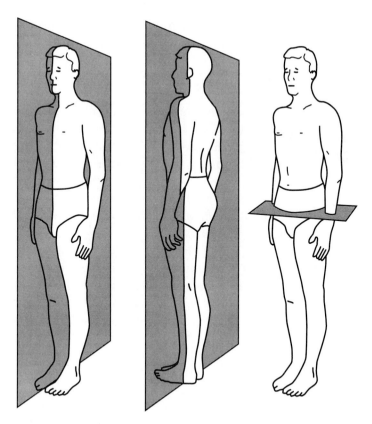

FIGURE 3.3 The midsagittal, frontal, and transverse planes of the human body.

The **transverse plane** of motion, also referred to as the horizontal plane, divides the human body into top and bottom parts (Figure 3.3). The most common movement that occurs in this plane is turning the head to look from side to side. However, all rotation movements occur in this plane.

In the next chapter, on biomechanics, a detailed examination of the human's center of gravity will be presented. Biomechanists describe the center of gravity as the body's balance or pivot point. The anatomical kinesiologist also considers the center of gravity to be an important anatomical marker. From this latter perspective, the center of gravity might be thought of as the point through which all the planes of motion pass. This point is also referred to as the body's center of mass.

If a movement is rotary in nature it occurs around an axis. Each of the planes of motion also have an axis of rotation. The axis of rotation lies at right angles to the plane of motion of interest. For example, joint actions in the sagittal plane occur about a horizontal axis. Movements in the frontal plane occur about an anteroposterior axis. Finally, actions that occur in the transverse plane are performed about the longitudinal axis.

Anatomical Lever Systems

Taking a very simple approach, we can think of the human skeleton as consisting of a series of bony segments linked together at a pivot point called a joint. The segments can be considered straight lines between the joints. When muscles contract, the segments move about the pivot point. The diversity of bones, joints, and their interactions with particular muscles allows the human body to produce a wide range of movements. Much of this movement variation can be produced because the human body makes use of the basic principles of levers.

A **lever** is a rigid object that revolves around a fixed point called a fulcrum or axis. The length of the lever between the fulcrum and the resistance is called the **resistance arm.** In contrast, the length of the lever between the fulcrum and the applied force is called the **force arm.** An important lever concept is **mechanical advantage,** or the ratio of the length of the force arm to the resistance arm.

Using levers provides a twofold functional advantage. First, the lever serves to increase the effect a force has on an object to which it is being applied. Secondly, the lever can increase the speed with which an object is moved. If the force arm is longer than the resistance arm, the lever will increase the force produced. Alternatively, if the resistance arm is longer than the force arm, the lever will increase speed. In many situations in the move-

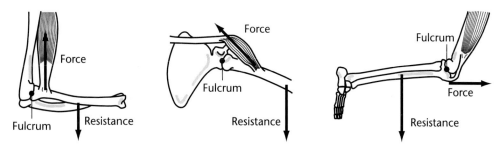

FIGURE 3.4 Most levers in the human body are third-class levers.

ment domain, the force arm is shorter than the resistance arm. For example, swinging an implement such as a tennis racquet or a baseball bat artificially increases the resistance arm, resulting in an increase in the speed of the striking point but requiring greater force to produce the movement. The make-up of the levers in the human body seems better suited to produce fast rather than forceful movements.

Levers can be classified into three different types (Figure 3.4), based on the relative position of the force, the fulcrum, and the resistance. A **first-class lever** consists of a fulcrum placed between the resistance and the applied force. A fulcrum at one end of the lever and the resistance applied closer to it than the force is called a **second-class lever.** When movements are a result of an eccentric contraction, a second class lever is involved. In these situations movements are quite efficient. A **third-class lever** is one in which the fulcrum is again at the end of the lever but the force is applied closer to it than the resistance. When concentric contractions are performed the human movement system works relatively inefficiently because this usually involves a third-class lever.

THE CENTRAL NERVOUS SYSTEM

The "control" center for movement in the human body is the **central nervous system (CNS),** which is composed of two important parts: the brain and the spinal cord.

The Brain

Figure 3.5 shows a drawing of a human brain, which is about three pounds of soft, spongy, pinkish-gray nerve tissue. At this point you will find it helpful

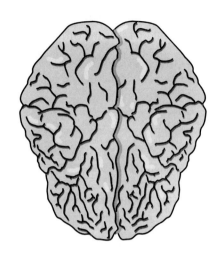

FIGURE 3.5   The human brain weighs approximately three pounds and consists of tightly packed nerve fibers.

to refer to Figure 3.6, which provides a flow chart of the important anatomical components discussed in the next sections. This figure will be useful to refer to as we discuss each part of the CNS.

The Cerebral Cortex.   The **cerebral cortex** accounts for about 80 percent of the brain's weight. Its many functions include abstract reasoning, speech, and the initiation of voluntary movement. The cerebral cortex has right and left cerebral hemispheres. These two halves are defined by a gap that runs from front to back. The **corpus callosum** is a nerve cable that crosses this gap to connect the hemispheres so that they can communicate.

Figure 3.7 illustrates two bands of nerve cells on the top of the cerebral cortex. One, the motor cortex, triggers our movements. The other, the somatosensory cortex, processes sensory information from the body. Penfield and Rasmussen (1950) determined the association between the motor and somatosensory cortexes and specific parts of the body. Their technique allowed patients to remain awake during brain surgery for treatment of epilepsy. They determined that stimulation of the motor cortex results in movement by specific muscles, and stimulation of the somatosensory cortex triggers sensations from specific body parts. Notice that some body parts, such as the thumb, cover large sections of these cortexes. Other parts, such as the forearm, account for much smaller sections.

The Forebrain.   The **hypothalamus,** located directly above the brainstem, contains nerve centers that control body temperature and rate of burn-

Structure   **Role in movement**

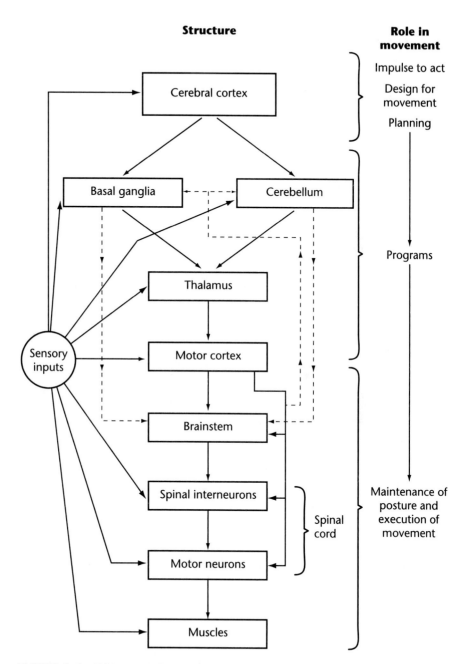

FIGURE 3.6   Diagrammatic representation of the organization of the motor system including its major structures and interconnections. (From Shea, Shebilske, & Worchel, *Motor Learning and Control,* Copyright © 1993 by Allyn & Bacon. Reprinted by permission.)

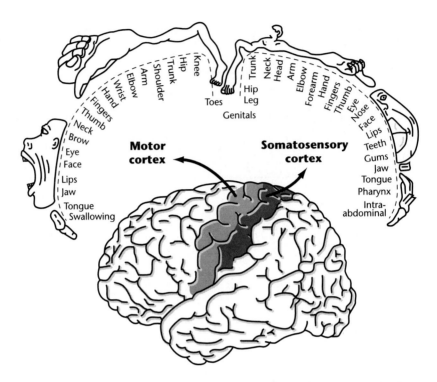

FIGURE 3.7   The motor and somatosensory areas are important parts of the cerebral cortex. (From Penfield & Rasmussen, *The Cerebral Cortex of Man,* New York: Macmillan, 1950)

ing fat and carbohydrates (see Chapter 5). Two egg-shaped structures make up the **thalamus,** which is located above the hypothalamus. The thalamus integrates incoming sensory information from all parts of our body. A damaged thalamus would distort our sensations of the world. The **basal ganglia** are four masses of gray matter located deep in the **forebrain.** This center modifies commands from other structures in the brain in ways that are not completely understood. One result of these modifications is to regulate "background" muscle tone. For example, when we write, the basal ganglia prepares the appropriate parts of the body for hand movements by tensing the upper part of our arm.

The Brainstem.   Figure 3.6 shows the **brainstem** connecting the rest of the brain to the spinal cord. The brainstem contains four important parts: the medulla, the pons, the cerebellum, and the midbrain. The medulla is a

HIGHLIGHT

Examining the Brain without Surgery—
Advancements in Neuroimaging

In the 1920s German psychiatrist Dr. Hans Berger demonstrated the use of an *electroencephalogram,* referred to as EEG. An EEG consists of amplified recordings of waves of electrical activity that are recorded via electrodes attached to an individual's head. Using EEGs, the researcher or clinician can examine the changes that occur in a variety of brain waves as a function of the type of activity being performed. In recent years major advancements have been made in neuroimaging techniques that provide a wealth of information about both the structure and the activity of the brain. One of these techniques involves the creation of a computer-generated representation of the brain structures using *computerized axial tomography,* or CAT scan. In a CAT scan, the brain is scanned with an X-ray beam while a computer

records how much of this beam is absorbed by different locations in the brain. The amount of absorption indicates the density of the scanned tissue, which can be captured in a computerized "picture" with a known color-coding system. An alternative neuroimaging procedure is *positron emission tomography,* or PET scan, used to provide a computer-generated image of the brain's metabolic activity. This procedure requires the administration of sugar that is temporarily radioactive. The brain is subsequently scanned to determine the amount of sugar absorbed by different areas of the brain. This technique is based on the assumption that since sugar is a fuel for activity, the more active areas will absorb a greater amount of sugar. Probably the most detailed view of the human nervous system at work can be obtained by using *magnetic resonance imaging,* or MRI, a procedure that permits detailed visualization of gross brain anatomy and pathology. MRI involves placing the head into a magnetic field that aligns the axis of rotation of all atoms with an odd atomic weight. A radio frequency then causes these atoms to spin. When the radio signal is terminated, a computer records the electromagnetic energy that is released as the atoms stop spinning. The structure of the pattern of energy released is ultimately displayed as a color-coded image that can be interpreted by the clinician or researcher.

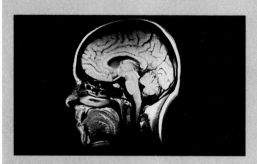

HIGHLIGHT 3.1 *Magnetic resonance imaging (MRI) is a neuroimaging procedure that provides great detailing of gross brain anatomy.* (Photo credit: Larry Mulvehill/Rainbow)

small, tube-like structure about the size of an index finger. It plays an integral role in controlling respiration and heartbeat and contributes to the maintenance of posture.

The pons has an important motor function. Damage to this location in the brainstem results in a movement disorder called "restless-leg" syndrome, which involves "thrashing about" during sleep. The cerebellum, sometimes called the small brain, is essential for regulating movements with respect to force, range, and rate of movements. Injury to the cerebellum results in problems with muscular tone, strength, and coordination. Prior to reaching the spinal cord the brainstem widens into an area called the midbrain, which contains the reticular formation central to regulation of arousal (see Chapter 9).

The Spinal Cord

The **spinal cord** is nerve tissue running from the brainstem through the backbone to the lower back. Figure 3.8 shows a cross section of the spinal cord. The white area contains myelinated fibers. **Myelinated nerve fibers** are surrounded by a myelin sheath that insulates them from other fibers. Myelin is made up of 70–80 percent lipids and 20–30 percent protein. The white matter carries information to and from the brain. Ascending nerves carry sensory information up to the brain. Descending nerves carry commands down from the brain to the muscles. There is also an area resembling a bent "H" that consists of gray matter. The gray area is composed of unmyelinated nerve fibers. Paralysis is the unfortunate consequence of injury to the descending nerves. For example, the viral disease polio attacks descending nerves.

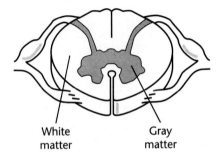

FIGURE 3.8 Cross section of the spinal cord showing the gray and white matter.

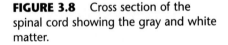

White matter   Gray matter

Spinal Reflexes. In order for us to turn the pages of this book, the brain and spinal cord must work together. However, our spinal cord can respond without waiting for the brain. This happens, for example, when we jerk our foot away from a thorn. Automatic action by the spinal cord is called a **spinal reflex.**

Spinal reflexes take advantage of the fact that muscles work in pairs. One muscle, an **agonist,** moves a joint in one direction when it is contracted. Contracting the **antagonist** muscle opposes the action of the agonist. Muscles also respond in groups of flexors that flex limbs and extensors that extend limbs. These muscle groups come into play during the seemingly simple action of pulling our foot away from a thorn. Figure 3.9 illustrates how this response is controlled by a withdrawal reflex, a spinal reflex that moves affected body parts away from painful stimulation. A sensory neuron stimulates interneurons in the spinal cord's gray matter. The interneurons stimulate the motor neurons of flexor muscles in the leg. They also innervate other interneurons that inhibit the leg's extensor muscles. This pattern of muscle innervations would withdraw our foot from the thorn. We also use an analogous withdrawal reflex to draw our hand away from a hot stove. The thorn example is more interesting, because we pull our foot up without falling down. We manage to stand because the withdrawal reflex in our legs always occurs with a **crossed extensor reflex.** This spinal reflex responds to painful foot stimulation by innervating the musculature to cause straightening of the leg on the unprovoked side, enabling it to bear weight. Figure 3.9 shows that the interneurons that stimulated flexors and inhibited extensors on the injured side simultaneously inhibited flexors and stimulated extensors on the other side.

If you have ever had a doctor hit your knee with a rubber hammer, he or she probably explained that it was to test a reflex. Figure 3.10b illustrates the neural circuitry involved in this reflex. It is a stretch reflex, a spinal reflex that ultimately results in a dramatic contraction in a stretched muscle. In Figure 3.10a, notice that the hammer tap causes an extensor muscle to be stretched, which in turn results in a signal being sent to the spinal cord. The afferent fiber that carries this signal synapses directly on the motor neuron that stimulates the muscle, causing it to contract. This monosynaptic (i.e., single-synapse) reflex is different from the other reflexes we have considered. The previous examples were polysynaptic (many synapses), since they had at least one interneuron between the sensory and motor neurons. Even though the stretch reflex is monosynaptic in contracting the stretched muscle, it does employ interneurons to inhibit the antagonists of the stretched muscle.

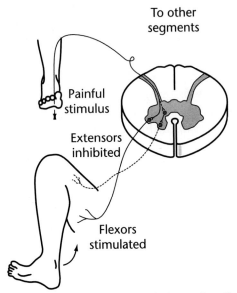

The withdrawal reflex

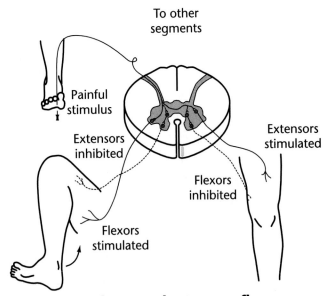

The crossed extensor reflex

FIGURE 3.9   The withdrawal reflex (top) and the crossed extensor reflex (bottom). (From Shea, Shebilske & Worchel, *Motor Learning and Control,* Copyright © 1993 by Allyn & Bacon. Reprinted by permission.)

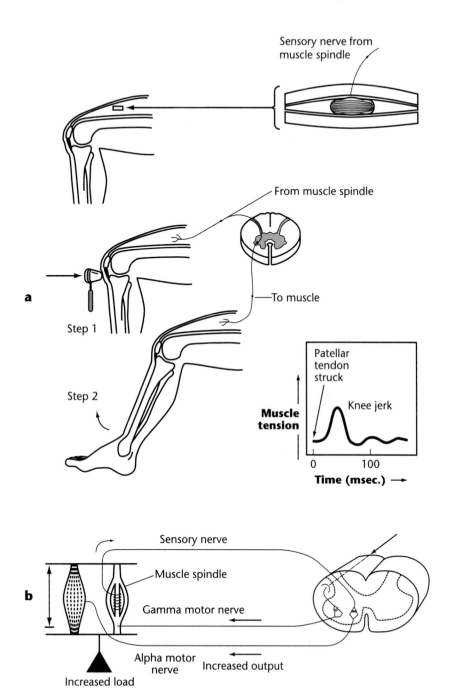

FIGURE 3.10 (a) The patellar tendon reflex is an example of a monosynaptic reflex (top), and (b) the neural circuitry involved in the stretch reflex (bottom). (From Shea, Shebilske & Worchel, *Motor Learning and Control,* Copyright © 1993 by Allyn & Bacon. Reprinted by permission.)

THE PERIPHERAL NERVOUS SYSTEM

While the CNS is the "control center" for producing movement, this system could not execute its wishes without an efficient communication network. The communication network transmits information to (i.e., sensory) and from (i.e., motor) the CNS and is called the peripheral nervous system. The **peripheral nervous system (PNS)** is made up of sensory nerves that relay messages from the senses, throughout the body, and back to the CNS. In addition, the PNS also contains motor nerves that take the commands from the CNS to the muscles that will be involved in executing a movement. Together, the CNS and PNS provide the necessary tools to control movements ranging from those such as getting up out of a chair to a tumbling pass performed by a gymnast. Let's start our examination of the PNS with the main unit of communication—the neuron. We will then take a look at the sensory receptors, followed by a look at the neuromuscular system.

Neurons: The Communication System

Neurons are cells that receive and send messages throughout the nervous system. Your brain contains 100 to 200 billion neurons, and each one connects with many others. As a result, your nervous system has more connections between neurons than there are stars in our galaxy (Hoyenga & Hoyenga, 1988). Figure 3.11 shows the parts that make up a neuron. Some features are in common with most cell types: a cell nucleus, a cell membrane, and a cell body. Other components are unique to the neuron's function of receiving and sending messages. **Dendrites** are tiny branchlike fibers extending from the cell body that receive messages. An **axon** is a single extension that carries messages to thousands of terminal branches that reach out to dendrites of other neurons. The illustrated axon has a fatty covering called a myelin sheath, which has gaps called nodes of Ranvier. Myelinated axons carry neural messages faster because the impulses skip from one node to the next.

Functional Types of Neurons.   Three categories of neurons carry neural messages between the brain, spinal cord, and muscles. Sensory neurons, also called **afferent neurons** (the prefix "a-" means "to"), carry signals to the brain or spinal cord. Motor neurons, also called **efferent neurons** (the prefix "e-" means "from"), carry signals from the brain or spinal cord. **Interneurons** originate and terminate in the brain or spinal cord. We will

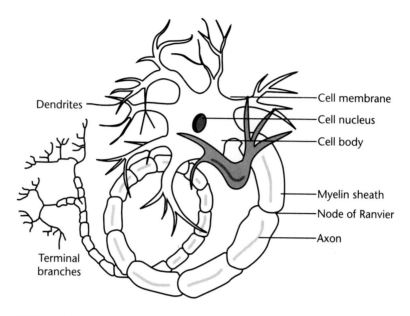

Dendrites

Cell membrane

Cell nucleus

Cell body

Myelin sheath

Node of Ranvier

Axon

Terminal branches

FIGURE 3.11   A myelinated neuron, which provides the main form of communication throughout the central and peripheral nervous system.

encounter many examples of these categories when we consider the larger structures of the nervous system.

Neural Impulses.   Neural impulses are responsible for sending and re-turning messages throughout our nervous system. They are enabling you to read and understand at this moment. In fact, they are the basis for all our perceptions and actions. It is rather astonishing, therefore, that the language of neural messages is a simple binary "off-on" code. The off and on states are defined by the distribution of ions, or charged particles (sodium and potas-sium) at the surface of the nerve fiber. Ions, with positive and negative charges, are inside and outside every neuron. An imbalance of these charges creates a **membrane potential,** which is an electric tension across the cell membrane. During the off state, also called the resting state or the state of polarization, negatively charged ions are concentrated on the inside and positively charged ions are concentrated on the outside. During the on state, also called the action potential or state of depolarization, sodium ions rush inside one spot in the neuron, then potassium ions rush out to bring the neuron back to its resting state. This process is immediately repeated at a

HIGHLIGHT

Carpal Tunnel Syndrome

Do you spend a great deal of time at the computer keyboard? Have you ever experienced pain, numbness, or weakness in your fingers? Has this pain sometimes radiated up your arm and sometimes to your neck? If so, you may have what is commonly referred to as *carpal tunnel syndrome.* This condition has received a great deal of attention in recent years since it seems to be a pervasive problem in the workplace, especially for individuals who perform repetitive hand activities such as typing. The carpal tunnel is an opening in the hand that consists of the bones of the wrist on the bottom and the transverse carpal ligament at the top. The median nerve and flexor tendons project through this opening to the hand. A number of situations can cause the material surrounding the tendons, called tenosynovium, to become irritated or inflamed; for example, arthritis, wrist fractures, repetitive use of the hands, or placing the arms and wrists into uncomfortable or unnatural positions for extended periods of time. When inflammation of the tenosynovium occurs, the tendons swell or thicken, and the pressure in the carpal tunnel begins to increase. More importantly, as the pressure increases, the result is "squeezing" of the median nerve against the transverse carpal ligament. This can eventually reach a point at which the nerve can no longer function as it should, resulting in pain and numbness in the hand. Currently a great deal of research is being conducted to find a remedy for this problem. In the case of typing, numerous new computer keyboards and attachments have recently surfaced that are specifically designed to maintain the hands in a normal orientation. Hopefully these design modifications will lower the occurrence of carpal tunnel syndrome.

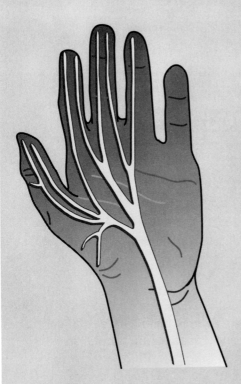

HIGHLIGHT 3.2   *Carpal tunnel syndrome occurs when the median nerve is "squeezed" against the transverse carpal ligament.*

neighboring area until the action potential travels the entire length of the cell membrane (see Figure 3.12).

Synaptic Transmission. When an action potential reaches the end of an axon, it meets a **synapse,** which is a junction between two neurons. Movement of a neural impulse across this junction is called synaptic transmission. The process has four steps. First, the action potential reaches an axon terminal, a tiny knob at the end of an axon's terminal branch. Second, a synaptic vesicle releases a chemical transmitter such as acetylcholine. Third, the neurotransmitter crosses a synaptic space, a very small gap between neurons. And fourth, the neurotransmitter binds with receptor sites on the dendrite.

A sufficient release of chemical transmitter substances at the synapse will cause an action potential in the receiving cell. The strength must be above a minimum or threshold level. This threshold is sometimes compared to the minimum trigger pull required to fire a gun. A bullet will not fire if the trig-

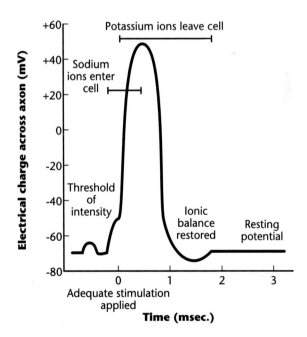

FIGURE 3.12 The neural message carried by the neuron must be above a certain threshold to reach its destination.

ger is not pulled hard enough. Similarly, an action potential will not fire unless synaptic transmission is strong enough.

The initiation of an action potential is an all-or-none event, which again is similar to firing a gun. A trigger pulled hard enough to fire a gun is hard enough to fire it at full force. Pulling the trigger harder will not make the bullet go faster or farther. Similarly, a neuron either fires an action potential at full force or it doesn't fire it at all. Stronger stimuli do not trigger stronger action potentials. They do, however, trigger them at a faster rate. Thus, the strength of a stimulus is indicated by the rate at which neurons fire.

The Sensory System

Before we make a voluntary movement (i.e., compared to involuntary movements or reflexive actions) we must gather information from the environment to assess the current state of affairs. The way we sense the world around us is via the transmission arising from thousands of sensory receptors. These receptors can be divided into two broad classes based on the kind of information they provide: exteroceptors and proprioceptors. **Exteroceptors** are sensory receptors that receive stimuli that provide a description of the environment, such as vision and hearing. **Proprioceptors** are sensory receptors that receive stimuli that provide information about the current state of our body. These include the vestibular apparatus, muscle spindles, and golgi tendon organs, as well as various pressure and temperature receptors.

Exteroception.   We all use exteroception to detect, identify, and locate objects in the world around us. So let's think about how our sensory abilities allow us to do this.

Vision.   Figure 3.13 highlights some of the important parts of the human eye. The sclera is the white opaque outer wall of the eye. The cornea is a transparent curved surface on the front of the eye that bends light to focus it as it enters the eye. In a chamber directly behind the cornea is a clear fluid called the aqueous humor, which nourishes the cornea. The iris is a doughnut-shaped muscle, and the pupil is the opening in the middle of the iris. The iris opens and closes the pupil to regulate the amount of light that enters the eye. Directly behind the iris is a transparent structure called the lens. The lens is held in place by ciliary muscles that stretch between the sclera and lens. The ciliary muscles can change the shape of the lens in order to make fine adjustments in focus. The lens gets rounder to focus closer objects and flatter to focus farther ones. These fine adjustments are called accommoda-

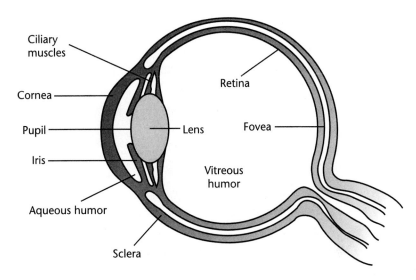

Ciliary
muscles

Retina

Cornea

Pupil — Lens

Fovea

Iris

Vitreous
humor

Aqueous humor

Sclera

FIGURE 3.13   The human eye is an important exteroceptive device.

tion. The vitreous humor is a transparent gel that fills the eye's main chamber and keeps it from collapsing.

The retina covers most of the eye's inner wall and contains tissue, blood vessels, receptors that respond to light, neurons that process information from receptors, and nerve fibers that carry information to the brain. Most blood vessels and nerve fibers are routed around the fovea, a very sensitive area of the retina. The retina contains two kinds of receptors: (1) cones located mostly in the fovea, and (2) rods located everywhere except the fovea. Cones in the fovea serve central or focal vision, which is the center of the total area that we see at any one time. When we look at something, we move our eyes so that the image of the object falls on the fovea. We see that object in the center of everything else that we see. The area of central vision covers about 30 letter positions up and down when this book is held at a normal reading distance. This area corresponds to the fovea and some of the retina immediately surrounding it (about 8 degrees). Everything seen outside of central vision is defined as peripheral or **ambient vision.**

Hearing.   Our ears also provide important exteroceptive information. Figure 3.14 displays important components of the human ear, which has three subdivisions: the external ear, the middle ear, and the inner ear. The external ear consists of the pinna, which is the elastic flap we usually refer to as the ear, and the ear canal, a tubular passage that funnels sound from the pinna

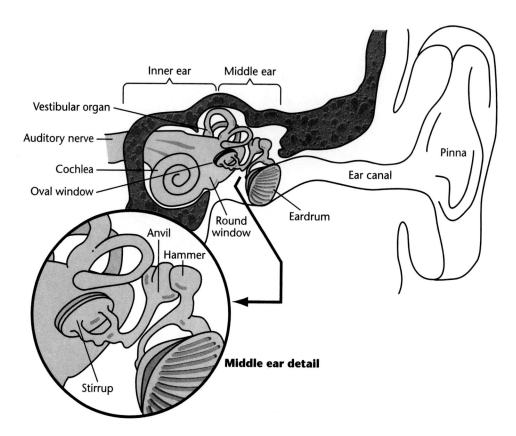

FIGURE 3.14   The ear has three parts: the external ear, the middle ear, and the inner ear.

inward. The eardrum is a thin membrane stretched over the innermost end of the ear canal. Sound waves strike the pinna and are funneled through the ear canal to the eardrum. Turning the ears toward a sound source and cupping the hands around the ears helps to catch more sound waves. The ear drum converts the sound from waves in air to waves in a membrane.

The middle ear is a small air cavity containing a chain of three bones: the hammer, anvil, and stirrup. The hammer is connected to the eardrum so that waves in the eardrum move the bones, which carry the waves inward. The inner ear, which looks like a snail shell, is called the cochlea, the Latin word for snail. The cochlea has an oval window that is an opening covered by a membrane connected to the stirrup. Thus sound crossing the bones in the middle ear make waves in the oval window. These vibrations then make waves in a fluid inside the cochlea. The fluid carries the waves to the basilar membrane, which stretches from one end of the cochlea to the other. Finally, the basilar membrane carries the wave to hair cells, which are receptor cells on the basilar membrane.

Cutaneous Senses.   Cutaneous senses refer to the senses of the skin: temperature, pain, and pressure sensations. Figure 3.15 shows a cross section of skin. It contains a variety of nerve endings that play a role in the cutaneous senses: cold (End bulbs of Krause), warm (Ruffini endings), pain (free nerve endings), and pressure (Pacinian corpuscles, free nerve endings, and Meissner corpuscles). This list does not account for all the data on cutaneous sensitivity. For example, cold spots are found in areas that have few or no End bulbs of Krause. The list is therefore only a simplified first approximation to the link between cutaneous sensitivity and specific receptors.

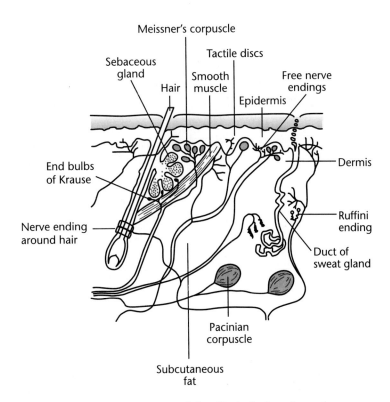

FIGURE 3.15   Cross section of the skin including the various cutaneous receptors.

Proprioception. Traditionally, the term *proprioception* applies to perception of individual body parts or the whole body, whether stationary or in motion. Another term, *kinesthesia* (from the Greek *kinein*, "to move" and *aisthesia*, "perception") refers to the sensations of position, tension, and movement of body parts. Originally the term only applied to moving body parts, but today it is applied to both moving and stationary situations. Thus, the terms *proprioception* and *kinesthesia* are practically synonymous as they are used today.

Sense organs in the vestibular system, which is located in the inner ear, determine our ability to perceive orientation and rotary acceleration. Figure 3.16 shows three major components of the system: the utricles, saccules, and semicircular canals. The utricles and saccules mediate perception of orientation with respect to gravity; the semicircular canals mediate the perception of angular accelerations. The pull of gravity moves stonelike calcium deposits in the utricles and saccules. This movement bends hair cells, which send neural messages to the brain. Angular acceleration moves fluid in the semicircular canals relative to hair cells, causing them to bend and to send

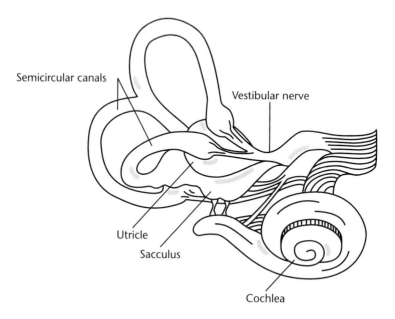

FIGURE 3.16 The semicircular canals of the vestibular system provide information concerning head position that helps the human maintain upright posture.

messages to the brain. The vestibular system plays an important role in maintaining a particular orientation with respect to our surroundings.

Sensations of position, tension, and movement of body parts are perceived through receptors in joints, tendons, and muscles. Joints contain a variety of receptors (e.g., Ruffini and Pacinian corpuscles, and free nerve endings). These receptors respond to both changes in joint angles and to muscle forces in the absence of joint movement. Tendons have simple receptors located between the muscle and the bone. The **golgi tendon organ** (GTO) responds to changes in muscle force, which can be created by passively pulling the muscle, actively changing the muscle length, or actively contracting the muscle without changing its length, as in isometric exercises.

Probably the most important proprioceptor is contained in the muscle. Called a **muscle spindle,** this device not only sends information to the CNS but can also receive information from the central nervous system. The spindles, depicted in Figure 3.17, run parallel to the main muscle, so that they are stretched when the main muscle is stretched. Stretching of the muscle spindle activates the receptors that send messages to the central nervous system. These receptors are in the middle of the spindle and they can also be stretched by contracting the tiny muscles at the ends of the spindle. The spindle muscles are innervated whenever the main muscle fibers are innervated. This dual innervation pattern causes the spindle to respond to changes in either muscle length or muscle force.

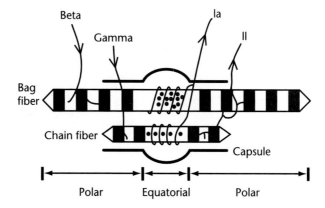

FIGURE 3.17 The muscle spindles, which lay parallel to the main muscle fibers, are a primary source of proprioceptive stimuli.

THE MUSCULAR SYSTEM

We tend to take for granted the extraordinary range of movements that the human body can perform. Each movement is a function of a series of complex events that occur before a muscle actually contracts. This section will focus on the muscular system. The nerve fiber provides the means by which a neural impulse can be transmitted to the appropriate muscle. As a result of neural stimulation, groups of muscle fibers contract to produce particular movements. Together the nerve and muscle fibers make up the motor unit. This is the fundamental "package" that is essential for producing coordinated movement.

Structure of Skeletal Muscle

Let's turn our attention for a moment to the movement effector, the muscle. Each muscle cell is composed of many thousands of threadlike structures called **myofibrils** that contain the proteins essential for contraction (see Figure 3.18). The myofibrils are the very site of the contractile process, which will be discussed in the next section. Many myofibrils comprise a muscle cell or fiber. A **muscle fiber** is a cylindrical cell with a cell membrane called a

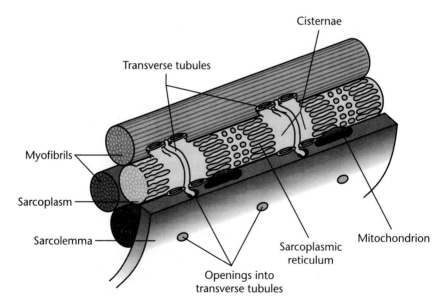

FIGURE 3.18   The muscle is made up of thousands of small fibers called myofibrals.

sarcolemma. Fibers lie in parallel and are separated by a layer of connective tissue called the **endomysium.** The **perimysium** surrounds a bundle of up to 150 fibers called the **muscle fasciculus.** These bundles are grouped to form the entire muscle and are surrounded by a fibrous connective tissue called the **epimysium.** This connective tissue becomes tapered at the ends of the muscle to form the connective tissue called tendons.

We must return to the myofibrils to discover the true site of contraction. Myofibrils contain two types of protein filaments important to the contraction process. The first is called **myosin.** Myosin molecules make up the thick filaments. The other protein is **actin,** which makes up the thin filaments. The arrangement of these two protein filaments gives the muscle myofibril a striated appearance. The myofibril is further subdivided into segments called **sarcomeres.** Sarcomeres are separated by a thin disc of protein referred to as a z-line. Within each sarcomere are areas in which the actin and myosin filaments overlap and regions in which they do not overlap. It is the sarcomere unit that actually shortens during contraction.

The sarcoplasm is served by a network of membranes called the **sarcoplasmic reticulum** that surround and run parallel with the myofibrils. The sarcoplasmic reticulum is the storage site for calcium. The **transverse tubules,** which extend into the myofibrils, can be considered the plumbing for spreading the action potential from the outside to the inner regions of the cell. When a nerve impulse crosses the neuromuscular junction it travels down the transverse tubules to the sarcoplasmic reticulum. This causes the release of calcium, which is the "trigger" for contraction to occur.

Sliding Filament Theory.   Contraction is a complex set of processes that involve a number of proteins and energy production systems. While some details of this process are understood, a detailed explanation of the process is beyond the scope of this chapter. The end result, however, is actin filaments sliding over the myosin filaments. This results in a shortening of the sarcomeres as the z-lines move closer to each other. It is generally believed that sliding occurs because numerous cross bridges extend out from the myosin filaments and attach (or bind) to the actin filaments. Energy for this process comes from the breakdown of **adenosine triphosphate (ATP)** into adenosine diphosphate (ADP) and phosphate. The liberation of stored energy will be discussed in detail in Chapter 5, in the section on energy systems.

The most commonly accepted model of contraction proposes that as cross bridges are established when the action potential moves down the muscle, other cross bridges are released and subsequently reattached. This process of attachment, release, and reattachment, called **cross-bridge cy-**

cling, can result in a significant shortening of the entire muscle. A single cycle of cross-bridge attachment across the length of a muscle will only result in about 1 percent shortening, but cross-bridge cycling can shorten a muscle by as much as 60 percent (Powers & Howley, 1990). It is important that all the cross-bridge attachments do not occur at the same time. The attachment-release-reattachment that results in a "ratcheting" of the filaments closer together must be cycled in such a way that a relatively large number of attachments remain while a few are released and reattached. This cycling has been likened to the movement of the legs of a centipede. It is important to note that this process seems to be limited primarily by the availability of free calcium and ATP. Relaxation occurs when the nerve impulse no longer triggers the release of calcium. The calcium is once again reabsorbed by the sarcoplasmic reticulum. In the absence of calcium, the cross bridges are deactivated and slide back to their resting position.

Fiber Types.   Muscle fibers can be differentiated in terms of their biochemical characteristics, which in turn determines their performance capability. **Fast twitch fibers** in humans have a more limited capacity for aerobic metabolism and are more easily fatigued. These fibers are activated by larger neurons, are generally richer in energy stores, and generally contain more myofibrils. Thus, fast twitch fibers have a large anaerobic capacity because these fibers can develop a great deal of force very rapidly. Slow twitch fibers are better equipped to shuttle nutrients and essential elements from the blood to the muscle cells than fast twitch fibers. Thus **slow twitch fibers** have the capacity for relatively high aerobic metabolism that results in a high resistance to fatigue. The neuron that activates slow twitch fibers is generally smaller and slower conducting than that of fast twitch fibers. In addition, slow twitch fibers are generally smaller than fast twitch fibers. The slower release of calcium in slow twitch fibers is a factor in a slower and ultimately reduced capacity to produce force when compared with fast twitch fibers. **Intermediate twitch fibers** have characteristics that are somewhere in between the fast twitch and slow twitch fibers. In fact, fiber type should be viewed as a continuum with muscle fiber characteristics ranging from slow to fast twitch.

The Motor-Unit

A group of muscle fibers are innervated by one neuron, called a motor neuron. The stimulus is an action potential sent along the motor neuron to the fibers. A motor neuron and the muscle fibers it innervates is called a **motor-**

unit. The number of muscle fibers in a motor-unit varies. More than a thousand fibers may comprise a motor-unit in the lower leg, while a motor-unit in the hand or eye may contain one hundred or less muscle fibers. Generally, the fewer muscle fibers in the motor-unit, the more precisely the muscle can be controlled. The force exerted by a muscle usually comes from the combined activity of many motor-units, called a **motoneuronal pool.** Next we must consider how particular motor-units are selected and "called into action."

Motor-Unit Recruitment.   To recruit motor-units means to activate them. They are usually activated and deactivated in a set sequence. The **size principle** is the most popular theory of how this orderly recruitment is controlled. Accordingly, the sequence depends on the size of the motor neurons. Motor-units with the smallest motor neurons are recruited first and deactivated last. Motor-units with the largest motor neurons are recruited last and deactivated first. Figure 3.19 shows a simplified motoneuronal pool with five motor-units. The smallest motor-unit is 1; the largest is 5; and the intermediate ones are 2, 3, and 4 in order. The figure represents a special case in which motor-unit recruitment is the only factor affecting muscle force. Motor-units are recruited in the order 1, 2, 3, 4, and 5. Then motor-unit 5 is the first to be deactivated; motor-unit 4 is deactivated next, and so on. Notice motor-unit 1, the smallest, is active from the beginning to the end of the contraction, and motor-unit 5, the largest, is only active during the brief

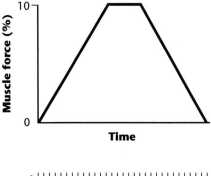

FIGURE 3.19   Simplified motoneuronal pool with five motor-units. The selection of these units is in part based on size. (From Powers, Scott K. & Howley, Edward T., *Exercise Physiology: Theory and Application to Fitness and Performance,* 2d ed. Reprinted by permission of Leland G. Johnson, Augustana College.)

period of maximal force. According to the size principle, the order of recruitment is predetermined by size and is not directly controlled by the brain. However, there is evidence that under some conditions motor-units can be selectively recruited.

Remember, motor-unit size corresponds to specific muscle characteristics or fiber type. For example, the smallest motor-units, slow twitch, are slow-contracting, low-force, and fatigue-resistant. In contrast, the largest motor-units, fast twitch, are fast-contracting, high-force, and fatigable.

Stimulation Frequency.   Muscle force depends not only on the number of active motor-units, but also on the rate at which motor-units discharge action potentials. Figure 3.20 shows the changes in force accrued as the muscle is repetitively stimulated at different frequencies. At very slow frequencies, the muscle develops force, relaxes, then develops force again. As the frequency is increased, the force from one stimulation adds to the force from a previous stimulation. This addition process is called **summation** and the blending together of contractions is called **tetanus.** It has also been suggested that muscle force increases when motor-unit stimulations are synchronized.

Although we have described recruitment and stimulation frequency separately, these two options are executed at the same time. That is, muscle forces are often determined by a combination of both kinds of control processes. You will use both kinds at the same time as you go about your activities today.

Length-Tension Relationship.   It is important to note that the force or tension that a muscle exerts under tetanus is also related to the length of the muscle prior to stimulation, because the forces exerted in whole muscle–

FIGURE 3.20   A recording of muscle tension being gradually increased with simple twitches initially followed by tetanic or fused stimuli. (From Powers, Scott K. & Howley, Edward T., *Exercise Physiology: Theory and Application to Fitness and Performance,* 2d ed. Reprinted by permission of Leland G. Johnson, Augustana College.)

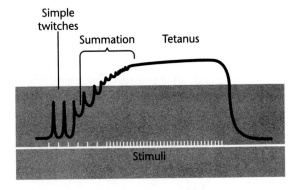

tendon units can be classified into two general categories: forces attributable to contraction of the muscle fibers and those attributable to the elastic properties of the muscles-tendons. The potential force resulting from isometric contraction is greatest when the muscle is at an optimal length. However, as Figure 3.21 indicates, force decreases as the muscle is lengthened or shortened. At optimal length, a maximum number of cross bridges between the muscle filaments is available and maximum tension can be produced. The filaments are pulled apart as the muscle is lengthened and the tension that can be generated via contraction decreases. Likewise, the cross bridges overlap as the muscle is shortened, which interferes with the production of force.

The muscles-tendons also have elastic qualities that can be exploited in the control of movement. This elastic quality can serve two purposes. First, it serves to dampen or "smooth out" the process of shortening or lengthening the muscle. Second, these connective tissues can exert passive forces when stretched. For example, during most human movement, the force exerted by the connective tissue is not too significant, but during high-performance movements such as jumping, it is may be responsible for storage of energy as a muscle lengthens immediately prior to rapid shortening.

These forces can be used alone or in conjunction with forces derived from muscle contraction to produce a controlled result. The resulting force available to the performer is the sum of the active (contraction) and passive (elastic) components. It is interesting to note that children will rapidly lower themselves after completing a pull-up in an attempt to "bounce-up" for the

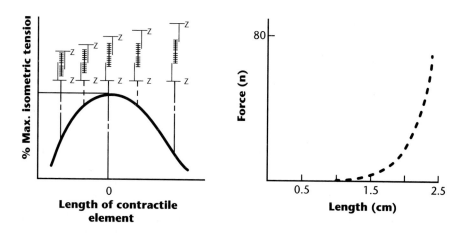

FIGURE 3.21   Tension produced by the contractile elements of the muscle (left), and by the elastic properties of the muscle-tendon complex. (Data from Winter, 1990 and Ralston, Inman, Strait, & Shaffrath, 1947)

next attempt. Apparently they have learned that a certain amount of force can be generated by stretching the muscle-tendon. It is much more difficult if the instructor requires the child to come to rest at the bottom. It is also interesting that children often get "stuck" just before their chin gets to the bar. This is the point at which the muscle is shortened to the extent that the force generated via contraction is reduced and few if any forces are available from elastic qualities of the muscle-tendon.

Classifications of Movement.   Movement occurs because each end of a skeletal muscle is attached to a bone by connective tissue called tendons. **Flexion** occurs when the shortening of the muscle tissue causes a joint angle to decrease. **Extension** is when the activation of the muscle results in an increased joint angle. **Concentric contractions** result when the active muscle shortens, and **eccentric contractions** occur when the active muscle lengthens. Performing a biceps curl involves bringing the weight up (concentric contraction of the flexor muscles) and slowly returning the weight to the lowered position (eccentric contraction of the flexor muscles). The second phase of the lift is eccentric because the active muscle lengthens as the force produced by the muscle resists the pull of gravity on the weight. Recall that in the latter situation (i.e., eccentric contraction), a second-class lever system is involved. In this case, the mechanical advantage is greater than one, thus movements resulting from eccentric contractions are very efficient. In the example provided, the activation of the muscle results in an **isotonic** (or dynamic) **contraction.** However, if the forces generated as a result of activation of the muscle are insufficient to cause movement, it is an **isometric** (or static) **contraction.**

FINAL COMMENT

In one sense the human mover might be considered a "complex machine" because so many different parts are involved. Each of these structures makes a unique but important contribution to the production of movement. This chapter looked at each of the fundamental components of our movement machinery. First we examined the role of the skeletal system. The skeleton of the human mover can be viewed as the "scaffolding" of the system. The skeleton consists of many bones that are connected to form joints, which are supported and strengthened by material such as cartilage and ligaments. This scaffolding provides numerous benefits for the human performer. For example, it provides our characteristic shape, offers protection for the inter-

 **HIGHLIGHT**

Gray's Anatomy

In this chapter the general make-up of the skeletal, nervous, and muscular systems has been reviewed both in terms of structure and function. Obviously in an introductory text such as this the depth of information is quite limited. This is not the case in what is probably the most famous of human anatomy textbooks, *Gray's Anatomy*. This textbook was first written by Dr. Henry Gray, a Fellow of the Royal College of Surgeons in England and a lecturer on anatomy at St. George's hospital medical school. The book includes a thorough discussion of general anatomy as well as detailed descriptions of all the major systems in the human body. This incredible detail is supplemented by over 700 illustrations, many in color, which allow the student to easily discriminate unique parts of the anatomy being discussed. In essence, *Gray's Anatomy* leads the reader through the dissection of the human cadaver.

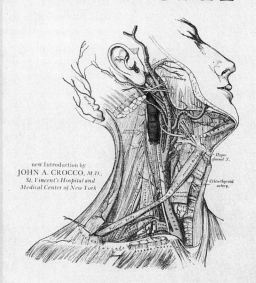

HIGHLIGHT 3.3   Gray's Anatomy *should be on every movement scientist's bookshelf.* (Photo credit: The Granger Collection, New York)

The success of this book is demonstrated by the fact that it has been an international best-seller for over 100 years. Moreover, it is used as a primary reference in a variety of fields, including medicine, neuroscience, and other allied health fields such as exercise science. This is probably one reference book that should be on the shelf of every movement scientist.

nal organs, acts as a production unit of red blood cells, and plays a critical part of movement production.

Another important role of the skeletal system is that it provides sites onto which the muscles attach. The muscles can be viewed as the "motors" of our movement architecture. These motors come in many different sizes and shapes but are usually well designed for their intended purpose. Movement about a joint is the result of contraction of the muscles. At this point it is only important to understand that the occurrence of a muscle contraction is the product of a complex set of processes that involve a number of proteins and energy production systems. (Obtaining the energy or "fuel" for muscle contraction will be detailed in Chapter 5.)

While the "fuel" for contracting the human "motors" or muscles was not discussed, the "communication" system that allows information to be passed between the "control center" or the brain and the muscle was reviewed. Communication is maintained via the nervous system, more specifically by the nerves that make up this system. Efferent nerves carry information away from the central nervous system to a variety of locations including the muscles. In contrast, afferent nerves allow information to be delivered to the central nervous system from specially designed sensory systems. These systems provide visual, auditory, and proprioceptive information that can impact how movements are subsequently executed. For example, fast movement modifications can be made via spinal level processes, as in the case of reflexive actions. Alternatively, voluntary movement adjustments, based on information derived by the sensory systems, can be instigated by the main control center, the brain.

This chapter provided an overview of the architecture of the human, highlighting the scaffolding (the skeleton), the motors (the muscles), and the communication link (the nervous system). Subsequent chapters will consider how to optimize the functioning of this system by more closely examining some of the mechanical (e.g., biomechanics), physiological (e.g., exercise physiology, fitness and health, motor development), and psychological (e.g., sport psychology, motor learning and control) issues that impact the behavioral capability of the human mover.

QUESTIONS FOR THOUGHT

- The skeleton provides a number of important functions for the human. Discuss these functions.
- There are three classes of levers. Describe the important characteristics of each lever type. For human movement, comment on how the type of lever involved changes with the type of muscle contraction being performed.

- Identify examples of movements that occur in each of the three cardinal planes of movement.
- The "communication" system (the nervous system) and the human "motors" (muscles) interact in the form of a motor-unit. What is a motor-unit? If someone gradually squeezed an object harder and harder, how would the person recruit the motor-units for this action?
- If the mass of an object that an individual is holding in his or her hand is suddenly increased, what happens? How does the individual compensate for this?

KEY TERMS

actin
adenosine triphosphate (ATP)
afferent neurons
agonist
amphiarthrodial articulation
antagonist
appendicular skeleton
articulation
axial skeleton
axon
basal ganglia
biaxial joint
brainstem
central nervous system (CNS)
cerebral cortext
concentric contraction
condyle
corpus callosum
cross-bridge cycling
crossed extensor reflex
dendrites
diarthrodial articulation
eccentric contraction
efferent neurons
endomysium
epimysium
extension
exteroceptors
fast twitch fibers
first-class lever
flexibility
flexion
foramen

force arm
forebrain
fossa
frontal plane
golgi tendon organ (GTO)
hypothalamus
intermediate twitch fibers
interneurons
isometric contraction
isotonic contraction
lever
ligaments
mechanical advantage
membrane potential
midsagittal plane
mobility
motoneuronal pool
motor-unit
muscle fasciculus
muscle fibers
muscle spindle
myelinated nerve fibers
myofibris
myosin
neurons
nonaxial joint
perimysium
peripheral nervous system (PNS)
proprioceptors
range of motion
resistance arm
sarcolemma
sarcomeres

sarcoplasmic reticulum
second-class lever
size principle
skeleton
slow twitch fibers
spinal cord
spinal reflex
summation
synapse
synarthrodial articulation

tendons
tetanus
thalamus
third-class lever
transverse plane
transverse tubules
triaxial joint
tuberosity
uniaxial joint

RESOURCES

Textbooks

Enoka, R. M. (1994). *Neuromechanical Basis of Kinesiology* (2nd ed.). Champaign, IL: Human Kinetic Publishers.

Hinson, M. M. (1981). *Kinesiology* (2nd ed.). Dubuque, IA: W. C. Brown Publishers.

Kreighbaum, E., & Barthels, K. M. (1990). *Biomechanics* (3rd ed.). New York: Macmillan Publishing Company.

Luttgens, K., & Wells, K. F. (1992). *Kinesiology: Scientific Basis of Human Motion* (8th ed.). Dubuque, IA: W. C. Brown Publishers.

Pick, T. P., & Howden, R. (Eds.). (1977). *Gray's Anatomy.* New York: Bounty Books.

Journals

Muscle and Nerve
Brain and Behavioral Sciences
Experimental Brain Research
Journal of Applied Physiology
Journal of Bone and Joint Surgery
Physical Therapy

Professional Societies

American Association of Anatomists
American College of Sport Medicine
American Physical Therapy Association
American Physiological Society
Society for Neurosciences

Internet

World Wide Web (WWW) Home Pages
http://www.nlm.nih.gov/extramural_research.dir/visible_human.html
http://www.meddean.luc.edu/lumen/MedEd/GrossAnatomy/LowerLimb/
    LECases.html

http://ivory.lm.com:80/~nab/
http://ccwfc.utexas.edu/~cwright/physicaltherapy.html
http://info.lut.ac.uk/research/paad/home.html

Listservers
Athletic Training
send: subscribe athtrn-l <your name>
to: listserv@iubvm.ucs.indiana.edu

American Society of Sport Medicine
send: subscribe amssmnet <your name>
to: listserv@msu.edu

Occupational Therapy
send: subscribe occup-ther <your name>
to: occup-ther@ac.dal.ca

Physical Therapy
send: subscribe pther-l <your name>
to: listserv@vm.ucs.ualberta.ca

Neuromuscular Aspects of Movement
send: subscribe neuromus <your name>
to: listserv@sjuvm.stjohns.edu

REFERENCES

Caine, D. J., & Lindler, K. J. (1985). Overuse injuries of growing bones: The young female gymnast at risk? *Physician and Sportsmedicine,* 13, 118–123.

Hoyenga, K. B., & Hoyenga, K. T. (1988). *Psychobiology: The neuron and behavior.* Pacific Grove, CA: Brooks/Cole.

Penfield, W., & Rasmussen, T. (1950). *The Cerebral Cortex of Man.* New York: Macmillan.

Powers, S. K., & Howley, E. T. (1990). *Exercise Physiology: Theory and Application to Fitness and Performance.* Dubuque, IA: W. C. Brown.

Ralston, H. J., Inman. V. T., Strait, L. A., & Shaffrath, M. D. (1947). Mechanics of human isolated voluntary muscle. *American Journal of Physiology,* 151, 612–620.

Shea, C. H., Shebilske, W. L., & Worchel, S. (1993). *Motor Learning and Control.* Englewood Cliffs, NJ: Prentice Hall.

Winter, D. A. (1990). *Biomechanics and Motor Control of Movement.* New York: John Wiley & Son.

Woods, G. W., Tullos, H., & King, J. (1973). The throwing arm: Elbow joint injuries. *Journal of Sports Medicine,* 1, 43–47.

CHAPTER 4

Biomechanics

CHAPTER OBJECTIVES

- To examine the contribution made by the study of biomechanics to our understanding of human movement
- To examine the contribution of center of gravity and balance to human movement
- To understand the role of both kinematic and kinetic factors for linear motion
- To understand the role of kinematic and kinetic factors for angular motion
- To provide an introduction to fluid mechanics

INTRODUCTION

Take a moment to imagine some of the problems facing long jumpers. These athletes wish to run down a runway and propel themselves into the air in order to take their bodies the farthest distance possible before landing. Why do they run as fast as possible prior to take off? What angle at take off will allow them to jump the greatest distance? Why do some athletes rapidly rotate their legs in the air, while some do not? What will happen to the athlete's performance if they jump into a headwind or with a strong tailwind?

One field that provides some important insight into these questions is **biomechanics,** "the study of the structure and functions of biological systems by means of the methods of mechanics" (Hatze, 1974). We might think of biomechanics as the "physics" of human movement. For this reason, information obtained in this area of study is crucial to our understanding of human movement. Research on biomechanics not only enhances our knowledge about human movement per se, it also allows an examination of the mechanical characteristics of the human to help optimize our interaction with a work device or machine. Most of us are aware of the television advertisements for new cars on the market that have "ergonomic" appeal. This is intended to suggest that the vehicle is appropriately designed to optimize human performance while driving. In addition to biomechanists being concerned with movement optimization, they are also interested in helping to prevent, control, and reduce the occurrence of injury.

Applying mechanics to the human system can be accomplished by initially considering two aspects of movement: statics and dynamics. **Statics** is the study of a system when it is in a state of constant motion, as when the body is either motionless (at rest) or moving with a constant velocity. In contrast, **dynamics** is the study of the system when the system is in a state of acceleration or deceleration.

To describe motion, we must also consider both the kinematic and kinetic aspects of action. **Kinematics** is concerned with providing an appropriate description of movement with respect to time and space. For example, consider the forehand tennis stroke. Is the acceleration of the hitting arm different during the execution of a topspin and slice tennis shot? A kinematic analysis of a movement disregards the forces that produce the movement. In essence, kinematics refers to the geometry of an action. **Kinetics** focuses on the forces that are associated with a movement: the forces that produce the movement and those that result from the movement. For example, the tennis instructor might like to know if the force produced by the hitting arm is the same during the topspin and slice forehand strokes.

Types of Motion

Most human movement is rather complex and composed of a number of fundamental types of motion. Therefore, before considering complex movements, it is essential to address the more fundamental movement "building blocks." Let's begin with differentiating between linear, angular, and general motion.

Linear Motion.   **Linear motion** occurs when the body moves in such a way that all parts of it travel the same distance in the same time as well as following the same directional path. Another term often used for linear

Straight-line (or rectilinear) translation

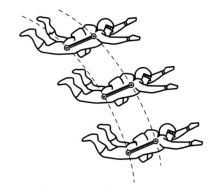

Curved-line (or curvilinear) translation

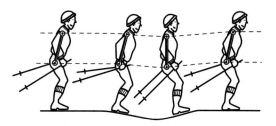

Nonlinear motion

PICTURE 4.1 *Examples of rectilinear and curvilinear movement can be found throughout the sporting world.*

motion is **translation,** which refers to movement of the body as a unit without individual parts of the unit moving in relation to one another. Linear motion can be in a straight line or a curved path. **Rectilinear motion** occurs when movement follows a straight line. If the movement path is curved, it is referred to as **curvilinear motion.**

Angular Motion.   **Angular motion** involves the body rotating around a point called an axis of rotation. For angular motion, also called rotary motion, the body moves in a circular fashion with all parts of the body moving through the same angle, in the same direction, within the same time frame. A good example of this type of motion is the gymnast executing giant swings on the high bar. In this case the axis of rotation is the point at which the gymnast's hands are placed on the bar.

General Motion.   Movements are rarely as uncomplicated as strict linear or angular motion. This is particularly true for athletic and many everyday activities. More common is a combination of the two. **General motion** is the term used to refer to movements that include both linear and angular components. For example, a sprinter is translated (linear motion) by the production of rapid rotary motion (angular motion) that occurs at the hip, knee, and ankle.

Measurement in Biomechanics

Being able to evaluate the kinematic and kinetic aspects of human movement is critical to the biomechanist. How is this achieved? One simple method to obtain a brief but not detailed kinematic analysis of movement is through observation. For example, why does the gymnastic coach carefully watch the athlete perform the vault during practice? What is the clinician looking for when a patient being rehabilitated goes through prescribed exercises? Observation allows the coach or the physical therapist to make judgments on the appropriateness of the movement mechanics exhibited by the athlete or the patient. However, it is important to note that some of the important kinematic and kinetic aspects of a movement cannot be discerned by the naked eye. Thus, the coach and the clinician may well miss some pertinent information about the actions they observe.

To obtain more detailed information about movement mechanics, the biomechanist uses a variety of elaborate instrumentation. Let's take a look at some of the procedures that facilitate both kinematic and kinetic analysis of human motion.

Measuring Kinematic Variables.   Arguably the most important instrumentation used to study human kinematics is that of cinematography or motion picture photography. **Cinematography** requires camera(s) that are specifically designed to film actions at very fast rates to allow the researcher to examine the kinematics of a movement. The most common 16mm cameras operate at 500 frames per sec (fps). However, cameras can run as low as

 **HIGHLIGHT**

Gideon B. Ariel and Ariel Dynamics, Inc.

Dr. Ariel received his Ph.D. in Exercise Science in 1972 at the University of Massachusetts-Amherst, specializing in biomechanics and computer science. Prior to this he was a member of the Israeli national track and field team and participated in the 1960 and 1964 Olympic Games. With this background it is not surprising that Ariel developed an interest in applying computer technology to enhance both analysis and assessment of human movement. His first step toward addressing this interest occurred in 1971 when he founded *Computerized Biomechanical Analysis*. With the explosion in the personal computer industry in the 1980s Dr. Ariel founded *Ariel Dynamics, Inc.,* and began marketing both the *Ariel Performance Analysis System (APAS)* and the *Ariel Computerized Exercise System (CES).* The APAS is a sophisticated computer-video-based system that offers the researcher the opportunity to measure, analyze, and display movement kinematics. This system is now a popular research tool used by a variety of movement scientists. The APAS also plays an important role in the clinical setting for disability assessment and in the areas of occupational and forensic biomechanics. In

addition, a number of athletes including Jimmy Conners (tennis), Al Oerter (discus), and Edwin Moses (track) have used the APAS system to evaluate their techniques. As a result of his innovations in the area of movement analysis, Dr. Ariel has become a popular spokesperson for technology in sport. In 1977 he was the focus of a *Sports Illustrated* article entitled "Gideon and His Magic Machine." Recently he has appeared on *Good Morning America,* compared the long-jump techniques of Carl Lewis and Bob Beamon on *20/20,* and appeared with Tom Brokaw on a NBC special discussing the black athlete.

From Gideon and his magic machine, *Sports Illustrated* (1977) and from the Ariel Dynamics, Inc., WWW homepage at http://www.arielnet.com/~ariel/

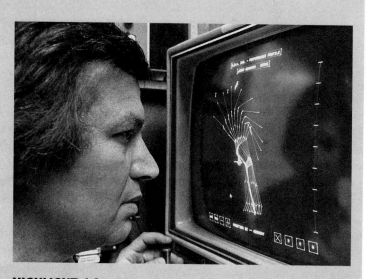

HIGHLIGHT 4.1 *Gideon Ariel has used his experience in track and field as well as his computer expertise to develop tools to enhance movement analysis.* (Photo credit: UPI/Corbis-Bettmann)

1–10 fps to as high as 10,000 fps. It is also important to consider the film that will be used to capture the action being documented. Deciding on the film rate will depend on the movement being filmed. Most human movements can be filmed at approximately 200 fps. This means that there is 0.005 sec between each frame of the film. However, if aspects of a movement such as point of contact between a tennis racket and the ball need to be determined, film rates of 500 fps are often used. Can you think of other activities that would require fast film speeds?

Filming can be conducted to obtain a two-dimensional (2-D) or three-dimensional (3-D) analysis of a movement. A two-dimensional analysis requires only one camera. This allows the image of the action to be examined along the X and Y axes. When using a three-dimensional analysis two time-synchronized cameras simultaneously record the action. This affords the experimenter the opportunity to describe a movement in the X, Y, and Z planes.

One of the major advances in recent years with cinematography instrumentation is the appearance of **videography.** Drawbacks of traditional fast-film analysis include the cost of developing the film and its inflexibility of use, such as its lack of immediate playback capability. However, with the emergence of video as a medium for conducting movement analysis, the biomechanist is afforded the chance to obtain a permanent record of the activity that can be examined immediately at relatively low cost.

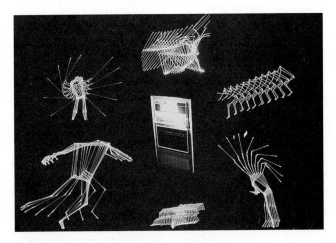

FIGURE 4.1 Computer generated "pictures" of movements can be obtained from traditional cinematographic or from videographic techniques. (Photo credit: Dan McCoy/Rainbow)

PICTURE 4.2 *Stroboscopy can be used to evaluate many different activities including those in gymnastics.* (Photo credit: © Bruce Curtis/Peter Arnold, Inc.)

While cinematography and videography are the techniques of choice for obtaining kinematic data, we would be remiss if we did not mention instrumentation that has historically been used for similar purposes but is much more limited. **Stroboscopy** is a technique that enables the experimenter to superimpose many images on a single photograph. Essentially, during the movement, a flashing light (strobe) turns on or off at a predetermined rate (e.g., 60 Hz). The camera records each image during the lighted period on top of the previously recorded image. Displacement measurements similar to those used in cinematography can be assessed, as well as velocity, if the time between the capture of each image is known. A primary limitation of this method is that the performer must be filmed in the dark, which restricts the type of movements that can be examined. Common actions that have been investigated using this technique are the golf swing and a variety of throwing actions.

Measuring Kinetic Variables.   There are numerous types of instrumentation for assessing the forces produced during a movement. The two most popular devices are the force transducer and the force platform. The **force transducer,** a device sensitive to forces, converts the amount of force into an electrical signal or voltage.

Force platforms, also called force plates, can measure the forces produced in three dimensions: vertical, mediolateral, and anteroposterior directions (see Figure 4.2). Force plates are quite useful for examining the force

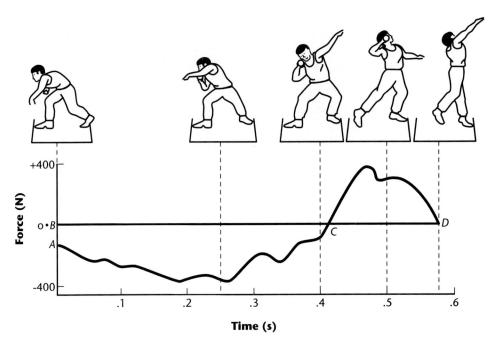

FIGURE 4.2   Force plates can be used to conduct a kinetic analysis of movements such as shot putting. (From Hay, *The Biomechanics of Sport Techniques.* Copyright © 1978 by Allyn and Bacon. Reprinted by permission.)

pattern over time, which is referred to as an impulse. The use of force platforms is quite important in many activities containing fundamental movements such as walking, running, jumping, or abrupt stopping. Unfortunately, the use of such devices in many cases is restricted to the laboratory since they are difficult to move between locations. Portable systems are available so that these systems can be inserted or attached to shoes, for example. However, a major problem with these devices is their lack of precision and hence their limited use for research purposes.

Another important technique for evaluating force production during a movement is **electromyography (EMG),** which is used to identify the magnitude and timing of activation in muscle groups that contribute to a movement. Figure 4.3 depicts EMG and muscle tension recordings for the biceps during both gradual (e.g., 2 sec) and short-burst (e.g., 400 msec) isometric contractions. Recall that Chapter 3 described an isometric contraction as one that involves generating forces as a result of activating muscles that are insufficient to cause movement. The basis of EMG is the electrical impulses generated by contracting muscles.

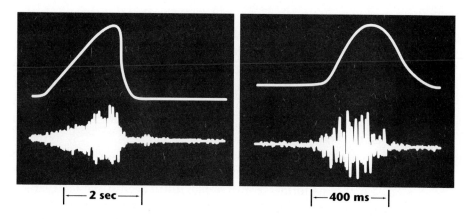

|—— 2 sec ——| |—400 ms—|

FIGURE 4.3   Electromyographic and muscle recordings during isometric contractions of the bicep muscle. (Adapted from Winter, 1990)

CENTER OF GRAVITY, STABILITY, AND BALANCE

When conducting a kinematic analysis of a human movement, one of the most commonly monitored locations for any body is the center of gravity, also called the center of mass. Probably the easiest way to think about the center of gravity is as the body's balance or pivot point. A more technical definition for **center of gravity** is the point about which a body's weight is equally balanced in all directions (Hall, 1995). In the human body the center of gravity is not fixed, because the body is made up of many segments that can move or remain stationary at any moment in time. For example, if you raise your arms from your side to above your head, you will shift your center of gravity in the direction your arms moved.

Center of Gravity

While identifying the center of gravity for a rigid structure is relatively easy, this is not the case for the human body with its many moving parts. Two methods that have been used extensively to locate the center of gravity for the human body are the reaction board method and the segmental method. The reaction board method makes use of the principle of moments that states that the sum of the moments acting on a body in equilibrium is zero.

For a body that remains motionless the reaction board method is sufficient for locating the center of gravity. However, the human body is often in a state of motion. In order to determine the center of gravity of someone in action, the segmental method is often used. This approach works on the assumption that the location of the body's center of gravity is a function of the center of gravity of each of the segments (e.g., upper arm, lower leg) of the body. The heavier segments of the body will exert a greater influence on the position of the whole-body center of gravity. When the products of segmental center of gravities location and mass are summed and divided by the sum of all the segmental masses (total body mass), the result is the location of the body's center of gravity.

Describing the location of the center of gravity over time is also useful and is one method of identifying differences between a skilled performer and a novice performer. For example, it has been suggested that an expert long jumper will lower his or her center of gravity approximately 10 percent of normal height during the last stages of the approach (Hay, 1986). Highly skilled runners appear to demonstrate less vertical oscillation of the center of gravity during performance. High jumpers make use of body flexion to increase the time of foot contact at take-off and to lower the center of gravity to maximize their take-off impulse when using the "Fosbury flop" technique. Monitoring the movement of the center of gravity is one aspect of performance that biomechanists provide to assist the athlete selection and coaching process.

Stability and Balance

Many activities that we perform day to day require the human body to be in a state of equilibrium or exhibit stability. **Stability** can be defined as resistance to a disruption in the equilibrium of the body. **Balance,** on the other hand, is an individual's ability to control stability. Let's use an example to clarify the difference between stability and balance.

Many situations necessitate the establishment of stability. The football lineman wants to maximize stability prior to blocking an opposing player. By contrast, a swimmer preparing for the start of a 50m freestyle race might compromise stability to facilitate a quick exit from the starting block at the sound of the gun. The process of being able to adjust stability to meet the demands of the situation is a function of balance. There are a number of different factors that affect an individual's stability. Some of these factors are addressed in the next section.

Mass of the Body.   The amount of matter that makes up a body is its mass. **Mass** is also considered to be a measure of the body's resistance to a change in its current state of motion, which is called the inertia of the body.

The most common unit of measurement of a body's mass is the kilogram (kg). Consider whether you would prefer to have a 130-kg or 80-kg lineman on your football team? While you make your decision, keep in mind that stability is the resistance to a disruption in equilibrium. It doesn't take an NFL coach to appreciate that in a contact activity such as football, an individual of greater mass is more likely to be able to counteract the forces that might compromise stability. This is consistent with Newton's second law (discussed later in this chapter), which basically states that the force required to cause a change in motion is proportional to the mass being moved.

Height of the Center of Gravity.   When considering the stability of a body, it is important to take into account how high the center of gravity is above the base of support. Increasing the height of the center of gravity above the base of support will make a body less stable. In many athletic activities, the performer will move the center of gravity higher to accomplish a position in which stability is reduced to improve the chances of moving quickly. In baseball for example, the shortstop prepares to field a ground ball by extending at the hips and knees slightly without moving in one particular direction. This raises the center of gravity and achieves an unstable but mobile position in space.

Size and Shape of the Base of Support.   Why does the archer or the golfer stand with feet spread wide apart rather than close together? The reason is to improve stability while they execute their activities. Martial artists also establish a wide base of support during defensive situations to maximize stability. Compare this to the sprinter, who minimizes the base of support to in order to compromise stability at the start of a race. In this case, the sprinter is preparing for a rapid movement away from the current starting posture. These examples highlight the importance of the size and shape of the base of support in order to control stability.

Friction.   The amount of friction between a surface and an object contacting a surface will also influence stability. Generally, the greater amount of friction, the more stability. Can you think of any situations in which low friction is the primary reason an object looks unstable? Anyone who has been skiing or ice skating knows about the effect of lack of friction and the resultant instability. In contrast, the climber tries to avoid instability by wearing rubber-soled climbing boots, thereby increasing the friction between the climber and the mountain face. This will hopefully facilitate the climber's chance of reaching the summit without falling.

LINEAR MOTION

At this point it is important to recall the definition of linear motion provided earlier in this chapter. Remember, linear motion occurs when the body moves in such a way that all parts of it travel the same distance in the same time and follow the same directional path. Linear motion is also called translation. Usually the study of linear motion includes both kinematic and kinetic analyses. We will examine each of these independently, beginning with linear kinematics.

Linear Kinematics

As previously discussed, kinematics provide an appropriate description of movement with respect to time and space. Kinematics descriptions can be useful to many other movement scientists as well as to biomechanists. For example, researchers interested in motor development use kinematic analyses to examine fundamental movement development such as throwing and catching.

The scientist concerned with motor learning and control might consider monitoring the changes in the movement kinematics as an indicator that learning is taking place. This type of information is also used in the "real world" by ergonomists or industrial engineers to evaluate whether a partic-

PICTURE 4.3   *Ergonomists also use kinematic analyses of movement to evaluate the execution of many everyday activities.* (Photo credit: ©Laima Druskis/Photo Researchers)

Biomechanics and Injuries in Industrial Settings

Techniques that are central to biomechanics are being used not only to enhance the production of movements in the athletic domain, but also to improve the execution of repetitive motions used in industrial settings. For example, a major problem in some workplaces is the occurrence of lower back problems from extensive lifting activities. It has been reported that this problem can account for as much as $20 billion a year in lost wages, productivity, and medical costs. Recent work by McGill & Norman (1993) has used many biomechanical techniques, including kinematic and kinetic analyses, in combination with anatomical data obtained from cadaver dissections and magnetic resonance images (MRI), to provide some guidelines that can be used to avoid some of these problems in the workplace. Based on this work they recommended that workers should perform rotations at the trunk when lifting, exercise great care in lifting after prolonged flexion or when rising from bed, lightly co-contract the stabilizing musculature to stiffen the spine, and avoid twisting. McGill & Norman suggest that these guidelines still need to be rigorously tested, but should prove to be more versatile than the old adage "bend the knees—not the back."

HIGHLIGHT 4.2   *A subject lifting a load with a lateral blending motion.* (Photo reprinted from *Journal of Biomechanics*, 25(1), 1992, with permission from Elsevier Science Ltd.)

ular everyday task is performed correctly. For example, in many industrial settings one might want to ensure that the proper mechanics are used when lifting heavy items to reduce the chance of injury (see "Highlight: Biomechanics and Injuries in Industrial Settings").

When these different researchers examine linear motion, what is involved in conducting a kinematic analysis? A number of different variables need to be considered. First, **displacement** is calculated by drawing a straight line from the initial position of an object to its end location. If you reach with your hand for a milk carton positioned 12 inches directly in front of you, your hand would undergo a displacement of 12 inches. However, if you return your hand to the starting location along the same path, displacement would be zero. In contrast, the **distance** covered by a movement refers to just that, the distance covered. In the previous example the hand would have traveled a distance of 24 inches.

Many people use the terms *speed* and *velocity* interchangeably. However, the biomechanist makes a distinction between these terms. **Speed** is calculated by dividing the distance covered by the time it takes to cover the distance. For example, if an athlete completed a 400-meter race in 50 seconds, average speed for the race would be 8 m/s. However, when velocity is examined a different picture emerges. **Velocity** is defined as the amount of displacement across time. Using the previous example, the athlete running the race experienced no (zero) displacement, therefore, the resultant average velocity was 0 m/s.

In many cases, just knowing displacement and velocity is not enough. Sometimes it might be informative to describe the **acceleration** of a body, which is defined as the change in velocity over time. Since velocity is always displacement divided by time, then acceleration is displacement divided by time, divided by time. The units of measurement reflect this. Acceleration is expressed as feet per sec per sec, which can also be stated as feet per sec^2.

Consider what might happen to the center of mass of the basketball player leaping up to block an opponent's shot. Prior to initiating the blocking action, the player has zero velocity and therefore zero acceleration. As the center of mass is raised by leaping to block the shot, there is a rapid increase (change) in velocity. The athlete is therefore undergoing acceleration. However, as the player nears the peak of the jump he or she undergoes deceleration. At the peak of the jump, the player experiences, for a brief moment, zero velocity. After making the block, the player's center of mass moves in a downward direction. Now the player again experiences a change in velocity over time, which might be interpreted as the player accelerating back toward the ground. Eventually the player returns to the ground and reaches a state of rest.

Why does the basketball player accelerate back toward the ground after a blocking a shot? Why does the high jumper accelerate toward the mat after leaping over the bar? Gravity, of course! This is the pulling influence the earth exerts on objects. Acceleration due to gravity is assumed to be constant at approximately 32.2 feet per second^2 (or 9.8 meters per second^2). Can you think of other activities in which acceleration due to gravity would be important? We will examine a subset of activities that are influenced by gravity when we discuss projectile motion in the next section.

Projectile Motion

What is a projectile? Most of us think of inanimate objects such as a baseball, an arrow, or a javelin when we consider projectile motion. However, it is important to remember that in many athletic events the human body can be considered to be the projectile, as in the case of a figure skater executing a triple axle jump, or a diver performing a double twist from the 10-meter board.

Flight paths of projectiles—inanimate objects or athletes—are curvilinear. More specifically, in the absence of air resistance the projectile flight path is parabolic. Figure 4.4 shows how changing the angle of release affects the vertical and horizontal displacement of a projectile. Notice that there is a complex interplay between the projection angle and the resultant vertical

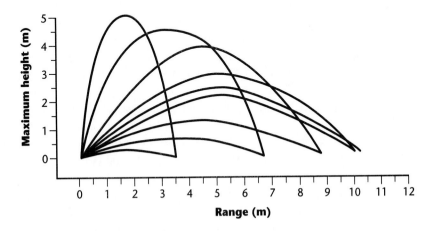

FIGURE 4.4 Changing the angle of release can affect the vertical and horizontal displacement of a projectile. (From Hay, *The Biomechanics of Sport Techniques.* Copyright © 1978 by Allyn and Bacon. Reprinted by permission.)

and horizontal distances. The projection angles of 30 and 60 degrees lead to the same horizontal displacement. However, there is a large difference between the vertical components of these projection angles. Figure 4.4 also points out that the greatest horizontal displacement is achieved with a projection angle of 45 degrees. In this situation the contribution of the horizontal and vertical components is equal.

Obviously the angle of projection that an individual might select for a specific activity depends on the goal of the action. For example, if maximum horizontal distance is required, as in the long jump, the previous discussion would suggest that a take-off angle of 45 degrees would be optimal. What other activities involve maximizing horizontal displacement?

When we are concerned with horizontal displacement, we are interested in what biomechanists call "range." In many practical situations the range of the projectile is a critical factor. We have already addressed the role of projection angle for horizontal displacement or range. More specifically, 45 degrees is the appropriate angle of release if the range needs to be maximized. However, this remains true only if we ignore air resistance. What other factors can you think of that might affect the range of a projectile? Two factors are particularly important: the height from which the projectile is released and eventually lands, and the velocity of the projectile at the time of its release.

What activities involve different release and landing heights? There are many examples. In track and field, there are events such as the shotput, javelin, or hammer throw in which the projectile is released from a position above the ground. When the height of release is different from the landing height, an adjustment needs to be made in the projection angle. In general, the greater the difference between the release and landing heights, the more the angle of release should be decreased.

The second factor, projectile velocity at the time of release, appears to be a very critical factor. Assuming all other things equal, if two javelins are projected with the same release angle but with different velocities, the throw with the greatest velocity will result in greater range. This has serious implications for the coach. Concentration on changing the release velocity would be most beneficial if range is the most crucial concern. This would seem to be more advantageous than adjusting the athlete's throwing actions to meet particular projection angles or heights. However, it is also important to note that projection velocity will probably take some time to change, since it is a function of the athlete's strength (Hinson, 1981).

Figure 4.4 also has implications for the projection angle when the goal is to increase the projectile "air time." For example, the intention of a punter in football when kicking from certain locations on the field is to keep the ball in the air for as long as possible. In this case, vertical displacement is critical. Which flight path in Figure 4.4 would achieve this goal?

Linear Kinetics

Since kinetics focuses on the concept of force, it seems appropriate that some time is spent trying to understand this term. **Force** is a push or pull acting on the body. If the push or pull is sufficient enough, the body will alter its state of motion. We measure the amount of force in newtons (N) or pounds (lbs). One pound is equal to 4.45 N. It takes approximately 22 N of force to push open a door (Kreighbaum & Barthels, 1990). Force allows inertia to be overcome, which affords an individual the opportunity to change the state of motion of the system (e.g., the human body). Forces have both magnitude (e.g., 50 N) and direction (e.g., 20 degrees from vertical). In addition, the force has a point of application such as the forehead when "heading" the ball in soccer. Finally, the force is applied along a line of action that extends indefinitely from the point of application along the direction of the force.

It is common to distinguish between internal forces and external forces. An internal force is one that exists within the system being examined. In the human system, for example, the contraction of a muscle causing a force to be created at the bone would be considered internal. Conversely, an external force is one that is a function of something outside the system being studied. Common causes of external forces on the human body are air resistance, gravity, and contact with other objects, such as the ground.

In the seventeenth century, Sir Isaac Newton noted that motion is associated with force in a very systematic fashion. His work led to three laws of motion that provide an explanation about why objects move as they do. Newton's laws of motion are now universally accepted. Let's examine each of them.

Newton's First Law: Inertia.   **Newton's first law: inertia** states, "a body continues in a state of rest or uniform motion until acted upon by an external force of sufficient magnitude to disturb this state." The first part of Newton's first law is relatively obvious to most people. We are all aware that a barbell will remain still until the weightlifter applies the appropriate force. The second part of this law, however, that the object will continue with uniform motion, is often misunderstood. This can result because we know that objects usually come to rest at some point in time even though no force appears to have been applied. However, in the "real world," external forces such as friction and air resistance are continually acting on the object and are sometimes overlooked.

Newton's Second Law: Acceleration.   **Newton's second law: acceleration** states, "the acceleration of the body is proportional to the force exerted on it and inversely proportional to its mass." This statement provides a description of the relationship between force, acceleration, and mass. Based on the relationship between these concepts, we can consider force to be the product of mass and acceleration. How does this impact human performance? The following example of kicking a soccer ball offered by Kreighbaum & Barthels (1990) provides insight into the answer to this question. Assuming the mass of a soccer ball remains constant, a greater amount of force is required to kick the ball with greater acceleration (see Figure 4.5a). Figure 4.5b demonstrates that as the mass of the soccer ball is increased, it will be kicked with less acceleration for any given amount of force. Finally, when the mass of the soccer ball is increased, the force that is exerted with the kick will need to be increased to ensure a particular acceleration (see Figure 4.5c). In most soccer games, the mass of the ball remains constant. Therefore, modifying the force or acceleration to execute a pass would be the critical concerns of the soccer player.

Another important concept that is worthy of mention at this time is momentum. **Momentum** is the product of a body's mass and its velocity. Essentially, momentum is the quantity of motion a body possesses (Hay, 1993). Newton's second law states that a force can be applied to a mass that results in a change in velocity of that mass. Essentially, when an external force is acting on the body to change velocity, the force is creating a change in the body's momentum. As the previous discussion highlighted, a change in a body's momentum will occur when an external force is applied to it. This is only part of the story, however. In addition to considering the magnitude of the force that influences momentum, it is also important to consider the time over which the force is exerted. The product of force and time is called an **impulse.**

Newton's Third Law: Action–Reaction.   **Newton's third law: action–reaction** states, "every action has an equal and opposite reaction." This law refers to the way in which forces act against each other. A volleyball player who "digs" or "bumps" the ball following an opponent's spike is exerting a force on the ball. The ball in turn exerts on the player's arms a force of equal magnitude but in the opposite direction. To understand the consequence of Newton's third law one need not look any further than a high jumper who uses the "Fosbury flop" technique. As the high jumper clears the bar, he or she drops the hips sharply to cause the legs to rise quickly, which enhances the likelihood of clearing the bar.

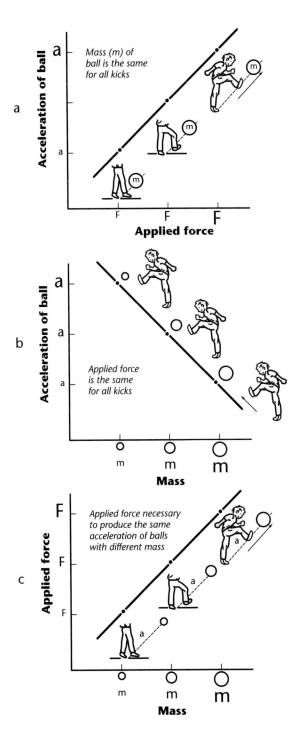

FIGURE 4.5a–c The relationship between force, mass, and acceleration. (From Kreigbaum, E., & Barthels, K. M. *Biomechanics.* Copyright © 1990 by Allyn and Bacon. Reprinted by permission.)

A principle that is an outgrowth of Newton's third law is called the conservation of momentum principle. **Conservation of momentum** states that in a system in which forces act on each other, the momentum in the system remains constant. An example that captures the essence of this principle is the impact of two balls in pool. When a ball is struck by the cue, it approaches the target ball with a certain amount of momentum. After impact, the momentum that exists between the two balls must remain the same. This assumes, of course, that no momentum is lost through other external forces such as friction or air resistance.

ANGULAR MOTION

When the direction of an external force applied to the body is in line with the body's center of gravity, linear motion occurs. However, forces acting in this way are not always the norm. It is also important to consider what happens to the body when a force is applied along a line that is not at the body's center of gravity. In this case angular motion will occur. This type of motion is also called rotary motion. Remember, angular motion is a result of applying an eccentric force to the body. An **eccentric force** is defined as "a force whose direction is not in line with the center of gravity of a freely moving object or the center of rotation of an object with a fixed axis of rotation" (Luttgens & Wells, 1992). Many of the principles of angular motion are similar to those identified for linear motion. A discussion of some of these follows.

Angular Kinematics

Just as with linear motion, our "tour" of the concepts central to angular motion begins with distinguishing between angular distance and displacement. **Angular distance** is equal to the angle between the initial and final positions when measured by following the path taken by the body. **Angular displacement** is the change in location of the rotating body.

In order to satisfactorily evaluate angular motion, appropriate units need to be used. There are three common sets of units used for angular motion: degrees, revolutions, and radians. One radian is equal to 57.3 degrees. One revolution is equal to 360 degrees. It is therefore not difficult to calculate the number of radians that would equal a revolution. How many? One revolution is equal to 6.28 radians.

When angular displacement is considered as a function of time, it is referred to as **angular velocity,** expressed in degrees/sec, radians/sec, or revolutions/sec. If a softball pitcher moves his or her arm 150 degrees in .2 sec, what is the angular velocity using revolutions and radians?

As with linear motion, angular motion also incorporates a second derivative called angular acceleration. **Angular acceleration** is the rate of change of angular velocity and is specified as degrees per sec per sec or degree per sec^2 (this could also be stated in terms of revolutions or radians). In the spiking action of the volleyball player, the arm undergoes angular acceleration as it is directed toward the ball. The player wishing to hit the volleyball hard should attempt to strike the ball with maximum velocity. After the ball is struck, the player's arm experiences a period of angular deceleration to avoid contact between the net and the arm.

Integrating Angular and Linear Kinematics.   When addressing angular velocity, the biomechanist can also consider the corresponding linear velocity of the object that is rotating. An important factor that influences linear velocity during angular motion is the length of the object that is undergoing rotation. Most people are aware that a softball hit near the end of the bat travels a greater distance than a ball hit in the middle of the bat. This occurs because for a given angular velocity, the resultant linear velocity at the end of the implement (e.g., the bat) will increase as the length of the implement is increased. From a practical standpoint then, if linear velocity is important, maximizing the length of the device would be most appropriate. This assumes that the implement of greater length can still be swung with the same angular velocity as the shorter implement. Do you think that this information would be useful to the softball player and coach. Certainly!

Consider the other side of the coin for a moment. What would happen if linear velocity of the rotating object was held constant and the length of the object was increased? The object would now exhibit an increase in angular velocity. There are many examples in which the radius of the body is increased or decreased to change the rotary motion. High divers execute layout, pike, and tucked somersault dives that have different rotation velocities. Basically, the longer the body (i.e., radius), the slower the rotation (less angular velocity). Therefore the diver lengthens the body to slow angular rotation. Conversely, divers shorten their bodies, by tucking, to increase the body's speed of rotation. Using the same principle, a figure skater can manipulate the velocity of a spin by extending the arms to the side or bringing them close to the body.

Angular Kinetics

In the introduction, a brief mention was made about torque, a crucial kinetic element when reviewing angular motion. Torque was referred to as the turning effect that can be exerted on a body. More precisely, **torque** is a product of force and the length of the moment arm. A **moment arm** is the perpendicular distance from the point of the applied force to the axis of rotation. Therefore, one way of increasing the torque of a baseball bat is to exert more force during execution of a swing. Alternatively, the torque can be increased by lengthening the moment arm. When torque is increased a great deal, it is often difficult to control the resultant rotary motion of the bat or racquet that is created. It is not uncommon in situations such as this to hear the teacher instruct the player to "choke up" on the bat or racquet, which effectively reduces torque by shortening the moment arm, thus enhancing control of the movement.

The resistance of a body to a change in its current state of linear motion is called **inertia.** A body's inertia is a function of its mass. Resistance to angular motion is a little more complicated. In addition to the object's mass, its resistance to angular motion will also be dictated by how far the mass is distributed away from the axis of rotation. The combination of the object's mass and distribution of the mass is referred to as the object's **moment of inertia.**

So, in the case of baseball, it will take more effort to start swinging the bat when the moment of inertia is greater. The moment of inertia can be increased by increasing the mass of the bat or by distributing the bulk of the mass away from the axis of rotation. Given this, why is it a good strategy for young children to "choke up" on the bat to help them swing?

As was the case for linear momentum, the body also possesses a certain amount of angular momentum. This concept is central to most swinging, kicking, and throwing activities. **Angular momentum** is the product of the body's moment of inertia and its angular velocity. Just as with linear momentum, angular momentum is initiated by an external force or torque. Once the external torque is exerted, the body continues to rotate until a new torque is applied to the system or another resistive force is experienced. This refers to conservation of angular momentum.

Let's take a look at an example described by Hay (1993). When divers perform a forward somersault off the 3-meter board, they achieve a tucked position early in the dive. The tucked position effectively reduces the divers' moment of inertia by moving their mass closer to the axis of rotation. Since only an external torque can change the body's angular momentum, how is

PICTURE 4.4   *Children can "choke up" on the bat to reduce the moment of inertia of that bat.* (Photo credit: ©Ken Cavanaugh/Photo Researchers)

this latter quantity conserved? Think about what happens to the rotation of the diver in the tucked position—they rotate faster or they increase angular velocity.

Conservation of angular momentum is also implicitly involved when we consider how the body transfers angular momentum. More specifically, what happens if one particular body segment's angular momentum is changed? How is total angular momentum conserved? Let's return to the diving example used in the previous paragraph to find the answer to these questions. Assume the diver is executing a pike front dive (see Figure 4.6). Notice that as the diver moves toward the pike position the legs undergo a drastic reduction in angular momentum. Note, however, the corresponding increase in angular momentum in the upper extremities. This reverses as the diver

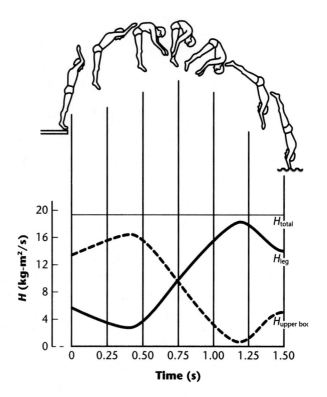

FIGURE 4.6   In a piked front dive the total angular momentum (H) is conserved but the contributions from the upper and lower limbs are quite different. (From Hay, *The Biomechanics of Sport Techniques.* Copyright © 1978 by Allyn and Bacon. Reprinted by permission.)

prepares for entry to the water. That is, the arms appear to remain stationary while the legs undergo an increase in angular momentum. Figure 4.6 reveals that the body's total angular momentum remains intact.

FLUID MECHANICS

This section begins with an important question. What athletic activities take place in a fluid environment? It is likely that you immediately think of activities such as swimming or scuba diving since they occur in water. However, it is important to realize that activities such as basketball, gymnastics, and parachuting also take place in a fluid environment. In this case air is the fluid. More importantly, for some activities such as swimming, optimizing performance requires consideration of both water and air as fluid environments.

Most of us think of the forces that are exerted on the body by fluids as having a negative effect. For example, the swimmer is slowed by having to move through the water. However, by obtaining a thorough understanding of the principles of fluid mechanics, we can actually take advantage of some of these fluid forces. More specifically, the baseball pitcher can purposefully make the baseball curve, the golfer can "slice" the ball around a tree, and the skydiver can perform very complex acrobatics. Furthermore, athletes in some activities can adopt alternative or innovative techniques to counteract the potentially detrimental effect of the fluid forces. For example, skiers, designers of bobsleds, and even track and field stars attempt to streamline their equipment and bodies to minimize fluid resistance.

What are the specific forces that exist in fluid environments? The primary forces that we will address are drag, lift, and buoyancy. The first two exist in both air and water. Buoyancy, however, is related to performing in water. Let's examine each of these types of fluid forces.

Drag

What is often referred to as fluid resistance is also called drag. **Drag** can be defined as the fluid force that opposes the forward motion of the body and reduces the body's velocity. One simple demonstration of the effect of drag is to hold your hand out of a car window so that it is perpendicular to the air flow. You can feel considerable pressure against the hand in this situation. When your hand is placed in a horizontal position, the air pressure is reduced considerably. The drag force when the hand is held in a vertical position exerts two important sources of force. The obvious one is the force that is exerted directly against the front of the hand impeding the forward motion.

A second effect that contributes to drag is a "sucking" force, which is a function of the displaced air filling the pocket or vacuum that is created behind the hand. Overcoming drag is an important consideration not only for the movement of the body through the fluid environment but also movement of any other type of object, such as those discussed in the earlier section on projectile motion. We can examine drag in a more specific manner. In fact, there are three different types of drag force that influence human performance: surface drag, profile drag, and wave drag. Wave drag is particularly important for water activities. Let's examine surface drag and profile drag first.

Surface Drag.   As the term suggests, **surface drag** is the resistance experienced by a body that is a result of the fluid rubbing against the surface of that body. Imagine the Olympic swimmer gliding through water. When you watch these athletes it appears as though the water just slides past the swimmer's body with each stroke. In reality, a thin layer of water actually "sticks" to the swimmer's body. This layer in turn attracts other water particles, which attract other water particles. The result of all this "attraction" is a reduction in the smooth passage through the water of the swimmer. Rather than a "smooth" ride, turbulence is created that slows down the swimmer.

Generally surface drag will increase if the surface area of the swimmer moving parallel to the surface of the water is increased. Skin friction will be further increased as the roughness of the skin increases. Hence, shaving of body hair is a common practice in swimming to maximize the swimmer's "streamlining." However, after extensive examination, it is generally assumed that surface drag is not the primary source of drag in most sporting endeavors. It would seem then that the body-shaving practice of the swimmer provides only a minimal benefit at best.

Profile Drag.   In contrast to surface drag, **profile drag** exerts a severe limitation on performance in a number of different sporting activities. In cycling, for example, drag accounts for as much as 90 percent of the resistive force encountered by the cyclist when racing (Kyle & Burke, 1984). Much of this is profile drag.

Profile drag plays a critical role in many high-speed activities in addition to cycling, including skiing, speed skating, and running. To understand how

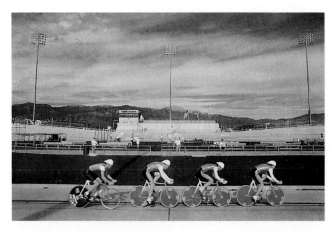

PICTURE 4.5   *Cyclists are always concerned with profile drag.*
(Photo credit: Will Hart)

this type of drag exerts its influence, imagine what happens to the air when a discus is thrown. The air is rapidly displaced around the sides of the discus and subsequently reunites behind the discus. It is here that a low-pressure pocket of air is formed that functions in the direction opposite to the flight of the discus. The greater the pressure created in this pocket, the greater the resistance to the forward motion of the discus. It is as if the profile drag actually "holds back" the discus as it tries to move forward.

There are number of factors that coaches, instructors, and athletes can consider to help counteract the negative influence of profile drag, including the cross-sectional area of the body that moves perpendicular to the flow of air, the shape of the body, and the smoothness of the surface of the body.

You are probably familiar with the horizontal position over the handle-bars adopted by cyclists when sprinting at the end of a race. In this case, profile drag is minimized by reducing the surface area exposed to the resistive force. Can you think of a situation in which an individual might like to increase profile drag? During a free fall the parachutist adopts a body position that exposes the largest surface area possible to the oncoming air in order to use profile drag to reduce the rate of descent. This technique would be especially important for skysurfers.

Object shape was also mentioned as a contributor to profile drag. A great deal of money is spent in sports such as yachting and kayaking in order to find an appropriately shaped piece of equipment that reduces profile drag. This enhances streamlining, which is a must in many of these activities. In the same light, athletes performing in luge competition and in some cycling events wear bullet-shaped helmets, which help reduce the pocket that forms behind the object and impedes its forward progress.

Smoothness of the object also seems to affect the profile drag an object experiences. Speed skaters wear suits made of slick, shiny material to reduce drag (see "Highlight: A "'Stretched' Stitch in Time"). The designers of bobsleds use fiberglass to achieve the same effect. Smoother objects do not necessarily result in less profile drag. In fact, putting dimples in golf balls turns out to be useful because it results in the turbulent air pocket being formed further behind the ball than would occur if the ball was smooth. This means that this low pressure pocket exerts less suction on the ball moving forward. While the skin friction is increased by the dimples on the ball, this does not outweigh the benefit of reducing the profile drag.

Wave Drag.   **Wave drag** is particularly important for the swimmer, who moves through both the air and the water at the same time. When the swimmer is in the air, during a dive, or submerged under the water, just after the dive, he or she is subject to both surface and profile drag. However, when the swimmer begins the swimming action along the surface of the water, a new drag is created by the production of waves. It is interesting to note that a major rule change occurred for the breaststroke because swimmers were adopting a strategy to reduce wave drag. Essentially, swimmers would swim

HIGHLIGHT

A "Stretched" Stitch in Time

In 1949, a DuPont chemist named Dr. Joe Shivers was given the task of creating "stuff" that would be the future material for an improved women's girdle. The result of this project literally transformed both the look of the clothing worn by athletes, rock stars, and even the "average person" on the street, as well as the physical appearance of those same individuals. Some ten years after Joe Shivers began

HIGHLIGHT 4.3 *Clothing that includes Lycra is now commonplace in most exercise settings.* (Photo credit: Tony Neste)

the project, the product now referred to as Lycra was christened. Lycra, more generically termed *spandex,* is a synthetic elastomer which is a material or fiber that can change shape when exposed to a force but will return to its original shape when the force is no longer present. How stretchable is Lycra? A ball of this material weighing only 975 pounds would be sufficient to stretch from the earth to the moon! The market for such a product is enormous. For example, in addition to women's girdles, DuPont scientists considered using Lycra in golf balls and condoms! However, the most lucrative market for Lycra has been exercise clothing and swimwear. A piece of workout clothing containing approximately 25 percent Lycra is particularly useful because it allows the material to conform to our muscles, stretching and contracting as necessary. Just as important, this material helps keep the muscles warm while enhancing the removal of sweat. Lycra is commonly incorporated into the clothing worn by sprinters, gymnasts, and swimmers because of its "second skin" quality that helps reduce drag by flattening and smoothing the surface of the body.

From "A long stretch of the imagination," Sports Illustrated (1990).

under water for as long as they could. This diminished wave drag and effectively made skin friction and profile drag the limiting forms of fluid forces that influenced their performance. Subsequently the rules were changed to limit the number of strokes that can be taken under water. This of course reintroduces wave drag as a factor the swimmer must contend with when swimming the breaststroke.

Lift

While many performers attempt to eliminate drag, many athletes try to take advantage of an alternative fluid force called lift. **Lift** is the component of air resistance that is directed at right angles to the drag force. Ski jumping is an ideal activity to use to examine the influence of lift. In ski jumping, drag should be minimized. This is facilitated by the streamlined position jumpers adopt and by the tight-fitting clothing they wear. In addition to reducing drag, it is essential to use lift to elicit superior performance in ski jumping. For example, jumpers are always looking to place their skies at an angle that encourages lift. The more lift, the longer "air time," which presumably results in greater jumping distance.

The angle of a projectile that maximizes lift while minimizing drag is called the **angle of attack.** Ganslen (1964) examined the optimal angle of attack for throwing a discus. This study suggested that the optimum lift–drag ratio (best combination of small drag and large lift forces) is at approximately 10 degrees for this track and field event. Ganslen also indicated that a discus flying at an angle greater than 30 degrees reaches what is called the **stall angle,** which is the point at which the discus literally stops because the lift force is eliminated and the drag force increases abruptly. This sort of information is obviously very important to athletes in a variety of other sports, such as javelin throwing.

An interesting aside concerning lift is provided by Hay (1993). Hay reveals that the "airfoils" on grand prix racing cars modify the use of lift to ensure the car stays in contact with the racing surface during fast turns. The airfoils are mounted upside down so that rather than the car being lifted, it is "pushed down" when a lift force occurs, as in the case of a turn. This is a prime example of how, with a little ingenuity, an understanding of basic principles of fluid mechanics can be used to one's advantage.

There is one additional phenomenon worthy of mention in this section on lift. This is the **Magnus Effect,** which refers to the production of lift due to spin being imparted on an object such as a ball. It is this effect that is primarily responsible for the "curve" in the curveball in baseball (Allman,

PICTURE 4.6 *The magnus effect has particular importance for throwing a curveball in baseball.* (Photo credit: Robert Harbison)

1982). It is also the effect that is quite embarrassing to many of us who play golf and have a difficult time keeping the ball flying straight.

Essentially, this phenomenon occurs because different pressures exist at the opposite sides of a spinning ball. When a ball is spinning from right to left, a low-pressure zone forms on the left side of a ball and a high-pressure zone exists on the right side of the ball. As the ball moves through the air, it tends to drift in the direction of the low-pressure zone. Using the current example, that means the ball would move from right to left.

While the Magnus Effect has been identified as the culprit of "slicing" and "hooking" in golf, it can also serve a very useful purpose in golf. For example, imagine a golf shot in which back spin is imparted on the ball. This creates a high-pressure zone under the ball and a low-pressure zone on top of the ball. Keep in mind the ball will drift in the direction of the low-pressure zone. This means the ball will experience lift, thereby increasing flight time. The influence of the Magnus Effect has also been investigated for the flight of a discus (Dyson, 1977), as well as for pitching in baseball (Briggs, 1959).

Buoyancy

In many aquatic activities, it is crucial that the body can float. Almost everybody has at some time laid back in a swimming pool and tried to float. Some people appear to float quite easily; others, like the proverbial brick, drop right to the bottom of the pool. What determines whether a body floats or sinks? This question is at the heart of buoyancy.

When an individual lies horizontally in the pool, the legs begin to sink until at some point the body appears to remain motionless, almost suspended in the water. At this point the upward force exerted by the water is equal to the weight of the individual floating. The upward force is called buoyancy. According to Archimedes' Principle, the magnitude of the buoyancy force is equal to the weight of water displaced by the floating body. In some cases, the object cannot displace the amount of water equivalent to body weight before the body settles at the bottom of the pool. This defines the "sinker." Another important consideration in determining the "floater" or the "sinker" is the specific gravity of the individual. **Specific gravity** is the ratio of body weight and the weight of an equal volume of water. An individual will float if his or her specific gravity is less than or equal to one but is doomed to sink if it is greater than one. Generally, women have lower specific gravities than men; therefore, women usually float better than men.

Before concluding this brief discussion on buoyancy, we need to mention the center of buoyancy. The center of buoyancy is the point in the body through which buoyancy acts. This location is particularly important in determining the way in which the body will lie when finally coming to rest in the floating position. If the center of gravity and the center of buoyancy coincide, the individual will float in the horizontal position at the surface of the water. This would seem particularly useful for improving the effectiveness of the swimmer. However, studies by Whiting (1963, 1965) demonstrates that this is a very uncommon occurrence. More than likely, the center of buoyancy is closer to the head than the body's center of gravity, resulting in the legs dropping until equilibrium is reached. This means that most individuals need to exert some force to achieve the horizontal position in water.

FINAL COMMENT

At the conclusion of Chapter 3 it was pointed out that obtaining a thorough knowledge and understanding of the basic architecture of the human mover was essential before "moving" on to assess the behavioral capabilities of this system. This architecture included the scaffolding or skeletal system; the motors, or muscles; and the communication system, or nervous system. Chapter 4 began our examination of the behavioral consequences of having to support movement with such an architecture. This chapter focused on the mechanical characteristics of the human and the associated limitations these mechanics exert on the types of movement that can be performed successfully. In essence, biomechanics can be considered the "physics" of human movement.

Biomechanists describe movement from both a kinematic and kinetic perspective. Kinematics refer to how a movement is performed in both time and space. When using this category of analysis the biomechanist is concerned with issues such as limb displacement, velocity, and/or acceleration. In order to obtain a more complete picture of the movement, a profile of the forces associated with a movement can also be obtained by examining movement kinetics. In this case, the researcher can discuss issues such as limb force, momentum, and/or torque.

Movements are generally a combination of two "building block" categories of motion that are termed linear and angular motion. Linear motion occurs when the body moves in such a way that all parts travel the same distance, in the same time, following the same path. In contrast, during angular motion the body undergoes a circular motion in which all parts travel through the same angle, in the same direction, within the same time frame. It is important to remember that the examination of either linear or angular motion involves examining similar kinematic and kinetic variables. For example, one can consider linear or angular acceleration or the conservation of linear and angular momentum. Establishing a link between linear and angular motion by considering each of the kinematic and kinetic variables that were discussed in this chapter will provide a useful study framework to aid your understanding of this information.

The final section of this chapter discussed fluid mechanics. We considered both water and air as fluids that are frequently encountered by the human performer. Drag was identified as a pervasive factor that limits movement in a fluid environment. In contrast, the performer can take advantage of lift to facilitate movement. In both cases, however, knowledge of both human mechanics and equipment design has enabled us to move more effectively in fluid environments.

At the beginning of this chapter it was suggested that the goal of research in the area of biomechanics is to optimize performance, as well as to help prevent, control, and reduce the occurrence of injury. Some of the current research trends exemplify this goal. This is particularly true for contemporary work that involves developing computer models of human locomotion.

A particularly attractive element of this type of research is that it provides an opportunity for movement scientists from different areas of study to interact. For example, many of the computer simulations are based not only on known mechanical parameters but also on known physiological parameters. It should be noted that the information on muscle physiology presented in Chapter 3 is central to these efforts (see also Chapter 5 on exercise physiology). This type of work will play a critical role in redefining our general understanding of the physics of movement. Moreover, data from these endeavors should also impact clinical or rehabilitative settings by enhancing our understanding of particular movement disorders as well as ergonomic settings related to the design of safer equipment.

QUESTIONS FOR THOUGHT

- Describe the difference between kinematic and kinetic analyses of movement.
- How does the biomechanist obtain the necessary information to discern the kinematic and kinetic aspects of a movement?
- Are there other movement sciences that might benefit from using similar measures of movement kinematics and kinetics? How?
- From the standpoint of the kinematic and kinetic variables used to describe a movement, how are linear and angular motion similar?
- Discuss the interaction of drag and lift and the effect of these factors on movement in a fluid environment.

KEY TERMS

acceleration
angle of attack
angular acceleration
angular displacement
angular distance
angular momentum
angular motion
angular velocity
balance
biomechanics
center of gravity
cinematography
conservation of momentum
curvilinear motion

displacement
distance
drag
dynamics
eccentric force
electromyography (EMG)
force
force platforms
force transducer
general motion
impulse
inertia
instantaneous angular velocity
kinematics

kinetics

lift

linear motion

Magnus Effect

mass

moment arm

moment of inertia

momentum

Newton's first law: inertia

Newton's second law: acceleration

Newton's third law: action–reaction

profile drag

rectilinear motion

specific gravity

speed

stability

stall angle

statistics

stroboscopy

surface drag

torque

translation

velocity

videography

wave drag

weight

RESOURCES

Textbooks

Hall, S. (1995). *Basic Biomechanics*. St. Louis: Mosby.

Hay, J. G. (1993). *The Biomechanics of Sport Techniques* (4th ed.). Engelwood Cliffs, NJ: Prentice Hall.

Kreighbaum, E., & K. M. Barthels. (1990). *Biomechanics* (3rd ed.). New York: Macmillan Publishing Company.

Luttgens, K., & K. F. Wells. (1992). *Kinesiology: Scientific Basis of Human Motion* (8th ed.). Dubuque, IA: W. C. Brown Publishers.

Journals

Ergonomics

Exercise and Sport Science Reviews

International Journal of Sport Biomechanics

Journal of Biomechanics

Medicine and Science in Sport and Exercise

Research Quarterly for Exercise and Sport

Professional Societies

American Society of Biomechanics

European Society of Biomechanics

International Ergonomic Society

International Society of Biomechanics

National Association for Sport and Physical Education: Kinesiology Academy

Internet

World Wide Web (WWW) Home Pages
http://gpu.srv.ualberta.ca/~pbaudin/biomch.htm
http://www.arielnet.com/~ariel/
http://tucker.mech.utah.edu/

Usenet/Listservers
biomech-l@nic.surfnet.nl
send: subscribe biomch-l <your name>
to: listserv@nic.sufnet.nl

REFERENCES

Allman, W. F. (1982). Pitching: The untold physics of the curve ball. *Science* 82, 32–39.

Briggs. L. (1959). Effect of spin and speed on lateral deflection (curve) of a baseball, and the magnus effect for smooth spheres. *American Journal of Physics, 27,* 589–596.

Dyson, G. (1977). *The Mechanics of Athletics.* New York: Holmes & Meier.

Ganslen, R. V. (1964). Aerodynamic and mechanical force in discus flight. *Athletic Journal,* (April), 88–89.

Grabiner, M. D. (Ed.). (1993). *Current Issues in Biometrics.* Champaign, IL: Human Kinetic Publishers.

Hall, S. J. (1995). *Basic Biomechanics.* St. Louis: Mosby.

Hatze, H. (1974). The meaning of the term biomechanics. *Journal of Biomechanics, 7,* 189–190.

Hay, J. G. (1978). *The Biomechanics of Sport Techniques* (2nd ed.). New York: Macmillan.

Hay, J. G. (1986). The biomechanics of the long jump. In K. B. Pandolf (Ed.), *Exercise and Sport Science Reviews* (vol. 3, pp. 401–446). New York: Macmillan.

Hay, J. G. (1993). *The Biomechanics of Sport Techniques* (4th ed.). Englewood Cliffs, NJ: Prentice Hall.

Hinson, M. M. (1981). *Kinesiology* (2nd ed.). Dubuque, IA: W. C. Brown.

Kreighbaum, E., & Barthels, K. M. (1990). *Biomechanics* (3rd ed.). New York: Macmillan.

Kyle, C. R., & Burke, E. (1984). Improving the racing bicycle. *SOMA,* 1, 34–45.

Luttgens, K., & Wells, K. F. (1992). *Kinesiology: Scientific Basis of Human Motion* (8th ed.). Dubuque, IA: W. C. Brown.

McGill, S. M., & Norman, R. W. (1993). Low back biomechanics in industry: The prevention of injury through safer lifting. In M. D. Grabiner (Ed.), *Current Issues in Biomechanics* (pp. 69–120). Champaign, IL: Human Kinetics.

Whiting, H. T. A. (1963). Variations in floating ability with age in the male. *Research Quarterly, 34,* 84–90.

Whiting, H. T. A. (1965). Variations in floating ability with age in the female. *Research Quarterly, 36,* 216–218.

Winter, D. A. (1990). *Biomechanics and Motor Control of Human Movement* (2nd ed.). New York: John Wiley & Sons.

CHAPTER **5**

Exercise Physiology

CHAPTER OBJECTIVES

- To develop an appreciation for the anaerobic and aerobic processes that provide energy for working muscle
- To identify the role the heart, lungs, vascular system, and blood play in the delivery of oxygen, nutrients, and the elimination of by-products to the working cells of the body
- To characterize the factors that inhibit or facilitate an individual's capacity to perform work

INTRODUCTION

Exercise physiology is perhaps the most well known of the disciplines involved in the scientific study of human movement. This is due in part to the relatively long history of physiology, the significant scientific advances in exercise physiology that have resulted in enhanced training methods, and because this discipline has received a great deal of good press in recent years. It is not uncommon for major television sporting events like the Olympics or a professional sporting event to allot a few minutes of air time to extol the advances in exercise physiology.

"**Exercise physiology** is the description and explanation of the functional changes brought about by a single (acute) or repeated exercise sessions (chronic exercise or training), often with the objective of improving the exercise response" (Lamb, 1984, p. 2). Note that this definition emphasizes both the description of the changes that occur as the body responds to exercise and the explanation of how the changes occur. For example, an individual who engages in an aerobic activity like running, walking, swimming, cycling, or aerobic dance relies on a complex interaction of many biological systems to produce the responses and to compensate for the changing demands and changing internal conditions. As exercise begins we are all aware that our heart rate and respiration increase. As exercise continues we may begin to sweat and sometime later we become fatigued. A day or so after an exercise session, we may even experience some muscle soreness. What we are not always aware of are the many complementary and interactive processes that accompany an exercise bout and the subtle but important adaptations that occur as a result of exercise. This chapter will outline some of the systems that support these processes.

EXERCISE METABOLISM

Exercise requires the expenditure of energy. In some cases exercise may increase energy expenditures by as much as 25 times in the entire body and as much as 200 times in specific working muscle. Each of us recognizes that the expenditure of energy requires fuel and results in the production of heat. Indeed, **energy** is defined as the capacity to perform work and is measured in terms of heat produced. A common unit of measurement of energy is the **calorie,** which is the amount of heat energy required to raise the temperature of a gram of water 1 degree centigrade. A kilocalorie (KCAL) is equal to 1000 calories. In the next chapter, the energy content of various foods will be discussed.

Since energy is defined in relation to work, it is necessary to briefly discuss the concept of work. Mechanical **work** is defined as the product of

PICTURE 5.1 *During vigorous exercise large amounts of energy are expended with heat and waste as the by-product.* (Photo credit: Tony Neste)

force acting across distance. Note, however, that this definition has only limited utility in relation to biological energy expenditures because work is often performed in the absence of movement. For example, mechanical work as defined by the formula above does not occur in isometric contractions because no external movement occurs. Yet it is clear that energy is liberated, heat is produced, and forces are applied.

The breakdown of adenosine triphosphate (ATP) into adenosine diphosphate and phosphate is the fuel for the contractile process. The chemical energy stored in ATP comes originally from food. All biological work requires energy derived from the breakdown of ATP.

Anaerobic and Aerobic Metabolism

Metabolism refers to the sum of the chemical reactions that include energy production and energy utilization. **Aerobic metabolism** refers to the chemical reactions that result in the breakdown of carbohydrates and fats into carbon dioxide, water, and energy. This reaction occurs in the mitochondria and requires the presence of oxygen. **Anaerobic metabolism** involves a complex series of chemical reactions that partially break down carbohydrates to provide small amounts of energy. This process does not require oxygen. However, there are clear trade-offs between anaerobic and aerobic metabolism. In the following sections we will discuss three series of reactions that result in the availability of ATP. The first two could be described as anaerobic and the last as aerobic. The involvement of the following energy systems in exercise of various duration is summarized in Figure 5.1.

Immediate Energy System

High-intensity activity results in ATP being utilized more quickly than it can be produced under normal conditions. Under these conditions another high-energy compound stored in the muscle cell, creatine phosphate, can be broken down to produce phosphate and creatine. The free phosphate can then bond with ADP to reform ATP. As quickly as energy is released by the breakdown of ATP into ADP and phosphate, ATP can be synthesized by the energy liberated during the breakdown of creatine phosphate and the phosphate produced.

This energy system is relatively efficient; however, the stores of creatine phosphate in the muscle are very small. Thus, energy derived via this system could be depleted in as little as 10 seconds. The utility of the system lies in

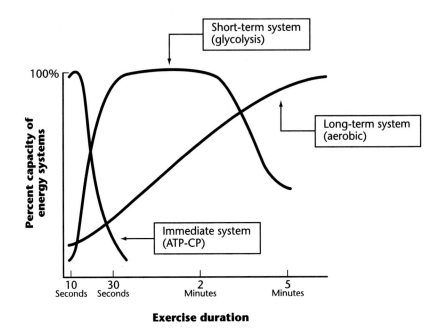

FIGURE 5.1 The role of the various energy systems during an all-out exercise bout of different durations. (From McArdle, Katch, & Katch, *Exercise Physiology: Energy, Nutrition and Human Performance.* Lea & Febiger, 1991. Reprinted by permission of Waverly.)

its immediate availability and relatively rapid recovery rates rather than the quantity of energy available.

Lactic Acid System

Another anaerobic energy system results in the production of ATP but at the expense of producing an unwanted by-product. This process is called **anaerobic glycolysis.** Glycolysis involves the breakdown of glycogen (carbohydrate) into pyruvic acid and ATP. Anaerobic means in the absence of oxygen.

The energy produced is used in the resynthesis of ATP (see Figure 5.3). This system of ATP production has two major limitations. First, only a small amount of ATP can be produced from a given amount of glucose in the absence of oxygen. Secondly, **lactic acid** is a by-product of this process. High concentrations of lactic acid in the muscle and blood result in fatigue. It is important to note that one of the biggest problems with the accumulation of lactic acid is the relatively long period of time required to eliminate it from the cells of the muscles and blood. However, each of us is dependent

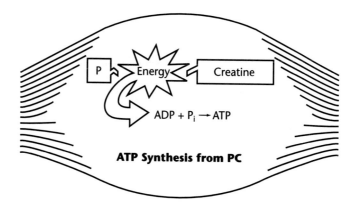

FIGURE 5.2   Illustration of the immediate energy system.

on this system to provide large amounts of energy for tasks that last beyond a few seconds but less than a couple of minutes.

Oxygen System

The amount of ATP produced for a given unit of glycogen under anaerobic conditions is only about one-twelfth of that provided in the presence of oxygen. The process involved in the complete breakdown of glycogen into water and carbon dioxide is called **aerobic glycolysis,** which differs from anaerobic glycolosis because lactic acid does not accumulate in the presence of oxygen. By accepting hydrogen, oxygen, in essence, diverts pyruvic acid

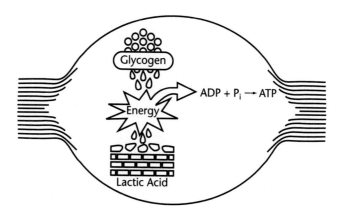

FIGURE 5.3   The lactic acid system (anaerobic glycolysis).

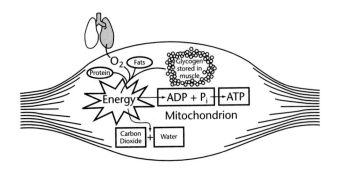

FIGURE 5.4   The aerobic system, which requires oxygen.

(precursor to lactic acid) into aerobic pathways. In a process called the **Krebs Cycle,** pyruvic acid is metabolized, as are other fuel sources including fats and protein. In summary, the aerobic system utilizes food sources for resynthesizing ATP without producing fatiguing by-products like lactic acid. Although carbohydrate stores in the body are relatively small, the utilization of fat stores could potentially provide nearly limitless energy supplies.

The aerobic system is limited in two ways (see Figure 5.4). First, fuel sources and oxygen must be available for aerobic metabolism. Second, and perhaps most important, the rate of ATP utilization must be slow enough for the process to meet the energy demands. As such, the aerobic system is particularly well suited to producing ATP during prolonged low- to moderate-intensity activity.

In the beginning of this section we noted that each of us recognizes that the liberation of energy requires fuel and results in the production of heat. In this section, we found that oxygen was utilized in the breakdown of fuel sources. We will now address the relationship between oxygen consumption and energy expenditure. It should come as little surprise that aerobic capacity or work capacity can be assessed by measuring or estimating an individual's maximal oxygen consumption. The method of using maximal oxygen capacity to estimate work capacity has become a well-established and valuable practice. In the next chapter this method will be outlined in more detail.

THE CARDIOVASCULAR SYSTEM

The cardiovascular system is involved in the delivery of oxygen, fuel, and other important nutrients to the living tissue, as well as removal of heat and waste products. This system is composed of the heart, lungs, vascular circuits, and of course the "delivery vehicle"—blood (see Figure 5.5).

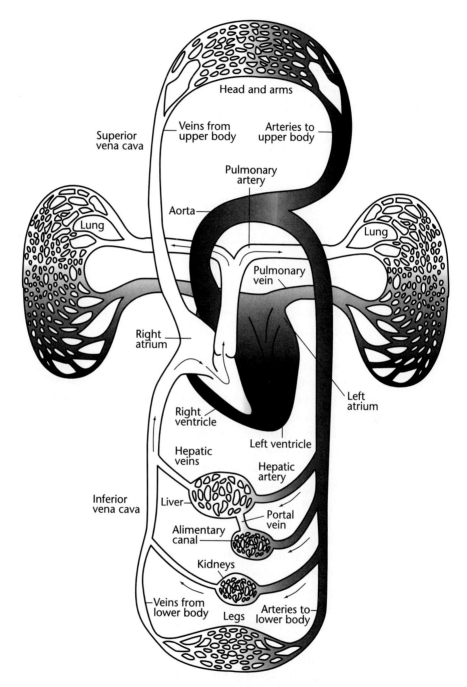

FIGURE 5.5 Representation of the cardiovascular system including the heart, lungs, and blood vessels. The dark shading indicates oxygenated blood.

Cardiac Function

The systematic contraction of the heart muscle provides the forces that initiate blood flow throughout the vascular system. "Even for a person of average fitness, the maximum output of blood from this remarkable organ is greater than the fluid output from a household faucet turned wide open" (McArdle, Katch, & Katch, 1991).

In many respects the heart muscle, or **myocardium,** is similar to skeletal muscle. However, heart cells are interconnected such that an action potential spreads throughout the muscle tissue. In this way heart muscle works as a unit. In essence the heart works as two pumps. The right side of the heart receives blood returning from the body and pumps the blood to the lungs for oxygenation. The left side of the heart receives the blood from the lungs and pumps it for distribution throughout the body. Each pump is composed of two chambers called the **atrium** and the **ventricle.** The atrium serves to collect blood while the ventricle pumps the blood to the lungs or body. The atrium then contracts to move blood into the empty ventricle. Valves located between the atrium and ventricle assure that blood only moves in one direction.

Contractile Rhythm.   Because of the way an action potential is transmitted throughout the myocardium, the heart contracts rhythmically. Stimulation of specialized heart tissue called the **sinoatrial node (S-A node)** causes the action potential to spread throughout the atria. This causes the atria to contract and in turn stimulates a second specialized tissue called the **atrioventricular node (A-V node).** Stimulation of the A-V node causes the action potential to move across other specialized tissues that branch into both the right and left ventricles (see Figure 5.6). This conduction system results in a coordinated contraction that efficiently pumps the blood.

Pressure Changes.   The contractile phase of the cardiac cycle is called **systole** and the relaxation phase **diastole.** During systole the pressures in the respective ventricles increase rapidly until they exceed the pressure in the pulmonary artery and the aorta. At this point blood is pumped into both the pulmonary and systemic circulation. During diastole, pressure in the ventricles is low, allowing the chamber to refill with blood from the atrium. Of course, these pressures are transmitted to varying degrees throughout the vascular system. The pressure is highest in the arterial system and can be estimated by the use of a **sphygmomanometer** (blood pressure cuff). Systolic blood pressure is measured during systole, and diastolic blood pressure

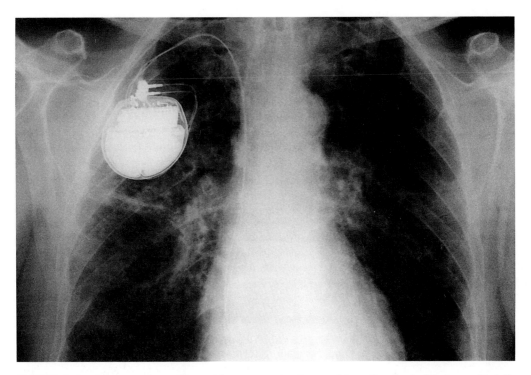

FIGURE 5.6   An x-ray of a patient with a pacemaker inserted into the chest. (Photo credit: Jeff Dunn/Stock Boston)

is measured during diastole. Normal blood pressure in an adult male is 120/80 (systolic/diastolic) and 110/70 in adult females. Chapter 6 will discuss the clinical interpretations of blood pressure.

Cardiac Output.   The amount of blood pumped from the left ventricle of the heart in one minute is called **cardiac output.** The heart will pump about five or six liters of blood per minute when the individual is at rest and up to 35 liters per minute in a highly trained individual during heavy exercise. As does any muscle, the heart responds to training. In the case of heart muscle, a training effect is reflected in terms of greater cardiac output. To understand the effects of training, it is important to note that cardiac output is the product of stroke volume and heart rate. **Stroke volume** is defined as the amount of blood pumped by the heart in one beat. Stroke volume increases as a result of training and is related to both the increased contractile capacity of the heart muscle and the increased venous return to the heart. **Heart rate** is expressed as the number of cardiac cycles occurring in one minute. Note from Figure 5.7 that training tends to decrease heart rate both at rest and during exercise. Thus increased cardiac output with training results primarily from increased stroke volume.

Circulation

The circulatory system is composed of an intricate series of tubules especially suited to transport and distribute blood to the living tissue. **Arteries** are the large vessels that carry the blood away from the heart. **Veins** are the vessels that return blood to the heart. In between is a series of smaller and smaller vessels that branch out to serve all living tissue. **Capillaries** are the microscopic vessels that connect the arteries to the veins. It is in the capillaries that blood/tissue gas exchange occurs.

Gas Exchange in the Capillaries.   Gas exchange between tissue and blood occurs in the capillaries. One gas of interest is oxygen, which is needed for metabolism. Another is carbon dioxide, which is the by-product of metabolism. The direction the gas moves (diffuses) across the capillary membrane is a result of differences in partial pressure of the gas across the membrane. Partial pressure is determined both by the concentration of a gas

Subject	HR (beat/min)		SV (ml/beat)		Q (l/min)
Rest					
Untrained Male	72	×	70	=	5.00
Untrained Female	75	×	60	=	4.50
Trained Male	50	×	100	=	5.00
Trained Female	55	×	80	=	4.50
Max Exercise					
Untrained male	200	×	110	=	22.0
Untrained Female	200	×	90	=	18.0
Trained Male	190	×	180	=	34.2
Trained Female	190	×	125	=	23.9

FIGURE 5.7   Heart rate, stroke volume, and cardiac output at rest and maximum exercise for trained and untrained males and females. (From Powers, Scott K. & Howley, Edward T., *Exercise Physiology: Theory and Application to Fitness and Performance,* 2d ed. Copyright © 1994 Times Mirror Higher Education Group, Inc., Dubuque, IA. All Rights Reserved. Reprinted by permission.)

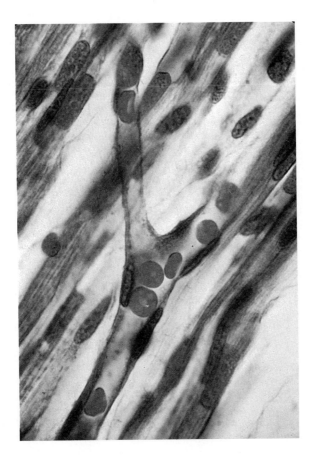

PICTURE 5.2 *Most capillaries are finer than a human hair, which forces red blood cells to pass through single file.* (Photo credit: Lennart Nilsson/Bonnier Alba AB)

and the pressure. If pressure is constant, gas moves from areas of greater concentration to areas of lesser concentration. Blood poor in oxygen and rich in carbon dioxide entering the capillaries in the lung meets high partial pressure of oxygen and low partial pressure of carbon dioxide. The result is that the blood is oxygenated and carbon dioxide is diffused into the lung. Essentially, the opposite occurs in the muscle tissue during exercise; oxygen diffuses from the blood to the tissue and carbon dioxide from the tissue to the blood.

Distribution of Blood Flow. The diameter of the arteriole can be altered to a limited degree. This constriction and dilation of the vessels is driven by both the brain and local factors. This capability is the key to diverting blood to the contracting skeletal muscle and away from less active tissue (see

Under Pressure

Scuba diving has become very popular but it is a potentially dangerous pastime. Decompression illness is the consequence of bubbles that form within the tissues. Inert gas, usually nitrogen or helium, enters the body through the lungs during a dive. When pressures increase during descent the gas dissolves in the blood and is circulated to body tissue. As pressure is relieved during ascent the gas is diffused out of the tissue into the blood and released during expiration.

After surfacing from a dive the tissues of a diver may contain a significant amount of excess nitrogen. Typically, the excess nitrogen is "washed out" by the blood and transported to the lungs, where it is exhaled. However, if the tissues become saturated with nitrogen because the diver has ascended too quickly, stayed down too long, made a number of dives in a short period of time, or some combination of the above, bubbles can form.

The bubbles themselves are not the problem, and paradoxically bubbles do not appear to form in the blood. Problems arise when a large amount of nitrogen reaches the capillaries in the lungs. When this supersaturation occurs bubbles are formed and the lung capillaries may not be able to exchange into the lungs all the gas bubbles. This results in the bubbles reaching the arterial system. It is only when the bubble reaches this side of the capillaries that trouble may occur.

Limb pain may occur because bubbles are impinging on the nerve endings and/or stretching the surrounding tissues. Numbness or paralysis results from bubbles reaching the spinal cord, where they affect circulation and disrupt the nerve cells. If many bubbles clog the capillary system in the lungs, coughing and shortness of breath result. The spinal cord and brain are especially susceptible because these tissues are well profused with capil-

HIGHLIGHT 5.1   *Technical diver shows what is needed to dive to 70m below the surface of the sea.* (Photo credit: © F. Stuart Westmorland/ Photo Researchers)

lary blood flow. Clogs in the brain or heart tissue may result in death.

The answer to these problems is to allow your body time to decompress fully. This can be accomplished by limiting the amount of time you spend at greater depths, ascending from your dive slowly, and allowing sufficient time in between dives. All divers are familiar with decompression tables that provide this information.

From Richard Moon, Richard Vann, and Peter Bennett, The physiology of decompression illness, Scientific American (August 1995).

Figure 5.8) during exercise. Vasodilation results in a decreased resistance and therefore increased blood flow. Vasodilation, coupled with an increased recruitment of capillaries, can increase blood flow to working muscle by as much as 40 times above that of rest.

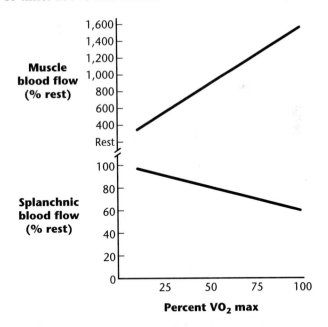

FIGURE 5.8 Blood flow to the muscles increases as a result of exercise. (From Powers, Scott K. & Howley, Edward T., *Exercise Physiology: Theory and Application to Fitness and Performance*, 2d ed. Copyright © 1994 Times Mirror Higher Education Group, Inc., Dubuque, IA. All Rights Reserved. Reprinted by permission.).

Blood

Blood is the messenger that carries oxygen to the tissue and removes lactic acid, carbon dioxide, and other by-products of cell metabolism from living tissue. Blood is transported by the circulatory system but does its job in the capillaries. Blood is composed of plasma (55 percent), erythrocytes (45 percent), and other proteins (<1 percent).

Hemoglobin.   The most important component of blood for exercise purposes is the erythrocytes or red blood cells. These cells contain an iron-protein compound called **hemoglobin,** which is responsible for transporting oxygen. For each liter (1000 ml) of blood, hemoglobin is capable of temporarily storing about 200 ml of oxygen. Oxygen is captured or released by the hemoglobin in the capillaries dependent entirely on the partial pressure of oxygen. In a later section we will discuss the changes in the partial pressure of oxygen at altitudes and its effect on the transfer of oxygen to the hemoglobin.

Hemoglobin concentrations in the blood do not change during exercise but the amount of oxygen carried changes as the partial pressure of oxygen changes. However, the number of red blood cells and therefore the amount of hemoglobin available in the blood may increase slightly with training. The practice of artificially increasing the number of red blood cells via the practice called "blood doping" will be discussed later in this chapter.

Blood Volume and Exercise.   Acute exercise does not cause a change in the number of red blood cells in the blood but may cause a shift of plasma water out of blood vessels, especially in untrained persons. The accumulation of water in the tissue is partially responsible for the "pumped up" feeling that results from lifting weights. However, endurance training may cause as much as an 8 percent increase in blood volume, due to small increases in red blood cells and relatively large increases in plasma volume. Remember, an increase in blood volume will result in an increased stroke volume because the filling of the chambers of the heart is more complete prior to systole.

Pulmonary Function

The lungs of an average person weigh about 1 kg but have a surface area about the size of a badminton court. In a highly trained distance runner, the lung surface is responsible for exchanging 3 to 4 liters of gas per minute.

The most obvious mechanical function of the pulmonary system is to move air into and out of the lungs. Air enters through the nose or mouth,

PICTURE 5.3   *The spongy air sacs or alveoli conduct the real business of gas exchange or respiration.* (Photo credit: Art Siegel)

where it is filtered, humidified, and adjusted to body temperature in the **trachea.** The **bronchi** and the smaller passages, the bronchioles, conduct the air to the terminal branches of the lungs, called **alveoli.**

Millions of alveoli comprise the surface area of the lungs and are the sites of gas exchange in the lungs. The membrane of the alveoli are served with a rich supply of blood located in capillaries. At rest approximately 250 ml of oxygen is diffused through the alveoli membrane into the blood and 200 ml of carbon dioxide is returned. During vigorous exercise this exchange rate may increase by as much as 25 times in endurance athletes.

Ventilation Mechanics.   Ventilation is characterized by inspiration and expiration. The forces driving inspiration come primarily from the diaphragm with some assistance from the intercostal muscles, which increase the size of the chest cavity by raising the ribs and lowering the diaphragm. The increased size of the chest cavity results in decreased pressure in the lungs, which causes air to rush in. As the muscles and tendons that were stretched during inspiration recoil, the volume of the chest cavity decreases, forcing air out of the lungs. Under resting conditions, expiration is a somewhat passive process, but under heavy exercise the intercostal and abdominal muscles are required to support the increased rate of ventilation. In normal healthy individuals the capacity of the ventilatory muscles does not appear to limit exercise. However, the ventilatory muscles of individuals with respiratory disease, like asthma, may become fatigued during even moderate exercise.

FACTORS AFFECTING PERFORMANCE

There are a large number of factors that directly or indirectly affect physical performance. Fatigue is perhaps the most common, but other factors arise directly from the environment in which we perform (e.g., temperature, humidity, altitude) or are a result of substances we ingest (e.g., stimulants, anabolic steroids, growth hormones). Athletes are always looking for a performance edge. In many types of competition only a small difference divides the world-class athlete from the large pack of hopefuls. A substance or procedure that improves performance is called an ergogenic aid. Unfortunately, ergogenic aids are often viewed as a shortcut to training. The following sections will highlight a few of the many factors that affect performance.

Fatigue

We are all aware of the concept of fatigue. When we lift weights, run, or perform any kind of work, we eventually reach a point at which our performance suffers. That is, there are limits to the intensity of exercise we can maintain (power), and there are limits to the amount of exercise we can perform (work). **Fatigue** is defined as the inability to maintain power output or work during extended or repeated contractions. Sustained work is also associated with subjective sensations often referred to as fatigue. In fact, there is some evidence that the site of fatigue may be **central** (brain, brainstem, spinal cord) and/or **peripheral** (motor neuron, neuromuscular junction, muscle). The following sections will briefly discuss the evidence for and against each of these sites contributing to fatigue.

Central Fatigue.   In the late 1800s, Mosso recorded two fatigue curves on an associate. One fatigue curve was recorded during the morning and the other immediately after the associate had presented an important lecture (see Figure 5.9). Clearly the amount of work performed during the second testing period was greater. Mosso concluded that an increased "mental energy" had permitted the muscle to endure better.

Later physiologists attempted to answer this question by electrically stimulating the ulnar nerve leading to the thumb and finger muscles. They reasoned that if there is no central contribution to fatigue, then electrical stimulation of the muscles should result in forces that are no different than forces elicited by voluntary contraction under rest and fatigue conditions. Data from Ikai, Yabe, and Ishii (1967) are provided in Figure 5.10. Note that the difference between forces exerted with voluntary contractions and under electrical stimulation increases as "fatigue sets in." This data, just like that of Bigland-Ritchie, Jones, Hosking, and Edwards (1978), suggests that there appears to be both a central and peripheral site of muscle fatigue.

Setchenov (1903) noted when the muscles of the right arm became exhausted from sawing wood they recovered faster if the individual exercised with the left arm during the interval between bouts of sawing with the right arm rather than simply resting. As with Mosso's earlier explanation, Setchenov proposed that afferent nerves from the active but not fatigued arm played a role in "recharging with energy" the fatigued nerve centers. Data from an experiment by Asmussen and Mazin (1978) is presented in Figure 5.11. Exercise preceded with active pauses (a.p.) resulted in greater accumulated work than bouts preceded by passive pauses (p.p.). Perhaps most interesting were the findings that three kinds of activity during active pauses

FIGURE 5.9 Two fatigue curves. The first was recorded before an important address and the second directly after. (From Asmussen, *Medicine and Science in Sport,* 11, 313–321, 1979, Williams & Wilkins. Reprinted by permission of Waverly.)

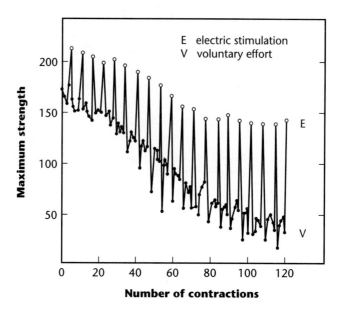

FIGURE 5.10   Maximum voluntary contractions of the thumb interrupted by electrical stimulation of the nerve serving the thumb muscle. (From Asmussen, *Medicine and Science in Sport,* 11, 313–321, 1979, Williams & Wilkins. Reprinted by permission of Waverly.)

resulted in essentially the same effect on the subsequent bouts of exercise. The first two types of active pauses were composed of exercise with large and small muscles of the opposite hand and the last was composed of mental activity (problem solving, counting backward, or the like).

Asmussen suggested that during passive pauses, the feedback from the fatigued limb impinges on a part of the brain called the reticular formation to cause an inhibition of voluntary effort. Alternatively, active pauses result in increased feedback from the nonfatigued site that shifts the balance between inhibition and facilitation to facilitation.

Peripheral Fatigue.   While many exercise physiologists regard the evidence in support of central fatigue with caution, the evidence for at least some sites of peripheral fatigue is much clearer. Potential sites for peripheral fatigue are the motor neuron, neuromuscular junction, and the muscle. Most physiologists note that, at least theoretically, there is a stimulation frequency at which a motor neuron will no longer conduct an impulse, but most agree that this point does not occur under natural conditions (Simonsen, 1971). Thus the motor neuron is generally ruled out as a site of periph-

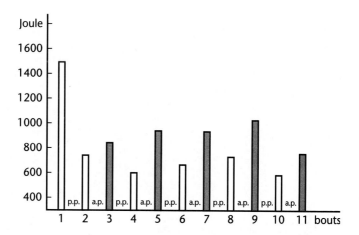

FIGURE 5.11   Accumulated work preceeded by passive and active pauses. (From Asmussen, *Medicine and Science in Sport,* 11, 313–321, 1979, Williams & Wilkins. Reprinted by permission of Waverly.)

eral fatigue. Similarly, evidence suggests that the neuromuscular junction could be the weak link if acetylcholine (neural transmitter) is depleted or the motor endplate experiences reduced excitability. However, evidence from studies that have measured the electrical activity (EMG) arising from the fatigued muscle suggests that the neuromuscular junction is not a site of peripheral fatigue (Bigland-Ritchie, 1978).

The system of calcium delivery to the muscle as well as the rate of cross-bridge cycling in the sarcolemma are implicated in muscle fatigue. High rates of stimulation may lead to a slowing of the action potential along the sarcolemma and the transverse tubules. This may be a result of an increased threshold derived from an accumulation of potassium (see neural impulses in Chapter 3). In addition, high stimulation rates appear to slow the relaxation process. Also, increased production of lactic acid in the cell interferes with calcium's role in the binding process. Calcium is required for cross bridges to be established and for the dissociation of the cross bridges during relaxation.

Fatigue and ATP Production.   The last and perhaps most obvious factor in the development of fatigue is the availability of ATP. Without ATP, the contractile process shuts down. ATP is implicated in the fatigue process during "all-out" anaerobic and aerobic performances. The reader is referred back to the immediate energy system that requires creatine phosphate to produce ATP,

PICTURE 5.4   *A weightlifter is faced with both central and peripheral fatigue.* (Photo credit: Nathan Benn/National Geographic Image Collection)

the lactic acid system that uses anaerobic glycolysis to produce small amounts of ATP with lactic acid as a by-product, and aerobic glycolysis, which produces large amounts of ATP but at a relatively slow rate. In activities of less than 10 seconds nearly 100 percent of the available ATP is derived from anaerobic energy systems. If the activity lasts up to a few minutes only about 70 percent of the ATP comes from anaerobic energy sources. In longer-lasting activities more than 90 percent of the ATP is derived from aerobic glycolysis. Any interruption in the ATP supply clearly results in fatigue. Exceed the rate of ATP supply and fatigue promptly intervenes.

Stimulants

A number of drugs can improve specific types of performance. Some of these drugs are commonly available and are legal (e.g., caffeine). Other performance-enhancing drugs can be dangerous and are controlled (e.g., amphetamines). All of these drugs have unwanted side effects and should be avoided. Two of these drugs will be discussed below.

Caffeine.   **Caffeine** is a stimulant available in many over-the-counter drinks, including coffee, tea, and cola products. Normal or even high usage of these products results in mild central nervous system stimulation within 15 minutes. Athletes have been known to receive higher dosages via injection or suppositories. High blood or urine concentrations of caffeine are presently outlawed by the International Olympic Committee. Caffeine, like many stimulants in small dosages, usually results in perceived increases in alertness and decreased drowsiness. The presence of caffeine also seems to play a role in the elevation of fatty acid utilization, effectively resulting in increased total work time. Thus the most likely ergogenic effect of caffeine is due to the facilitated use of fat as fuel, thus sparing the body's limited carbohydrate reserves. In addition, caffeine may increase the contractile capability of skeletal muscle by increasing the availability of calcium. However, this latter effect, while reproducible in isolated muscle preparations, has not been clearly demonstrated in intact humans.

Amphetamines.   **Amphetamines** are powerful stimulants that are both banned from use in athletics and controlled by law. These drugs stimulate the central nervous system, resulting in increased heart rate and elevated blood pressure, and play a role in altering the synthesis and metabolism of natural central nervous system stimulants (catecholamines). Amphetamines may be found in a number of prescription drugs and black market "pep pills." In a review of the studies involving human subjects, Ivy (1983) concluded that amphetamines tend to delay the onset of fatigue and hasten recovery from fatigue. However, a significant number of studies have reported little or no affect of amphetamines on exercise performance or simple psychomotor skills.

Growth-Enhancing Drugs

Two drugs act in a way that enhances growth of muscle tissue. The drugs were developed and studies were conducted as a result of legitimate, and in some cases very successful, clinical applications. Later, these drugs were used in the food industry to increase the lean–fat ratio in cattle and chicken. However, in recent years some athletes have exploited the effect of these drugs, often with severe outcomes.

Anabolic-Androgenic Steroids—A Historical Perspective

Various forms of natural and synthetic testosterone have received widespread attention in recent years. Ben Johnson was stripped of his 100-meter gold medal in the 1988 Olympics in South Korea, the Chinese swimmers were banned from the pre-Olympic international competition in 1995, and there have been widespread reports of anabolic-androgenic steroid use in American high schools and colleges. The performance-enhancing effects

HIGHLIGHT 5.2 *Charles Eduoard Brown-Sequard claimed that injection of testosterone extracts resulted in remarkable rejuvenating effects.* (Photo credit: Culver Pictures, Inc.)

of these drugs and the reported deleterious side effects have led to their ban in athletic competition throughout the world. Is the use of these drugs a recent phenomenon?

Records dating from as early as 1,000 B.C. indicate that Egyptian, Roman, and Greek cultures touted the medicinal and aphrodisiac powers of natural extracts of testosterone. The *Pharmacopoea Wirtenbergica,* a compendium of remedies published in 1754, included the therapeutic uses of testosterone. Charles Edouard Brown-Seguard, a prominent French physiologist, announced a rejuvenating therapy at the Société de Biologie in 1889. The therapy involved the injection of testosterone extracts derived from dogs and guinea pigs. He claimed that his use of the extracts increased his physical strength and intellectual energy, relieved his constipation, and even lengthened the arc of his urine. In 1896 Austrian physiologist Oskar Zoth and Fritz Pregly injected themselves with a testosterone extract from a bull. They found that the extract improved muscular strength.

By the early 1900s, the market value of these extracts was recognized. In 1935 three pharmaceutical companies separately sponsored research teams to isolate the hormone responsible for the wondrous ergogenic effects. One research team, headed by Adolf Butenandt, was sponsored by Schering Corporation in Germany and another, headed by Leopold Ruzicka, was sponsored by Ciba in Switzerland. In 1939 Butenandt and Ruzicka shared the Nobel Prize in Chemistry for their work.

In the 1950s Soviet weightlifters were provided with a testosterone-based product in an attempt to build strength. At the 1954 World Championships the physician for the Soviet team reported to John Ziegler, physician for the American team, about the drugs. This was apparently the first introduction of this type of drug to American sports.

From John Hoberman and Charles Yesalis, The history of synthetic testosterone, Scientific American (February 1995).

Androgenic-Anabolic Steroids.   Androgenic-anabolic steroids are drugs that function in a manner similar to the male hormone testosterone. Androgenic refers to compounds that result in effects associated with the development of secondary male sex characteristics. Anabolic refers to compounds with growth-stimulating characteristics. This class of drugs was developed to promote muscle growth and delay atrophy in bed-ridden patients, but were soon exploited because of their effect on muscle mass and their reported, but not fully documented, effects on strength. A 1988 study by Buckley and colleagues estimated that 1 in 15 high school students have used steroids to enhance athletic performance and/or to enhance appearance.

The side effects of androgenic-anabolic steroids are many and varied. In men, sperm production may be reduced, resulting in sterility, and estrogen levels may be increased, resulting in breast development. Females may experience a deepening of the voice, beard growth, and/or a disruption of the menstrual cycle. The most serious side effects are an increased risk of coronary heart disease, prostate cancer, and liver disease.

Various versions of the drug have been synthesized in an attempt to minimize the unwanted side effects. These versions may appear particularly appealing to athletes and may be difficult to detect with traditional drug tests. Almost all athletic organizations and professional societies in medicine and sports medicine have issued position papers stating that any potential gain in exercise performance from steroids is outweighed by the probability of acquiring severe side effects.

Growth Hormone.   Growth hormone, also known as somatotrophic hormone, is produced in the pituitary gland. It is involved in the normal tissue-building process. In the past only natural forms of growth hormones were available for clinical purposes but synthetic forms are now available. The new synthetic forms have drastically reduced the cost of growth hormone and dramatically increased the likelihood of their abuse. In a 1988 study, Crist and colleagues administered well-trained men, engaged in a strength-training program, either a placebo or growth hormone in concert with a high-protein diet. No changes in body composition were noted after 6 weeks for the placebo group but the growth-hormone group experienced a reduction in body fat and an increase in lean body weight.

The negative effects arising from various dosages of growth hormone are not well documented. However, acromegaly, a disease of the pituitary gland that causes an excess secretion of growth hormone, results in permanent deformities and may be associated with an increased incidence of diabetes and a shortened life span.

Oxygen, Altitude, and Blood Doping

Oxygen is diffused into the blood in the capillaries of the lungs and subsequently transferred from the capillaries to living tissue throughout the body. This section will briefly discuss the possible ergogenic effect of breathing higher than normal concentrations of oxygen, breathing in lower than normal partial pressures of oxygen at high altitudes, and the process of blood doping.

Higher than Normal Oxygen Concentrations.   It is not uncommon to see professional football players after a brief but intense bout of exercise rush to the sidelines and inhale oxygen-enriched gas mixtures. This practice is supported by the belief that higher concentrations of oxygen in the blood—**hyperoxia**—will delay fatigue and/or enhance recovery from fatigue. Yet the arterial blood in normal individuals breathing air at sea level is about 95 to 98 percent saturated, so richer concentrations of oxygen will increase the saturation levels only about an additional 1 or 2 percent. In fact, research does not support the use of oxygen-enriched gas mixtures as an ergogenic aid prior to a fatiguing event or to enhance the recovery from a fatiguing event. However, breathing an oxygen-enriched gas mixture during exercise (see Figure 5.12), even though impractical in many situations, does appear to enhance performance (Weltman et al., 1978). The higher than normal oxygen concentrations appear both to decrease the work required for ventilation and to enhance the oxygen available in the muscle cell to sup-

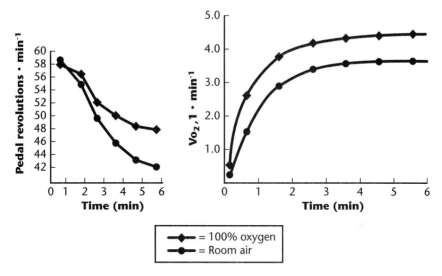

FIGURE 5.12   Bicycle ergometer performance increased as a result of breathing 100% oxygen versus room air. (From McArdle, Katch, & Katch, *Exercise Physiology: Energy, Nutrition and Human Performance.* Lea & Febiger, 1991. Reprinted by permission of Waverly.)

port aerobic glycolysis. This is especially true at high altitudes; mountain climbers typically require supplemental oxygen.

High Altitude and Oxygen Diffusion.   The challenges of exercise at high altitude are readily apparent to anyone who has visited higher elevations. At high altitudes it is not uncommon for a visitor to experience a variety of symptoms, including lightheadedness, headache, nausea, and insomnia. At altitudes above 18,000 feet, the effects can be quite severe. Even though the concentration of oxygen in the air at sea level and at higher elevation is about the same (20.9 percent), the partial pressure of oxygen decreases as altitude increases. Remember from our discussion of oxygen diffusion earlier in this chapter that partial pressure is the key to oxygen diffusion. Lower partial pressure of oxygen in the alveoli due to high altitude results in significant reductions in hemoglobin saturation. For example, at 6500 feet above sea level, hemoglobin is only about 90 percent saturated with oxygen, as compared to 95–98 percent at sea level. At 18,000 feet, hemoglobin saturation drops to below 75 percent and may result in as much as a 40 percent reduction in aerobic capacity. Indeed, work capacity may decrease by as much as 3 percent for every 1,000 feet above the altitude of 5,000 feet (Buskirk et al., 1967).

Adaptations to Altitude.   With exposure to altitude, individuals quickly experience physiological and metabolic changes that permit them to adjust successfully to the new environment. **Acclimatization** is a term used for the collective adaptive responses that improve an individual's tolerance to a new environment. Altitude acclimatization may require from days to months, depending on the specific adaptation and the altitude.

Immediate changes resulting from altitude include an increased respiratory drive, which may lead to hyperventilation and increased blood flow. Longer-term adaptations include a decrease in blood plasma volume and an increased formation of hemoglobin and red blood cells (see Figure 5.13). As little as one week at 7,000 feet above sea level may result in a decrease in plasma of about 8 percent and an increase in red blood cells and hemoglobin of 4 and 10 percent, respectively. At 14,000 feet plasma volumes may decrease by as much as 25 percent and red blood cells and hemoglobin increase by as much as 6 and 20 percent, respectively (Buskirk et al., 1967; Hannon, Shields, & Harris, 1969). This relatively large increase in the blood's ability to transport oxygen results in an increased tolerance to altitude and an increased ability to work.

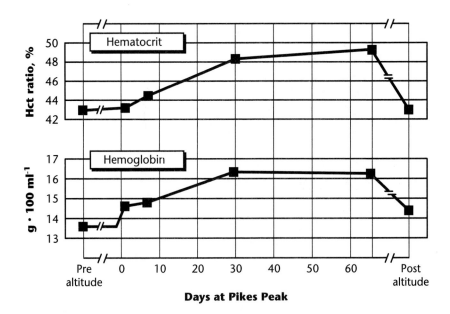

FIGURE 5.13   Exposure to altitude results in increases to hemotocrit and hemoglobin. (From McArdle, Katch, & Katch, *Exercise Physiology: Energy, Nutrition and Human Performance.* Lea & Febiger, 1991. Reprinted by permission of Waverly.)

Performance upon Return to Sea Level.   Exposure to altitude results in an increase in the oxygen-carrying capacity of the blood, which in turn results in an increased work capacity at altitude. How might these adaptations influence performance upon return to sea level? Many athletes, coaches, and researchers reasoned that training at altitude should enhance performance at sea level. Research, however, has found few if any positive effects of altitude training on performance at sea level.

Adams and colleagues (1975) measured maximal oxygen uptake in two groups of six highly trained middle-distance runners (see Figure 5.14). Group 1 was trained for three weeks at an altitude of 7,200 feet, while Group 2 was trained at sea level. After three weeks the groups exchanged training sites for an additional three weeks. Altitude initially resulted in about a 17 percent decrease in maximum oxygen uptake. A posttest at sea level led the authors to conclude that there was no synergistic effect of training and short-term exposure to altitude when compared with training at sea level. Note also that exercise at altitude is restricted. Highly trained athletes may not be able to exercise at an intensity high enough to get positive training effects and may even detrain.

Blood Doping.   Even though the research on altitude indicated that increasing the oxygen-carrying capacity of the blood via acclimatization at

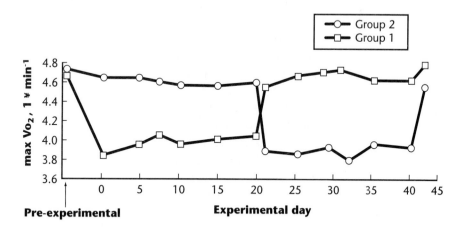

FIGURE 5.14   Effects of training at altitude and sea level for three weeks on maximal oxygen consumption. Group 1 trained for three weeks at an altitude of 7,200 ft while Group 2 was trained at sea level. After three weeks the groups exchanged training sites. (From McArdle, Katch, & Katch, *Exercise Physiology: Energy, Nutrition and Human Performance.* Lea & Febiger, 1991. Reprinted by permission of Waverly.)

altitude was not beneficial to performance at sea level, many athletes, coaches, and some researchers viewed the notion of oxygen-enriched blood as an ergogenic aid. A practice called **blood doping** involves infusing red blood cells into the athlete prior to competition. The blood is typically taken from the athletes about 5 to 7 weeks prior to competition and stored. Before the competition, the athlete's system restores the lost blood cells by natural processes. Just prior to competition the blood cells are transfused back into the athlete.

The time course of this process is described in Figure 5.15. Two aspects of this time course are critical. First, approximately 6 weeks is required for red blood cells and hemoglobin levels in the blood to normalize after 500 ml of blood are removed. Second, a significant amount of the viable blood cells are lost during extended storage. Traditional blood storage techniques resulted in as much as a 40 percent loss in viable blood cells after only three weeks. This resulted in a trade-off between waiting for the athletes' hemoglobin to return to near-normal levels and the time course of the rapidly deteriorating stored blood. It has been reported that three weeks was a typical time between removal and infusion. Under these conditions, controlled studies involving blood doping found small, if any, benefits of blood dop-

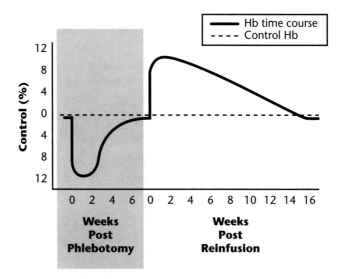

FIGURE 5.15 Decreases in hemoglobin levels following removal and increases following reinfusion. (From N. Gledhill, Blood doping and related issues: A brief review. *Medicine and Science in Sports and Exercise,* 14, 183–189, 1982. The American College of Sports Medicine.)

ing. However, more recent advances in blood storage techniques have significantly increased the life of stored blood. Blood storage techniques now allow blood to be stored for a year or more with less than a 15 percent loss of red blood cells. More recent research has indicated that reinfusion of about one liter of blood, well after the subject has recovered from the withdrawal of blood (> 6 weeks), results in significant improvements in middle-distance running performance. The effect, however, seems to diminish within a few days after reinfusion.

It is important to note the differences between the effects of acclimatization to altitude and the effects from blood doping. Both procedures result in an increased capacity of the blood to transport oxygen. However, altitude acclimatization does not translate into a beneficial effect on aerobic performance at sea level, while blood doping appears to enhance aerobic performance. Two factors may contribute to this difference in performance effects. First, altitude acclimatization results in significant reductions in total blood volume, and blood doping results in increases in total blood volume. Increased blood volume may lead to more complete filling of the ventricles of the heart prior to contraction, resulting in increased stroke volume and cardiac output. Secondly, altitude adaptations include a number of minor changes in the acid base balance, resulting in an elevated cell and blood pH (becomes more alkaline). This and other adaptations that occur at altitude are not present as a result of blood doping.

Heat and Humidity

During exercise we become hot, begin to sweat, and tend to become flushed even in relatively cool environments. Body temperature measured on the surface of the skin is called **skin temperature.** Temperature measured rectally is called **core temperature.** Normal core body temperature ranges from about 97 to 100 degrees but with strenuous exercise in moderate environments may reach 105 degrees. However, during exercise in hot and humid environments, core temperature may exceed 106 degrees, resulting in heat exhaustion or heatstroke. Core temperatures above 108 degrees may result in death.

One of the products of energy metabolism is heat. During exercise the production of heat within the body can be substantial. If the heat generated within the body is coupled with high environmental temperatures, heat stress may occur. The factors that result in increased body temperature and the factors that reduce heat stress will be discussed in this section.

Thermoregulation in Heat and Humidity.   The processes that protect an individual from heat stress by regulating core temperature are called **thermoregulation.** When exercising in a hot and/or humid environment there is competition between the mechanisms that regulate blood flow to the muscles and those that direct blood flow to the surface of the skin. This competition typically results in decreased performance in endurance events in hot and/or humid environments. Body heat can be lost or gained by radiation, conduction, convection, and/or evaporation (see Figure 5.16).

   Radiation is a form of heat transfer through the air from one object to another. For example, heat radiation from the sun is transferred to a person exercising in the sun as well as to the ground and other objects. This type of heat is apparent when walking across the sand at the beach on a hot summer day. **Conduction** is heat transferred from warmer to cooler objects that come in direct contact. Walking on the hot sand transfers heat to the soles of your feet by conduction. **Convection** is the transfer of heat from the surface of the skin to the air or water circulating next to the body. Upon entering the water, convection results in the transfer of body heat to the water.

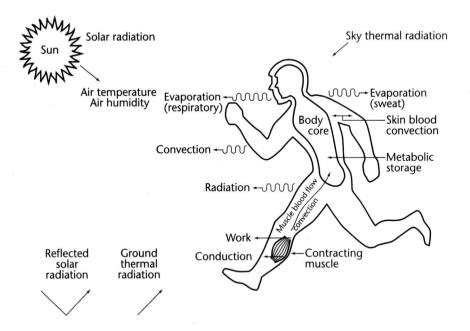

FIGURE 5.16   Factors affecting the build-up and dissipation of heat during exercise in hot weather.

Evaporation is the transfer of heat to the environment as water is vaporized from the respiratory passages and the surface of the skin. Evaporation provides the major natural defense against overheating in hot relatively dry environments. To lesser extents, heat is transferred to the environment via radiation, conduction, and convection. In fact, evaporation is the only way to lose heat when the environment is hotter than you are. Evaporation is assisted by approximately 3 million sweat glands distributed on the surface of the body. Sweat glands secrete a weak saline solution on the surface of the skin. The evaporation of sweat results is a cooling effect that serves to cool the blood circulating near the surface of the skin. This blood in turn cools the core of the body as it is circulated throughout the vascular system.

Evaporation is greatly facilitated by air currents and can be severely decreased by increased relative humidity and clothing. Remember evaporation, not sweating, cools the skin. Relative humidity is the percent of moisture carried in the air relative to the total amount of moisture that can be carried. Obviously, if the relative humidity is high the air can accept less additional moisture from the surface of the skin than if the relative humidity is low. Air currents also tend to take moisture-laden air away from the skin. In the absence of air currents, the air next to the skin becomes increasingly saturated with moisture until further evaporation is not possible. Tight-fitting clothing or uniforms can also decrease the amount of evaporation that occurs. This may be a particular problem for football players or other athletes wearing restrictive clothing who exercise in hot and humid environments (see Figure 5.17).

Heat Acclimatization and Heat Stress.   Work bouts that can be performed relatively easily in cool environments may be difficult to complete in hot/humid environments. However, the body quickly adapts to the new environment by shunting increased amounts of blood to the surface of the skin. In addition, a lower threshold for sweating accompanies both more evenly distributed sweating and an increased sweat rate. With as little as a week of heat stress, sweating may increase twofold. This allows the heat-acclimated individual to exercise with a lower core temperature (rectal) and lower heart rate in the hot environment.

Replacing Body Fluids.   Ingesting fluids serves two major purposes in hot environments. First, fluids replace important electrolytes and fluid balances in the body. In fact, it is recommended as a general rule to match fluid

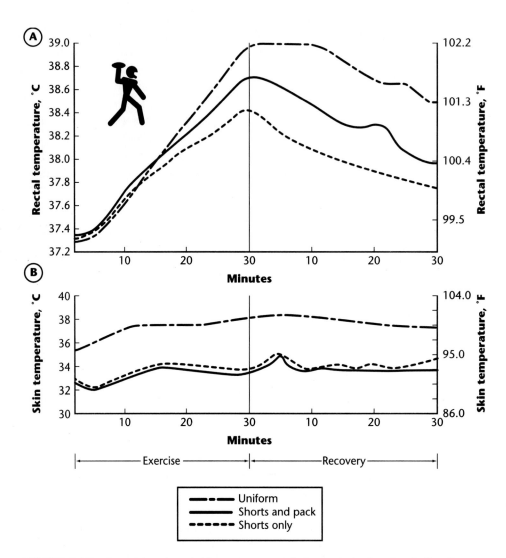

FIGURE 5.17   Rectal (core) and skin temperature during exercise in a football uniform, short and pack, or shorts only. The top line in each graph (indicating higher core and skin temperature) represents the group wearing the football uniform. (From McArdle, Katch, & Katch, *Exercise Physiology: Energy, Nutrition and Human Performance.* Lea & Febiger, 1991. Reprinted by permission of Waverly.)

intakes to fluid loss in long-term exercise in hot environments. Second, fluid ingestion can serve to cool core body temperature, particularly if the fluids are relatively cold. In fact, cool liquids are emptied from the stomach and absorbed more quickly than liquids at body temperature.

FINAL COMMENT

In the previous chapter we discussed the biomechanical principles that apply to the study of human movement. In that chapter, motion was discussed in terms of the kinetics of human movement. Remember, kinetics is a description of movement with respect to the forces that are associated with the movement. However, Chapter 4 did not describe *how* the human body produces these forces during exercise. This chapter presents some of the answers to how our body can sustain movements. The breakdown of ATP into adenosine diphosphate and phosphate is the fuel for the contractile process. In high-intensity activities of a relatively short duration ATP is provided via anaerobic metabolism. Energy from anaerobic metabolism is limited and in some cases results in unwanted by-products like lactic acid. On the other hand, aerobic metabolism can produce very large quantities of ATP but the process is relatively slow. Thus anaerobic metabolism supports high-intensity activities of short duration (e.g., 100-meter dash) and aerobic metabolism provides the fuel for longer lasting activities of lower intensity (10,000-meter race).

When we exercise the cardiovascular system responds to support the increased demand for fuel and oxygen. This system is also crucial for dissipating heat and removing waste products that accumulate as we increase our activity. A major benefit that results from training is that physiological systems adapt in subtle but often profound ways to accommodate the increased demands placed on the body. With training, transport of essential elements (oxygen and fuel) are improved by enhancing the functioning of the heart, circulatory system, and the volume and oxygen-carrying capacity of the blood and the working muscle.

While training can lead to dramatic improvements in how well the physiological systems function, the system can be positively or negatively affected by a number of factors including fatigue level, the presence of stimulants or drugs, altitude level, and/or heat and humidity levels. Obviously, for a performer, a coach, and/or an instructor to take full advantage of the capability of the physiological systems, they should be very aware of both the benefits and limitations these factors have on human physiology. For example, 10,000-meter track athletes would adopt quite different acclimatization approaches for an important meet in Colorado (8000 feet above sea level) and Texas (sea level).

It is important to note that the goal of this chapter was to provide a broad overview of exercise physiology and its contribution to the working of the cardiovascular system at rest and during exercise. At this stage we have not discussed what type of exercise and nutritional programs help us to achieve a healthy physiological system. The next chapter attacks this issue as well as how we can monitor the capacity of our system, ultimately allowing us to suggest programs that are most appropriate for enhancing longevity and quality of life.

QUESTIONS FOR THOUGHT

- Name different activities and determine the primary energy system that would be utilized to support the activity.
- List and discuss factors that will result in increased oxygen to the muscles of the human performer. When untrained people first engage in a weightlifting or aerobic running program, they are often able after only a few days to sustain higher-intensity exercise or exercise at a given intensity for longer. This adaptation occurs too quickly to be accounted for by changes in physiology. What could account for the improved performance?
- Discuss the contributions of central and peripheral sites of fatigue. In a weight-training class, can you lift more weight when the whole class is cheering you on or when you are alone? Why?
- Discuss ergogenic aids that you have tried or have heard of others using. What is the basis for enhanced performance with these aids? What are the potential side effects? Should some ergogenic aids be legal and others banned from competition?
- Explain the effects altitude has on the physiological functioning of an individual. In Chapter 4 we discussed projectile motion. What effect will performing at high altitude have on projectile motion?
- When exercising in a hot and humid environment, what can be done to reduce core body temperature? Are the methods discussed a result of radiation, conduction, convection, or evaporation?

KEY TERMS

acclimatization

aerobic glycolysis

aerobic metabolism

alveoli

amphetamines

anaerobic glycolysis

anaerobic metabolism

androgenic-anabolic steroids

arteries

atrioventricular node (A-V node)

atrium

blood doping

bronchi

caffeine

calorie

capillaries

cardiac output

central fatigue

conduction

convection

core temperature

diastole

energy

evaporation

exercise physiology

fatigue

growth hormone

heart rate

hemoglobin

hyperoxia

Krebs Cycle

lactic acid

metabolism

myocardium

peripheral fatigue

radiation

sinoatrial node (S-A node)

skin temperature

sphygmomanometer

stroke volume

systole

thermoregulation

trachea

veins

ventricle

work

RESOURCES

Textbooks

Bowers, R. W., & Fox, E. L. (1992). *Sports Physiology.* Dubuque, IA: W. C. Brown.

Lamb, D. R. (1984). *Physiology of Exercise: Responses and Adaptations.* New York: Macmillan.

McArdle, W. D., Katch, F. I., & Katch, V. I. (1991). *Exercise Physiology: Energy, Nutrition, and Human Performance.* Philadelphia: Lea & Febiger.

Powers, S. K., & Howley, E. T. (1990). *Exercise Physiology: Theory and Application to Fitness and Performance.* Dubuque, IA: W. C. Brown.

Journals

Exercise and Sport Science Reviews

Journal of Applied Physiology

Journal of Physiology

Medicine and Science in Sport and Exercise

Research Quarterly for Exercise and Sport

Professional Organizations

American Alliance of Health, Physical Education, Recreation, and Dance

American College of Sports Medicine

The American Physiological Society

Internet

World Wide Web (WWW)

http://physiology.med.cornell.edu/WWWVL/physioweb.html

http://www.faseb.org/

Listservers
Physiology
send:join physiology <your name>
to: mailbase@mailbase.ac.uk

Thermal Physiology
Send: sub thpysio <your name>
To: listserv@frmop11.cnusc.fr

MacLab Hardware for Physiologists
Send: sub maclab <your name>
To: Listserv@irlearn.ucd.ie

REFERENCES

Adams, W. C., Bernauer, E. M., Dill, D. B., & Bomar, J. B. Jr. (1975). Effects of equivalent sea-level and altitude training on VO_2 max and running performance. *Journal of Applied Physiology, 39*, 262.

Asmussen, E. (1979). *Medicine and Science in Sports, 11*, 313–321.

Asmussen, E., & Mazin, B. (1978). Recuperation after muscle fatigue by diverting activities. *European Journal of Applied Psychology, 38*, 1–8.

Bigland-Richie, B., Jones, D. A., Hosking, G. P., & Edwards, R. H. T. (1978). Central and peripheral fatigue in sustained maximum voluntary contractions of human quadriceps muscle. *Clinical Science and Molecular Medicine, 54*, 609–614.

Buckley, W. E., Yesalis, V. E., Friedl, K. E., Anderson, W. A., Streit, A. L., & Wright, J. E. (1988). Estimated prevalence of anabolic steroid use among male high school seniors. *Journal of the American Medical Association, 260*, 3441.

Buskirk, E. R., Kollias, J., Akers, R. F., Prokop, E. K., & Reategui, E. P. (1967). Maximum performance at altitude and on return from altitude in conditioned runners. *Journal of Applied Physiology, 23*, 259–266.

Crist, D. M., Peake, G. T., Egan, P. A., & Waters, D. L. (1988). Body composition response to exogenous GH during training in highly conditioned adults. *Journal of Applied Physiology, 65*, 579.

Hannon, J. P., Shields, J. L., & Harris, C. W. (1969). Effects of altitude acclimatization on blood composition in women. *Journal of Applied Physiology, 26*, 540–547.

Hoberman, J. M., & Yesalis, C. E. (February 1995). The history of synthetic testosterone. *Scientific American, 212*, 76–81.

Ikai, M., Yabe, K., & Ishii, K. (1967). Muskelkraft und muskuläre ermüang bei wickürlicher anspanning und elektricher reizung des muskel. *Sportartz und Sportmedizin,* 197–211.

Ivy, J. L. (1983). Amphetamines. In *Ergogenic Aids in Sport.* Champaign, IL: Human Kinetics.

Lamb, D. R. (1984). *Physiology of Exercise: Responses and Adaptations.* New York: Macmillan.

McArdle, W. D., Katch, F. I., & Katch, V. I. (1991). *Exercise Physiology: Energy, Nutrition, and Human Performance.* Philadelphia: Lea & Febiger.

Powers, S. K., & Howley, E. T. (1990). *Exercise Physiology: Theory and Application to Fitness and Performance.* Dubuque, IA: W. C. Brown.

Setchenov, I. M. (1935). Zur frage nach der einwirkung sensitiver reize auf die muskelarbeit des menschen. In *Selected Works* (pp. 246–260). Moscow.

Simonson, E. (1971). *Physiology of Work Capacity and Fatigue* (p. 571). Springfield, IL: Charles C. Thomas.

Tesch, P., Thorsson, A., & Kaiser, P. (1984). Muscle capillary supply and fiber type characteristics in weight and power lifters. In R. Giles (Ed.), *Circulation, Respiration, and Metabolism* (pp. 227–239). New York: Springer-Verlag.

Weltman, A. L., Katch, V., & Sady, S. (1978). Effects of increasing oxygen availability on bicycle ergometer endurance performance. *Ergonomics, 21,* 427.

CHAPTER 6

Fitness and Health

CHAPTER OBJECTIVES

- To develop an appreciation for the many and varied benefits of regular exercise
- To understand the tools and procedures that are used to assess exercise capacity and health risk
- To characterize the methods of training that result in an increased performance capability and an increased potential for good health
- To highlight the interaction of exercise, nutrition, and body composition

INTRODUCTION

Records from more than two thousand years ago reveal that humans speculated on the health and medical benefits of exercise. Early Chinese history noted a series of medical exercises called Cong Fu. The Chinese thought that diseases were the result of inactivity. Thus, movement combined with breathing exercises (i.e., Cong Fu) were intended to keep the internal organs functioning and to prolong life. In the United States in the 1800s, physical training programs known as Swedish and German gymnastics became popular. These exercise programs used physical and mental exercises performed in progression from easy to difficult. By the early 1900s, a few progressive companies provided exercise facilities and offered exercise programs for their employees. This was the beginning of corporate fitness programs that became popular in the 1980s.

EXERCISE AND HEALTH

Today research has documented many of the physiological and psychological benefits of exercise (for further discussion see Chapters 5 and 9). This section will discuss health and fitness from an exercise perspective. **Health** is typically defined as physical, mental, and social well-being, not just freedom from disease. **Fitness** is defined as the capacity to perform the activities required of an individual. Thus this chapter will be concerned with the interaction between exercise, fitness, and disease in relation to longevity, quality of life, and prevention of disease. **Wellness** encompasses health and fitness as well as emotional, intellectual, spiritual, interpersonal, social, and environmental well-being.

Longevity and Quality of Life

For many people, both longevity and quality of life are important. These notions are of increasing concern as we grow older. Obviously we would prefer to live longer and maintain a good quality of life as we age. For many of us, quality of life is directly related to our physical, mental, and social health. The question of concern in this section relates to the role exercise plays in increasing longevity and quality of life. In general, research indicates that regular physical activity throughout life results in increased longevity and offers some degree of protection from health problems.

Harvard Alumni Study.   Paffenbarger and colleagues (1986) reported a study of 17,000 Harvard alumni who entered college between 1916 and 1950. The study found regular exercise countered the life-shortening effects of cigarette smoking and excess body fat. Even for people with high blood pressure, those who exercised regularly reduced their death rate by one-half. Genetic tendencies toward an early death were countered by regular exercise. For individuals who had one or both parents die before the age of 65 (a significant health risk), a lifestyle that included regular exercise reduced the risk by 25 percent. A 50 percent reduction in mortality rate was observed for those whose parents lived beyond 65 years.

The results clearly indicated that regular exercise can result in reduced risk of death. In fact, mortality rates decreased as the amount of exercise increased; active men lived an average of one to two years longer than sedentary men. It is interesting to note, however, that very active men had higher death rates than moderately active men (See "Highlight: Walk Don't Run").

PICTURE 6.1 *Regular exercise can result in increased quality of life and reduced risk of cardio-vascular disease.* (Photo credit: Will Hart)

In a review of a number of studies concerning the relationship between physical inactivity and coronary heart disease, Powell and colleagues. (1987) concluded that regular exercise contributes to the prevention of heart disease to such an extent that a sedentary individual is more than two times more likely to develop heart disease than an active and fit individual. In fact, the American Heart Association now considers physical inactivity a primary risk factor at least as powerful as hypertension, smoking, and high cholesterol.

The Framingham Study. Kannel and Gordon (1974) monitored the health of the Framingham community, a suburb of Boston. They reported that increasing levels of physical activity were associated with decreasing incidence of death, particularly death attributed to cardiovascular disease. In addition, the authors of the Framingham study noted an increased incidence

It's Never Too Late

He's a world champion. Jesse Coon of College Station, Texas, is a world champion swimmer in his age group of 80–84. Eighty-four-year-old Coon has been swimming competitively since the ripe old age of 64. The former physics professor at Texas A&M University holds the world record for the 50-meter butterfly. His time of 58.05 seconds beat Shokei Yoshida, a Japanese swimmer who held the record with the time of 59.50 seconds. In the past 20 years he has won more than 150 medals and he expects to keep on winning. Coon swims 5 days a week for 90 minutes a day. Besides his workout in the pool, Coon gets exercise by mowing his lawn and sailing.

Not all mature Americans need to be world record holders to benefit from a more active lifestyle. Recent studies indicate that regular exercise and physical activity can reduce or slow down the biological process of aging. Decreased body fat and increased muscle mass make everyday tasks easier. Increased bone density decreases the possibility of getting osteoporosis. Increased flexibility that comes with activity decreases risk of injury. Aerobic capacity, psychomotor skills, and a controlled body weight due to regular exercise all contribute to possible choices of activity for the older adult. Because Jesse Coon swims, he doesn't have to hire someone to mow his lawn for him and he is able to enjoy a day at the lake sailing.

The extent to which exercise increases lifespan is still being debated. To be sure, a more active lifestyle improves quality of life. Older adults can experience increased life satisfaction, happiness, and self-esteem, along with reduced stress with a regular activity. The many benefits of exercise are evidenced by mall walkers, square dance hoedowners, ballroom dancers, league bowlers, pedestrian golfers, and the mature weightlifter. Simple lifestyle choices such as taking the stairs instead of the elevator or hiding the remote control can increase activity for some sedentary individuals.

More people are living longer. By the year 2000,

HIGHLIGHT 6.1   *A more active lifestyle improves quality of life.* (Photo credit: ©Tim Brown/Tony Stone Images)

15 percent of Americans will be over the age of 65. Jesse Coon says, "The older you get, the more important it is to exercise." Coon is living proof! More importantly, Coon expects his next 20 years to be better than his last 20 years. He is an example not only to others of the gray-haired set, but also for those of us who are considerably younger than he.

of cardiovascular heart disease as the number of risk factors increased (see Figure 6.1). Risk factors were defined as high cholesterol (>250 mg/dl^{-1}), high blood pressure (>160 mmHg), smoking (>1 pack per day), and incidence of coronary heart disease in one's family.

More on Fitness and Longevity.   Blair and colleagues (1989) conducted one of the few large-scale longitudinal studies that obtained actual fitness

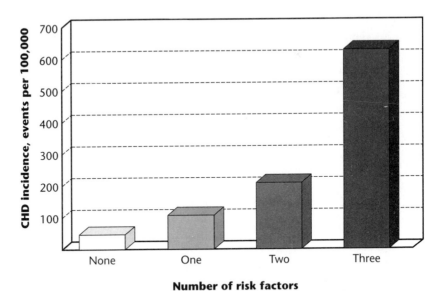

Number of risk factors

FIGURE 6.1   Increases in the number of risk factors like high cholesterol, high blood pressure, and smoking are associated with an increased incidence of coronary heart disease. (From McArdle, Katch, & Katch, *Exercise Physiology: Energy, Nutrition and Human Performance.* Lea & Febiger, 1991. Reprinted by permission of Waverly.)

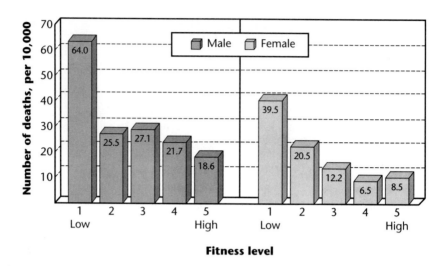

FIGURE 6.2   Even small increases in fitness appear to result in increased longevity. (From McArdle, Katch, & Katch, *Exercise Physiology: Energy, Nutrition and Human Performance.* Lea & Febiger, 1991. Reprinted by permission of Waverly.)

information from the individuals rather than survey or self-reported information. The study followed more than 13,000 men and women for an average of eight years. The most important finding was that even moderate levels of fitness resulted in significantly lower mortality rates than those for individuals in the sedentary category. In fact, the death rates for the most fit individuals were about three times lower than for the sedentary individuals. These results should be very encouraging for sedentary individuals, suggesting that they, as a group, can decrease their death rate with only moderate-intensity exercise like walking, riding a bicycle, swimming, or jogging for as little as 30 minutes a few times a week (Figure 6.2).

Potential Risks of Exercise

Most exercise physiologists and physicians recognize the many and varied benefits of moderate regular exercise. However, there are potential risks associated with exercise. For our purposes these will be classified as risks associated with physiological stress and with anatomical stress.

Physiological Risks.   Physiological risks of exercise are dependent on a number of factors including exercise intensity/duration, environmental conditions (temperature, humidity, altitude), fitness level, and degree of cardiovascular heart disease. Death rate from vigorous exercise occurs at a rate of approximately 1 death per year in a population of 15,000 to 20,000 adult exercisers. Exercise-related death is extremely rare in individuals without underlying cardiovascular disease. Although rare, most exercise-related deaths occur in middle-aged and older individuals with advanced coronary artery disease. In fact, exercise-related death is more likely to occur from daily work activities (e.g., yard work, shoveling snow, moving furniture) than from fitness related activities like walking, swimming, or jogging. This is particularly true if the individual adheres to an exercise prescription from a physician or exercise specialist.

Anatomical Risks. With exercise there is always the risk of injury to the muscle, tendon, bone, or joint structures. This type of injury can be classified as chronic or acute. **Chronic injury** lasts a long time or recurs with some regularity. Usually chronic injury begins gradually and is often difficult to relate to a specific incident. Chronic anatomical injury is often referred to as "overuse" injury. Examples of chronic injury are shin splints, bursitis (irritation of the bursa in the knees, hips, shoulder, or elbow), low back pain, and tendinitis (inflammation of the tendon). **Acute injury** is characterized by a sudden onset and can typically be related to a specific incident. The symptoms of acute injury are localized pain, swelling, and limited ability to use the injured area. Examples of acute injury are a sprained ankle or knee and a pulled muscle.

In many cases chronic injury can be avoided by wearing proper shoes and engaging in appropriate warm-up and warm-down activities. Most importantly, however, those who exercise should "listen" to their body's warning signals. Pain should not be viewed as a positive consequence of exercise but as a warning sign not to be ignored. It is time to reassess the usefulness of the adage "no pain, no gain" so often heard in exercise settings.

GRADED EXERCISE TESTING

The purpose of **graded exercising testing** is to determine an individual's response to a standardized exercise workload. Various forms of exercise testing are routinely administered to determine the exercise capacity and cardiopulmonary response of healthy individuals and various patient populations in laboratory and hospital settings. Exercise testing may be used prior to beginning an exercise program to determine a safe level of exercise or as a diagnostic test by a physician in an attempt to evaluate the presence of heart disease. The choice of tests included in the exercise test battery is dependent on specific purposes of the testing and the individual being tested. Clearly different tests would be chosen for a healthy college age student and for an elderly person with symptoms of coronary heart disease.

In all cases, the guidelines for administering exercise testing discussed in this chapter will be based on those established by the American College of Sports Medicine (ACSM). The reader is referred to the *Guidelines for Exercise Testing and Prescription* (1991) written by the Preventive and Rehabilitative Exercise Committee of the American College of Sports Medicine.

Preexercise Screening

Prior to exercise testing it is important to determine an individual's potential risk through a careful screening procedure. This is important so that the safety of the testing program to the individual can be assessed, an appropriate test battery can be administered, and a physician can be present if required. In addition, the person responsible for test administration should inform the individual being tested of the potential risks in all procedures that will be administered. The person should be offered an opportunity to ask questions and be provided sufficient information to make an **informed consent.** In the case of a minor or other person legally under the supervision of a guardian, the parent or guardian must provide consent. (See "Highlight: Ethical Treatment of Human Subjects" in Chapter 2.)

Health History.   An initial step in the prescreening sequence is to administer a **health history** questionnaire. This is used to determine an individual's past and present history on factors that might impact their potential risk of cardiovascular disease and/or might limit the utilization of exercise testing as a diagnostic tool. The ACSM guidelines suggest that items like history of stroke, chest discomfort, lightheadedness, shortness of breath, high blood pressure, ankle swelling, caffeine use, alcohol use, and tobacco use be included in the health history. Also included should be information concerning the level of activity in which the individual typically engages. This should include frequency, duration, and intensity of the exercise as well as the type of exercise preferred.

Assignment of Risk.   On the basis of the health history an individual can be classified into one of three risk categories; apparently healthy, individuals at higher risk, and individuals with disease. An **apparently healthy** individual does not have symptoms suggestive of cardiopulmonary or metabolic disease and has no more than one major coronary risk factor.

Exercise testing is not suggested prior to engaging in strenuous exercise for apparently healthy men below the age of 40 and women below the age of 50. In fact, under the ACSM guidelines older apparently healthy individuals may engage in moderate exercise without an exercise test. **Moderate exercise** is defined as intensities of between 40–60 percent of VO$_2$ max. **Vigorous exercise** is defined as intensities greater than 60 percent of maximum. Even though exercise testing and medical examinations are not suggested for younger apparently healthy individuals, exercise testing may provide a basis upon which an effective and safe exercise program can be established.

Individuals at **higher risk** have symptoms of possible cardiopulmonary or metabolic disease and/or two or more major coronary risk factors. An exercise test and medical examination are suggested for higher-risk individuals before engaging in a vigorous exercise program. Individuals with symptoms suggestive of coronary, pulmonary, or metabolic disease should have a medical examination and exercise test with a physician present before engaging in any exercise program.

Individuals **with disease** are those who have diagnosed cardiac, pulmonary, or metabolic disease. An exercise program for individuals with disease should only be initiated with a physician's approval. Exercise testing for these individuals is important to assess the safety of an exercise program and to monitor the progress of the disease's effect on functional capacity.

Physical Examination.   An abbreviated cardiovascular and pulmonary physical examination by a physician is suggested for some individuals prior to an exercise test or participation in an exercise program. The examination should focus on the signs and/or symptoms of cardiovascular heart disease. In addition, the examination should include an evaluation of body weight/fat, edema, pulse rate, cardiac rhythmicity, blood pressure (supine, sitting, and standing), and an evaluation of heart and lung sounds.

Laboratory Tests.   Laboratory tests may play an important role in determining health and exercise risk. Laboratory tests should include blood analysis for glucose, uric acid, total cholesterol, high- and low-density lipoproteins, triglycerides, hemoglobin, hematocrit, and erythrocytes. These analyses can be conducted on a small amount of blood typically taken from a vein in the arm.

Perhaps the most talked about, and one of the most important, laboratory measurements is that of cholesterol. **Total cholesterol** in the blood serum can be divided into two classes depending on the compound called lipoprotein that is carrying the cholesterol. One type of **lipoprotein** is a compound of cholesterol and protein. Lipoproteins are important because they are the main form of transport for fat in the blood. **Low-density lipoprotein (LDL)** carries more cholesterol than **high-density lipoprotein (HDL).** LDL, the bad cholesterol, carries cholesterol from the liver to other body cells. High concentrations of LDL are associated with cardiovascular risk. This is because LDLs may be taken up by the muscle cells in the arteries and have been implicated in the hardening of the arteries, called **atherosclerosis.** Diets high in saturated fats will increase LDL. High levels of HDL, the good cholesterol, are associated with protection from cardiovascular disease. HDL transports cholesterol in the opposite direction from LDL. HDL removes cholesterol from the tissue and returns it to the liver for possible degradation. Exercise appears to result in increased levels of HDL.

Because the total amount of cholesterol is composed of good (HDL) and bad (LDL) cholesterol, many scientists feel that the ratio of LDL to HDL is a sensitive index of possible coronary heart disease. This ratio is improved with a low-calorie, low-saturated-fat diet and moderate levels of aerobic activity.

Preexercise Evaluation

After an individual has completed a health history, a medical examination (if required), and blood has been drawn for laboratory tests, pulmonary function, resting blood pressure, and resting electrocardiogram (ECG) are typically assessed. These tests may provide a basis on which the potential risks associated with exercise testing may be reevaluated and the need for a physician's presence during exercise testing may be determined.

Pulmonary Function.   A **spirometer** is a device used to measure the volume and capacity of the lungs. This device, and the measurements it provides, may be helpful in detecting and quantifying lung disease. For the present purposes only a few basic ventilation measures will be discussed (see Figure 6.3).

Tidal volume (TV) is the amount of air moved during inspiration or expiration during normal ventilation. The additional (above TV) amount of air moved during a maximal inspiration is called the **inspiratory reserve volume (IRV)** and the additional air moved during a maximal expiration is termed **expiratory reserve volume (ERV).** Together these reserve volumes produce the **forced vital capacity (FVC),** which is the total amount of air that can be moved in one breath. Even after maximal exhalation, over one liter of air remains in the lungs. The remaining volume is called the

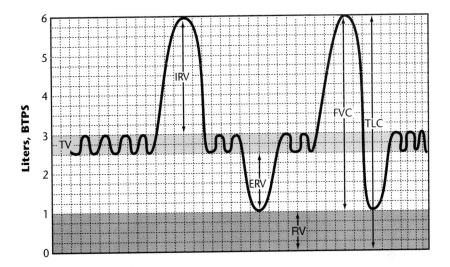

FIGURE 6.3 Measures of lung volume. (From McArdle, Katch, & Katch, *Exercise Physiology: Energy, Nutrition and Human Performance.* Lea & Febiger, 1991. Reprinted by permission of Waverly.)

residual volume (RV). Residual volume tends to increase with age. Thus, inspiration and expiration reserves become smaller with age. The sum of the residual lung volume and vital capacity is called the **total lung capacity (TLC).**

When lung volumes are adjusted for the size of the individual, no differences are detected for trained and untrained individuals. Even the capacities of trained marathoners and distance runners does not differ from the untrained (e.g., Mahler et al, 1982). Thus it appears that the normal capacity for ventilation does not limit exercise. However, decreased volume and/or capacity may indicate chronic obstructive pulmonary disease like emphysema, chronic bronchitis, or asthma.

Resting Blood Pressure. Remember that the pressures created by blood being pumped out of the heart are transmitted to varying degrees throughout the vascular system. These pressures are referred to as **blood pressure.** The pressure is highest in the arterial system and can be estimated by the use of a **sphygmomanometer,** or blood pressure cuff. Systolic blood pressure is measured during systole and diastolic blood pressure is measured during diastole. Normal blood pressure in an adult male is 120/80 (systolic/diastolic) and 110/70 in adult females. Blood pressure is the product of cardiac output and peripheral resistance. Therefore blood pressure is elevated by increased cardiac output and/or increased peripheral resistance. **Hypertension** is a disease characterized by abnormally elevated blood pressure. Individuals with chronic (prolonged) hypertension have an increased probability of stroke and coronary artery disease. In some cases hypertension can be effectively treated with a combination of exercise and diet. However, some individuals require medications that dilate the blood vessels, reduce cardiac output, and/or reduce the volume of blood and thus decrease blood pressure.

Resting Electrocardiogram.   Electrodes placed on the surface of the chest can be used to monitor the time course of the action potential as it is transmitted across the heart muscle. An **electrocardiogram (ECG)** is a recording of the electrical activity of the heart as sensed by these electrodes. The ECG is an integral component of exercise testing because of its use in diagnosing various heart problems, especially those associated with cardiac rhythm, electrical conduction, oxygen supply to the heart muscle, and actual heart muscle damage. The preexercise resting ECG is typically taken while lying down, sitting, and standing. This is done to assure that the electrodes are responding correctly and to detect any abnormalities that may preclude continuing the exercise test.

The ECG can be recorded from three electrodes. However, generally a 12-lead ECG is used for diagnostic purposes because of its increased sensitivity to changes in the heart during exercise. In essence, a 12-lead ECG takes an "electrical picture" of the heart from a number of different angles, while a 3-lead ECG provides a single perspective. A typical ECG is provided in Figure 6.4. The **P-wave** represents the depolarization and subsequent contraction of the atria. The **QRS-complex** is caused by the depolarization and subsequent contraction of the ventricles. The **T-wave** represents the repolarization of the ventricles.

Exercise Testing Protocols

Exercise tests are usually performed in a laboratory or hospital setting. The test is typically conducted on a bicycle ergometer or treadmill. In both cases the test involves a number of progressively more difficult stages of exercise. For this reason this type of exercise test is referred to as a "graded" exercise stress test. In the case of the bicycle ergometer, the stages involve increasing the resistance on the pedals and/or increasing the rate of pedaling. When a treadmill is used, exercise is graded by increasing the treadmill speed and inclination.

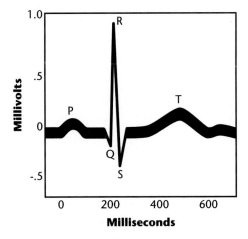

FIGURE 6.4 A normal electrocardiogram during rest.

    In most graded exercise protocols, exercise stages are usually maintained for a period of 3 to 5 minutes. **Maximum aerobic capacity (VO₂ max)** is recorded when oxygen uptake plateaus and does not increase with further increases in workload, heart rate increases to age-predicted maximum (220 – age), or volitional exhaustion. Subjects who reach their maximum aerobic capacity cannot continue to work at that intensity for more than a minute or two because their demand for oxygen exceeds their ability to supply oxygen. Many low-fit individuals will be unable to achieve or will not be permitted to achieve VO₂ max. **Functional aerobic capacity** is used to estimate VO₂ max when the test is terminated early. For diagnostic purposes it is recommended that the individual achieve at least 85 percent of age-predicted maximal heart rate because some ECG abnormalities do not appear until the cardiovascular system is stressed to this point (Pollock, Wilmore, & Fox, 1978).

Bruce Protocol.   The **Bruce protocol** (1971) is considered a continuous exercise test because the workload increases steadily during the test with no rest between stages. This treadmill protocol is used with a wide variety of subjects/patients ranging from normal risk to high risk. With normal risk subjects, the Bruce protocol starts at 1.7 mph and 10 percent inclination. The inclination increases by 2 percent and the speed by .8 mph each 3 minutes. For high risk individuals the starting inclination can be decreased to 0–5 percent but the increase each 3 minutes is the same (2 percent and .8 mph).

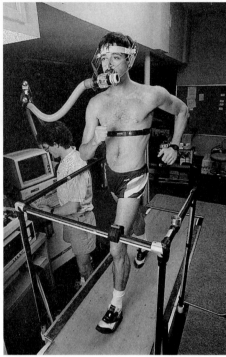

PICTURE 6.2   *Bicycle ergometers (above) and treadmills (right) are convenient devices to control work load during a graded exercise test.* (Photo credits: Will Hart)

Naughton Protocol.   The **Naughton protocol** (1972) is a discontinuous exercise test because after the first 15 minutes of relatively slow walking, the 3-minute stages alternate between rest and walking at increasing treadmill speed and inclination. This treadmill protocol is used with cardiac and high-risk patients. Note that the intensity of the exercise in the Naughton protocol is substantially less than Bruce protocol at comparable stages.

Monitoring During and After an Exercise Test

During a typical graded exercise test, heart rate, ECG, and blood pressure are monitored to detect abnormalities and signs of excessive stress. In addition, subjective rating of perceived exertion is recorded.

Blood Pressure.   Blood pressure is typically taken every 2 to 3 minutes during the test and recovery period. A normal blood pressure response to exercise is for the systolic blood pressure to increase as exercise intensity increases. Typically, systolic blood pressure increases from 110–120 mmHg at rest to 180–200 mmHg at peak exercise. Diastolic blood pressure normally does not increase much (10mmHg) in healthy individuals. Abnormalities in blood pressure response during exercise may provide hints of cardiovascular heart disease.

Heart Rate and Electrocardiogram.   Heart rate is typically taken from the ECG record but can be taken from palpitation (feeling the pulse in the wrist or neck). As treadmill speed and inclination increase, heart rate must also increase to meet the increased demands for oxygen. If heart rate increases too rapidly early in exercise or does not increase with increases in exercise intensity, heart problems may be implicated. Age-adjusted maximal heart rate (220 – age) is also used as marker for terminating the exercise test. In the absence of other warning signs, the test is typically terminated at between 85 percent and 100 percent age-adjusted maximum heart rate.

The ECG is monitored continuously during a diagnostic exercise stress test. Changes in the normal pattern of the heart's electrical pattern are often an indication of a lack of oxygen to the heart muscle. In many cases, abnormalities in the ECG are not noted until an individual is sufficiently stressed by exercise. It is important that a trained technician or cardiologist monitor the ECG record because important warning signs often appear in very subtle forms.

One of the most common ECG abnormalities is called an ST segment depression (see Figure 6.5), which occurs when the slope between the S and T segments is more gradual than in a normal ECG. This abnormality may suggest at least a 70 percent reduction in the blood flow of the coronary artery.

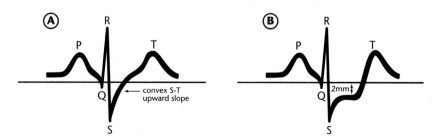

FIGURE 6.5   A normal ECG tracing (left) and an abnormal tracing (right) indicating a S-T segment depression.

Robb and Marks (1964) predicted that a 1–2 mm ST segment depression was associated with a 4.6-fold increase in mortality from cardiovascular heart disease and a 2 mm depression with a 19.1-fold increase. Remember, however, that these probabilities represent only an association between the ST segment depression and coronary artery occlusion. In other words, this type of ECG abnormality does not mean there is coronary artery disease but rather that more detailed tests should be conducted under the supervision of a cardiologist in a hospital setting.

Dialogue and Ratings of Perceived Exertion.   After each minute of the exercise test the subject is asked to rate on a numerical scale their perceived exertion. The original **ratings of perceived exertion (RPE)** scale was developed by Swedish psychologist Gunnar Borg (1982). Subjects rate their effort according to how they feel. Physiological measures of fatigue are relatively objective, whereas the RPE scale (Figure 6.6) is a subjective rating taking into account the psychological and emotional state of the individual being tested (see Chapter 9). The scale ranges from very, very light to very, very strong (or hard). This dialogue informs the technician and/or physician of the subject's perception of his or her exertion. In general, subjects' ratings of perceived exertion coincide well with objective measures of exercise stress.

Category RPE Scale		Category-Ratio RPE Scale	
6		0	Nothing at all
7	Very, very light	0.5	Very, very weak
8		1	Very weak
9	Very light	2	Weak
10		3	Moderate
11	Fairly light	4	Somewhat strong
12		5	Strong
13	Somewhat hard	6	
14		7	Very strong
15	Hard	8	
16		9	
17	Very hard	10	Very, very strong
18		•	Maximal
19	Very, very hard		
20			

FIGURE 6.6 Original RPE scale (left) and revised scale (right). (From McArdle, Katch, & Katch, *Exercise Physiology: Energy, Nutrition and Human Performance.* Lea & Febiger, 1991. Reprinted by permission of Waverly.)

Regularly asking the subject for ratings of perceived exertion also opens the door to dialogue between the exercise technician/physician and the subject. Of particular interest are reports of pain in the heart area, left shoulder, and/or the neck. **Angina pectoris** is a temporary but often intense pain in the area of the heart that may indicate that the oxygen supply to the heart has reached a critically low level. Typically, angina subsides after a few minutes of rest.

Because the RPE scale tends to correlate with heart rate, it is being used more often in exercise classes to complement heart rate measures. For example, an individual attempting to attain a training intensity of 170 bpm in an exercise class would like to achieve an RPE score of 17—very hard. When the individual reports an RPE score of 17, heart rate should be at about 170 bpm. In fact, fitness instructors use RPE scales almost exclusively for participants who use medications that affect heart rate.

Postexercise Consultation

After an exercise stress test, it is important for the exercise specialist or physician to review the results with the individual. This consultation should occur soon after the exercise stress test but because a considerable amount of data has to be reviewed, the consultation may occur a few days after the administration of the test. During the consultation the test results should be reviewed in nontechnical terms, additional tests may be advised, changes in exercise and health behavior will be discussed (diet, stress, workout habits, and so on), medication or surgical options will be discussed if called for, and/or an individualized safe exercise program will be established. This is also an opportunity for the individual to ask questions and express concerns.

TRAINING FOR HEALTH AND FITNESS

There are two complementary reasons for exercise training. One is to improve health through exercise. Clearly exercise can play a powerful role in reducing the incidence of disease and can contribute to both longevity and quality of life. The other reason is to improve one's capacity to achieve an extrinsic goal. Body builders, power lifters, football players, track athletes, and many average persons wish to achieve higher levels of fitness for reasons not directly related to health. For these reasons it is important to differentiate between the training goals as they relate to health and fitness and extrinsic exercise goals related to improving exercise capacity.

Basic Concepts of Training

Safe, effective training programs all incorporate a few basic principles. Although the principles of training are translated slightly differently for strength, aerobic, and anaerobic training, the general principles of training remain relatively constant across training programs.

Frequency, Duration, and Intensity.   All exercise programs should be carefully planned to ensure the acquisition of the exercise objectives. In planning an exercise program, frequency, duration, and intensity of exercise should be considered. **Exercise frequency** refers to the number of sessions performed in a given time period (e.g., a week). **Exercise duration** is the total time devoted to an exercise at a single session. In strength training duration is a product of the number of sets and number of repetitions per set. **Exercise intensity** relates to the physiological stress placed on the body during exercise. A careful balance of these factors can contribute to the desired training effect without increasing the likelihood of acute or chronic injury. It should be obvious that the condition of the participant, the exercise objectives, and the activity engaged in will be considered in the determination of frequency, duration, and intensity. Clearly these factors would be balanced differently for a senior citizen interested in improving health and fitness and a competitive college athlete interested in competing in distance running events. In the following sections some useful principles will be discussed in relation to specific exercise goals.

Overload and Specificity Principles.   A physiological system responds with what is called a training effect when the system is stressed. The **overload principle** refers to the finding that training effects only occur when a physiological system is exercised at an unaccustomed level. A system that experiences overload, within some limits, responds with gradual adaptations that increase the capacity of the system. In most cases, moderate overloads that are gradually increased as the system adapts produce the best results. Overload may be adjusted by manipulating exercise frequency, duration, and/or intensity. One of the keys to positive adaptations from exercise overload is that exercise should progressively induce moderate to high but not excessive stress. Excessive stress may result in the physiological system having to expend a great deal of energy repairing injured tissue.

Alternatively, a system that is continually understressed (underloaded) will gradually lose the capacities that it once possessed. The finding that gains in capacity from overload are quickly lost when the overload is

PICTURE 6.3   *To increase strength experts recommend 3 sets with a resistance that requires a maximal effort to complete between 3 and 9 repetitions every other day.* (Photo credits: Tony Neste)

removed is often called the principle of reversibility or detraining effect. It is interesting to note that, in general, the time course of detraining adaptations are more rapid than the positive adaptation from training.

No one would expect that strength training exercises involving the arms would increase leg strength or that running long distances would improve sprint speed. The **specificity principle** states that physiological adaptations are specific to the components of a system that are overloaded during exercise. Thus, an arm exercise like the biceps curl, including many repetitions and relatively low weight, stresses the endurance capacity of the arm, which in turn elicits specific adaptations that increase the endurance capacities of the involved limb. Although there may be some generic adaptations that may increase the capacity of other muscle groups or the same muscle group in different ways (e.g., strength), the correlated adaptations occur only to the extent that the system is overloaded. The primary adaptations are in response to the specific stress. The specificity principle also seems to apply to exercise modalities. For example, aerobic stress induced by bicycling, swimming, or running seems to result in adaptions that are most effectively demonstrated in the same activity that was used during training. This is not to say that the development of cardiovascular fitness through swimming will not increase your ability to endure an exercise bout involving running. However, the benefit of a swimming program to running performance is dependent on the extent to which the systems involved in running are stressed by swimming. It is easy to see that a swimming program that involves relatively long duration and moderately high-intensity exercise will result in adaptations to the cardiovascular system but not necessarily to the strength or endurance capacity of the leg muscles. Thus, swimmers that are given a fitness test on the treadmill (running) often complain of their legs "giving out" before they feel really tired.

Muscle Strength, Power, and Endurance

Weight training programs have become very popular in recent years. This increased popularity has been the result of a number of factors. ACSM guidelines now recommend that everyone should do resistance training two times a week. Research and practical experience has indicated that properly constructed weight training programs do not reduce mobility, flexibility, or speed. For a number of years coaches in a variety of sports did not include weight training in their conditioning program, especially during the season, because they believed that performance would suffer. Today many coaches utilize weight training as an integral part of their total in-season and out-of-season conditioning package. For many years women were told that weight training was not a proper activity for them. Anyone who visits a fitness facility today can see that this myth is no longer with us. This is verified in a later discussion on gender issues that appears in Chapter 9. Another myth is that weight training is relatively dangerous. While this might have been the case for free weights, today's weight machines are extremely safe when used properly and offer some advantages over free weights. Even free weights are safe when used correctly with a partner.

Weight training equipment can be divided into three categories. Category I includes free weights, barbells, and some machines that simply limit the movement of the weights (Universal). This equipment keeps the weight constant but does not regulate the resistance. With a constant weight the resistance placed on the muscle changes as the joint angle and the orientation with respect to gravity is changed. Category II includes equipment where speed of movement is controlled and resistance is variable (Cybex) or speed of movement is constant and the individual controls the resistance (Othotron). Category III involves machines where speed is variable and resistance is variable (Nautilus). These later two categories are probably the safest for use with general populations.

Muscle Strength.   The most common method of strength training involves **progressive resistance exercise.** This method represents the practical application of the overload principle. As the exercised muscle group becomes stronger the resistance is increased correspondingly. A great deal of research has been done to determine the optimal frequency, duration (repe-

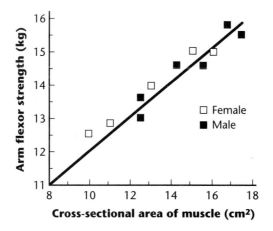

FIGURE 6.7 Arm strength as a function of cross-sectional area. (From Wilmore, J. Figure from J. Wilmore et al., Alterations in strength, body composition and anthrometric measurements consequent to a 10-week weight training program. *Medicine and Science in Sports, 6,* 133–139, 1974. The American College of Sports Medicine.)

titions multiplied by sets), and intensity for strength training. That is, should three sets of 10 repetitions using a given resistance be used? Should the resistance be changed between sets (increased or decreased)? Should fewer or more than 10 repetitions be used? Should fewer or more than 3 sets be used? While there is no consensus among researchers concerning the most effective workout for increasing strength, many experts recommend that you complete 3 sets with a resistance that ensures a maximal effort to complete between 3 and 9 repetitions.

Strength training programs stimulate a complex set of adaptations that result in an increase in the cross-sectional area of the muscle (Figures 6.7 and

FIGURE 6.8 Strength changes as a result of a 10-week training program. (From M. Ikai & T. Fukunaya, Calculation of muscle strength per unit of cross sectional area of a human muscle by means of ultrasonic measurement. *Internationale Zeitschrift fuer Angewante Physiologie, 26,* 26–31, 1988. Copyright © Springer-Verlag, Heidelberg, Germany.)

6.8). In fact, the cross-sectional area of a muscle seems to one of the most reliable ways to predict the contractile capacity of the muscle. (It might be useful to review the structure of the muscle provided in Chapter 3.) This is probably a result of **hypertrophy,** an increase in the size of the muscle fibers due to an increase in the number and size of the myofibrils. An alternative view is termed **hyperplasia.** This notion suggests that progressive resistance exercise promotes an increase in the number of muscle fibers. Training also appears to result in a better utilization and synchronization of the motor units by the central nervous system.

Power.   Many sports require not only high force production but that the forces are generated very rapidly. **Power** is the ability to generate force very rapidly and is calculated as the product of force and velocity. Consider that two individuals move a given amount of weight through a range of motion as quickly as possible. If the first individual completed the lift in 1 second and the other individual completed the lift in 2 seconds, the first would have exerted much more power. Sports like the shotput, discus, high jump, long jump, sprinting, and even blocking in football, place a premium not only on strength but also on power.

In order to increase power, an individual needs to increase strength and/or speed of contraction. In general, strength may be more trainable than speed of contraction. Although training may minimally enhance speed of contraction, this factor may be dependent on what type of fiber the muscle is composed of. A muscle largely composed of fast twitch fibers will exhibit faster speeds of contraction than a muscle predominately composed of slow twitch fibers. In general, however, training programs designed to increase power should consider the specificity principle. Thus training for power should include fewer repetitions with greater resistance performed as fast as possible.

Muscle Endurance.   Some individuals engage in a training program with the objective of increasing the number of repetitions they can execute. **Muscular endurance,** defined as the ability to sustain a resistance for a period of time, implies that a given level of muscular work can be continued for a relatively long period of time. Muscular endurance is, however, closely related to muscular strength with correlations between muscular strength and endurance between .75 and .97. Thus increases in strength tend to result in increases in muscular endurance. Just as power is enhanced by a large percentage of fast twitch fibers, muscular endurance is enhanced by a large percentage of slow twitch fibers. However, prudent application of the specificity principle is the key to obtaining increases in muscular endurance. Hence, training for muscular endurance should include more repetitions with less resistance.

Aerobic and Anaerobic Training

Aerobic and anaerobic training increase different performance capacities. In keeping with the specificity principle, activities that demand high levels of aerobic activity for extended periods of time increase the capacity to perform this type of work. Likewise activities that require high intensity activity for short periods of time result in an increased capacity for anaerobic metabolism.

Aerobic Activities.   Aerobic training improves a variety of capacities related to the transport and utilization of oxygen. Research indicates that regular aerobic activity results in an increased capacity to generate ATP aerobically, increased capacity to mobilize and utilize the energy stored as fat, and a greater capability to store and utilize carbohydrates. In addition, regular aerobic activity results in increases in cardiovascular function and increases in blood volume, stroke volume, cardiac output, oxygen extraction, and total blood flow to the working muscles.

Designing an aerobic training program, just as designing a strength training program, must take into account the principles of overload and specificity, as well as exercise intensity, duration, and frequency. These factors must be considered in terms of an individual's initial fitness level, preferred activities, and purpose for training. For example, a sedentary adult wishing to reduce his or her risk of cardiovascular disease can benefit from low-intensity exercise twice a week for as little as 20 minutes. Does this sound familiar? It should, because the study by Blair et al. (1989) discussed earlier revealed similar findings. On the other, hand, an active adult wishing to participate in road races may require aerobic exercise as much 4 or 5 times a week for 40 minutes or more at a moderate to high intensity to produce fitness gains and/or weight loss.

One general rule of aerobic training for the average person is to train at between 70 and 90 percent of one's age-predicted maximum heart rate (see Figure 6.9). Remember **age-predicted maximum heart rate** can be determined by subtracting your age from 220. When an individual maintains heart rate between 70 and 90 percent of age-predicted maximum heart rate, he or she is in what is called the **training-sensitive zone.** Heart rates in this zone assure people that they are exercising at an intensity sufficient to overload the aerobic system and therefore invoke a training effect. The lower

 **HIGHLIGHT**

Walk Don't Run

Often referred to as the "father" of aerobics since writing the 1968 bestseller *Aerobics,* Kenneth Cooper is responsible for getting scores of Americans to start pounding the pavement in the name of better health. With *Aerobics* and several other books touting the benefits of exercise for total well-being, Cooper outlined the many benefits of regular exercise "essential to good health and an effective life." At that time, Cooper believed that more exercise meant better health. Recently, Dr. Cooper and others have begun to question if more is really better.

The untimely death of Cooper's 52-year-old friend Jim Fixx caused many to question the benefits of running. Jim Fixx, the author of *The Complete Book of Running,* was an avid 60-mile-a-week runner. He died of a heart attack while running in 1984. Most authorities wrote off his death to genetic factors. Upon learning of other highly trained athletes succumbing to various deadly disorders, Cooper began to look for a connection. Why were elite athletes dying?

Cooper starting collecting evidence that indicated that very vigorous exercise can in some cases be fatal. The type of people documented are typically highly trained and among the best at what they do. The Institute for Aerobics Research released interesting data from a long-term study in 1989. That study showed that death rates dropped off with increased exercise except in one category: the elite athlete. Death rates actually increased slightly for the exceptionally active.

Cooper believes that very high intensity exercise can break down the body's immune system and develop "free radicals," which are highly reactive compounds caused by stress such as cigarette smoke, car exhaust, or excessive exercise. Cutting back on exercise and taking antioxidants are two of his current recommendations to increase the body's immunity. Antioxidants are vitamins C, E,

HIGHLIGHT 6.2   *Dr. Kenneth Cooper at his world famous Aerobic Institute and Clinic in North Dallas.* (Photo credit: The Cooper Aerobics Center).

and beta-carotene, which combat the effects of free radicals in the body.

So what are we to do? Health professionals have long debated the optimal amount of exercise. For many people, Cooper now advocates walking rather than jogging. Or jogging rather than running. Or decreasing the amount of intensity in any exercise program. Cooper runs or walks an average of 15 miles a week. To be sure, the jury is still out on the optimal amount of exercise necessary for a high quality of life. It is prudent to be aware that more than exercise or lack of it contributes to good health. Total well-being means applying healthy lifestyle habits such as not smoking, managing stress, and eating a smart diet, as well as exercising regularly.

From Helen Thompson, Walk don't run, Texas Monthly *(June 1995).*

and upper limits should be used only as a guideline for healthy, active individuals. Sedentary individuals just beginning an exercise program should probably attempt to maintain about 50 to 60 percent of their age-predicted heart rate. Of course, individuals with cardiovascular disease or significant risk factors should consult a physician before engaging in an aerobic training program. The 90 percent range should be considered the upper limit for aerobic training even for highly fit individuals because at this point oxygen demands start to exceed oxygen supply.

Note that increased aerobic fitness results in lower resting and exercise heart rates. Therefore, a more fit individual will have to exercise at a higher absolute intensity to achieve his or her training heart rate than a lower-fit person. Note also that research has indicated that some activities like swimming do not generally result in as large a heart rate response as walking, running, or cycling. In fact, some experts have suggested that about 10 beats per minute need to be added to your heart rate during swimming to achieve a comparable heart rate response.

In order to develop moderate to high levels of aerobic fitness a great deal of time must be devoted to training, because aerobic training is by definition at a lower intensity and of long duration. Thus it is especially important for individuals involved in aerobic training to engage in activities that they enjoy. The most popular forms of aerobic activity are walking, running, cycling, swimming, and aerobic dance. Although each of these activities can

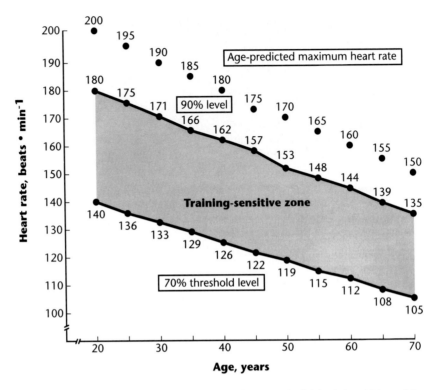

FIGURE 6.9   For an effective, vigorous workout, an individual should keep his or her heart rate in the training-sensitive zone.

be used effectively as a exercise modality, many individuals find that engaging in a combination of activities, called **cross training,** helps to prevent boredom and decreases the likelihood of overuse injuries. Cross training involves alternating between two or more aerobic activities such as running and swimming.

Anaerobic Activities.   Anaerobic training improves a number of capacities important to brief, high-intensity exercise. Anaerobic training has become popular as a component of sports fitness programs because many sport activities like football, wrestling, basketball, soccer, and sprinting require large anaerobic capacities. Anaerobic training, in general, is believed to be much less effective in reducing risk of cardiovascular heart disease than lower-intensity aerobic activity. Anaerobic training does result in increased

PICTURE 6.4   *Experts agree that regular participation in aerobic dance classes can result in increased aerobic fitness and increased longevity.* (Photo credit: Tony Neste)

ability to do anaerobic work, in hypertrophy, and in increased tolerance for lactic acid.

Can you think of a training procedure that we have already considered that might fit the definition of anaerobic training? Strength training is generally considered to fall into this category. In most cases weight training sets last 60 seconds or less and another set is completed after a short rest. This type of high-intensity activity spaced between relatively short rest periods is characteristic of anaerobic training. Many sports include short dashes or other short duration all-out activities to maximize ATP production via the ATP-CP pathway (see the section on immediate energy systems in Chapter 5).

EXERCISE AND NUTRITION

It has long been realized that optimal nutrition will enhance athletic performance. Unfortunately, over the years athletes, coaches, and the average sedentary person have continually changed their opinions concerning optimal nutrition practices. Milo of Croton, a seven-time Olympic champion in 532 B.C. was said to have consumed 20 pounds of bread, 20 pounds of meat, and 18 pints of wine each day. In the 1970s high-protein, low-carbohydrate diets were popular with many dieters who ended up gravely ill. Some people actually died on this type of a diet due to heart failure. To this day some athletic coaches still encourage a steak dinner as a pregame meal. Another popular regimen with some coaches was to restrict water intake during practices. Thankfully, most coaches now practice sound and reasonable eating and drinking regimens for their athletes.

Participants in the athletic world are not the only people subject to radical ideas in nutrition. We are a society hungering for a shortcut to health and prosperity, as evidenced by the multibillion-dollar fitness industry. A large proportion of that industry deals with miracle diets and wonder pills to "melt away" or "burn off" unwanted fat. As consumers, we are susceptible to misleading advertising. Even within the fitness industry many professionals listen to their heart instead of their head in the hopes that a particular food or supplement may really have some magical fat-burning powers.

A proper diet is well-balanced and includes a variety of foods. **Nutrients** are components of food needed by the body. There are six classes of nutrients: protein, carbohydrates, fats, vitamins, minerals, and water.

Energy Nutrients

Proteins, carbohydrates, and fats are the only sources of food energy. Called the **energy nutrients,** they come from the foods we eat and provide the fuel for our bodies to function.

Carbohydrate.   **Carbohydrate,** one of the basic foodstuffs, is defined as any of a group of chemical compounds, including sugars, starches, and cellulose, containing carbon, hydrogen, and oxygen only. One gram of carbohydrate provides 4 calories. There are simple and complex carbohydrates. The simple sugars are glucose, fructose, and galactose, also called monosaccharides. The double sugars are maltose, lactose, and sucrose, also called disaccharides. Glycogen and starch are the complex sugars or polysaccharides. Starch is the storage form of sugar in plants. Glycogen is the storage form of glucose in humans.

Carbohydrate is the most readily available source of food energy. When eaten, carbohydrate is broken down to glucose through digestion and metabolism. Glucose is then stored in the human body in the form of glycogen in the liver and the muscles. Glycogen is depleted during intensive muscular activity. Since glycogen is the preferred fuel during aerobic exercise, a diet rich in carbohydrates is optimal for aerobic performance.

Most people do not eat enough carbohydrates. At least 60 percent of daily caloric intake should be in the form of carbohydrates, especially complex carbohydrates, which provide both nutrients and dietary fiber. Good sources of complex carbohydrates are whole-grain breads, rice, pasta, potatoes, vegetables, and fresh fruit. Although sugar and sweets are composed of carbohydrates, they should be kept to a minimum in the diet. Simple carbohydrates that are refined and processed are often added to foods that have relatively little nutrient value such as cookies, candies, and pies; these foods are said to contain "empty" calories.

Fat.   **Fat** is the most concentrated form of food energy. One gram of fat provides 9 calories while protein and carbohydrate each provide 4 calories per gram. Dietary fat is essential for the functioning of each cell in the body. Fat, also known as lipids, protects and cushions internal organs. Body fat also acts as insulation against extremes in temperature, both hot and cold. Fat supplies energy for the muscles and is necessary for the transport of the fat-soluble vitamins A, D, E, and K. Dietary fat is the only source of the essential fatty acid called lineoleic acid, which plays a role in growth and skin maintenance. It is found only in polyunsaturated fats such as vegetable oil.

When fats are metabolized in the body, they must first be broken down from triglycerides. Triglycerides consist of one glycerol backbone and three molecules of free fatty acids (FFA). Depending on the chemical structure of the FFA, it is considered saturated or unsaturated. Saturation means the carbon atoms are full with hydrogen atoms. Unsaturated fats have a carbon double bond, which decreases the number of hydrogen bonding links available.

Saturated fats include most of the animal fats such as the fat in meats, dairy products, and eggs. Vegetable sources include palm oil and coconut oil and their derivatives. Saturated fats are more solid at room temperature; unsaturated fats are more liquid at room temperature. Examples of unsaturated fats are vegetable oils like corn oil, peanut oil, cottonseed oil, and soybean oil. Unsaturated fats include both monounsaturated and polyunsaturated fats. There is evidence that monounsaturated oils such as olive oil and canola oil can enhance HDL cholesterol. It is generally accepted that dietary fat should be kept to 24 to 30 percent of daily caloric intake. The American Heart Association recommends that 10 percent or less of your total fat intake should be saturated. Saturated fats have been shown to raise blood cholesterol, while monounsaturates seem to have no effect at all. A high-fat diet is associated with greatly increased risk of cardiovascular disease as well as colon and breast cancer.

Protein.   **Protein** is a compound composed of complex chains of amino acids, which are the major structural components of all body tissue. Every

Synthetic Protein—Great News for Obese Mice

One of the great quests in the twentieth century has been to find a quick and easy method of losing weight. Scientists, health/fitness experts, and con artists have attempted to find the quick fix for being overweight. Have you ever taken grapefruit pills or gorged on bran muffins? The fact is, more and more of the population is becoming over-weight. We find it difficult to eat appropriate foods and exercise regularly. As a result we give in to fast foods and little exercise. Couch potatoes, there is now hope!

Ever since the discovery of a mutant strain of mice that is prone to extreme weight gain, scientists have been looking for ways to reduce the weight of the mice. The hope is that if they can discover what causes the mice to gain weight, they will be one step closer to understanding weight gain in humans. This strain of mice generally weighs twice as much as control mice even though their diet and exercise is carefully controlled.

In the summer of 1995, scientists discovered a synthesized version of a natural protein that caused obese mice to lose up to 40 percent of their body weight in one month without going on a diet or experiencing side effects. The "Ob protein" injected into the mice is very similar to a protein found in humans. Douglas Coleman, who identified the strain of mice in 1950, states "the gene that encodes the protein in the mouse is 92% the same as in humans." The hope is that this is the first miracle drug that will facilitate an individual's efforts to control weight. Hopes are so high that Amgen Corp has paid $20 million for the rights to develop products based on the Ob protein. In the not too distance future, weight control may be as close as an injection away.

From Jerry Adler and Amy Salzhauer, Escaping the diet trap, Newsweek (August 7, 1995).

HIGHLIGHT 6.3   *Mutant mouse before (left) and after (right) one month treatment with Ob hormone.* (Photo credit: John Sholtis, The Rockefeller University, New York, NY © 1995 Amgen, Inc.)

cell in our body contains protein, which is necessary for tissue growth and repair. Proteins are components of hormones, enzymes, cellular structures, and blood transport systems.

Most Americans eat more protein than is necessary. Approximately 12–15 percent of daily calories should be in the form of protein. Most high-protein foods are associated with fat, especially saturated fats in animal products, so high-protein consumption often correlates with high fat intake. Choose lean cuts of meats and lower-fat versions of dairy products to reduce fat intake.

Competitive athletes and weightlifters often take extra protein in the hopes of enhancing performance and increasing muscle mass. The truth is that excess protein cannot be stored in the body. What is not used is converted to fat and glucose. High-protein diets put a tremendous strain on the liver and kidneys and can cause dehydration due to the increased production of urea. Urea is excreted in the urine to rid the body of the extra nitrogen from eating too much protein.

It is interesting to note that the average person will benefit most from the same diet recommendations that an elite athlete will benefit from, that is, a high-complex-carbohydrate, low-fat regimen on a daily basis. To meet daily protein requirements, the average individual can follow this formula: 0.9 to 1.0 g of protein per kg of body weight. Pregnant or nursing women need up to two to three times as much as normal.

Vitamins, Minerals, and Water

Vitamins, minerals, and water are the remaining three nutrients. Each is critical for the proper functioning of the body. All the essential nutrients can be obtained from a balanced diet.

Vitamins.   **Vitamins** are organic substances that the body needs in small amounts but cannot manufacture itself. Vitamins play a role in proper functioning of nerves and muscles, in releasing energy from foods, and in promoting normal growth of body tissues. Vitamins provide no calories and cannot be used as a fuel; however, they play an important role as metabolic regulators. All vitamins must be obtained from the foods that we eat.

Vitamins are categorized as either fat-soluble or water-soluble. Fat-soluble vitamins are A, D, E, and K. These vitamins are stored in the liver as well in the body's fat cells. Taking megadoses of vitamins can be dangerous because any extra fat-soluble vitamins that the body doesn't need may build up to toxic levels within the body.

Water-soluble vitamins are the B-complex and C vitamins. Since these vitamins cannot be stored they must be replaced on a daily basis from the foods that are eaten. Whatever the body does not use is excreted in the urine. There are many well-meaning vitamin "poppers" with very expensive urine! The vitamin industry may be guilty of misleading many consumers hoping to have better health through a bottle. The bottom line is that a well-balanced diet will normally provide all the vitamins necessary for good health.

Minerals.   **Minerals** are inorganic substances that perform a wide range of vital functions throughout the body. There are two forms of essential minerals: macrominerals, which are needed in relatively large amounts (greater than 100 mg per day), and microminerals or trace minerals, which are needed in very small amounts (less than 100 mg per day). Calcium, by far the most abundant mineral in the body, plays a role in the functioning of the muscles and also joins with phosphorus to form the bones and teeth. Phosphorus also functions to release energy from carbohydrates. Iron is a key component in hemoglobin. Iodine, magnesium, sodium, chloride, zinc, selenium, and copper are also important to the normal functioning of the body.

Water.   Water is the most vital nutrient, second in importance only to oxygen for survival. Our body is made up of approximately 60 to 75 percent water. Water is critical to the functioning of every cell within the human body. Water provides the means to transport nutrients and oxygen to cells and removes waste products. It also plays a major role in regulating the body's temperature. Perspiration is actually a way to cool the body. Dehydration—excessive loss of body fluids—is an extremely dangerous and potentially life-threatening condition. Endurance athletes must be especially careful to stay hydrated during training and competition. Water is needed before, during, and after competition. Water has no calories and therefore is often overlooked as a basic nutrient requirement. The average person should drink at least eight 8-ounce glasses every day. An athlete will require even more water to replace lost fluids during training. A good rule is to drink water *before* you are thirsty.

Fueling for Exercise

Coaches and athletes have often put much emphasis on the 24-hour period preceding competition. Sometimes pregame rituals and eating habits are more comforting and psychologically sound than physiologically based. The fact is that an athlete with a poor overall diet that is nutritionally deficient will benefit little from a pregame meal. Wise coaches today are concerned with the athlete's diet during the season as well as during the off-season.

Studies have shown that the pregame meal is ineffective in enhancing an athlete's performance. The one exception is the practice of **carbohydrate loading.** To increase glycogen storage in the muscle, and therefore enhance endurance, many long-distance athletes like marathoners or triathletes will go through a succession of exhaustive workouts to deplete the muscle stores of glycogen. The athlete then eats a carbohydrate-free diet for three days, followed by three days of a carbohydrate-rich diet. This process actually "supersaturates" the muscle glycogen stores. The normal range of glycogen storage is 0.95 to 2.0 g per 100 g of muscle. After carbohydrate loading the glycogen storage has been found to be 3.70 g per 100 g of muscle. Similar results can be seen when the carbohydrate-free portion of the carbohydrate loading regime is omitted. Carbohydrate loading is probably not necessary or even beneficial to an athlete competing in an event that takes less than 60 minutes to complete and less than 70 percent VO_2max. This is because muscle glycogen depletion does not occur with lower intensity or shorter bouts of exercise. Carbohydrate loading is not recommended on a regular basis because the process may be stressful on the kidneys.

During prolonged exercise, fluid replacement is imperative for optimal performance and also to avoid dehydration. It is popular to have glucose drinks like Gatorade at community races such as 10-kilometer or marathon runs. Is drinking a glucose drink a good way to ward off fatigue? Most drinks on the market have a concentration of glucose too high to allow quick gastric emptying. Taking in more than a 2.5 percent glucose solution will actually cause the sugar to "lie in the stomach" and possibly cause cramps. Unless the athlete is doing a long or ultra-endurance event, cool water is the replacement fluid of choice. Water loss can be over 2 liters per hour with a total loss of 6 to 7 percent of body weight with heavy exercise, so fluid replacement is very important.

The thirst mechanism does not naturally stimulate a person to drink enough to hydrate completely. To avoid heat stress and dehydration, an athlete exercising in hot and humid conditions should drink a quart of water prior to an event and also in 15-minute increments throughout the activity. After the activity, carbohydrate-rich drinks and a normal diet may be ingested to replete muscle glycogen.

The recommendations for the athlete's diet are not far from what is optimal for the average person. It is recommended that both the athlete and the average person eat a diet high in complex carbohydrates and low in saturated fats and limit foods high in refined sugar and sodium. In fact, some evidence suggests that 3–6 small meals may fuel the body better than 1–2 meals, as is common with today's hectic schedules. Eating more frequent meals is thought to have a beneficial effect on metabolism. Eat a variety of foods with the four basic food groups represented, and everything in moderation.

Fuel for Low-Intensity Exercise.   Energy for low intensity exercise below 50 percent VO$_2$max comes primarily from fat. Both fat and carbohydrate contribute to the energy needs of the muscle at 50 to 70 percent VO$_2$max. As the intensity of the exercise increases, so does the carbohydrate utilization. At intensities above 85 percent VO$_2$max, carbohydrates are the primary source of energy. Stored glycogen is readily depleted at high intensities. Studies are inconclusive as to whether there are other factors that limit exercise capacity. The roles of liver glycogen and blood glucose are being investigated. It has been shown that an untrained person will deplete muscle glycogen stores much faster than a trained person. A "fit" person is more adept at utilizing fat as a fuel source than an untrained person. This concept is known as glycogen sparing.

Fuel for High-Intensity Exercise.   During short bursts of energy such as sprinting, glycogen is depleted, but it is selectively depleted from the fast twitch fibers. The ATP and PC stores in the muscle are the primary energy sources. During an anaerobic event such as the sprint very few slow twitch fibers are recruited.

Nutrition, Body Composition, and Weight Control

The human body is composed of lean body mass and fat mass. **Lean body mass** is comprised of muscle, bone, and organs. Excess body fat is associated with increased risk of cardiovascular heart disease and some forms of cancer. Increased lean body mass is associated with increased resting metabolism and increased performance capacity.

Body Fat.   Some fat is necessary in the body. The fat within the nerves, brain, liver, and bone marrow is called **essential fat.** When fat levels drop below the essential level some physiological functions are altered. Essential fat for males is 3 percent of total body weight. Essential fat for females is 11 to 13 percent because of additional fat in the female reproductive organs. When a female's body fat drops below that amount, she usually becomes

amenorrheic, or ceases to have menstrual periods. It is not unusual for young female gymnasts, distance runners, and dancers to be amenorrheic. In a young athlete with low body fat, onset of menstruation is often delayed. Studies have shown that long periods of low estrogen as a result of amenorrhea decrease the risk of breast cancer and increase the risk of osteoporosis. It is believed that between one-third and one-half of all female athletes have some form of menstrual irregularity.

Fat is stored as adipose tissue and serves to protect the internal organs, to insulate the body, and to provide a potent fuel source. Fat stored under the skin and outside the muscle is called subcutaneous fat. Fat stored within the muscles is called interstitial fat. Males in the general population should strive for about 15 percent body fat and females about 25 percent. Athletes and other extremely active individuals may exhibit significantly lower body fat percentages. In many cases, these levels may be much lower than those recommended and in extreme cases can be considered dangerous.

Determining Percent Body Fat.   The only exact method of determining body composition is by extracting the fat deposits from a human cadaver. However, there are many indirect methods of estimating body composition. Three of the most popular methods will be briefly discussed: hydrostatic weighing, skinfold methods, and bioelectical impedance analysis.

Hydrostatic weighing is considered the gold standard for determining body composition. Before being weighed, the subject's residual volume is determined. The subject is then weighed under water to determine **body density,** which is the ratio of body mass to body volume. Hydrostatic weighing is based on the Archimedes principle of water displacement. That is, a body submerged in water will float if its weight is less than the weight of the water that it displaces. Essentially, fat is less dense than water and lean body mass is more dense than water. Thus fat floats and lean body mass sinks. Note that if two people weigh the same on land and have the same body volume but one has a higher percentage of body fat than the other, the leaner individual will weigh more under water than the individual with greater fat. This is the one time you want to weigh more, not less!

Even with hydrostatic weighing there may be an error in the equations used to determine percentage of body fat. This appears to be true for heavily muscled athletes and individuals with particularly dense bone structure. Furthermore, individuals who are not comfortable being submerged in water may not fully expire air. This is a critical problem for this method. For these reasons, it is important to consider hydrostatic weighing as well as the other methods of determining body fat merely as "estimates" of percent body fat.

PICTURE 6.5   *The hydrostatic method of determining body fat requires a person to be weighed underwater. In the picture the man is attempting to expire as much air as possible prior to the measurement of his underwater weight.* (Photo credit: © Nathan Benn/Stock Boston)

Other methods of determining body fat are useful because hydrostatic techniques require special equipment. One popular field method is called the **skinfold** method because it utilizes a special pair of calipers to determine the thickness of folds of skin at various sites on the body surface. The sites used to take skinfold measurements may be weighted differently in the calculations used for males and females, because men tend to store fat in the stomach, whereas females tend to store fat in the upper legs, upper arms, and buttocks. The skinfold measurements are entered into equations in order to estimate body density and percentage of body fat. When performed by a skilled technician, skinfold estimates of body fat are typically within 3 to 5 percent of the estimates derived from hydrostatic weighing.

Another popular method of determining percentage of body fat is **bioelectric impedance.** This method is based on the concept that an electrical current will be conducted better by hydrated fat-free tissue (lean body mass) than by fat. Muscle tissue contains almost three times as much water as fat. Two distinct disadvantages of the bioelectric impedance method must be considered. First, the level of hydration or dehydration of the body as well as the skin or ambient temperature affect the body fat prediction with this method. Second, the method is probably not as accurate as either the hydrostatic weighing or skinfold methods.

Weight Control and Body Composition.   Body composition can be altered with regulation of diet and regular exercise. Consistent aerobic activity and resistance training are both critical to a change in body composition. If the exercise component is left out, significant losses in lean body mass can occur. In fact, it is actually possible to increase your percentage of body fat while losing overall body weight. Studies have shown that dieters who lose weight have a greater chance of keeping the weight off if exercise is part of their maintenance program.

Dieting seems to have become a national pastime for many Americans. There always seems to be a new diet book on the best-sellers list. It seems that for many of us, "buying" a shortcut to weight loss is more palatable than restricting dietary intake and increasing exercise. Millions of people support the multibillion-dollar diet industry. The bottom line is that to maintain your present weight, caloric intake must equal caloric expenditure. Weight loss or gain is the result of an unbalanced caloric budget. A realistic goal would be to lose one pound a week. Someone who uses 500 more KCAL per day than is consumed would see a weight loss of one pound after 7 days, since it takes 3,500 KCAL to lose one pound. Increasing exercise while restricting caloric intake would add to the total caloric deficit and increase weight loss. By combining exercising with dieting, the weight loss tends to be more permanent and will also help maintain lean body mass.

Set-Point Theory.   **Set-point theory** is a concept introduced by researchers who realized that each individual may react differently to the same conditions. Fit individuals seem to utilize fat as a fuel source more efficiently than sedentary, less fit individuals. Genetics, body type, body size, gender, and dietary habits all may affect how an individual reacts to energy imbalances. Many middle-aged individuals who have lost and gained 10–20 pounds several times throughout their lives have probably increased their percentage of body fat and reduced their metabolism. It is thought that every individual has an internal hypothalamic thermostat regulating weight. The body is comfortable at this point and may even defend that particular weight even when dietary changes begin to invoke weight change. Most of us hover around the same weight. This would explain why dieters initially lose weight easily and then reach a frustrating plateau. It is theorized that when an individual overeats on a particular day, the body gives off more heat to expend the extra energy. On a day when the caloric intake is less than usual, the body may attempt to conserve energy. The body's set point is difficult to change. Frequent aerobic activity, resistance exercise, and meals high in complex carbohydrates and low in fat are all thought to help.

Anorexia Nervosa.   An alarming statistic indicates that more than one million teenagers are affected by the eating disorder called **anorexia nervosa.** The precise cause is still undetermined but the possibilities are complex. Societal pressures to live up to the unrealistic "thin is beautiful" model are often blamed. Other possibilities involve depression, impulsive behavior, and the inability to cope. Anorexia nervosa is a serious medical condition that requires intervention to prevent permanent damage or death. Diagnosis and treatment are often difficult because the anorexic is obsessed with self-control and full of denial about the condition. Although anorexia nervosa is most often seen in teenage females, the number of young men with anorexia is increasing. Treatment requires cooperation between physicians, nurses, psychologists, and dietitians. Residential treatment centers are especially successful.

Bulimia.   **Bulimia,** which was not even recognized or named until 1980, shares some of the same characteristics as anorexia nervosa and is much more common. Bulimics are usually of normal weight, think constantly of food, and alternate between starving themselves and binging. After eating too much food the bulimic "purges" the food by forced vomiting. Estimates suggest that between 5 and 20 percent of young women are affected by bulimia. Repeated binging and subsequent purging presents serious health hazards, including abnormal heart rhythms and kidney failure as well as irritation and infection of the pharynx, esophogus, and salivary glands. Bulimia is often considered a "closet" disease because this problem affects seemingly healthy individuals. It is interesting to note that both anorexia nervosa and bulimia are known only in developed nations and are typically more common among the wealthy. Sadly, both eating disorders affect all ages but more and more preteenagers are becoming afflicted.

FINAL COMMENT

The previous chapter provided a broad overview of exercise physiology, focusing in part on how the cardiovascular system works during rest and exercise. In this chapter our focus shifted to the type of exercise programs used to try to optimize the functioning of the systems discussed in the previous chapter. It appears clear that a well-planned exercise program can increase longevity and improve an individual's quality of life. A particularly note-worthy finding is that just experiencing moderate exercise a few times a week can significantly decrease your risk of cardiovascular disease. Moderate exercise does not have to entail running around the local track; it can be achieved by regularly walking up the stairs rather than always taking the elevator.

It is imperative that a graded exercise test is administered to individuals classified as "at risk" and "with disease." This type of test is significantly less important for "apparently healthy" individuals. However, for all individuals a graded exercise test can provide the basis for a carefully planned and safe exercise prescription. Exercise programs should consider the initial condi-tion of the individual and his or her exercise preferences. Regardless of the type of exercise program, exercise frequency, duration, and intensity should be carefully balanced to progressively overload the system being trained. This overload should be sufficient to induce a training effect but not so large as to stress the system severely. Exercise programs should also consider the specificity principle. That is, an exercise program will produce training ef-fects only in those systems that are sufficiently stressed.

Regular exercise has a very important companion—a good diet. The diet provides the human performer with the necessary nutrients that both fuel the human motors called muscles and provides the essential elements that maintain the human skeletal, nervous, and muscular systems. These nutri-ents include carbohydrate, fat, protein, vitamins, minerals, and water. Car-bohydrates, fat, and protein are the foodstuffs that power the muscles. Proteins and vitamins are crucial for the upkeep of both nerves and muscles. Finally, minerals such as calcium are crucial to the maintenance of bone as well as being involved in the contractile process (see Chapter 3).

QUESTIONS FOR THOUGHT

- Discuss the sequence involved in conducting a graded exercise test. At what points might a physician's presence be required or the test be terminated? What are the purposes of conducting a graded exercise test?
- Explain the overload principle and the specificity principle.
- Identify the classifications of nutrients that should be present in a "good" diet. In Chapter 3 we discussed the scaffolding, communication system, and motors of the human architecture. Which nutrients are important for each component of this ar-chitecture? Why?

- Explain how exercise and nutrition interact to determine body composition. Discuss the various methods of determining percentage of body fat.
- In order to reduce the risk of cardiovascular disease, does an individual have to engage in an intensive exercise plan? Explain.

KEY TERMS

acute injury
age-predicted maximum heart rate
amenorrheic
angina pectoris
anorexia nervosa
apparently healthy
atherosclerosis
bioelectric impedence
blood pressure
body density
Bruce protocol
bulimia
carbohydrate
carbohydrate loading
chronic injury
cross training
electrocardiogram (ECG)
energy nutrients
essential fat
exercise duration
exercise frequency
exercise intensity
expiratory reserve volume (ERV)
fat
fitness
forced vital capacity
functional aerobic capacity
graded exercise testing
health
health history
high-density lipoprotein (HDL)
higher risk
hydrostatic weighing
hyperplasia
hypertension

hypertrophy
informed consent
inspiratory reserve volume (IRV)
lean body mass
lipoprotein
low-density lipoprotein (LDL)
maximum aerobic capacity (VO_2max)
minerals
moderate exercise
muscular endurance
Naughton protocol
nutrients
overload principle
power
progressive resistance exercise
protein
P-wave
QRS-complex
ratings of perceived exertion (RPE)
residual volume (RV)
set-point theory
skinfold
specificity principle
sphygmomanometer
spirometer
tidal volume (TV)
total cholesterol
total lung capacity (TLC)
training-sensitive zone
T-wave
vigorous exercise
vitamins
wellness
with disease

RESOURCES

Textbooks

American College of Sports Medicine. (1991). *Guidelines for Exercise Testing and Prescription* (4th ed.). Philadelphia: Lea & Febiger.

Bowers, R. W., & Fox, E. L. (1992). *Sports Physiology*. Dubuque, IA: W. C. Brown.

Heyward, V. H. (1991). *Advanced Fitness Assessment and Exercise Prescription*. Champaign, IL: Human Kinetics.

Lamb, D. R. (1984). *Physiology of Exercise: Responses and Adaptations*. New York: Macmillan.

McArdle, W. D., Katch, F. I., & Katch, V. I. (1991). *Exercise Physiology: Energy, Nutrition, and Human Performance*. Philadelphia: Lea & Febiger.

Pollock, J. H., & Wilmore, J. H. (1990). *Exercise in Health and Disease: Evaluation and Prescription for Prevention and Rehabilitation*. Philadelphia: W. B. Saunders.

Powers, S. K., & Howley, E. T. (1990). *Exercise Physiology: Theory and Application to Fitness and Performance*. Dubuque, IA: W. C. Brown.

Journals

Journal of Applied Physiology
Medicine and Science in Sports and Exercise
Nutrition

Professional Organizations

American Alliance for Health, Physical Education, Recreation, and Dance
American College of Sports Medicine

Internet

World Wide Web
http://www.dgsys.com/~trnutr/index.html

Listservers
Fitness and Wellness
send: subscribe fit-L <your name>
to: Listserv@etsuadmn.etsu.edu

Fitness
send: subscribe fitness <your name>
to: listserv@indycms.iupui.edu

Physiology
send: subscribe physl-tr <your name>
to: listserv@cc.itu.edu.tr

Newsgroups
news:sci.med.nutrition
news:misc.fitness.misc

REFERENCES

American College of Sports Medicine. (1991). *Guidelines for Exercise Testing and Prescription* (4th ed.). Philadelphia: Lea & Febiger.

Blair, S., Kohl, H. W. III, Paffenbarger, R. S. Jr., Clark, D. G., Cooper, K. H., & Gibbons, L. W. (1989). Physical fitness and all-cause mortality: A prospective study of healthy men and women. *Journal of the American Medical Association, 262,* 2395.

Borg, G. A. V. (1982). Psychological bases of perceived exertion. *Medicine and Science in Sports and Exercise, 14,* 377–381.

Kannel, W. B., & Gordon, T. (1974). *The Framingham Study: An Epidemiological Investigation of Cardiovascular Disease.* DHEW No. (NIH) 74-599. Washington, DC: Public Health Service.

Mahler, D. A., Moritz, E. D., & Loke, J. (1982). Ventilitory responses at rest and during exercise in marathon runners. *Journal of Applied Physiology, 52,* 388.

McArdle, W. D., Katch, F. I., & Katch, V. I. (1991). *Exercise Physiology: Energy, Nutrition, and Human Performance.* Philadelphia: Lea & Febiger.

Paffenbarger, R. S. Jr., Hyde, R. T., Wing, A. L., & Hsieh, C. C. (1986). Physical activity, all-cause mortality, and longevity of college alumni. *New England Journal of Medicine, 314,* 605.

Pollock, M. L., Wilmore, J. H., & Fox, S. M. (1978). *Health and Fitness through Physical Activity.* New York: John Wiley.

Powell, K. E., Thompson, P. D., Caspersen, C. J., & Kendrick, J. S. (1987). Physical activity and incidence of coronary heart disease. *Annual Review of Public Health, 8,* 253.

Powers, S. K., & Howley, E. T. (1990). *Exercise Physiology: Theory and Application to Fitness and Performance.* Dubuque, IA: W. C. Brown.

Robb, G. P., & Marks, H. H. (1964). Latest coronary artery disease determination, its presence and severity, by the electrocardiogram. *American Journal of Cardiology, 13,* 603.

CHAPTER 7

Motor Development

CHAPTER OBJECTIVES

- To differentiate between traditional and contemporary developmental perspectives
- To introduce some of the current issues that are capturing the attention of motor developmentalists
- To examine the changes in motor development across the lifespan
- To examine the factors that mediate motor development

INTRODUCTION

As adults we take for granted how easy it is to move around the environment. We can hop on a bicycle and perform what, to a child, seems to be an amazing balancing act. However, it doesn't take a young child long to begin producing a variety of movements. At first the movement is rather crude, but soon even children master walking, grasping, and throwing, to name but a few movements. Have you ever wondered how the child develops so quickly?

On the other end of the continuum, many individuals must face the regression that occurs as they "pass their prime" and get older. What factors contribute to this process? Why do some people age better than others in terms of their motor capabilities? These questions as well as those related to the development of the child's motor capacity are of great interest to the researchers and teachers of motor development.

PICTURE 7.1   *The development of a child's motor skills is one area of interest to the motor developmentalist. But not the only one!*

Motor development is defined as the study of changes in human movement behavior across the lifespan and the influence of these changes on motor performance. The field of motor development is often thought of as involving the study of children. Though this is certainly true, motor development involves much more than merely studying the changes in children's motor behavior. More contemporary approaches involve what is called a "lifespan perspective," which examines the progression and regression in behavior by focusing not only on children but also on adolescence and adulthood. This position recognizes that development continues beyond the time when physical growth begins to slow down. Interestingly, this area has received very little attention from motor developmentalists and is ripe for some extensive study. However, before we examine behavioral changes throughout the lifespan, the theoretical perspectives that dictate the way in which this examination occurs need to be addressed.

Theoretical Perspectives

Most chapters in this book contain theoretical frameworks from which to generate research. Motor development is no different in this respect. In fact, the area of human development has enjoyed the luxury of a diverse set of theoretical perspectives from which to pose research questions. In the following sections we will examine the positions that impact the research being conducted today.

Maturational Theory. **Maturational theory** played an important role in the thinking of researchers working in the area of child development. This position basically contends that a child reaches particular developmental landmarks dictated by their genetic make-up. This perspective does not include a primary role for environmental factors in the development process. Gesell (1928) was one of this theory's biggest advocates. The maturational theory is the cornerstone of many of the general development charts that are available today (see Figure 7.1). For example, the idea of human locomotion progressing from an infant initially being able to roll over to eventually being able to walk is consistent with this theoretical position. It is generally assumed that this fundamental activity cannot be significantly accelerated by special training. This theory has important implications for the use of specially designed programs of motor activities for children that are common in many school settings. More specifically, it suggests that these programs would provide no benefits and thus could be eliminated.

Biological and Social Development Theory. In contrast to the position held by Gesell, Robert Havighurst (1952) considered development to occur due to the interaction of biological, social, and cultural factors. This position intimates that for proper development to occur, the child should master certain tasks within a specified time frame. Havighurst suggested that there are certain time periods when the body is optimally ready to experience certain activities. This proposal views play and physical activity as critical during infancy and early childhood.

Intellectual Development Theory. Perhaps the individual who exerted the greatest influence on the evolution of child development theory was Jean Piaget (1963). His position on the underlying mechanisms of development is still tantamount to much of the thinking that occurs today regarding modern developmental psychology. In essence, Piaget considers development to be a function of a problem-solving process used by the learner when interacting with the environment. Piaget places great emphasis on the individual's capability to seek the necessary experiences to solve a problem, as opposed to being a passive recipient of information.

As the name of this position indicates, Piaget was particularly interested in obtaining an understanding of intellectual development. A major contribution of Piaget's work was the introduction of the stages of intellectual development. They are classified as the sensorimotor period (0–2 years), preoperational period (2–7 years), concrete operations (7–11 years), and formal operations (over 11 years). In which stage do you think Piaget considers movement experience to play its largest role? Of course, during the

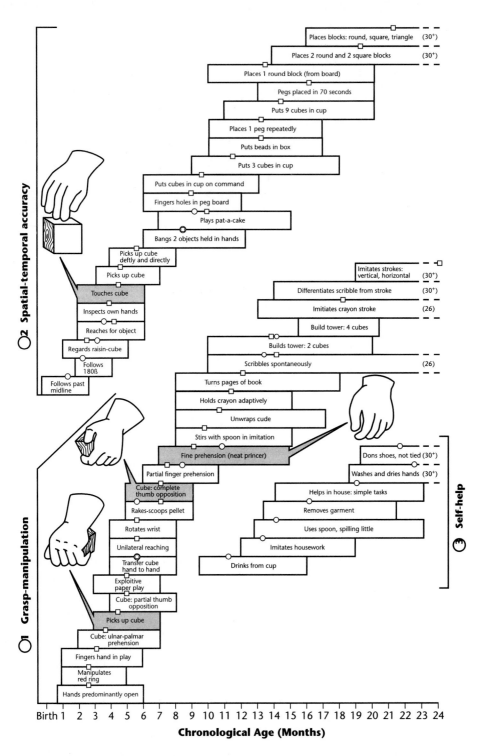

FIGURE 7.1 Progression of changes in manual control. Systematic changes such as those indicated in this chart are consistent with maturational theory. (From Keogh & Sugden, *Movement Skill Development*. Copyright © 1985 by Allyn & Bacon. Reprinted by permission.)

sensorimotor period. However, Piaget also felt movement activities were important during the preoperational period. This is a time when the individual is unable to use logical operations to transform information but can think in terms of images and symbols.

Information Processing Perspective. The **information processing perspective** was an outgrowth of the "cognitive revolution" in psychology that occurred as a direct opposition to researchers who refused to try to describe the mental events undertaken in the "black box" or the mind of an individual. While this perspective emanates from psychology it is now a prevalent position adopted by many motor behaviorists in the field of motor development, motor learning, and motor control (see Chapter 8). The information processing framework advocates the need to examine the influence of cognitive processes such as sensation, perception, attention, decision making, problem solving, and motor programming.

Attempting to understand the working of the mind by adopting the information processing approach has often been likened to the mind working as a computer (Schmidt, 1988). In fact, central to this position is the assumption that the human operator collects (i.e., senses), transforms (i.e., perceives), selects (i.e., makes decisions), and executes (i.e., programs motor responses) information much like a computer does. Obviously, from a motor development standpoint, the focus is on obtaining an understanding of how an individual gradually masters the capability to perform this higher order mental activity and implement its consequences via the motor system.

Dynamical Systems Perspective. The **dynamical systems perspective** is less inclined to attribute the developmental changes that occur to higher-order mental processing activity that is central to the information processing approach. This position proposes that the qualitative changes in motor behavior emerge from a complex interaction between the current status of the body systems, the nature of the environment, and the demands of the task (Newell, 1986).

The dynamical systems approach places special importance on the interplay between the many systems that make up the human mover. We consider many of these systems throughout this text. For example, we discussed the skeletal, nervous, and muscular systems in Chapter 3. In Chapter 5 we considered the impact that the cardiorespiratory system has on physical activity. Subsequently, we will discuss the role of the sensory and perceptual systems on behavior in Chapters 8 and 9 when we discuss motor learning and sport psychology. Each of these systems must cooperate to afford the individual the opportunity to move. However, it is essential to note that these systems do not develop at the same rate. Hence each system can potentially limit the type of activity that can occur at any particular point of development.

Biological Synchronization

Did you know that if a large number of fireflies are placed in a closed area they will soon begin to flash in synchrony? Although each insect starts with a rhythm of its own, the sight of the other lights flashing causes it to bring its rhythm into harmony with the other insects. This coupling of independent oscillators is at the heart of a large number of natural phenomenon. Indeed, the dynamical systems perspective of motor learning and control is based in part on the notion of coupled oscillators.

For example, the movement of our arms is thought to be coupled such that we experience little difficulty in moving both arms at the same time as long as

there is some degree of synchronization between the limbs. Let's consider a few very simple synchronization tasks with the first finger of each hand. We find it easy to tap our fingers in-phase or anti-phase. In-phase tapping is when the fingers hit the tabletop at the same time. We can easily increase or decrease the rate of tapping provided we do so with each hand. Anti-phase tapping is also easy. This is when we tap alternately with one hand then the other. Again, we can easily increase or decrease the rate of tapping. But try tapping in-phase or anti-phase with a different rhythm for each hand. This is tough unless you split one of the rhythms in parts. For example, you can tap with

HIGHLIGHT 7.1   *Two pendulum clocks placed near each other will become synchronized by forces or vibrations transmitted through the wall.*

your left finger, then twice with your right, left finger again, twice with your right, and so on. This type of tapping is still synchronized but the right finger is cycling twice as fast as the left.

Try patting your head and rubbing your stomach. This is a good bit more difficult because we must break the synchronization between the limbs to accomplish the task. The desynchronization is what is difficult. Try. I bet that if you are able to pat your head and rub your stomach at

the same time, you do so in a synchronized way. Observe carefully someone who can do this task. What do you notice? In some way they have synchronized the two movements. I'll bet that each time their hand hits their head their other hand is at the same point while rubbing their stomach.

From Steven Strogatz and Ian Steward, Coupled oscillators and biological synchronization, Scientific American *(December 1993).*

Perception-Action Perspective.   The fundamental premise underlying the perception-action perspective is that perceptual processes cannot be completely assessed without considering movement and vice versa. For example, moving around in one's environment provides a much richer perceptual array. Likewise, obtaining richer perceptual information enlightens the actor on the diverse movement opportunities available. This theoretical position is strongly supported by the work of J. J. Gibson (1966). The concept of affordance is critical to the perception-action position. An **affordance** describes to an individual the available functions (including actions) of particular objects within the current perceptual circumstances. For example, a chair affords the adult a place to sit. However, to the infant, this same object might merely afford an object to grasp. As the child grows, diverse behaviors emerge since the chair now affords a new action given the change in the status of the infant's body size.

Current Issues

What are the current developmental issues that researchers, adopting some of the theoretical positions discussed in the last section, are currently investigating? Haywood (1993) highlights four issues that are particularly interesting to the present day motor developmentalist. First, the issue of whether the emergence of a new activity is a function of **nature** or **nurture** has long interested the developmental scientist. If you have seen the film *Trad-*

ing Places starring Eddie Murphy and Dan Ackroyd you are probably familiar with this issue. In essence, this problem stresses the unique roles an individual's genetic make-up and learning experiences might play in acquiring new movement behaviors. What do you think the maturational theorist would conclude? Would this be the same as a researcher who supports a dynamic systems position?

A second theme currently capturing the attention of individuals studying motor development focuses on the search for sensitive or critical periods in the development process. A **sensitive period** is a time span during which an individual is most susceptible to the influence of a particular event or factor (Haywood, 1993). A **critical period** is a time span in which a particular movement behavior would have to be acquired if it was to achieve optimal performance. Should such time periods be identified, the implications for motor development would be enormous. More specifically, the identification of either a sensitive or a critical period would require that each individual is exposed to particular movement activities within very specific time frames in order to maximize human motor performance.

A third theme identified by Haywood (1993) is that of **continuity** versus **discontinuity** of motor development. While movement development progresses (continuous), it is quite amazing to watch the variety of movements that emerge and apparently disappear (discontinuous) as development moves forward. Some motor development researchers use the different skills and stagelike quality of development to examine this progression. However, one must be careful not to assume that all individuals will follow exactly the same sequence or reach the same motor milestones in exactly the same time frames.

The final theme that continues to confront the motor developmentalist is the **universality** versus **variability** issue. It is not uncommon for a layperson to assume intuitively that all individuals develop in a similar manner (universality). This is consistent with a stage-type approach discussed in the previous section. More specifically it is not uncommon for the layperson to assume that if a child is 12 months old he or she will be able to walk. However, it is becoming increasingly apparent that there is a great deal of individual difference (variability) in both the way and in the time frame that a child ultimately achieves a particular motor behavior. This can even be the case for twins. While a great deal of attention has focused on identifying generality in the developmental process (i.e., time frame to reach motor milestones), some of the recent work has shifted to examining developmental variability with the hope that this will shed some light on the developmental process (Thelen, 1989).

 **HIGHLIGHT**

Johnny and Jimmy

McGraw (1975) was interested in determining how important early training is for a child's motor development. She decided to attack this question by working with twins, Johnny and Jimmy, from the time they were 20 days old. Her idea was that Johnny and Jimmy would have very similar genetic make-up. Thus, any differences in their motor capacity would be a function of the different experiences to which she would expose them during the course of the experiment. The twins would spent eight hours a day in the laboratory for five days each week.

Johnny was selected as the "experimental" child. This meant that he would be exposed to the types of training that was the focus of McGraw's experiment. Jimmy was the "control" subject. In the early stages, while Jimmy was left in his crib, McGraw would try to stimulate Johnny's reflexes. However, periodic testing of these reflexes indicated that both Johnny and Jimmy were performing in a similar way. It appears that special training of reflexive responses does little to improve this type of action. In fact, this trend in the data appeared true for many

movements the children performed in the first year.

However, the role of specialized training early in a child's life seems to have an important influence on the acquisition of more complex, coordination-type skills such as jumping, swimming, and skating. Johnny seemed to show more interest in these activities and was less fearful when performing these activities. In contrast, Jimmy did not show the same motivation or enjoyment toward these activities. These differences continued to exist between Johnny and Jimmy through age 6 and 10 years.

What can be concluded from this now classic work? It appears that behaviors controlled by lower brain centers (i.e., not the cerebral cortex; see Chapter 3 for discussion) are unaffected by early training. In contrast, coordinated actions that are acquired later in life can benefit from early intervention similar to that experienced by Johnny.

McGraw, M. B. (1975). Growth: A Study of Johnny and Jimmy. *New York: Arno Press. Originally published in 1935.*

Methods of Study

It would seem appropriate at this time to consider some of the common methodological approaches used in the motor development arena to examine some of the issues highlighted in the previous section. We will focus on three major methods—longitudinal, cross-sectional, and sequential—reviewing the advantages and disadvantages of each.

Longitudinal Method.   The **longitudinal method** is probably the most reliable since inherent in motor development research is the study of changes in motor behavior over time. The obvious strength of this method is that specific individuals can be selected as the focus of a study and followed over a set period of time. The time course of a study may vary from weeks to years. When the longitudinal method is used, development can be directly observed and recorded and not just inferred.

Even with methods that "seem" foolproof there are always drawbacks. The major problem with the longitudinal design is the potential for attrition. More specifically, as the years pass, many of the subjects participating in these studies find reasons to drop out of the experiment. Moving out of town, children becoming ill or disabled, or just becoming bored with being a participant are all common reasons for the high dropout rate characteristic of this design. A second concern when using this design is ensuring that "learning" or "practice" effects are not prevalent. This can occur when the same test is administered at each meeting and the children being tested become familiar with the requirements of the test. A final issue that needs to be attended to is the individual who administers the tests. If changes in the experimenter occur this can impact the reliability of the measures being taken (see Chapter 2 for discussion on validity and reliability).

Cross-Sectional Method.   The **cross-sectional method** probably accounts for the majority of studies conducted in the area of motor development. Using this method the experimenter collects data on different groups of individuals at the same time but the subjects differ in age. The researcher thus obtains a "quick fix" on the developmental changes while only needing a very short period of time to conduct the experiment. In general, this method provides an overview of the typical behavior of the age groups used in the study. The major disadvantage of the cross-sectional design is that the different age groups might differ in their motor behavior for a variety of reasons (e.g., educational, social, physical activity) other than the development factor of interest (i.e., age).

Sequential Method.   The **sequential method** is really a protocol that incorporates the best of both the longitudinal and cross-sectional methods. This procedure involves studying several different samples (i.e., cross-sectional) over a number of years (i.e., longitudinal). This design allows subjects differing in age or educational background, for example, to be compared at the same time in order to identify any current behavioral differences.

A LIFESPAN EXAMINATION OF MOTOR DEVELOPMENT

Before examining the developmental process from a lifespan perspective it is important to consider how components of the lifespan are categorized. This is not as easy as one might think; there is considerable disagreement among motor developmentalists on how to label the components of the lifespan. Gabbard (1996) identifies five "stages" of the lifespan: the prenatal stage, infancy stage, childhood stage, adolescent stage, and the adulthood stage. These stages correspond to approximate age ranges. For instance, the childhood stage includes both early and late stages and extends from approximately 2 years to 12 years of age (see Figure 7.2). Furthermore, Gabbard identifies particular phases of movement that might be expected to emerge during each of the lifespan stages. The adolescent stage, for example, involves movement growth and refinement.

In contrast, Haywood (1993) points out that the term "stage" has been used rather inconsistently in the literature and has often been taken to imply a very stereotypic development process. Haywood refers to the prenatal stage, **infancy, childhood, adolescence,** and **adulthood** as developmental periods that can also be associated with *approximate* age ranges. For example, Haywood describes the childhood period as extending from approximately 1 year to 10 years old. Whether one prefers "stages" or "periods" is unimportant at this point. However, it is essential to appreciate that development through the categories of the lifespan (i.e., infancy, childhood, adolescence, and adulthood) should not be restricted to particular ages. In the following sections we will explore the movement development issues that surface during each of these categories.

Infancy

Newborns are capable of producing a number of basic movements, many of which are automatic or reflexive. A **reflex** is an involuntary movement response elicited by a variety of sensory stimuli including a sound, light, or touch. Some of the early reflexes exhibited by the child are termed **primitive reflexes** (see Table 7.1). This type of reflex is associated with ensuring that the child can obtain nourishment and secure protection.

The earliest primitive reflex elicited by the fetus is the sucking reflex. This has been demonstrated as early as the fetal age of four months. Three different reflexes appear around seven fetal months: the moro, palmar grasp, and tonic neck reflex. The moro reflex consists of a sudden extension and

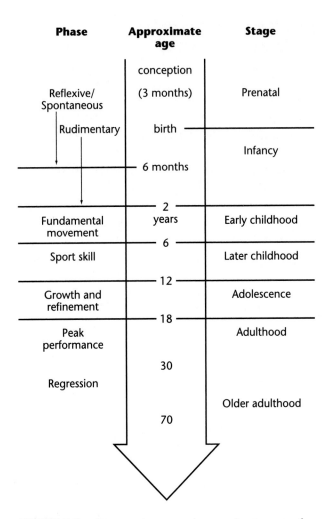

Phase	Approximate age	Stage
Reflexive/ Spontaneous	conception (3 months)	Prenatal
Rudimentary	birth	Infancy
	6 months	
Fundamental movement	2 years	Early childhood
Sport skill	6	Later childhood
Growth and refinement	12	Adolescence
Peak performance	18	Adulthood
Regression	30	
	70	Older adulthood

FIGURE 7.2 Stages, phases, and approximate ages of motor development as proposed by Gabbard (1996). (From Gabbard, Carl P., *Lifelong Motor Development,* 2d ed. Copyright © 1996 Times Mirror Higher Education Group, Inc., Dubuque, IA. All Rights Reserved.)

bowing of the arms and spreading of the fingers. The legs execute a similar action only less noticeable. This reflex usually lasts through the first three months after birth. Placing a rod or stick against the palm of a newborn will cause the child's fingers (not the thumb) to close around the object. This is known as the palmar grasp reflex. If you have ever had a young child grip your finger you know that this grip is very strong. The strength of the grip

TABLE 7.1   The primitive reflexes.

Reflex/ reaction	Starting position (if important)	Stimulus	Response	Time	Warning signs
Primitive Reflexes					
Asymmetrical tonic neck reflex	Supine	Turn head to one side	Same-side arm and leg extend	Prenatal to 4 mo	Persistence after 6 mo
Symmetrical tonic neck reflex	Supported sitting	Extend head and neck Flex head and neck	Arms extend, legs flex Arms flex, legs extend	6 mo to 7 mo	
Doll-eye		Flex head Extend head	Eyes look up Eyes look down	Prenatal to 2 wk	Persistence after first days of life
Palmar grasping		Touch palm with finger or object	Hand closes tightly around object	Prenatal to 4 mo	Persistence after 1 yr; asymmetrical reflex
Moro	Supine	Shake head, as by tapping pillow	Arms and legs extend, fingers spread; then arms and legs flex	Prenatal to 3 mo	Presence after 6 mo; asymmetrical reflex
Sucking		Touch face above or below lips	Sucking motion begins	B to 3 mo	
Babinski		Stroke sole of foot from heel to toes	Toes extend	B to 4 mo	Persistence after 6 mo
Searching or rooting		Touch cheek with smooth object	Head turns to side stimulated	B to 1 yr	Absence of reflex; persistence after 1 yr
Palmar-mandibular (Babkin)		Apply pressure to both palms	Mouth opens; eyes close; head flexes	1 to 3 mo	
Plantar grasping		Stroke ball of foot	Toes contract around object stroking foot	B to 12 mo	
Startle	Supine	Tap abdomen or startle infant	Arms and legs flex	7 to 12 mo	

(Reprinted by permission from K. M. Haywood, 1993, *Lifespan and Motor Development,* 2d ed., Champaign, IL: Human Kinetics Publishers, pp. 93–94)

begins to diminish after the first month and is gradually replaced by voluntary movements that are the beginning of manual control.

Finally, the tonic neck reflex is a little more complex than the other reflexes because it has a number of variations. This reflex is related to stretching the neck muscles and joints. The asymmetrical tonic neck reflex has a characteristic extension of the arm and leg on the side to which the head turns. Moreover, the arm and leg on the side opposite the head turn will flex. This results in a position similar to the "on guard" position adopted by the fencer.

A few more primitive reflexes surface just after birth, including the rooting, babkin, and babinski reflexes. Other primitive reflexes that appear at a later stage are the planter grasp and startle reflexes. The latter is somewhat similar to the moro reflex. However, in the case of the startle reflex, the infant initially flexes arms and legs rather than extending them, as is the case with the moro reflex.

The **postural reflexes** help the infant maintain an upright position with respect to the environment (Twitchell, 1965). Many of these reflexes persist through the infant's first year. This class of reflexes includes head and body righting reflex, labyrinthine reflex, and parachute reflex.

The **locomotor reflexes** resemble the voluntary locomotor movements that subsequently appear. These responses are associated with crawling, stepping, and swimming movements. Most of us are familiar with the stepping reflex, which can be elicited by holding the infant upright and allowing the feet to touch the floor. Pressure on the surface of the infant's foot will cause it to produce a movement that is characteristic of the stepping motion used for locomotion.

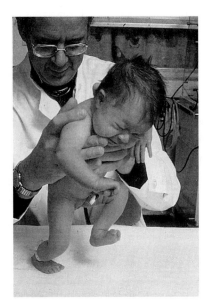

PICTURE 7.2   *Testing for the occurrence of the stepping reflex has offered the opportunity to investigate the reason for the appearance and disappearance of reflexes.* (Photo credit: © Taeke Henstra/Petit Format/Photo Researchers)

A great of deal of debate has surrounded the appearance and disappearance of reflexes. Maturational theorists believe that reflexes come and go depending on the structure of the nervous system. As the nervous system matures the reflexes are systematically eliminated as voluntary control takes over (Pontius, 1973; Wyke, 1975). However, some researchers suggest that there is a natural progression of the reflexes into an integrated and organized system that controls movement (Zelazo, 1983). From this perspective reflexes do not actually "disappear" but are merely modified and reorganized. Furthermore, the work of Zelazo and colleagues intimates that stimulating the stepping reflex early may encourage voluntary walking at an earlier age.

Esther Thelen (1983), a strong proponent of the dynamical systems approach, has provided an alternative proposal regarding the disappearance of reflexes and in particular the stepping reflex. She demonstrated that adding weights to the ankles of 4–6-week-old infants reduced the display of this reflex. From this, Thelen concluded that the stepping reflex may surface or disappear based on the child's leg strength. Early on, the child has sufficient strength to lift the mass of the leg, thus, the reflex exists (unless additional weight is added!). As the child develops, leg mass reaches a point at which there is insufficient strength to lift it, at which point the reflex seems to "disappear." At this point in development it is assumed that the leg strength of the child is a "rate controller." Essentially, the rate controller is the system that is dictating the array of behaviors that a child can elicit at any particular periods during development. The rate controller will of course change over time.

Random but Voluntary Movement. Some movements performed by the infant are not reflexive in nature and are often referred to as random or spontaneous movements. These movements are common with newborns when they are lying on their back and consist of movements of the legs or arms in a seemingly disorganized fashion. However, Thelen and her colleagues have demonstrated that these movements are actually more coordinated than initially meets the eye. In fact, the kicking movements made by the child, while not the same, are remarkably similar to walking steps taken by adults (Thelen, 1985; Thelen & Fisher, 1983). More specifically, the supine kicking motion of the infant is quite rhythmical and has a definite pattern of coordination (see Figure 7.3).

Motor Behavior Landmarks During Infancy. Probably one of the most significant contributions of the work conducted by maturational the-

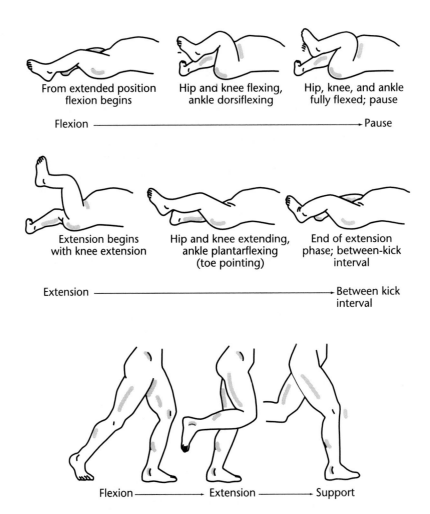

From extended position   Hip and knee flexing,   Hip, knee, and ankle
flexion begins   ankle dorsiflexing   fully flexed; pause

Flexion ──────────────────────────────────────► Pause

Extension begins   Hip and knee extending,   End of extension
with knee extension   ankle plantarflexing   phase; between-kick
                          (toe pointing)   interval

Extension ──────────────────────────────────────► Between kick
                                                    interval

Flexion ──────────► Extension ──────────► Support

FIGURE 7.3   Random leg movements of the child strike a remarkable resemblance to the walking action of an adult with respect to rhythmicity and coordination. (Reprinted by permission from K. M. Haywood, 1993, *Lifespan and Motor Development,* 2d ed., Champaign, IL: Human Kinetics Publishers, pp. 93–94)

orists is the identification and description of landmark activities that occur during an infant's early "adventures." These landmarks are very prevalent for locomotion as well as manual control. Researchers Shirley (1931), Bayley (1935), Ames (1937), Gesell (1939), and McGraw (1940) were all instrumental in documenting the sequential occurrence of these landmark events.

However, it is interesting to note, that even these authors did not necessarily agree on the age at which some of these milestones emerged. This once again supports the idea that age is not necessarily a reliable marker for the process of motor development.

Locomotion.   Important events in an individual's capacity for **locomotion** include crawling, creeping, and walking. **Crawling** can be described as a movement in which infants use their arms to pull themselves forward while their legs push. An important characteristic of crawling is that the child's stomach stays in contact with the ground. In essence the crawling child resembles the soldier training to stay low when moving across a battlefield. Generally crawling occurs prior to **creeping,** which involves keeping the stomach and chest off of the surface on which the child is ambulating. Figure 7.4 displays two quite distinct creeping methods: homolateral and contralateral. A characteristic of homolateral creeping is the alternating motion of the arm and leg of one side of the body with the arm and leg of the opposite side. In contrast, contralateral creeping involves alternating left arm and right leg movements with right arm and left leg movements. Most efficient creepers appear to use a contralateral style but approximately 20 percent of children adopt the homolateral method (Cratty, 1979).

One of the most monumental landmarks in a child's development is walking unaided. This usually is preceded by the necessary postural adjustments that are fine-tuned by standing in a supported position and ultimately unsupported. **Walking** has been defined as a movement that shifts weight from one foot to the other, with at least one foot contacting the surface at all times (Gabbard, 1996). However, when observing an infant and adult walking there are some marked differences. The infant generally compensates for a great deal of instability by establishing a wide base of support and taking very short steps. If necessary, review the appropriate section in Chapter 4 that discusses the relationship of balance, stability, and base of support. Moreover, upper body rotation, in particular swinging the arms, is reduced or eliminated once again to lessen the chance of instability.

We would be remiss if at this time we failed to mention a study conducted by Shirley (1931) on infant development. This study contained a great deal of information regarding the development of walking. A wealth of anthropometric and movement data was collected on 25 babies from birth to two years of age using a longitudinal design. From a total of 743 walking records a very comprehensive walking record for each child was obtained. Based on this data Shirley offered a detailed description of walking development. The first stage involves taking steps while supported, but the child cannot bear weight. The second stage is standing with support. According to Shirley, reaching this stage is an important correlate and therefore predictor

Pioneers in Motor Development—
Dr. Lolas E. Halverson and Dr. Esther Thelen

Lolas E. Halverson was one of the initial researchers to concentrate on the study of children's motor development. Dr. Halverson made many contributions to the field of motor development. She conducted a now classic "decades-long" longitudinal study of "just" seven people. Most of Halverson's research was conducted in the Motor Development and Child Study Laboratory at the University of Wisconsin-Madison, where she achieved the rank of professor in 1965. She also chaired the Department of Physical Education at the University of Wisconsin from 1963 to 1970. During her career she received numerous honors, including an Honor Award from the American Alliance for Health, Physical Education, Recreation, and Dance (AAHPERD), a Joy of Effort Award from the National Association for Sport and Physical Education (NASPE), and the University of Northern Iowa Alumni Distinguished Service Award. Dr. Halverson died in September 1993. The National As-

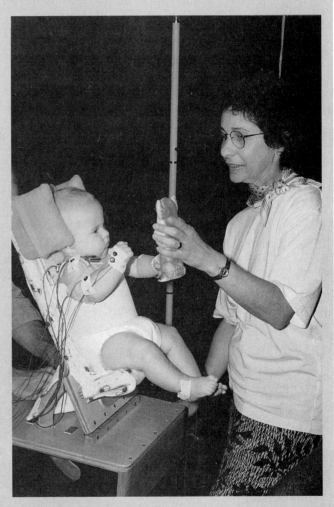

HIGHLIGHT 7.3   *Dr. Esther Thelen is a strong proponent of the dynamical systems perspective.* (Photo courtesy of Dr. Esther Thelen)

sociation for Sport and Physical Education has since honored her contribution to motor development with the establishment of the Lolas E. Halverson Young Investigator Award.

Halverson's work focused on identifying movement landmarks in order to describe the sequencing of movement acquisition. More recently motor developmentalists have concentrated on the process of movement acquisition as opposed to the movement product (e.g., jumping). An emerging theoretical framework that is being used to address this issue is the dynamical systems perspective. As described earlier, this position places special importance on the self-organizing capacity of the human system. A major proponent of this perspective is Dr. Esther Thelen (see picture), a professor of psychology and cognitive science at Indiana University. Dr. Thelen's work has been instrumental in raising questions about the veracity of the

commonly held notion that maturation of the nervous system is the driving force behind development using clever experimental paradigms such as submerging infants in chest-high warm water or adding weights to their ankles. Using this approach Thelen has demonstrated that asynchronous physical growth exerts an important influence on the patterns of behavior that are exhibited by the child. This work has attracted a broad audience, exemplified by the recent collaborative effort with Dr. Linda Smith, a psychologist specializing in cognitive development, that resulted in a book entitled *A Dynamic Systems Approach to the Development of Cognition and Action.* This is one further demonstration of the expanding influence of the movement scientist in today's scientific community.

From North American Society of Psychology of Sport and Physical Activity (NASPSA) Newsletter *19 (Winter 1994).*

of walking alone. Walking when led by an external source is the third stage. The final stage is walking alone.

Shirley (1931) also highlighted some important changes that occur as the infant moves toward becoming a mature walker. Initially, an acceleration in walking speed is observed as well as an increase in step length. In addition, step width increases to maintain stability but eventually decreases when the child walks alone. A toe-out walking motion also changes to more parallel foot alignment with a mature walking pattern.

Manual Control. **Manual control** is movement of the arms and hands in order to manipulate objects. The stages of progression for manual control are usually categorized as reaching, grasping, and releasing behaviors. Reaching

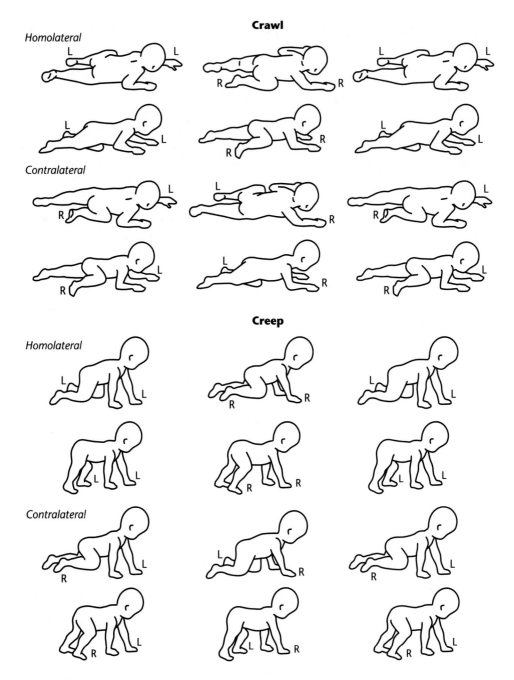

FIGURE 7.4 Homolateral and contralateral movement patterns for crawling and creeping. (From Keogh & Sugden, *Movement Skill Development.* Copyright © 1985 by Allyn & Bacon. Reprinted by permission.)

and grasping are initially combined into a unitary action. More specifically, an infant reaching for an object moves the entire body toward it. Moreover, the fingers are opened at the beginning of the reaching motion and begin to close as the object is located. Bower (1979; 1982) indicated that the reaching and grasping components begin to separate at approximately four months.

An important landmark during development of the grasping action is adopting the digital grasp as opposed to the palmar grasp. The digital grip allows for greater dexterity and manipulative power. Figure 7.5 reveals the different grasping techniques that an infant uses. Note that the initial attempts to grasp an object require the thumb and fingers to be used as a unit to force the object against the palm of the hand. Shortly after, approximately one month, the child uses what is known as a true opposition grip. In this case, the thumb opposes the fingers in order to grip the object. There is only minimal contact between the object and the palm of the hand in this situation. Finally, the infant uses a neat pincer grip in which objects are manipulated using the thumb and forefinger. Halverson (1931) revealed that true opposition for infants gripping actions occurred around eight months.

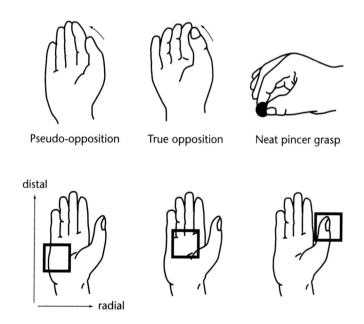

Pseudo-opposition   True opposition   Neat pincer grasp

distal

radial

FIGURE 7.5   Examples of grasping techniques that are adopted by a child.

Releasing objects appears to be a particularly difficult movement for the child to master. At about eight months one can usually observe crude attempts to release objects by merely opening the hand and letting the object drop. However, at close to fourteen months more precise digit control allows the child to place blocks on top of one another. More complex release capabilities are necessary at a later stage when releasing a thrown ball, for example. All this occurs within the first twenty-four months! No wonder parents often comment that their children change so rapidly. This is certainly true with respect to their motor capabilities. In fact, Halverson (1937) suggests that rudimentary reaching, grasping, and releasing actions can be well coordinated as early as eighteen months old.

Explaining the Occurrence of Motor Behavior Landmarks.   It is not difficult to notice that the work of the maturational theorists was very important for describing the sequence of events resulting in the achievement of particular behavioral landmarks. However, it is essential that the step beyond description is made and some explanation is offered to account for the appearance of these landmark actions. As one would expect, given our previous discussions, the maturational theorists suggest that the accomplishment of landmark activities is directly related to cortical development. In contrast, the perception-action proponent would intimate that the changes in posture with development offer new perceptual experiences, which in turn offer new motoric opportunities. This process would lead the individual to identify new affordances. How might the dynamical systems advocate explain these events?

Childhood

According to Gabbard (1996), childhood involves the improvements in fundamental movement skills and the practice of these movements for sport and recreational activities. A **fundamental movement** can be described as a common motor activity that involves a specific movement pattern (e.g., walking, running, jumping, and throwing). The **movement pattern** is defined as the basic functional structure of a fundamental motor skill (Gabbard, 1996). A great deal of effort has been expended both to categorize and delineate the time course of fundamental locomotor, nonlocomotor, and manipulative movement patterns that are used during early childhood. The status of these patterns at particular times determines whether the movement is classified as immature or mature. An **immature movement pattern** might be considered a minimal level of proficiency, whereas a **mature**

PICTURE 7.3   *Throwing is an example of a fundamental movement that an individual might experience during childhood.* (Photo credit: © Elizabeth Crews/Stock Boston)

movement pattern would be considered to meet sport skill form (Figure 7.6). By the age of three, most children display minimal characteristics for most of the fundamental movement patterns. Usually by the age of six the child can produce a variety of movement patterns that would be classified as mature.

In order to develop fundamental movements and use them appropriately, children must become aware of the effect of their own physical make-up, the task, and the environment (Newell, 1986). For example, during childhood the shape, size, and capacity of the individual's limbs change. This has to be taken into account in order to effect movement efficiently.

Phase I: The ball is thrown primarily with forearm extension. The feet remain stationary, body does not rotate, and there is a slight forward sway.

Phase II: Rotatory movement is added. The hand is cocked behind the head during the preparatory movement and the trunk then rotates to the left. The throwing arm swings around in an oblique-horizontal plane.

Phase III: A forward step with the right leg is added in a righthand throw. The step produces additional forward force for the throw.

Phase IV: Throwing arm and trunk rotate backward during preparation. A contralateral step moves body weight forward.

FIGURE 7.6 The stages that precede the production of a mature throwing movement pattern. (From Keogh & Sugden, *Movement Skill Development.* Copyright © 1985 by Allyn & Bacon. Reprinted by permission.)

Alternatively, the child must understand that gravity has an enormous influence on actions. This becomes quite obvious to them as they attempt to develop throwing and jumping movements.

The discovery of mechanical principles results in improvements in performance. Recall that we discussed many of these principles in Chapter 4 when we focused on biomechanics. For example, a child realizes that stepping into a throw propels the ball a greater distance. Is this consistent with any of Newton's Laws? What about when children learn that holding their arms out in the air rather than close to their sides makes them rotate slower? Can you explain why this will occur? While the child obviously cannot describe these mechanical principles verbally, through perceptual-motor exploration the child implicitly acquires this knowledge, which is manifest in the qualitative changes in the movement patterns used during childhood.

Adolescence

Early childhood brings with it some dramatic changes in the child's ability to produce movement. Voluntary control is now clearly evident, supporting a number of fundamental locomotor, nonlocomotor, and manipulative movement actions. In the early part of the childhood stage the primary concern of the researcher is to provide an account of whether a child can actually perform certain actions. As the child reaches the latter stages of childhood and early adulthood (approximately 7 to 17 years old), significant improvements in motor performance can be noted. Many of these are a function of body growth and changes in body structure. An important factor that surfaces during this period is age-related differences.

At about 10 to 12 years old, with the onset of the adolescent growth spurt, male–female differences in motor performance become apparent. Most motor developmentalists agree that there is a consistent trend indicating that males continue to improve their motor performance on a variety of tasks. In contrast, there is a general leveling off in performance for females at about the age of 14. This is clearly displayed in Figure 7.7, which shows throwing distance curves for males and females. Many of these differences can be attributed to the males possessing more muscle mass and less body fat than their female counterparts. This gives them a distinct advantage in the tasks requiring strength and power. Furthermore, males also gain a mechanical advantage over females due to structural differences such as longer arms, narrower hips, and wider shoulders. This is particularly important for throwing or striking activities requiring maximum leverage. (Chapter 3 discusses the concepts of mechanical advantage and leverage in more detail.)

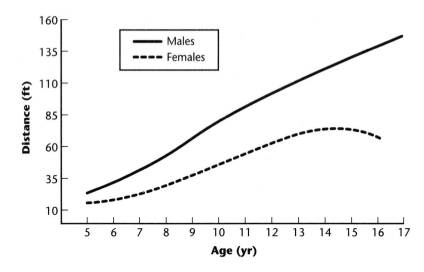

FIGURE 7.7   Throwing distance curves for males and females as a function of age in years. (From Johnson, Warren K. & Buskirk, Elsworth R., *Science and Medicine of Exercise and Sport,* 2d ed., HarperCollins Publishers, Inc., 1974. Copyright © 1974 by Warren K. Johnson and Elsworth K. Buskirk.)

Adulthood

As mentioned previously, much of the early work in the area of motor development concentrated on the stages up through adolescence. However, contemporary approaches in motor development have been particularly interested in the changes that occur in the latter stages of life. Gabbard (1996) incorporates two distinct but important phases during adulthood: peak performance and regression. Let's take a look at each of these.

Peak Performance.   It is generally accepted that between ages 25 and 30 an individual will demonstrate **peak performance.** Females tend to demonstrate peak performance levels a little earlier than males. Females peak at approximately 22 to 25 years old, whereas males peak at around 29 years old. There is a great deal of individual variability with these age ranges. At first glance this might seem rather surprising. Many people assume that our optimum performance capacity is much earlier. So why do we "peak" when we do? At least part of the answer lies in the maturing of three factors that play a big part in many aspects of motor performance: cardiorespiratory functioning, muscular strength, and perceptual-motor capacity.

Being tolerant of greater physical workloads that tax the cardiorespiratory system is indicative of superior physiological endurance. Figure 7.8

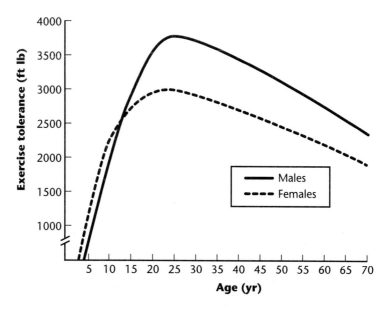

FIGURE 7.8 The relationship of exercise tolerance as a function of age for both males and females. (From Gabbard, Carl P., *Lifelong Motor Development,* 2d ed. Copyright © 1996 Times Mirror Higher Education Group, Inc., Dubuque, IA. All Rights Reserved.)

illustrates the relationship between age and exercise tolerance. While there are marked differences between the male and female functions, it is clear that both reach their peak in their third decade. A similar finding can be found for peak grip strength, which is often considered an appropriate index of muscle strength. Figure 7.9 shows grip strength as a function of age. The characteristic difference between males and females is again evident but both once again reach optimal levels between 24 and 29 years of age. Finally, two of the most common measures used to assess the functioning of the perceptual-motor system are reaction time and movement time. While perhaps not as pronounced as in the case of cardiorespiratory functioning and muscle strength, perceptual-motor capacity as assessed using reaction time and movement time shows a gradual improvement up to the early adult years with a gradual decline thereafter.

A rather unscientific method of deciding whether peak performance occurs at the time suggested in the present chapter is to observe the present-day athletic stars. What is the average age of these athletes? A similar approach was used by Hirata (1979), who studied the athletes who earned medals at the Olympic Games between 1964 and 1976. The average age for the males was 26 years old and 23 years old for the females.

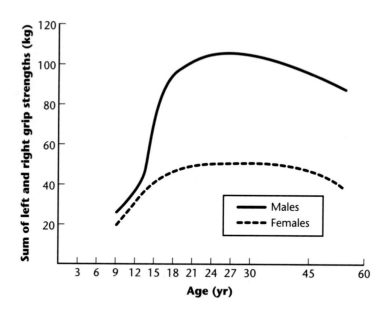

FIGURE 7.9   The relationship of grip strength and age for both males and females. (From *Research Quarterly for Exercise and Sport,* vol. 48, no. 109, 1977. Reprinted by permission of the American Alliance for Health, Physical Education, Recreation and Dance.)

A qualifier to the data offered by Hirata can be found in the work of Jokl (1964), who also studied Olympic athletes. Findings from this study indicated that the younger competitors were involved in the anaerobically demanding activities such as sprints in track and field and swimming, as well as boxing. In contrast, athletes over 30 years of age were commonly found in events such as fencing, marathon running, and horsemanship. In fact, an examination of the world record marathon times for different-aged males and females is probably one of the most convincing sets of data for peaking in the late 20s to early 30s. This data is depicted in Figure 7.10.

Regression.   The **regression** in motor performance that occurs as a function of age is not considered in many motor development textbooks (Corbin, 1980; Gallahue, 1989; Keogh & Sugden, 1985). However, if one considers that the number of people over the age of 65 will double by the year 2040, it would seem appropriate that some understanding of the aging process and its implications for development and motor performance be achieved (Payne & Issacs, 1991).

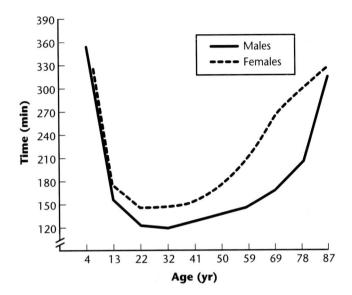

FIGURE 7.10 The world record marathon times for males and females in different age groups. (From McArdle, Katch, & Katch, *Exercise Physiology: Energy, Nutrition and Human Performance,* Lea & Febiger, 1991. Reprinted by permission of Waverly.)

In the case of peak performance we examined cardiorespiratory function, muscle strength, and psychomotor functioning. These same factors are also involved in the regression process that ultimately occurs for each and every one of us. After peak performance we see about 0.75 percent decline per year in physiological functioning. What does this means for the 70-year-old who is trying to complete a marathon? An approximately 30 percent decline in maximal aerobic power. Furthermore, there is also a 40 percent decrease in anaerobic power, which may be a function of the older individual's inability to control the lactic acid accumulation that occurs after acute bouts of intense exercise.

Males maintain peak strength until they are 45, after which there is a slow decline. At 65 years males have only lost 15 percent of their peak strength performance. In another study, Shock (1962) found that from the age of 35 to 90 there was approximately a 50 percent decline in hand-grip strength. Remember, we are assuming that hand-grip strength is indicative of overall muscle strength. What causes the loss in muscle strength with age? One hypothesis is the 25–30 percent loss in muscle mass that happens between the ages of 30 and 70.

The dynamical systems perspective once again provides a nice account for regression. Remember that this position suggests that the fastest regressing system will exert the greatest limit on behavior (Haywood, 1993). This is true if it regresses beyond some critical point. At this time the individual must adopt a new movement pattern in order to try to achieve a goal response. The breakdown might result from any one of a variety of systems such as a weakening muscular system, a slowing in the nervous system, or an insensitive perceptual system. Obviously, a disruption in the perceptual or muscular system might also impact the opportunity for perception-action integration and exploration. In this sense the aging individual will be exposed to a new set of affordances, which would certainly change that individual's movement repertoire.

Can some of these regression problems be reduced or eliminated? Clark, Lanphear, & Riddick (1987) examined whether exposing elderly individuals to training on reaction time and movement time tasks could reduce some of the problems associated with the aging process. Training reaction and movement time consisted of playing video games! The findings suggested that this training method actually improved the reaction time of the 70-year-olds who participated in the study. Maybe this will become a useful excuse for young children to persuade their parents to play "just one more game" in the arcade at the mall.

FACTORS MEDIATING MOTOR DEVELOPMENT

The development process is dependent on a number of important factors that in most cases result in predictable changes in development and function. We will look at two important categories influencing the progression of motor development. First, we must consider biological influences including growth and maturation. Second, we will examine the perceptual-motor changes that contribute to efficient movement production. Let's start by looking at the biological factors.

Biological Influences

There is a vast amount of information on the role of biological factors on human development and in particular motor development. In order to attack this problem we will review this information in three subsections: neurological development, physical growth and maturation, and physiological development. It is important to note that these factors, while examined independently, are highly interrelated.

Neurological Development.   It almost goes without saying that human development as a whole is highly reliant on the effective functioning of the central nervous system (CNS). We have already spent some time considering the role of the CNS in the chapter on anatomical kinesiology. You may recall that with respect to movement, this system provides the human architecture with the means of communication from the higher control centers to the human "motors," or muscles.

The CNS develops in a very orderly fashion passing through distinct stages called proliferation, migration, integration, differentiation, myelination, and cell death (Cowan, 1978). **Cell proliferation,** as the name suggests, refers to the rapid production of neurons that begins around the second prenatal month. This process is virtually complete by the time of birth, with the newborn having approximately 10 to 100 billion neurons. As proliferation progresses a second process begins, migration. During **cell migration,** cells begin to move to the location within the body for which they are designed. In essence, the cells migrate, like birds in the winter, to meet other cells that will have a similar function. Cells become more elaborate when they reach their terminal location within the system. An example of this is the rapid changes that occur in the axon and dendrite structures during this period.

Integration and differentiation occur next. **Cell integration** is defined as an interweaving of the developing neurons from agonist and antagonist muscle groups to allow the coordinated action of these muscles that is characteristic of mature movers. **Cell differentiation** is a further refining of the role and function of particular neurons. Moreover, differentiation is also linked with the more general progression of motor control from gross, often ill-defined movements to very coordinated and intricately controlled ones.

One important marker of neurological development is the extent of **cell myelination.** You should recall from Chapter 3 that myelin is a substance deposited around the neuron that speeds up transmission of impulses and offers some resistance to fatigue. The degree of myelination for different sites in the body varies considerably. However, the motor mechanisms of the spinal cord appear to be fully myelinated by the end of the first month of birth. *Lorenzo's Oil,* a highly acclaimed movie of several years ago, examined a genetic disorder called adrenoleukodystrophy (ALD). This disorder, passed from mother to son, causes a breakdown of myelin that ultimately causes the brain to shut down. A great deal of research at this time is being conducted in search of methods to regenerate myelin in the brain.

As an individual ages there is cell death. This is probably not that surprising to most of us. However, a rather startling suggestion by Cowan (1978) is that proliferating cells experience competition for the limited number of synaptic sites available in the body. The consequence of this is that some structures in the developmental process lose, through cell death, as much as 50 percent of the neurons that were initially produced.

Another important neurological development worthy of some attention occurs during the first two to three years of life. This development is termed **hemispheric lateralization.** This refers to the specialized function that each side of the brain adopts. For example, you may have heard that a particular individual is "right-brained." What does this mean? Generally, this refers to the fact that the individual in question seems to have heightened capacity for functions that are controlled by the right side of the brain, including music and art appreciation, creativity, emotion, and spatial awareness. In contrast, the left hemisphere is assumed to account for language, logical operations, and other processes requiring analytical processing such as cognitive activities related to science and math problems. Another aspect of hemispheric lateralization that is particularly crucial for movement production is the notion of contralateral control. Essentially this means that the right side of the brain governs movements on the left side of the body and vice versa. Figure 7.11 provides a nice overview of lateralization.

To conclude this section on neurological changes we should not forget to consider the consequences of the aging process. We provided part of the answer to this in an early section. Do you recall what happens to the nervous system with age? Remember, we discussed a reduction in the speed of neural transmission with an increase in age. This may occur because of increased synaptic delay. You might also recall that we briefly discussed the prevalent problem the elderly experience with maintaining their balance. This occurs because with age comes a degradation of the vestibular apparatus (i.e., the inner ear). This is a result of a deterioration in neurons in the cerebellum that contribute to the coordination of voluntary movement and vestibular functioning.

Physical Growth and Maturation.   **Growth** is generally considered to be an increase in size or body mass resulting from an enlargement of a biological unit, such as an arm. **Maturation,** on the other hand, is defined as progress toward the optimum integration and functioning of the body's systems. This section concentrates on what physical characteristics change as a function of growth and maturation. Moreover, the ramifications of these changes for motor performance are also discussed.

According to work conducted by maturationalists (i.e., Gesell and Ames), growth occurs in a cephalocaudal and proximodistal fashion. This refers to the orderly physical changes that occur from the head down

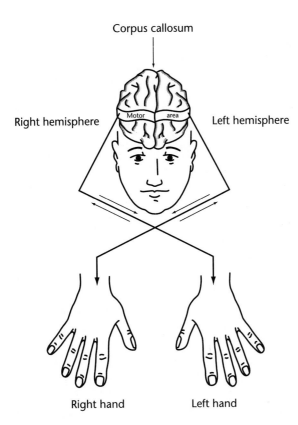

Corpus callosum

Right hemisphere   Motor   area   Left hemisphere

Right hand   Left hand

FIGURE 7.11 Hemispheric lateralization suggests that the two sides of the brain become specialized in terms of their function. The right side is important for control of movement on the left side of the body and vice versa. (From Gabbard, Carl P., *Lifelong Motor Development*, 2d ed. Copyright © 1996 Times Mirror Higher Education Group, Inc., Dubuque, IA. All Rights Reserved.)

through the trunk (i.e., **cephalocaudal**) and from the center of the body out to the peripheral areas such as the hands and fingers (i.e., **proximodistal**). There is rapid growth during gestation and during the first year. After this there is a lull until the onset of puberty, which brings with it a growth spurt. At the conclusion of puberty, in early adulthood, there is a gradual slowing in growth again.

As previously mentioned, anthropometric measures are an essential tool for studying growth and maturation. Growth curves are probably one of the most commonly used anthropometric measures. Almost all parents have learned from visiting the pediatrician where their children fall on the normative growth curves. Figure 7.12 shows both male and female stature by percentile for ages 2 to 18 years. Notice the rapid increase in height from approximately 2 to 13 years for females, with a much more gradual increase thereafter. You can also see a similar trend for the males. However, the rapid rise in stature continues until the age of 16.

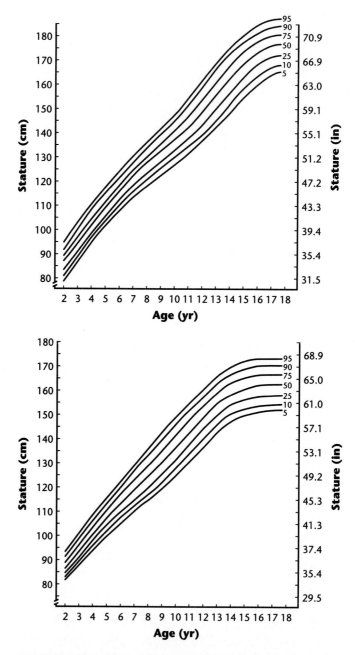

FIGURE 7.12   Males (top) and females (bottom) stature by age percentiles. (Data from National Center for Health Statisitics, June, 1976)

An additional factor that is monitored throughout a child's development is that of weight. At birth, a child weighs approximately 7–7.5 pounds. During the next six months the child's weight doubles. The next major change in weight that an individual experiences is during the adolescent growth spurt. It is during this stage that a male can increase his weight by as much as 50 pounds. A female also experiences this increase in body weight but to a lesser extent, gaining only 35–40 pounds. The increase in weight for males and females is displayed in the growth curve depicted in Figure 7.13. Notice that the growth spurt is characteristically earlier for females.

Most people have an intuitive idea, at least for adults, of how stature and weight influence motor performance. For example, most of us would conclude that a tall and skinny individual would most likely be better suited to long distance running than to throwing the discus. In contrast, a short and stocky individual who demonstrates a great deal of strength is more likely to excel in a sport such as wrestling as opposed to fencing. However, the relationship between aspects of stature and weight with motor performance is less clear for younger children.

One study by Jaffe and Kosakov (1982) examined the relationship between age at walking to stature and weight parameters. The findings from this study indicated that overweight and obese infants (6–18 months) exhibited a delay in motor development compared to their average weight and stature counterparts. While at first this picture appears straightforward, it is clouded by results obtained during a follow-up study. The subsequent study revealed that those individuals categorized as slow developers were developing normally one year later.

Deciding that an individual has reached maturity at first seems rather easy but in actuality is quite difficult to determine precisely. The most common method used to estimate a person's level of maturity is, of course, chronological age. Unfortunately chronological age is of little use because it merely identifies the number of days since birth but does little to address individual differences in the rate of maturation. Another measure of maturity that appears more reliable than chronological age is skeletal maturity, which is typically assessed by X-raying the bones of the left wrist and the hand complex. This method is particularly useful from about 18 months of age. Figure 7.14 shows X-rays of the hand–wrist complex for a 4- and a 13-year old.

What is the relationship of maturity to achieving successful motor performance? The answer to this can be found in almost any elementary, junior high, or high school gymnasium or playing field. More specifically, it is not uncommon to see the earlier maturer, the big strong child, dominate

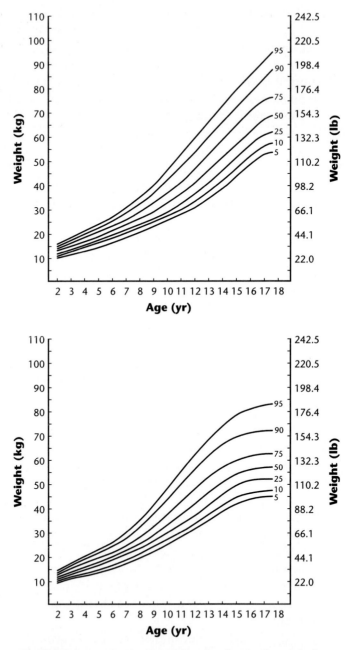

FIGURE 7.13   Males (top) and females (bottom) weight by age percentiles. (Data from National Center for Health Statistics, June 1976)

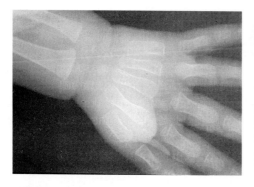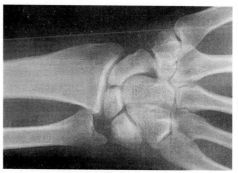

FIGURE 7.14   X-rays of the hand–wrist complex of a 4-year-old (left) and a 13-year-old (right). This method is commonly used to establish skeletal maturity. (Photo credit: Mark Burnett/Photo Researchers)

many athletic events. However, Malina (1984) suggests that as adolescence nears its conclusion, maturity exerts less influence because late maturers subsequently reduce the size differences that accounted for performance discrepancies. What this means is that the star athlete in junior high school may not be the star athlete in high school as well (Clarke, 1971). The advantages of early maturity for motor performance do not appear to be evident for females, however. In fact, in direct contrast to males, superior motor performance of females appears to be negatively related to biological maturity.

Physiological Development.   A major complaint of many adults today is that American children are less fit now than they were 20 to 30 years ago. For this reason, a great emphasis has been placed on health-related fitness activities and programs to encourage participation in physical activity. What do we mean when we say children are not fit? Payne & Isaacs (1991) suggest that in order to assess health-related fitness we must consider cardiovascular endurance, flexibility, and muscular strength.

   Cardiovascular endurance can be assessed by using a number of different physiological measures. Recall from the chapter on exercise physiology (Chapter 5) that **heart rate** (HR) is simply defined as the number of cardiac cycles that occur in one minute. Maximal HR decreases with age. This is also true for resting and submaximal HR, with males having slightly lower HRs than females. Speculation as to why HR decreases with age has focused on the changes in contractile properties of the cardiac muscle and fluctuations in the nervous control of the heart that occur as one gets older. Cardiac output can also be used to evaluate cardiovascular endurance. **Cardiac output** was defined in Chapter 5 as the amount of blood that can be pumped through the heart in one minute. As development progresses the volume of the heart increases, which brings with it a corresponding increase in cardiac output. Subsequent to adolescence there is a decline in both heart rate and stroke volume, which dictates cardiac output. Thus resting and maximal cardiac output will exhibit approximately 20 to 30 percent decline by 65 years of age (Fitzgerald, 1985).

Another physiological measure to consider when assessing cardiovascular endurance is that of maximal oxygen consumption, or VO_2max. This measure is an index of the maximal amount of oxygen the body can absorb at the tissue level. It appears that VO_2 max remains relatively constant during childhood and early adolescence (Payne & Isaacs, 1991). Peak capacity appears to occur between the ages of 18 and 25 years. There appears to be a gradual decline in the body's capacity to use oxygen after this time. Aerobic capacity, however, can be improved by as much as 20 percent for both children and adults given the right type of training.

You should recall from Chapter 3, which discussed anatomical kinesiology, that being able to move a joint through its full range of motion is important to motor performance and is known as **flexibility.** Clarke (1975) reported that general range of motion increases throughout childhood until about the age of 10 years for males and 12 years for females. One should keep in mind, however, that a general statement of an individual's flexibility is difficult to generate because it is very joint-specific. While most of us have observed the amazing flexibility of a young child, we assume that with age we become inflexible. Munns (1981) demonstrated that with light or moderate physical activity elderly individuals (65–88 years old) can experience improvements in their range of motion. This suggests that engaging in physical activity even when older offers the opportunity to maintain one aspect of basic motor functioning: flexibility. Clearly this is important since many everyday motor activities require some degree of flexibility, for example, tying one's shoes or reaching for an object on a high shelf.

Earlier in this chapter, grip strength as a function of age was discussed (see Figure 7.9). Remember that grip strength is commonly used as an index of muscle strength. Basically there is an increase in muscle strength from early childhood, with the rate increasing quite dramatically, especially for males, at the time of puberty. Methany (1941) reported a 359 percent increase in grip strength for males between the age of 6 and 18 years. Females,

PICTURE 7.4   *Children exhibit a great deal of flexibility.* (Photo credit: © Martha Cooper/Peter Arnold, Inc.)

by contrast, experience an increase of about 260 percent during the same period. This difference is attributed to greater muscle mass and androgen production by males.

Perceptual Influences

In order for us to move around the environment efficiently we rely a great deal on the receipt of sensory information. While the majority of the senses (vision, auditory, and kinesthetic) probably play a role in movement production at some stage, most experts would agree that the development of kinesthesis and vision are most important for the production of action (Keogh & Sugden, 1985).

The visual system and the functions it performs undergo a number of changes during the life span. For example, the size of the eye almost doubles from the time of birth to maturity (Gabbard, 1996). Structural changes occur to support visual functions such as acuity, spatial orientation, depth perception, movement perception, and visual–motor coordination. Object perception and discrimination as well as depth perception are particularly important for static visual displays. Obviously, once items in the environment are more dynamic, the role of movement perception becomes increasingly more important. Remarkably, children can deal with both static and dynamic visual displays quite adequately by the time they reach their first birthday.

A classic study examining the visual perceptual capabilities of children and focusing on depth perception was conducted by Gibson & Walk (1960). Basically, the study demonstrated that infants can utilize depth cues in the first year after birth. The study also used a piece of equipment known as the visual cliff, which has become a standard piece of apparatus for assessing visual perceptual capacity of young children. Essentially the device consists of a platform several feet off the ground. A checkerboard pattern is printed on the platform and on the ground next to the platform. A plastic cover extends across the checkerboard pattern on the platform and floor. Thus when a child crawls across the plastic on top of the platform, he or she eventually reaches a point at which there appears to be a dramatic drop to the floor. When the mother attempts to call the child across the plastic that spans the "cliff," the child refuses to move and often begins to cry. These data suggest that children can detect depth quite effectively.

As a person gets older, common visual problems impact their capacity to move. These problems include decreased visual acuity, decreased sensitivity to light, and poor depth perception. **Senile macular degeneration (SMD)** is one of the most prevalent causes of loss of visual acuity in the elderly. SMD is caused by a reduction in the number of photoreceptors, a reduced blood supply to the retina, and loss of ocular reflexes. While this affliction causes disruption of central vision, peripheral vision is left intact. This is good news for the elderly because movement is particularly reliant on the ambient visual system, which receives information from the peripheral part of the visual field.

Obtaining and efficiently interpreting information related to the awareness of movement and body position in space is crucial to successful motor performance. This type of sensory information is accumulated from a number of different proprioceptive sources, including the muscle spindles, Golgi tendon organs, and a variety of joint receptors as well as the vestibular apparatus in the inner ear. There appear to be two primary aspects of kinesthetic perception: acuity and memory (Keogh & Sugden, 1985).

Kinesthetic acuity can be described as our ability to differentiate proprioceptively between two different weights, locations, distances, or forces. An individual's optimal ability to perform this type of discrimination occurs at approximately 8 years of age. This is in stark contrast to kinesthetic memory, which does not reach mature levels until age 12. **Kinesthetic memory** is used when one is asked to reproduce a previously presented movement of particular force, location, or distance.

There are a number of other functions that we almost "automatically" control day to day via kinesthetic perception, for example, spatial awareness, balance and postural control, and temporal awareness. **Spatial awareness** is our ability to draw inference as to our location in space within the environment in which we are moving. Presumably an interaction between visual and kinesthetic information is very important to perform this function successfully.

There are few if any movements that do not require that we control posture or balance. We have discussed balance in Chapter 4 in some detail. However, it is important to reiterate that general improvement in balance appears to occur into the adolescent years. Unfortunately, a lack of control of balance is probably one of the major problems experienced by elderly individuals. This is usually due to malfunctioning of the vestibular apparatus in the inner ear (a review of the vestibular system is provided in Chapter 3).

Memory

Remember that at the beginning of this chapter we indicated that one of the contemporary theoretical positions in motor development is called the information processing position? This perspective likens the human mover to the computer in that we are assumed to accumulate information from the environment, interpret it, and then act on the information by executing a motor response. There are a number of critical information processing activities that are assumed to change as a function of the development process. In particular we will address the role of memory, processing and movement speed, and the capacity for advanced movement planning.

Presumably during the learning process, whatever is actually acquired must be stored in some location in order to access it when the same response is called for at a later time. In the information processing framework, this location is called **memory.** More specifically there are three different memory systems, termed sensory memory, short-term memory, and long-term memory. **Sensory memory** is characterized by capacity to hold an incredible amount of information for a very short period of time (~1 sec). **Short-term memory** has a limited capacity of about seven pieces of information that can reside in this storage space for 30–60 seconds. After this time information is either forgotten or transferred to **long-term memory,** which is presumably the human's permanent memory store. It has a wealth of space to hold a variety of types of information including that related to movement.

There is some evidence of primitive memory function in the formative months from studies investigating **habituation.** This method consists of presenting a stimulus to infants and monitoring the time they spend gazing at it. As the same stimulus is repeated habituation occurs, which is evident in the lack of time the infant spends looking at the stimulus. For habituation to occur one might assume that some prior knowledge or "memory" for the stimulus is necessary.

As we have pointed out earlier, short-term memory is restricted to approximately seven pieces of information at any one time. There is limited research on the development of short-term memory and movement. Sugden (1978; 1980), however, has conducted a number of studies indicating that short-term memory for younger individuals is not as efficient as that of the adult because of the poor use of rehearsal. It appears that young children use a few unsophisticated rehearsal strategies. Furthermore, the acquisition of more elaborate processing strategies seems to be part of the developmental process.

At the other extreme, short-term memory often fails the elderly person. It would seem that one major reason is a diminished ability to process the information as it resides in short-term store, therefore it doesn't get to long-term memory. This may also contribute to the well-known fact that older

PICTURE 7.5 *Children use a limited number of rehearsal strategies when attempting to solve problems.* (Photo credit: © Mimi Forsyth/ Monkmeyer Press)

adults exhibit long-term memory deficiencies. In this case, information is often not transferred to long-term memory because the elderly are less likely to spontaneously engage elaborate processing strategies—another example of regression with age.

Movement Planning and Execution

Assuming that in order for an action to be executed we must first process a sequence of information, the human performer is somewhat dependent on the speed with which information is processed. The most common index of processing speed is reaction time (RT). In contrast, movement time (MT) is used to assess execution speed. Many activities in everyday life require both quick processing and execution, such as slamming on the brakes of your car when someone pulls out in front of you, or catching a fragile object as it falls from a table toward the floor. There is a significant improvement in both RT and MT between the ages of 6 and 12. Information processing becomes less efficient from around 20 years, as evidenced by the increase in RT and MT. The rate of increase of RT and MT subsequently increases further at about 60 years.

A final information processing consideration is one that is slightly more difficult than some of the other mental operations that have been discussed. **Preprogramming,** or advanced planning, occurs when an individual organizes and prepares a response prior to the signal to respond. The advantage of this is that a faster initiation of the response can be made when the signal arrives. In addition, cognitive resources are freed for other mental activity that may have to be performed during the execution of the movement. Children seem to have the capacity to preprogram movements. However, the movement preprogramming of young children is not entirely efficient, resulting in greater attention being required during the execution of a movement because more errors are made and need to be corrected.

FINAL COMMENT

In this chapter we adopted a "life span" approach to assess motor development. This is consistent with the contemporary view that the development process continues well beyond the point at which growth and maturation slow down. While research in motor development traditionally focused on the young child, many researchers now feel that important insight into the developmental process can be garnered by close examination of the regression that is associated with adulthood as well as during infancy and childhood. For this reason a brief overview of some of the important characteristics of infancy, childhood, adolescence, and adulthood are provided in this chapter.

It should be understood that trying to map specific ages, activities, or capabilities to these developmental periods is very difficult and may be counterproductive. While maturationalists place great emphasis on providing detailed documentation of particular motor milestones, the current thinking attempts to stress the individual nature, both in terms of form and time frame, of motor development. This is particularly true in the case of the dynamic systems perspective, which is currently a popular theoretical framework. In this case, the resultant behavior exhibited by an individual is the outcome of a number of cooperating systems that are the focus of Chapters 3 (anatomical kinesiology) and 5 (exercise physiology), which all develop at a different rate. For these reasons, at any point in development, each system may act as a rate controller ultimately dictating the qualitative form of an individual's motor expression.

Biological, perceptual, memory, and movement-related factors can all influence the progression of motor development throughout the life span. Biological factors include neurological and physiological development as well as changes in growth and maturation. Recall that growth is defined as an increase in size or body mass resulting from an enlargement of a biological unit such as an arm. Maturation, on the other hand, is defined as progress toward the optimum integration and functioning of the body's systems. Growth and maturation influences are particularly pronounced during adolescence in which a number of gender differences emerge.

It appears that research in motor development is moving into an exciting new era. The emergence of the dynamical systems approach has sparked innovative new experimentation addressing age-old questions such as the role of reflexive movements and their association with voluntary control. It would seem that this theoretical perspective will provide the framework to examine the four key issues Haywood (1993) has highlighted as critical topics for future research: delineating the contribution of nature and nuture to the development process, identifying critical or sensitive periods during development, explaining the continuity and discontinuity in performance and motor capabilities, and assessing the role of movement variability as it pertains to movement development. These issues and others that surface will likely keep the current corps of motor developmentalists busy for many years.

QUESTIONS FOR THOUGHT

- There are a number of theoretical perspectives used to address motor development. How are they different? Are there some similarities among these positions?
- How are growth and maturation different? How do they contribute to motor development?
- Discuss the appearance and disappearance of reflexes from two different theoretical perspectives.
- In discussing the developmental process it is common to see terms such as developmental periods, stages, chronological age, and phases. How are these terms different?
- Childhood involves refining movement patterns. This requires that the child take into account the mechanical principles that can optimize motor performance. Describe some of the principles discussed in Chapter 4 that might be appropriate in this situation.
- Describe some of the gender differences that emerge during adolescence. Can these differences be accounted for by differential development of components of the human architecture discussed in Chapter 3?

KEY TERMS

adolescence
adulthood
affordance
cardiac output
cell differentiation
cell integration
cell migration
cell myelination
cell proliferation
cephalocaudal
childhood
continuity
crawling
creeping
critical period
cross-sectional method
discontinuity
dynamic systems perspective
flexibility
fundamental movement
growth
habituation

heart rate
hemispheric lateralization
immature movement pattern
infancy
information-processing perspective
kinesthetic acuity
kinesthetic memory
locomotion
locomotor reflex
longitudinal method
long-term memory
manual control
maturation
maturational theory
mature movement pattern
memory
motor development
movement pattern
nature–nuture
peak performance
postural reflex
preprogramming

primitive reflex
proximodistal
reflex
regression
senile macular degeneration (SMD)
sensitive period
sensory memory

sequential method
short-term memory
spatial awareness
universality
variability
visual cliff
walking

RESOURCES

Textbooks

Corbin, C. B. (1980). *A Textbook of Motor Development* (2nd ed.). Dubuque, IA: W. C. Brown.
Gabbard, C. (1996). *Lifelong Motor Development* (2nd ed.). Dubuque, IA: W. C. Brown.
Gallahue, D. L. (1982). *Understanding Motor Development in Children.* New York: John Wiley & Sons.
Haywood, K. M. (1993). *Lifespan Motor Development* (2nd ed.). Champaign, IL: Human Kinetics.
Keogh, J., & Sugden, D. (1985). *Movement Skill Development.* New York: Macmillan.
National Association for Sport and Physical Education (1996). *Looking at Physical Education from a Developmental Perspective: A Guide to Teaching.*

Journals

Child Development
Developmental Psychology
Journal of Experimental Child Psychology
Journal of Gerontology
Journal of Motor Behavior
Research Quarterly for Exercise and Sport

Professional Organizations

American Alliance for Health, Physical Education, Recreation, and Dance
North American Society for the Psychology of Sport and Physical Activity
Society for Research in Child Development

Internet

World Wide Web
http://www.tahperd.sfasu.edu/aahperd/naspe.html

Listservers
Motor Development
send: subscribe motordev <your name>
to: listserv@umdd.umd.edu

Dynamical Systems
send: subscribe dynsys-L <your name>
to: listserv@uncvm1.bitnet

Biomechanics
send: subscribe biomch-l <your name>
to: listserv@nic.surfnet.nl

REFERENCES

Ames, L. B. (1937). The sequential patterning of prone progression in the human in-
    fant. *Genetic Psychology Monographs,* 19, 409–460.
Asmussen, E. (1968). The neuromuscular system and exercise. In H. Falls (Ed.), *Exer-
    cise Physiology.* New York: Academic Press.
Bayley, N. (1935). The development of motor abilities during the first three years.
    Monographs of the Society for Research in Child Development, 1.
Bower, T. G. R. (1979). *Human Development.* San Francisco: Freeman.
Bower, T. G. R. (1982). *Development in Infancy.* San Francisco: Freeman.
Clark, J. E., Lanphear, A. K., & Riddick, C. C. (1987). The effects of videogame play-
    ing on the response selection processing of elderly adults. *Journal of Gerontology,*
    42, 82–85.
Clarke, H. H. (1971). *Physical and Motor Tests in the Medford Boys' Growth Study.* En-
    glewood Cliffs, NJ: Prentice-Hall.
Clarke, H. H. (1975). Joint and body range of motion. *Physical Fitness Research Digest,*
    5, 16.
Corbin, C. B. (1980). *A Textbook of Motor Development* (2nd ed.). Dubuque, IA: W. C.
    Brown.
Cowan, W. (1978). Aspects of neural development. In R. Porter (Ed.), *Neurophysiology*
    (vol 111, no. 17, pp. 149–191). Baltimore, MD: University Park Press.
Cratty, B. J. (1979). *Perceptual and Motor Development in Infants and Children* (2nd ed.).
    Englewood Cliffs, NJ: Prentice-Hall.
Fitzgerald, P. L. (1985). Exercise for the elderly. In L. Goldberg & D. Elliott (Eds.), *The
    Medical Clinics of North America.* Philadelphia: Saunders.
Gabbard, C. (1996). *Lifelong Motor Development* (2nd ed.). Dubuque, IA: W. C. Brown.
Gallahue, D. L. (1989). *Understanding Motor Development* (2nd ed.). Indianapolis:
    Benchmark Press.
Gesell, A. (1925). *The Mental Growth of the Preschool Child.* New York: Macmillan.
Gesell, A. (1939). Reciprocal interweaving in neuromotor development. *Journal of
    Comparative Neurology,* 70, 161–180.
Gibson, E. J., & Walk, R. D. (1960). The "visual cliff." *Scientific American* 202, 64–71.
Gibson, J. J. (1966). *The Senses Considered as Perceptual Systems.* Boston: Houghton-
    Mifflin.
Halverson, H. M. (1931). An experimental study of prehension in infants by means
    of systematic cinema records. *Genetic Psychology Monographs,* 10, 107–286.

Halverson, H. M. (1937). Studies of the grasping responses in early infancy. *Journal of Genetic Psychology,* 51, 437–449.

Havighurst, R. J. (1972). *Developmental Tasks and Education* (3rd ed.). New York: McKay.

Haywood, K. M. (1993). *Lifespan Motor Development* (2nd ed.). Champaign, IL: Human Kinetics.

Hirata, K. (1979). *Selection of Olympic Champions* (vol. 1). Santa Barbara, CA: Institute of Environmental Stress.

Jaffe, M., & Kosakov, C. (1982). The motor development of fat babies. *Clinical Pediatrics,* 27, 619–621.

Jokl, E. (1964). *Medical Sociology and Cultural Anthropology of Sport and Physical Education.* Springfield, IL: C. C. Thomas.

Keogh, J., & Sugden, D. (1985). *Movement Skill Development.* New York: Macmillan.

Malina, R. M. (1984). Human growth, maturation, and regular physical activity. In R. A. Boileau (Ed.), *Advances in Pediatric Sport Sciences: Biological Issues* (vol. 1). Champaign, IL: Human Kinetics.

McGraw, M. B. (1940). Neuromuscular development in the human infant as exemplified in the achievement of locomotion. *Journal of Pediatrics,* 17, 747–771.

McGraw, M. B. (1975). *Growth: A Study of Johnny and Jimmy.* New York: Arno Press. First published 1935.

Methany, E. (1941). The present status of strength testing for children of elementary and preschool age. *Research Quarterly,* 12, 115–130.

Munns, K. (1981). Effects of exercise on the range of joint motion in elderly subjects. In E. Smith, & R. Serfass (Eds.), *Exercise and Aging.* Hillsdale, NJ: Enslow Publishers.

National Center for Health Statistics. U. S. Department of Health, Education and Welfare, HRA, 25, 3, June 22, 1976.

Newell, K. M. (1986). Constraints on the development of coordination. In M. G. Wade & H. T. A. Whiting (Eds.), *Motor Development in Children: Aspects of Coordination and Control* (pp. 341–361). Amsterdam: Martinus Nijhoff Publishers.

Payne V. G., & Isaacs, L. D. (1991). *Human Motor Development: A Lifespan Approach* (2nd ed.). Mountain View, CA: Mayfield Publishing Company.

Piaget, J. (1963). *The Origins of Intelligence in Children.* New York: W. W. Norton.

Pontius, A. A. (1973). Neuro-ethics of walking in the newborn. *Perceptual and Motor Skills,* 37, 235–245.

Schmidt. R. A. (1988). *Motor Control and Learning: A Behavioral Approach* (2nd ed.). Champaign, IL: Human Kinetics.

Shirley, M. M. (1931). *The First Two Years: A Study of Twenty-five Babies: Postural and Locomotor Development.* Minneapolis: University of Minnesota Press.

Shock, N. W. (1962). The physiology of aging. *Scientific American,* 206, 100–110.

Sugden, D. A. (1978). Visual motor short term memory in educationally subnormal boys. *British Journal of Educational Psychology,* 48, 330–339.

Sugden, D. A. (1980). Developmental strategies in motor and visual short term memory. *Perceptual and Motor Skills, 51,* 146.

Thelen, E. (1983). Learning to walk is still an "old" problem: A reply to Zelazo (1983). *Journal of Motor Behavior, 15,* 139–161.

Thelen, E. (1985). Developmental origins of motor coordination: Leg movements in human infants. *Developmental Psychology, 18,* 11.

Thelen, E. (1989). The (Re)Discovery of motor development: Learning new things from an old field. *Developmental Psychology, 25,* 946–949.

Thelen, E., & Fisher, D. M. (1983). From spontaneous to instrumental behavior: Kinematic analysis of movement changes during very early learning. *Child Development, 54,* 129–140.

Twitchell, T. E. (1965). Attitudinal reflexes. *Physical Therapy, 45,* 411–418.

Wyke, B. (1975). The neurological basis of movement. In K. S. Hold (Ed.), *Clinics in Developmental Medicine* (no. 55). London: William Heinemann.

Zelazo, P. R. (1983). The development of walking, new findings, and old assumptions. *Journal of Motor Behavior, 15,* 99–137.

CHAPTER **8**

Motor Learning and Control

CHAPTER OBJECTIVES

- To develop an appreciation for the field of motor learning and control
- To understand the diversity of human motor performance and learning
- To understand the theoretical perspectives used to explain human motor performance
- To examine the way in which movement is controlled and the factors that influence that control
- To identify the factors that influence the performance and learning of motor skills

INTRODUCTION

Motor learning and control can be defined as the scientific discipline concerned with understanding the processes leading to the learning and control of skilled human movement. It is easy to see from the name and the definition that the discipline is really a combination of two very closely related subfields: motor learning and motor control. **Motor learning** focuses on understanding the way in which the processes that lead to skilled movement are developed and the factors that facilitate or inhibit this development. **Motor control** is concerned with understanding the execution of the processes that lead to skilled human movement and the factors that affect the execution of skilled performance. However, it is important to understand that the two subfields are so intertwined that it is often counterproductive to separate them. Factors that influence the control of a motor skill often influence the learning of that skill and vice versa. The processes responsible for movement are constantly changing in very subtle ways, with each new experience holding the potential to change the way we respond.

The emphasis in this field is on human motor learning and motor control. The concern is generally with the learning and control of goal-directed movements in healthy individuals. While the focus of this field is on a broad range of motor performances, not just those related to sport or work, the field tends to concentrate on skilled movements. Adams (1987), in a historical review of skilled motor behaviors, suggests that a definition of motor skill has two defining characteristics. First, a definition of skill must have wide boundaries but not so wide as to include "a physician making a clinical decision or the skill of a mathematician." Secondly, a skill is learned. Thus, there is tendency to deemphasize movements that are primarily reflexive and those that can be considered to be primarily genetically defined (e.g., walking). However, current research is concerned with all stages of learning across the lifespan.

Contemporary researchers tend not to concentrate on the highly skilled but rather on the processes and prior practice experiences that allowed that skill to be developed. The term *skill* also relates to tasks that require movement for goal attainment. Thus the field is more concerned with the processes of a pianist, athlete, or machinist than with a mathematician, philosopher, or writer. In addition, the field is more concerned with the learning of a task than with training. The changes in performance capabilities of a distance runner or powerlifter after intense training will be of less interest than a child learning to ride a bike or a teenager learning to drive a standard shift car.

As suggested in this discussion, the field of motor learning and control in recent years has tended to use a process-oriented approach to study motor

PICTURE 8.1 *The higher centers of the central nervous system activate the motor cortex in much the same way a pianist depresses piano keys to produce a melody.* (Photo credit: Will Faller)

skill. The **process-oriented approach** emphasizes the study of the cognitive processes and mechanisms underlying movement. Researchers that employ this approach feel that these processes and mechanisms can be exposed and ultimately understood by carefully manipulating experimental conditions and observing the changes in behavior. They reason that if the basic processes and mechanisms can be revealed then a wide range of skills/tasks can be understood without having to study directly each specific instance. This approach is contrasted with a **task-oriented approach,** which emphasizes the effect of environmental conditions and restraints on specific tasks without regard to the underlying cognitive processes. This approach appeared to guide much of the research in the 1940s to 1970s. However, in the mid-1970s dissatisfaction with this approach increased with the emergence of the process-oriented approach in cognitive psychology. The process-oriented approach guided much of the motor learning and control research into the 1990s. Only recently have a number of influential contemporary motor learning and control researchers begun promoting a return to the task-oriented approach because they feel that motor behavior can be shaped by the opportunities (affordances) and restrictions (constraints) imposed by the environment on tasks.

DIVERSITY OF MOVEMENT

Motor skills are very difficult to categorize. However, there have been a number of attempts to classify movements along different dimensions. Let's take a look at some of them.

Task and Environmental Dimensions

It is useful to describe motor skills on two somewhat independent continuums. One continuum involves the structure of the task and the other pertains to the environment in which the task is performed. The task dimension involves the extent to which the movement termination is known prior to movement initiation. **Discrete movements** have a distinct beginning and a distinct ending. Motor skills such as serving in tennis, driving in golf, shooting in basketball, or writing your name are discrete motor skills. The majority if not all of the processing activities for these movements can occur prior to movement initiation. On the other hand, **continuous movements** have no distinct ending. Attempting to catch a parakeet in a cage, running or tackling in football, or guarding an opponent in basketball are

HIGHLIGHT

The Life and Legacy of Franklin Henry

Franklin Henry is considered by many to be the father of the discipline of motor learning and control. The following is part of an "in memorium" article in the Winter 1994 newsletter of the North American Society for Psychology of Sport and Physical Activity.

Franklin M. Henry, Professor Emeritus, Department of Human Biodynamics, passed away in Oakland, California, on September 13, 1993. During his long and illustrious career, "Doc" Henry (as he was fondly known) directed more than eighty master's and doctoral degrees in his own and other departments. Former students hold distinguished professorships and chair departments at colleges and universities throughout the world. For more than three decades, Professor Henry's research significantly advanced our understanding of metabolism and cardiovascular function during exercise, fundamental tenets of motor learning, and the specificity of training. More than 120 articles appeared in such journals as *Science, American Journal of Physiology, Journal of Applied Physiology, American Journal of Psychology, Journal of Experimental Psychology,* and *Research Quarterly.*

His inquisitive nature was a source of inspiration for hundreds of young men and women. His inventive skills served him well. While still an undergraduate, he designed research instruments for Professor Harold Jones (Psychology) and Dr. Nathan Shock (Physiology). Like many scientists of his generation, Professor Henry constructed most of the equipment that

HIGHLIGHT 8.1   *The Father of Motor Learning and Control—Franklin Henry* (Photo credit: Hearst Gymnasium Historical Collection, Department of Biodynamics, University of California)

he and his students needed to carry out their investigations. He was intolerant of careless work and a thorough and demanding teacher. He was also exceedingly kind, providing for students both intellectual and material support.

Franklin Henry was also deeply committed to his profession. At a national meeting in 1964, he set forth a cogent assessment of why physical education must be conceived of as an academic field with roots in both the biomedical and the psychosocial sciences. This address, reprinted innumerable times, prompted wide-ranging discussions and fostered a number of significant developments in this country and abroad. He served on editorial boards of the *Journal of Applied Physiology, Journal of Motor Behavior,* and other publications. He was an Associate Editor of the *Research Quarterly* for well over a decade.

A Fellow of the American Psychological Association and the American Academy of Physical Education (which honored him in 1972 with the coveted Hetherington Award), Professor Henry was also a mem-ber of the American Association for the Advancement of Science, the American Alliance for Health, Physical Education, Recreation, and Dance, and other professional associations. The American College of Sports Medicine acknowledged his outstanding contributions in 1975 with its highest scientific distinction—the Honor Award. In 1983, a Physician and Sports Medicine feature article described him as a "pioneer" in the field. The North American Society for the Psychology of Sport and Physical Activity honored Franklin in 1981 with the first Distinguished Scholar Award.

examples of continuous motor skills. These skills cannot be completely preplanned. Changes in the environment dictate that information processing activities must be utilized throughout the movement.

Poulton (1957), in an attempt to characterize motor skills, classified movement on a second continuum related to the environment in which the skill is performed. **Closed environments** are relatively stable such that conditions do not change from moment to moment. For example, the environmental conditions you encounter in bowling are relatively fixed. The pins do not move unless you hit them with the ball and the condition of the lane remains somewhat constant from frame to frame. The tasks required in closed environments often require very precise movements. This affects the character of the task by necessitating special processing demands that may not be required in open environments. In bowling, very minor variations in the response production can result in poor performance. The same is true for golf, archery, and target shooting. In these latter examples, the environment is somewhat less stable than the environment in bowling. For example, changes in weather (gusty winds or rain) may vary from instant to instant such that a response prepared under one set of conditions may not be appropriate for the conditions a few minutes or even a few seconds later.

PICTURE 8.2 *Extremely skilled athletes appear to be able to uncouple the movements of their arms. As Michael Jordan uses one arm to gently tip the ball, he exerts a great deal of force with the other arm to fend off his opponent.* (Photo credit: Reuters/ Corbis-Bettmann)

In **open environments,** the conditions are continually changing. Responses cannot be planned very long in advance because the conditions under which the response is planned have the potential to change very rapidly. In many cases, open environments are created because an opponent is involved. Opponents in tennis, wrestling, basketball, and football attempt to make the skill environment unstable. They realize that by creating uncertainty as to what is happening or will happen, they can gain an advantage. In football, the offensive team varies the snap count and the play in order to create uncertainty as to what will happen and when. Disguise and misdirection are an integral part of many sports skills. Many plays in football are created to appear like some other play so as to disguise the true intention of the offensive team. It is interesting to note that continuous skills are demanded more often in open environments because the ending to the skill cannot be accurately defined prior to the initiation of the movement. Alternately, discrete motor skills are often more appropriate in closed environments because the performer is generally afforded enough time to pre-plan the movement and the movement plan can be specified in advance.

Gentile, Higgins, Miller, and Rosen (1975) have applied the concept of open and closed environments to a single skill (see Figure 8.1). Using batting in baseball as an example, they suggest that a progression from T-ball to baseball could be used to gradually introduce complexity to the skill of batting by reducing the information load that must be processed. T-ball presents fewer demands than normal baseball. Progressions like this are used extensively in youth sports programs and elementary physical education programs.

Stages of Learning

Think about a specific motor skill you have practiced many times. The motor skill may be typing, playing a piano, serving a tennis ball, or hitting a baseball. Many changes occur as a task becomes better learned. Compare your

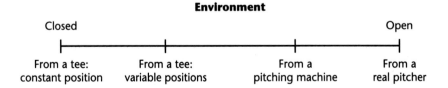

FIGURE 8.1 Diagram illustrating how hitting a baseball can be adapted from a closed environment to an open environment. This transition offers a good progression for skill development. (Adapted from Gentile, Higgins, Miller, & Rosen, 1975)

performance now and when you first attempted the task. In 1964, Fitts proposed three stages of learning: the cognitive stage, the associative stage, and the autonomous stage. At each stage, the manner in which we process information may change just as our performance changes.

Cognitive Stage. The **cognitive stage** begins when the learner is first introduced to the motor task. The learner must determine the objective of the skill as well as the relational and environmental cues that control and regulate the movements. Think about attempting a new video game. What do the changes in sound mean, the changes in color, or movement? What stimuli are important to attend to? What stimuli are simply distractions? What alternatives are available? What are the best choices to make? When? Which controls do what? Is speed, steadiness, or accuracy important? So many stimuli are available but so much is unimportant or distracting. The stimuli that you attend to must be carefully selected and then organized and interpreted. In this stage the performer is more concerned with what to do than how to do it. It is too soon to concentrate on refining the movement.

Associative Stage. The **associative stage** is concerned with performing and refining the skill. The important stimuli have been identified and their meaning is known. Conscious decisions about what to do become more automatic. Now the performer concentrates more on the task. How can the movements be timed better, made more efficient, or accomplished more quickly? For example, the typist begins to group letters or even words together to be typed as a single unit. As this integration process continues, attention demands appear to be reduced. The performer seems less rushed and better able to attend to other stimuli not related to the task.

Autonomous Stage. The **autonomous stage** is characterized by a nearly automatic kind of performance. The performer seems to be performing on "autopilot." It is not unusual to see a skilled typist, pianist, or even someone playing a difficult video game who can say hello to a friend without apparent interruption to the primary task. Their performance as well as the information they process have changed as a result of extensive practice. At this stage of learning, it may even be detrimental to attempt to consciously control the movement. For example, all of us can walk without difficulty under normal circumstances. However, if we have to walk across a stage in front of a group of people, we may attempt to consciously control our gait. The result may be that our normal gait pattern is disrupted and our walking is changed.

THEORETICAL PERSPECTIVES

The following section should serve as a review if you have just finished reading the previous chapter addressing motor development (Chapter 7). You should be familiar with the two most commonly adopted theoretical frameworks used in motor learning since they are the same as two contemporary positions used in the development area. These are the information processing and dynamical systems perspectives. Let's take a look at each of them from a motor learning and control viewpoint.

Information Processing

Recall that from the information processing perspective, humans are viewed as active processors of information rather than as passive recipients. We do not always respond to the same stimuli in the same way. We consider the current circumstances and past experiences stored in memory before formulating a course of action. We seek out information and interpret stimuli based on the context in which it is presented. The basic assumption of the information processing approach is that when an individual performs a movement, a number of cognitive processes are performed in order for the movement to be executed correctly.

Consider a tennis player about to receive a serve. The player must utilize sight and sound to determine how fast the ball is moving, where it is going, and what type of spin has been imparted to the ball. This information along with information stored in memory from similar past situations is used to plan and execute an appropriate return. Reflect on movements you make everyday. What are the processes involved in those movements?

The model presented in Figure 8.2 represents a simplified attempt to depict the major events in human information processing. The model assumes that the performer accepts sensory input (information) via the various sensory receptors. The information is transmitted to the central nervous system (CNS), where the information is processed. These processes result in commands transmitted to the musculature that are tailored to the specific environmental demands and the intentions of the performer. Hence the label **information processing.**

In describing the model, it is convenient to choose an arbitrary starting point for the flow of information. For example, while waiting at a traffic signal the light turns green (stimulus); the light from the traffic signal reaches the sensory receptors in the eyes. This stimulus information is transmitted to the CNS, where the information is processed. The end result is that

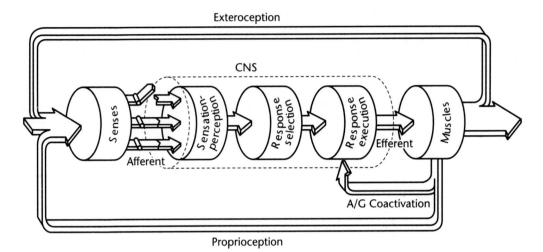

FIGURE 8.2   An information processing model. Note that information flows from left to right. (From Shea, Shebilske, & Worchel, *Motor Learning and Control.* Copyright © 1993 by Allyn & Bacon. Reprinted by permission.)

impulses are transmitted to the muscles in your legs and feet that cause your foot to be taken off the brake so that you may begin to depress the accelerator. However, the model does not necessarily suggest a point at which a sequence of events begins that ultimately result in movement, but rather depicts a continuous flow of information. Sensory receptors continually bombard the CNS with volleys of input and the result is a nearly constant output to the muscles. As a result of movement a whole new sensory perspective is available.

Traditional information processing models have generally depicted a serial flow of information (Martiniuk, 1976). The model illustrated in Figure 8.2 is a serial processing model. The model separates the processes into central and peripheral components. **Central processes** are categorized as sensation-perception, response selection, and response execution processes. **Peripheral processes** involve the activation of sensory receptors and muscles as well as the transmission to (afferent) and from (efferent) the CNS. This section will concentrate on the central processes, although an understanding of the important features of the peripheral components is important to understanding the processing of information. For example, it is important to understand that **exteroceptors** such as vision, audition (hearing), taste, and smell provide us with a description of the world around us and **proprioceptors** such as the muscle spindles, Golgi tendon organs, and various pressure and temperature receptors provide us with knowledge of the current state of our body.

Sensation-Perception.   The first major class of processing is termed sensation-perception. Neural transmission from tens of thousands of sensory receptors must first be sensed and then perceived. **Sensation** involves the detecting and/or selecting of specific sensory transmissions from the continual barrage of transmissions constantly impacting the central nervous system. So much information is available that the resources available for information processing cannot possibly act on all of them. What happens when a friend whispers to you in class? Do you hear what the professor is saying or do you listen to your friend? Can you do both?

Only after stimuli are sensed can they be perceived. **Perception** involves long-term memory such that the sensations are given meaning. Thus sensations can be organized, classified, and interpreted. The movement of a few dots on a computer monitor is perceived such that they are recognized as a moving ball, an outline of a hand, or a person (see Figure 8.3). A sound is no longer a simple auditory sensation but a bell indicating class is over. The visual information representing the contours of a face now represent a specific friend. A light touch on your arm might invoke fear when you are working around a wasps' nest, or warmth when in the company of a loved one. Perceptual processing considers the current circumstances and past experiences in interpreting sensations.

Response Selection.   The second class of processing, **response selection,** utilizes current information and past experiences to formulate a course of action or inaction. Consider a batter in baseball. The batter must utilize

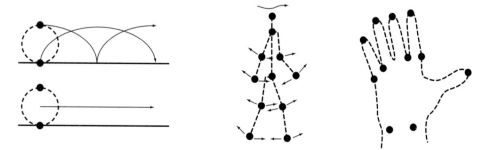

FIGURE 8.3   Three illustrations of how we actively impose organization on moving objects.

information from sensation-perceptual processing of the pitcher's motion, movement of the ball, instruction from the coach, situation in the game, position of the fielders, the count, and so on to plan an appropriate action. Swing or don't swing? Take it to right field or left? Bunt or hit away? As the number of alternatives and the complexity of the situation increase, so does the difficulty of response selection processing.

Response selection can involve a conscious decision or a nonconscious translation. Decisions are required when two or more alternatives are considered. Translation involves relating a particular stimulus to a particular response. Sometimes stimuli and responses are highly compatible. That is, a particular stimulus nearly automatically elicits a particular response. In Figure 8.4 (left), the compatibility between the lights and the response buttons is relatively high. However, responses to the light–button arrangement in Figure 8.4 (right) will require a good deal of translation. Subjects perform more slowly when the compatibility is low (right) than when the compatibility is high (left).

Response Execution.   The third class of processing is termed **response execution.** The product of the response selection stage can be likened to the floor plan an architect devises for a house. It provides the general features of what the final product should look like but does not include the detail necessary to actually construct the house. The **action plan** is the detail, the step-by-step sequence of events that make up the planned movement. The sequence of commands to the muscles must be coordinated both hierarchically and sequentially. In this context, hierarchical means that changes in posture must precede changes in limb position, or commands to stabilize

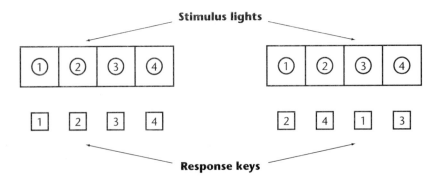

FIGURE 8.4   Two configurations of lights and keys. The one on the left offers higher compatibility than the one on the right.

the shoulder must precede commands to the arm and hand. Similarly, sequential organization involves the timing and ordering of the various muscle commands.

A Dynamical Systems Perspective

The notion that humans process information in much the same way that a computer processes data is not the only way to view motor performance and learning. A number of extremely well-respected scientists are critical of the information processing analogies used to explain motor behavior. These scientists propose an alternative viewpoint that has come to be known as the dynamical systems perspective (e.g., Bernstein, 1967; Kelso, 1984; Turvey, 1990).

The Degrees of Freedom Problem. Bernstein (1967) argued that many of the traditional views of motor control and information processing propose that subjects must directly control the many degrees of freedom in the human body in order to produce coordinated movement. Turvey (1990) proposes that the human body is comprised of nearly 100 degrees of freedom (joints), 1000 muscles, and 100 trillion cells that must be appropriately organized and controlled. Bernstein maintained that this direct control would place tremendous organizational and computational demands on the brain. The question then is, how is the human body controlled without placing overwhelming demands on the brain?

Synergies or Coordinative Structures. Muscle/tendons groups are functionally grouped to support movement across joints and neurologically linked as a result of the neural circuits in the spinal cord. The functional group formed by this linkage between muscle groups is termed a **synergy** or **coordinative structure.** What does this mean? The activation of one muscle group is related in subtle but potentially important ways to other muscle groups. Bernstein (1967; first published 1940) and later Turvey (1977) note that these linkages may play an important role in reducing the difficulty of controlling movement.

To understand the concept of synergies or coordinative structures, consider the example of a puppeteer attempting to control the movement of a marionette. Each joint or body part of the marionette is connected to a string that the puppeteer can use to control the movement. Do puppeteers attempt to control each string independently or have these artists learned that they can link the strings together in some fashion to decrease the difficulty but

PICTURE 8.3 *Each joint of the marionette is attached to a string that the puppeteer can use to control the movement. Puppeteers do not try to control each string independently, rather they attach the strings to a paddle in such a way that the movement of the paddle produces movements of the head, arms, and legs simultaneously.* (Photo credit: Photofest)

still achieve relatively complex movements? Indeed, they have found a way to configure the strings on a paddle such that relatively complex movements like walking—including not only leg movements but head and arm movements as well—can be realistically created by simply tilting the paddle back and forth.

Engineers use this principle whenever possible in designing machinery. Consider an airplane control example provided by Tuller, Turvey, and Fitch (1982). They noted that the ailerons on the wings, the elevators on the tail, and the rudder on the tailfin of an airplane must be coordinated to achieve efficient flight control. Would it be effective for the engineers to design the control system so that the pilot had to control the ailerons, elevators, and rudder independently? No! This would overload the pilot. Evasive maneuvers would be almost impossible.

Tuller and colleagues (1982) point out:

> What is needed is a way of organizing the parts of an airplane so as to simplify its control without losing its desirable maneuverability. One way to do this is to link parts of the system together. First, the aileron and the rudder can be linked into a functional relationship; when the aileron on the left goes up by one position, the rudder goes to the right by one position. . . . Next, the right aileron can be linked to the rudder so that when the right aileron moves up the rudder moves to the left. . . . Think of what we are attempting to do. We are trying to make the airplane manageable. . . . Initially, the airplane has five independent parts each capable of assuming nine different positions. . . . Now three of those parts have been banded together into a single entity, the aileron-rudder subsystem (p. 257).

The point of this discussion is not just about marionettes or airplanes but about efficient control systems. There is every reason to believe that the human control system is the most elegant system ever assembled and that synergies are an integral part of this system.

Bimanual Movements.   While the dynamical systems approach relying on coordinative structures potentially reduces the demands on the control system, it may pose difficulties under some conditions. Consider that your hands/arms are constrained to act as a functional unit. What happens when you wish to uncouple this functional unit? To answer this question simply try rubbing your stomach and patting your head. This is difficult without practice because it requires you to undo a long-established and coordinated structure between limbs. Even after practice on this task, you will find that your head patting is still linked in some subtle way to rubbing your stomach.

Kelso, Southward, and Goodman (1979) required subjects to make aiming movements with the left, right, and both hands. According to speed–accuracy relationships (to be discussed in a subsequent section), subjects' movement time should be reduced when the target is closer or larger. This was the case for single hand/arm movements (Figure 8.5, Conditions 1 through 4). This was also the case for bimanual movements with the same requirements (Conditions 5 and 6). However, when the movement of one hand required a different distance to be traversed or a different size target to be contacted than the other hand, both hands/arms appeared to be constrained to act as a unit. This resulted in longer movement time for the shorter distance or larger target (Conditions 7 and 8) than that occurring when the limb was acting alone.

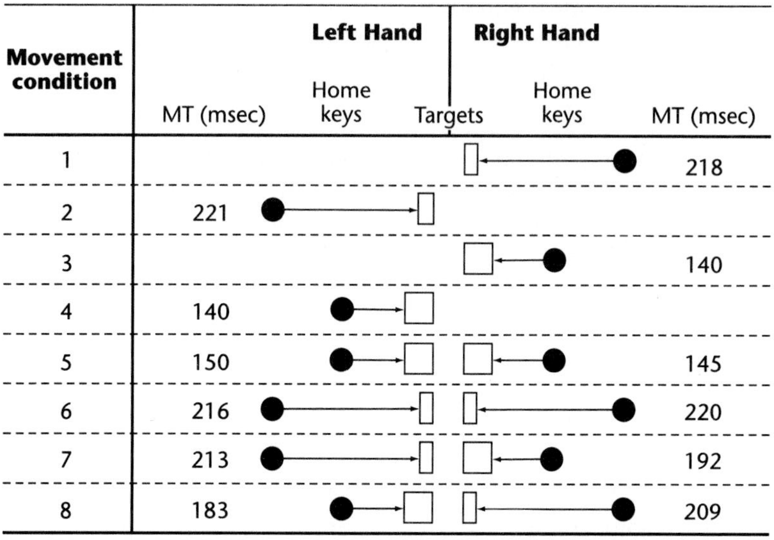

Movement condition	Left Hand			Right Hand	
	MT (msec)	Home keys	Targets	Home keys	MT (msec)
1				▯←⎯⎯⎯⎯●	218
2	221	●⎯⎯⎯⎯→▯			
3				▯←⎯⎯●	140
4	140	●⎯→▯			
5	150	●⎯→▯	▯←⎯→●		145
6	216	●⎯⎯⎯⎯→▯	▯←⎯⎯⎯⎯●		220
7	213	●⎯⎯⎯⎯→▯	▯←⎯⎯●		192
8	183	●⎯⎯⎯→▯	▯←⎯⎯⎯⎯●		209

FIGURE 8.5   Average movement times for one- and two-handed movements to targets of different distances and sizes. Note that in two-handed movements, the two hands move together. (From Shea, Shebilske, & Worchel, *Motor Learning and Control.* Copyright © 1993 by Allyn & Bacon. Reprinted by permission.)

In a related experiment, subjects were asked to move both hands from a home position to adjacent targets. Distance and target size were the same for both hands but a cardboard barrier was placed between the home position and the target for one hand but not the other. If the limbs were controlled independently, the limb without the barrier should take a direct route to the target and arrive before the other limb. This was not the case. Both limbs arrived at virtually the same time taking essentially the same route.

CONTROLLING MOVEMENT

When watching a young pianist play a complicated musical score, a grandmother crocheting, Michael Jackson performing dance steps, or even a child learning to walk, we all should be amazed at the degree of motor control required to perform movement. Remember, movement is our way of communicating with the world. Facial expressions, speech, and hand gestures are the basis of formal communication, but we communicate more subtly with movements when we play, work, or perform a skill. The following section will discuss important factors affecting our ability to move.

Role of Feedback in Motor Control

Recall from Chapter 3 that the central nervous system is continually receiving feedback from the various sensory receptors. Consider the information that an athlete's senses are relaying to their brain during competition. Feedback is unquestionably used in the selection of a response and the formulation of an action plan. The question that remains, however, is the extent to which this feedback is utilized in the control of an ongoing movement. Does the athlete actively process information during a movement or had they practiced the response to the extent that it could be executed nearly automatically? This question has been debated in the literature for years (see Adams, 1971, and Schmidt, 1976, for reviews).

Closed-Loop Control.   It is thought (see Adams's closed-loop theory) that feedback can be used not only to plan and initiate movements but to adjust the progress of an ongoing movement. Consider a task like threading a needle (Figure 8.6). As you move the needle and the thread closer together, it may become necessary to engage in additional information processing activities to complete the task. On the basis of feedback, it may become apparent that the thread is not moving on a trajectory to meet the eye of the needle. This information is then processed and a corrected trajectory is

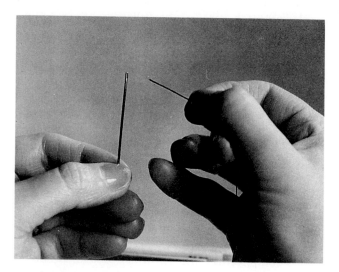

FIGURE 8.6   When attempting to thread a needle, you must continually compare the position of the head of the needle and the end of the thread to adjust your movement. (Photo credit: Corbis-Bettmann)

effected. The sequence may be repeated until the thread successfully passes through the eye of the needle. In a sense, athletes sometimes have to thread the needle with their response.

Adams (1971) states:

> A closed-loop system has feedback, error detection, and error correction as key elements. There is a reference that specifies the desired value for the system, and the output of the system is fed back and compared to the reference for error detection and, if necessary, corrected. The automatic home furnace is a common example. The thermostat setting is the desired value, and the heat output of the furnace is fed back and compared against this reference. If there is a discrepancy the furnace cuts in or out until the error is zero. A closed-loop system is self-regulating by compensating for deviations from the reference (p. 116).

Closed-loop control does not require detailed initial movement commands. Adjustments based on response-produced feedback can be used to adjust the progress of the movement. Thus, movement control is regulated by an error-nulling process and the movement is completed only when all perceptible error has been eliminated.

Advantages and Disadvantages.   Closed-loop control has three major advantages and two significant disadvantages. The first advantage is that closed-loop control can be utilized to produce movements in new situations. As long as the performer can determine the discrepancy between the current position and the desired position, a correction can be executed. Second, a great deal of movement flexibility can be exhibited under closed loop control. This is because movement control is not dependent on specifying in advance the exact movement path required to achieve a movement goal but rather involves nulling the error between a current movement state and a desired state. Consider the problem of catching a fish in an aquarium. The desired outcome is to catch the pet in a net. The movement required to achieve this goal may require a very flexible movement plan that is determined by the movement of the pet. Lastly, closed-loop control can be used to produce very accurate movement outcomes. Consider threading a needle or removing a small splinter in your finger. These movements require a great deal of precision and are clearly controlled by closed-loop processes.

The price that the performer pays for closed-loop control may be significant in some situations. First, the execution of corrections in closed-loop control appears to be attention-demanding. Moving to a small target is more attention-demanding than moving to a larger target, especially as the subject approaches the target. Presumably this is due to more corrections being required as greater accuracy is necessary. However, the greatest disadvantage of closed-loop control is the time required to execute successive corrections. Keele and Posner (1968) have suggested that approximately 200 milliseconds are required to produced visually based corrections. Later research suggests that correction can be affected more quickly than 200 milliseconds but the visual feedback loop is certainly not less than 100 milliseconds. Thus, closed-loop control may be limited to relatively slow movements.

Open-Loop Control.   Open-loop control is based on the concept of a motor program. The motor program concept has a long history in explaining behavior that is difficult to explain by closed-loop principles. A motor program was defined as a "set of muscle commands that are structured before a movement sequence begins, and that allows the sequence to be carried out uninfluenced by peripheral feedback" (Keele, 1968, p. 387). This definition suggested that a motor program was the biological analog to a computer program. This analogy may be unfortunate because the nervous system is quite different from a computer and a motor program may be quite different from the simple computer programs with which most of us are familiar. However, one useful aspect of the analogy is that more sophisticated computer programs can be programmed to be somewhat flexible in their operation and can be instructed to receive input from the operator or some sensing device.

Consider the many movements you execute each day that appear to be controlled almost automatically. These movements may be controlled by a motor program. Many experts believe that at least parts of a gymnastic routine would have to be controlled by a motor program. The routines are extremely well practiced and consistently performed. Indeed, many coaches tell their advanced gymnasts not to think about the routine: "Just do it, let it flow." Could it be that these athletes have developed motor programs?

Advantages and Disadvantages.   Open-loop control has two major advantages and two disadvantages. The first advantage is so obvious that it is easily overlooked. Open-loop control can produce very rapid movement or movements under conditions in which normal feedback sources have been eliminated or disrupted. Secondly, because open-loop control is prestructured, feedback does not have to be processed during the movement, and attention normally allocated to making corrections (and presumably other information-processing activities) is not necessary. This permits the performer to engage in other strategic processing that would not be possible if closed-loop control was employed.

The disadvantages of open-loop control are also somewhat obvious. As Adams (1976) states:

> An open-loop system has no feedback or mechanism for error regulation. The input events for a system exert their influence, the system effects its transformation on the input, and the system has an output. A traffic light with fixed timing snarls traffic when the load is heavy and impedes the flow when traffic is light. The system has no compensatory capability. (p. 89)

Open-loop control is not effective when the environmental conditions are constantly changing such that the demands of the movement cannot be determined in advance. Likewise, movements that require a great deal of precision may require extensive amounts of practice for an efficient motor program to be developed.

Schema Theory: Generalizable Motor Programs

In 1975 Schmidt proposed a schema theory of motor learning. A **schema** is an abstraction or a set of rules for determining a movement. Because the important features of a potentially large number of specific movements can be abstracted in a schema, memory and retrieval requirements are greatly reduced. In addition, Schmidt proposes that novel movements can be generated because the rules encapsulated in the schema can be applied to new movements within a class of movements. Thus schema theory proposes that movements are controlled by a generalizable motor program.

The product is a generalizable motor program that, when provided response specifications, produces a unique response. The program is composed of **invariant features** that define the generalizable characteristics of the motor program. These features are thought to include the hierarchical characteristics of the movement (termed order of elements by Schmidt, 1975), the relative forces, and relative timing. Since the invariant features consist only of the relative characteristics of the movement, the program must be scaled or parameterized in order to produce a specific movement. Based on the specific requirements, the **variant features** of the program that must be specified are thought to include the specific muscles to be used, the actual force, and actual timing of the movement.

Consider the handwriting example in Figure 8.7. Assume for the sake of the example that the writing (in cursive) of your name is controlled by a generalizable motor program. As a result of practice experiences, the generalizable motor program is well developed. The invariant features of the generalizable signature program consist of the hierarchical structure such

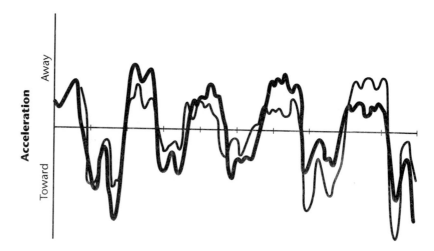

FIGURE 8.7   Vertical acceleration produced by subject's writing the word "hell" with one execution having half the amplitude of the other. (From Shea, Shebilske, & Worchel, *Motor Learning and Control.* Copyright © 1993 by Allyn & Bacon. Reprinted by permission.)

that the order of the elements (letters) does not change from one execution to another. Likewise, our signature results in a consistent but relative pattern of innervations both in terms of time and force. Specific points in the production of the signature are consistently produced with more force relative to other points and the flow of the pattern consistently maintains a relative timing or flow pattern.

By scaling your generalizable signature program, you can easily produce your signature within the lines of fine-lined paper or on the blackboard (specify muscle groups), with the light touch of a felt tip pen or by scratching onto a desk top (specify actual force). Similarly, your signature can be executed very quickly or very slowly (specify actual timing). Depending on the specific demands, you can produce your signature in many ways without violating the invariant features or basic structure derived from the generalizable motor program.

Speed–Accuracy Trade-Off

When we perform a skilled movement, we are often concerned with speed and accuracy. However, when we increase the speed with which we do something, we tend to increase the number of errors we make. To perform more accurately, we must slow down. This basic principle has come to be known as the **speed–accuracy trade-off** because performers must trade off speed in order to increase accuracy or trade off accuracy to increase speed.

In 1899, Woodworth studied the relationship between the speed and accuracy of a repetitive line-drawing task. Subjects were required to draw lines with a pencil back and forth between two lines (targets). The subjects attempted to stop each movement at the targets but were required to keep pace with a metronome. The speed of the movement was increased or decreased by varying the metronome. In one set of experiments, Woodworth had subjects perform with their eyes open or closed and movement velocity was manipulated by changing the setting on the metronome (Figure 8.8). When subjects were permitted to view their movements, the average distance from the target increased as movement velocity increased. When eyes were closed, errors were quite large. The findings that accuracy decreased as movement speed increased forms the basis for some of the fundamental principles of motor control.

Fitts' Law and the Index of Difficulty.   In 1954 Paul Fitts conducted a series of experiments on the relationship between speed and accuracy of simple aiming movements. Fitts, an industrial engineer, attempted to apply mathematical and information-processing concepts to the study of these simple movements. Subjects attempted to tap back and forth between two targets with a stylus as quickly as possible. The amplitude (A) between targets and the width (W) of the targets were manipulated. The task was scored as the number of taps in 20 seconds. This score could be transformed into average movement time (MT) by dividing the number of taps into 20 seconds.

FIGURE 8.8   As the velocity of the movement increases, the difference between the eyes-open and eyes-closed conditions is reduced. (From Shea, Shebilske, & Worchel, *Motor Learning and Control*. Copyright © 1993 by Allyn & Bacon. Reprinted by permission.)

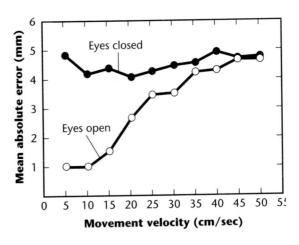

Fitts (1954) systematically manipulated target width and amplitude. His experiments suggest two fundamental points. First, subjects' performances are more sensitive to changes in target width than amplitude. Thus target width must be weighted more heavily than target amplitude. Second, Fitts found it useful to characterize the relationship as a linear function or straight line. To do this he multiplied the factors by Log_2. Thus, Fitts proposed an **index of difficulty (ID)** as the following equation:

$$ID = \log_2(2A/W)$$

Perhaps the most remarkable aspect of this relationship is the wide range of tasks that appear to follow **Fitts' Law.** The relationship seems to hold for single aiming movements in air or water; moving a joystick, handle, or cursor; throwing darts, and even for eye movements.

FACTORS AFFECTING LEARNING AND PERFORMANCE

When we plan practice sessions, we assume that the session will improve the participants' capability to perform the skill being practiced. In some cases research has questioned the efficacy of traditional practice formats. This section will introduce the reader to factors that should be considered in designing practice sessions that will optimize the later performance of the skill and increase the performers' ability to adapt to new movement demands.

Acquisition, Retention, and Transfer

One of the prime objectives in motor learning is to determine the acquisition conditions under which motor skills will be best learned. **Acquisition** refers to experiences provided to a learner that are thought to enhance learning. It will be helpful to view acquisition as the stage in which the concern is primarily with providing experiences that improve learning and not with demonstrating how well the player, student, or subject can perform. This is an important concept because some manipulations that ultimately improve learning result in poor performance during acquisition. In this regard it is useful to distinguish between two related learning objectives, retention and transfer. **Retention** refers to delayed practice experiences (test or game) on a task that was experienced during acquisition. If we practice a task and then are tested at a later time on that task, the test would be considered a retention test. **Transfer,** on the other hand, refers to practice experiences on a variation of the task or on another task that was not experienced during acquisition.

Transfer Paradigm.   Acquisition, retention, and transfer performance are evaluated in what is commonly termed a **transfer paradigm,** which involves two distinct phases (see Salmoni, Schmidt, & Walters, 1984). In the acquisition phase the independent variable of interest is manipulated. That is, different groups receive different treatments. After the acquisition phase is completed, the retention or transfer phase is conducted (Figure 8.9). Prior to this phase, a period of time is allowed to elapse so that any temporary effects of the acquisition conditions (e.g., fatigue, frustration) will dissipate. Then the groups are assessed under a common level of the independent variable. This permits evaluation of the relatively permanent effects of acquisition manipulations relatively uninfluenced by other, more temporary effects specific to the acquisition manipulations. An important consideration for the experimenter is under what common condition(s) should retention and/or transfer be assessed. This is a difficult question because a group(s) switched to a new condition may perform more poorly just because the condition is new. Likewise if subjects under one condition are tested under that condition, they may have an advantage simply because they are familiar with the conditions. The use of this paradigm is very important to the study of learning.

Distinction between Performance and Learning.   Before taking a closer look at the factors affecting the learning and performance of motor

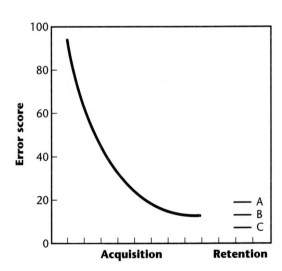

FIGURE 8.9   Possible outcomes in an experiment involving acquisition and retention tests.

skills, it is important to review the distinction between performance and learning. It will be especially important to distinguish between temporary factors that affect performance and the factors that contribute to the relatively permanent changes in performance, termed learning.

For example, a teacher could have a group of beginning bowlers wear a special visor that would not permit them to see the pins but would allow them to see the lane marks near the scratch line. Another group would not be required to wear the visor. Would there be a difference in the performance of the two groups? Would you expect a difference in learning? Surely the visor would at least temporarily affect performance; thus it would be considered a performance variable. It is not so clear, however, whether the use of the visor would affect learning. To assess the influence on learning, it would not be appropriate to simply look at the scores at the end of the bowling unit. The two groups are performing under different conditions. The performance of the two groups must be assessed under the same conditions; probably without the visor. What prediction would you make concerning temporary performance effects and more stable changes related to learning?

If differences are observed during practice, performance effects are indicated. If differences are observed during a retention test under common conditions, learning effects are indicated. This distinction is critical to the interpretation of the experiments conducted on information feedback (see Salmoni, Schmidt, & Walter, 1984 for review).

Information Feedback

Feedback is important for all aspects of motor behavior. Feedback, in one form or another, is our brain's only link to the body and to the environment. Feedback indicates that we are hungry, tired, fatigued, that we should do something, that we should do nothing, that we are in danger, that we are embarrassed, or that we are comfortable. Right now innumerable sensory receptors located throughout your body are communicating with various centers of your brain. Stop for a second and pay attention to the sensations. What do you feel? What you consciously feel is feedback, but many other sources of feedback of which you are not conscious play important roles in your life, in your control of movement, and in the process of learning.

Classifications of Information Feedback.   In our discussion of feedback we will be concerned with feedback sources that influence the performance and learning of motor skills. We do not mean to suggest that the many other sources of feedback that contribute to the regulation of bodily

Feedback and the Vitual World

Imagine you could sit in a chair at home and experience skiing down a mountainside in Colorado. Close your eyes for a short time. Imagine what this ski experience might be like. Your boots feel tight and there is a nip in the air. Now you feel light as you ride on the chair lift as the breeze moves by your face. Your eyes water because you are not wearing your goggles. At the top you begin your descent. Can you describe some of the sensations or feedback you will experience? Yet you are not in Colorado but at home

HIGHLIGHT 8.2   *VPL Research in Redwood City, CA has developed a virtual reality system that simulates driving a car. Is skiing far behind?* (Photo credit: © Bob Strong/The Image Works)

relaxed in a comfortable chair. How can this be?

Virtual environments or virtual reality already exist in many research laboratories around the United States and the rest of the world. Much of the work initially involved providing the visual stimulation an individual might experience in a particular situation such as skiing. This was achieved by having participants wear specially designed helmets through which very persuasive visual information could be displayed to convince them they were moving. However, more contemporary work goes beyond simulating just visual experiences, such as by using gloves specially outfitted with fiber optic devices that allow movements of the hand to be displayed in a virtual world. One area for which this technology has important implications is microsurgery in which a device might be controlled by the movement of the surgeon's hand while he or she views a realistic display of the inside of the heart.

Of course, there are many other important applications of this technology. One of the primary markets for this modern presentation of feedback is in the computer game industry.

function and homeostasis are not important to life or even movement behavior. However, we will eliminate from our discussion the many sources of sensory feedback that are not directly related to skill learning. We also will not concentrate on sensory feedback available prior to the initiation of movement even though this information is critical to the decision and planning process. Instead, we will concentrate on feedback sources that can be manipulated to improve performance and learning. This can take many forms in learning environments, but generally serves the role of providing information to performers about the proficiency with which they move.

For our purposes it will be helpful to classify information into two categories: knowledge of results and knowledge of performance. **Knowledge of results (KR)** is information received concerning the extent to which a response accomplished the intended movement goal. If you attempt to kick a football through the center of the goal posts, knowledge of results is that information you receive concerning your success. **Knowledge of performance (KP)** is information received about the actual performance and execution of the movement. Was the movement performed correctly or the way it was intended to be performed? This information provides a basis on which to assess the correctness of the movement pattern. Thus it is possible for the performer to receive positive KP and negative KR or vice versa. The movement can be performed correctly or the way it was intended and still not achieve its goal.

It is important to note that either KR or KP can arise from intrinsic or extrinsic sources. **Intrinsic feedback** is internal feedback normally received during and after the execution of a task. The normal sensory information received during and after hitting a baseball is intrinsic feedback. You feel the bat strike the ball and see where the ball goes without any special assistance. **Extrinsic feedback** is external feedback received during and/or after the response from some additional source. Coaches, teachers, experimenters, and even some special devices are capable of providing additional, augmented information to the performer.

Most of the researchers in motor learning consider information feedback to be a very important, if not the most important, variable affecting performance and learning. This is evident by the role information feedback plays in Adams's closed-loop theory (1971) and Schmidt's schema theory (1975). However, the important questions for most theorists concern why and how information feedback influences performance and learning. A theoretical attempt to answer this question will be discussed, but the reader should be warned that a comprehensive theory of feedback information has not yet been proposed.

Processing of Feedback.   Feedback can provide the performer with information on how to correct a movement or achieve a movement goal. That is, feedback can be used almost like a guide to follow to the correct movement and/or the movement goal. But does feedback that guides the performer positively increment performance and learning? It is relatively clear

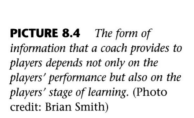

PICTURE 8.4   *The form of information that a coach provides to players depends not only on the players' performance but also on the players' stage of learning.* (Photo credit: Brian Smith)

that the guidance features of feedback can be used to influence performance positively when this source of feedback is present. However, the effects may be present only as long as the feedback is present. Indeed, research suggests that subjects may become overly dependent on KR if it is continually available. A number of experiments suggest that when KR is available that subjects fail to seek out other sources of feedback and to develop relationships between errors and responses and do not test alternative strategies.

Practice Scheduling and Composition

The purpose of practice, at least from the learning standpoint, is to improve the performer's capability to perform under game or test conditions. But what practice conditions will best improve these capabilities? Obviously there are a great number of ways in which we could spend our practice time. The important question, however, is how can we best maximize this time to improve learning? The focus of this section will be on two facets of this question: practice scheduling and practice composition. **Practice scheduling** is concerned with manipulations that cause the conditions under which, or the context within which, a specific task is executed to change. Manipulating the order with which tasks are learned or manipulating practice/rest intervals are examples of practice scheduling. **Practice composition** is manipulated by varying the task or task variations that are practiced or the manner in which tasks are practiced. Manipulations that vary the number of tasks or task variations intermingled in a practice session or vary the manner in which a task is practiced (physical, mental, observational, or simulated practice) involve practice composition.

Scheduling of Practice.   How can practice be scheduled to best enhance learning? This is a formidable question that learning psychologists have been asking at least since the time of Ebbinghaus (1885). Recent research has shown that the nature of the information processing and memory states responsible for learning are influenced by the scheduling of practice. Three interrelated types of practice schedule manipulations will be highlighted: practice distribution, contextual interference, and context effects. These areas do not comprise an exhaustive list of research involving manipulations of practice schedule but do represent classifications of research typical of recent research efforts.

Practice Distribution. **Practice distribution** concerns manipulations to the practice-rest intervals (see Adams, 1987; Lee & Genovese, 1988 for reviews and theoretical perspectives). Generally this involves changing the ratio of practice time to rest time within blocks of trials but also includes manipulations of the time between practice sessions. **Massed practice** is defined as ratios of practice intervals to rest intervals of greater than one. If practice intervals, perhaps practice trials, are packed together such that the time between practice is no longer than the time involved in actual practice, the session is said to be massed. **Distributive practice** is defined as ratios of practice intervals to rest intervals of less than one. That is, more time is devoted to the rest interval than to actual practice. While the cutoff of one has historically been used to distinguish between massed and distributed practice schedules, it may be useful to think of massed and distributed practice as the ends of a practice/time continuum.

In an analysis of the practice distribution literature, Lee and Genovese (1988) found that massed practice, relative to distributed practice, tends to depress acquisition performance. In addition, there was a tendency for distributed practice, particularly on continuous tasks, to result in better retention. The effect seemed to be the reverse for discrete tasks. It is difficult to isolate the reasons why distributed practice facilitates acquisition and retention while massed practice appears to enhance performance and learning of discrete tasks.

An alternative way to address the practice distribution question is to manipulate the number of sessions each day and the time between sessions. This question has interesting practical applications. Given that only a certain amount of practice can be allotted to a unit of instruction, teachers and coaches must decide whether to plan many short sessions or fewer longer sessions.

Baddeley and Longman (1978) taught postal workers a typing task used to sort mail. All subjects received 60 hours of instruction. Subjects were assigned to one of four groups comprised of two lengths (1 or 2 hours) and two

PICTURE 8.5 *Baddeley and Longman (1978) found that postal workers learned a typing task more quickly when taught in one hour/one session a day than a group taught in two hours/two sessions a day.* (Photo credit: Ellis Herwig/Stock Boston)

frequencies (1 or 2 sessions per day). Two groups practiced 1 hour each session. One group practiced one session a day for 12 weeks and the other group two sessions a day for 6 weeks. Two other groups practiced 2 hours a session. One group practiced one session a day for 6 weeks and the other, two sessions a day for 3 weeks.

The results related to two dependent measures are particularly interesting: time to learn the keyboard and typing speed. In terms of both time and speed measures, the 1 hour/one session group attained the criterion performance levels first. The 2 hour/two session group required the most time to attain the performance goals. Perhaps most interesting was that subjects tended to prefer the 2 hour/two session schedule better than the 1 hour/one session schedule. That is, the subjects tended to prefer the condition that resulted in the poorest performance! The Baddeley and Longman experiment may have direct application for teachers and coaches. It appears that students and athletes may benefit from shorter practice sessions distributed over more days.

Contextual Interference. When a number of tasks or task variations are experienced within practice sessions, the manner in which those tasks are organized may influence acquisition, retention, and transfer performance. At the extreme, practice schedules can be organized such that the tasks to be learned are practiced in a random order (C-A-B, B-C-A, A-B-C) or a blocked order (A-A-A, B-B-B, C-C-C). Note that both groups receive the same number of trials, spaced at the same intertrial interval. Which group would perform better during acquisition, retention, or transfer?

Shea and Morgan (1979) had subjects practice three variations of a task in either a blocked or random sequence. The task variations were similar in that each variation started (picking up a ball) and ended (placing the ball in a slot) the same, but varied in terms of the combinations and/or order in which three of the six barriers were "knocked down" (Figure 8.10). The movement time of subjects performing under random conditions was generally less than that of subjects in the blocked condition. After 10 minutes rest, retention and transfer were measured for one half of the subjects under blocked or random conditions. The other half of the subjects performed the retention and transfer tests after 10 days. Retention and transfer performance after both 10-minute and 10-day delays were significantly higher for subjects who learned the task variations under random conditions.

Shea and Morgan (1979) suggest the dramatic reversal of the random group from acquisition to retention and transfer arises as a result of the multiple and variable processing strategies adopted by subjects when faced with random conditions. Central to this theoretical position is the concept of **contextual interference.** Blocked conditions are thought to promote low contextual interference because the context remains relatively stable from trial to trial. Random schedules, on the other hand, generate high contextual interference because the context within which a given task is executed

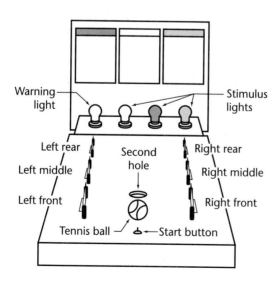

FIGURE 8.10 Barrier knock-down task used by Shea and Morgan (1979). (From Shea, Shebilske, & Worchel, *Motor Learning and Control.* Copyright © 1993 by Allyn & Bacon. Reprinted by permission.)

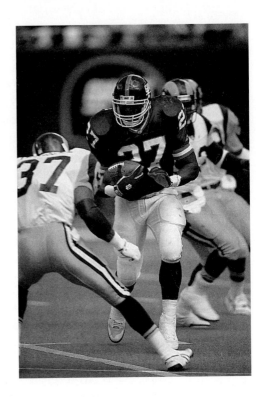

PICTURE 8.6   *Research on contextual interference suggests that football teams should practice their offensive plays in a random order. Do coaches do this?* (Photo credit: Will Hart)

changes from trial to trial. Under blocked schedules the subject is more likely to invoke similar strategies from attempt to attempt and the conditions under which memory operations occur is more likely to remain stable. This results in relatively good acquisition performance but does not enhance retention or transfer. Retention is facilitated under random schedules because the acquisition schedule induces the subject to engage in more varied processing strategies, under more varied contexts than blocked schedules.

Composition of Practice.   Another way in which practice schedules can be manipulated is by varying the composition of practice. Remember, practice composition is manipulated by varying the tasks or task variations that are practiced or the manner in which these tasks are practiced. Teachers and coaches must be concerned with the tasks that they include in practice sessions. The question of interest is, What should be practiced?

Specificity versus Variability of Practice.   Historically the question of practice composition has been discussed in terms of the specificity of learning principle, which appears to have been borrowed from the specificity of training principle in exercise physiology (Barnett, Ross, Schmidt, & Todd, 1973) and is best articulated in the work of Henry (1960) and Adams (1971). Henry's **specificity hypothesis** proposes that motor skills are specific and only superficially resemble other similar motor skills. This implies that changing the motor task only slightly produces a new motor task for which a new motor program must be developed. Adams (1971) also takes a specificity position in the formulation of the closed loop theory of motor skill acquisition. Adams emphasizes the use of sensory feedback and knowledge of results to build the perceptual trace of a specific movement. Adams (1987) reemphasizes the specificity notion and attributes the principle to the "identical elements theory" developed by Thorndike and Woodworth (1901). The central prediction of the specificity principle is that practice should be specific to the task and condition to be learned. This notion has received limited support with both gross motor and fine motor performance.

An alternative viewpoint is the variability of practice hypothesis. The **variability of practice hypothesis** states that variable but related practice experiences enhance the memory states responsible for motor control. This hypothesis was derived from schema theory. The variability of practice position, for the most part, has been discussed in terms of transfer to a novel variation of a task rather than the retention of a specific motor task. Schmidt (1975, 1976) posits that the subject does not store in memory the specific characteristics of each movement but rather abstracts the information along with knowledge of results to form a rule or schema capable of governing motor control for that class of movements. The schema notion postulates that the strength of the schema is directly related to the variability of practice that the subject receives with a particular schema class. The greater the variety of experiences, the more generalizable the response capabilities. Thus the prediction from schema theory is that increasing the variety of practice experiences leads to increased schema strength and better transfer capability.

Studies prompted by the prediction of schema theory and the variability of practice hypothesis were generally designed to determine the extent to which practice experiences contributed to transfer performance. Much more recently, studies have investigated the variability of practice hypothesis in terms of retention.

Transfer and Variability of Practice.   The typical paradigm used in the study of schema theory and variability of practice notions requires subjects to practice either one (constant practice) or a variety of task variations (variable practice) and then assesses transfer to a novel variation. According to the variability of practice hypothesis, the variable practice group should perform better on a transfer test than the constant practice group. Variable practice

 **HIGHLIGHT**

Simulators—Teaching Tools of the Future

The movie *The Last Starfighter* is about Alex Rogan, a young man especially gifted in playing video games. Alex lives in a rundown rural trailer park and is trying every way he knows to get away from home and "be something." To pass the time he plays a video game called "The

HIGHLIGHT 8.3 *Alex Rogan concentrates on mastering the Starfighter video game, unaware that it was placed on earth to recruit actual Starfighters for the Star League of Planets.* (Photo credit: The Kobal Collection)

Starfighter." One lonely night, the game salutes him as usual: "Greetings, Starfighter, you have been recruited by the Star League to defend the frontier against Xur and the Ko-Dan Armada." As Alex plays the game, he blasts enemy ships and incoming rockets; on and on he fights without defeat. Finally, breaking every previous record, he blasts the Command Ship.

As it turns out the "video game" was really a training simulator placed around the galaxy to train and test starfighters. After destroying the Command Ship, Alex is visited by a strange visitor from another world named Centari. As the movie progresses, Alex is recruited into the Star League and almost single-handedly defends the alien world from the Ko-Dan Armada.

This is certainly fiction, but how far from the truth is it? Today we use training simulators almost on a daily basis. If you took driver's education, you probably used a car simulator. If you go to the health club, you probably use a bicycle, jogging, or rowing simulator. If you were training to be a military pilot, you would log many hours in a flight simulator. Simulators are being developed at a very fast rate. As the cost of computers goes down and the power of small computers grows, the realism and utilization of simulation is increasing.

Computer-based simulator training devices are capable of carefully controlling the learning environment. The system can carefully space your practice and provide precise feedback when appropriate. In fact, systems available today are capable of prescribing practice that is specific to your strengths and weaknesses. For example, a simulator developed for the military by Lockheed Aerospace, designed to teach operators how to use the sophisticated control devices for the Patriot Missiles, keeps track of the strength and weaknesses of the operators. The system then provides realistic real-time engagements designed to test the operators' areas of strength and train them in areas of weakness. What next? A simulator for basketball? Tennis? Skiing? Keep your eyes open—it may be here before you know it.

experiences increment the memory states responsible for generating the new response to a greater extent than does constant practice. A number of studies have found that variable practice enhances the ability to transfer to a novel task variation.

Retention and Variability of Practice.   In general, teachers and coaches, preparing their students for a specific test, competition, or game, usually provide experiences specific to the game or test conditions. However, when the purpose is to develop a more general skill (e.g., throwing, jumping, hitting), variable practice is often prescribed. As discussed above, the variable practice scheme is thought to better equip the performer to produce novel task variations than specific practice. But what type of practice composition results in the best retention? Intuition and limited experimental evidence might suggest specific practice.

Part–Whole Practice.   Many motor skills, particularly complex skills, can be partitioned into relatively independent components. The question of interest is whether it is effective to design practice to include independent practice on the various components of the overall skill (see Chamberlin & Lee, 1993; Wightman & Lintern, 1985, for reviews).

Wightman and Lintern (1985) identified three methods for constructing part practice: fractionation, simplification, and segmentation. When practice is variously composed of one or more parts of the whole task, the practice is said to be fractionated. Thus the partitioning of the components to be practiced changes from practice session to practice session. A tennis coach may have his or her players practice cross-court shots (forehand then backhand and so on) or practice serve and volley segments. That is, the components are practiced in various combinations at subsequent practices.

Simplification involves reducing the demands of one or more of the task components so as to reduce the overall difficulty or complexity of the skill. In tennis, an instructor may simplify the demands by using a ball machine. The machine projects the ball to the same place at the same speed trial after trial. A similar tactic is often used in Little League baseball. The younger children play T-ball before progressing to a game in which the ball is consistently projected by a pitching machine. Eventually the Little Leaguers are introduced to the real game. Mane, Adams, and Donchin (1989) found no clear advantage of adapting the level of difficulty of a complex task (video game) by slowing the task down and then speeding it up as the subjects became more proficient. They also found substantial negative effects of practicing a simplified version when transferred to a higher level of difficulty. This negative effect, termed negative transfer, suggests that beginners develop habits and strategies as a result of practicing a simplified version of the task that is ineffective for more difficult versions.

Lastly, **segmentation** involves partitioning the skill along spatial or temporal dimensions. Segmentation strategies can be classified as pure part or progressive part. In pure part practice the segments of the task are practiced to criterion before moving to another part without regard to temporal or spatial progression. Progressive part involves either a forward or backward chaining. For example, in forward chaining the first part of a skill is practiced to some criterion before introducing the second part and so on. In backward chaining the last segment is learned first. Tennis instructors often teach students the serve by having them practice the ball toss first, then racquet motion before putting the whole skill together. This teaching method is used by many physical education teachers and coaches to teach sequential tasks. Sequential tasks, such as a tumbling, dance, or a skating routine, are composed of a set of tasks that are linked together to form a single performance.

Chamberlin and Lee (1993) suggest that the answer to this question of whether part–whole practice is more effective than whole practice hinges on the degree to which the components of the skill are independent. They maintain that as the degree of interdependence of the components increases, the value of part training decreases. Naylor and Briggs (1963) asked subjects to predict the appearance of images on a computer screen. They manipulated the interdependence of the type, number, and locations of the images. Whole practice was more effective than part practice when the characteristics of the images were highly interdependent. When the characteristics were independent part practice was more effective than whole practice. For example, Briggs and Waters (1958) found that independent practice on the pitch and roll components of a flight simulator was not nearly as effective as whole practice. Clearly, pitch and roll interact to maintain level flight.

Similar benefits have been found on a computer game currently being studied by the U.S. Air Force. The game, called "Space Fortress," is much like many video games available today (see Figure 8.11). The components of the

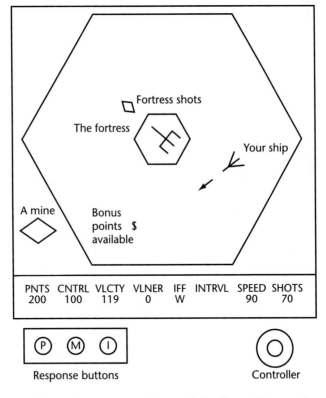

FIGURE 8.11 Screen and controls for "Space Fortress." The control on the right is a joystick used to control the ship and shoot missiles. The buttons on the left are used to collect bonuses by pushing either the points (P) or missiles (M) button at the appropriate time. The "I" button is used to identify whether a ship is friend or foe. (From Shea, Shebilske, & Worchel, *Motor Learning and Control*. Copyright © 1993 by Allyn & Bacon. Reprinted by permission.)

game include ship control, ship velocity, and response rate to "friends" and "foes." It appears that part–whole practice is effective for this game, but only to the extent that subjects are effective in "seeing" the connections between parts.

Shebilske, Regian, Arthur, and Jordan (1992) devised a modified part–whole practice scheme for the space fortress game that attempts to facilitate the learning of the connections between components. The method, termed active interlocked modeling (AIM), requires individuals to work in pairs. One subject controls one half of the task while being interlocked with a partner who controls the other half. Actions of one require reactions of the other and vice versa. Subjects learn the whole task while alternately practicing only one half of the task then the other half. This method facilitates the learning of the connections between the halves by viewing and responding to the actions and reactions of their partner. The AIM protocol can therefore be viewed as a **part–whole learning method** that is modified to establish connections between parts.

Mental and Observational Practice.   Remember, practice composition is concerned with what and how we practice. Constant and variable practice represented only one dimension of practice composition, that related to physical practice. Another dimension of practice concerns mental and observational practice where the subject engages cognitive operations related to the task but does not physically practice. Occasions arise in which it is not feasible to engage in physical practice. Mental practice may decrease the likelihood of injury and/or increase the opportunity for practice during inclement weather or when facilities are not available.

Mental practice refers to the processes associated with mentally rehearsing the performance of a skill in the absence of any overt physical practice. Mental practice is often associated with mental imagery, but this is not always the case. What appears to be important is that mental and physical practice share the same cognitive operations. Roland, Larsen, Lassen, and Shinhoj (1980) reported that when subjects mentally rehearsed learned finger sequences, blood flow to the supplementary motor cortex was similar to that during actual practice. However, mental practice did not increase blood flow to the motor cortex as did actual practice. The supplementary motor cortex is thought to be a site for high-level movement planning and/or the site of already developed movement plans.

An interesting experiment involving mental practice was conducted by Kohl and Roenker (1980). A physical practice group attempted 18 trials on a pursuit rotor task with their right hand. The pursuit rotor was set at 60 rpms, and trials were 30 seconds. The mental practice group held the stylus with their right hand and rehearsed performing the task for 18 trials. The mental practice subjects had only seen the experimenter perform the task for one trial but had never physically practiced the task. A control group was not permitted to practice the task physically or mentally. Following the acquisition period all subjects were given six trials on the task using their left hand.

The mental and physical practice groups performed similarly and both were superior to the control group. The results suggest that the cognitive activities associated with mental and physical practice are similar because similar benefits were observed.

Observational practice also appears to enhance retention. Much can be learned by observing others as they engage in motor tasks. I am always amazed at the number of observers who mass around a new video game in the arcades. Can they learn by observing others perform the video game? What about sports skills? What kind of information is gained by observing other players perform a task?

It has been argued by many theorists and researchers that the cognitive activities associated with observational practice are similar to the cognitive activities associated with actual practice. It has been proposed that as the performer (demonstrator) utilizes feedback, the observer can also observe some aspects of the feedback available. While subjects involved in actual and observational practice may perform similar cognitive operations, their perspective on the feedback is clearly different.

Newell, Morris, and Scully (1985) concluded that actual practice, a first person perspective on feedback, was a more effective practice method than observational practice when the processing of feedback was a critical factor for performance and learning. They noted that observational practice, a third-person perspective on feedback, was particularly valuable when the subject had to either execute previously learned skills under new conditions or when internal sensory feedback was not critical to the control of the movement.

Scully and Newell (1985) proposed that the most useful information conveyed by the demonstrator to the observer was the relative features of the movement pattern. They propose that "the problem for the learner of motor skills appears to be one of coordinating the body to reproduce the observed relative motion and scaling the relative motion appropriately" (p. 181). Therefore, it may be important to distinguish between error scores and the patterns of movement in interpreting the effect of demonstrations. Researchers who have measured error scores and movement patterns (Martens, Burwitz, & Zuckermen, 1976) have provided evidence consistent with Scully and Newell's proposal.

In summary, observational practice appears to be a viable practice method to improve particular characteristics of movement strategies and scaling relative features of movements. Observational practice, like mental practice, may also be important because physical injuries and fatigue are not experienced and actual practice facilities are not required.

FINAL COMMENT

The field of motor learning and control is concerned with the learning and control of a wide variety of movement produced at the various stages of learning. Motor learning is concerned with the changes that occur as a result of practice, and motor control is concerned with the production of the movement itself. In discussing movements, the researchers in motor learning and control have found it useful not only to describe the movement task but to describe the environment in which the task is performed. This information, coupled with information about the stage of learning of the performer, is important for the researcher to understand the demands placed on the performer. As in each of the fields discussed so far in this text, precise terminology is necessary for a thorough understanding of the processes leading to skilled motor behavior and control.

We actively seek and selectively process information. We choose what to do and what not to do. Under different circumstances or when we have more experience, we perceive things differently and choose different ways to react and respond. However, if a single link in the sequence of information processing fails, the end product, our movement, suffers. At times our movements are dependent on feedback and other times with practice we can produce movements without having to utilize feedback. The former mode of control is called closed-loop control and the latter is called open-loop control. Independent of how we control our movements, as we move faster we move with less precision. If we slow down, we regain accuracy. This finding is termed the speed–accuracy trade-off.

One of the major goals of research in motor learning and control is to find more efficient and effective ways to teach motor skills. One area that seems quite promising is that of information feedback. It appears that the spacing of feedback and the type of feedback provided to a learner affects performance, learning, and transfer. Likewise, the manner in which practice is scheduled and composed plays an important role in determining the effectiveness of the practice.

QUESTIONS FOR THOUGHT

- Describe the task and environmental dimensions for bowling, target shooting, playing a video game, wrestling, or football.
- Take a motor skill with which you are familiar and describe the information processing activities that would occur with a beginner and with an experienced performer. Discuss factors that would increase the sensation-perception processing demands, the response-selection processing demands, and the response-execution processing demands.
- Discuss tasks that are controlled primarily through closed-loop control and tasks that are more likely to be controlled by open-loop processes. What role does the environment in which the task is performed play in determining the mode of control?
- A great deal of money is spent on expensive simulators by the military (e.g., flight simulators) as well as by athletic groups (e.g., pitching machines). Do these devices contribute to motor learning? How?
- How are motor development and motor learning different? Are there any similarities?
- If you were a coach, what issues related to practice would the discussion in this chapter have highlighted for you?
- Is the practice specificity discussed in this chapter the same as the specificity principle discussed in Chapter 6?

KEY TERMS

acquisition
action plan
associative stage
autonomous stage
central processes
closed environments
closed-loop control
cognitive stage
contextual interference
continuous movements
coordinative structure
discrete movements
distributed practice
exteroceptors
extrinsic feedback
Fitts' Law

index of difficulty
information processing
intrinsic feedback
invariant features
knowledge of performance (KP)
knowledge of results (KR)
massed practice
mental practice
motor control
motor learning
observational practice
open environments
open-loop control
part–whole learning method
perception
peripheral processes

practice composition
practice distribution
practice scheduling
process-oriented approach
proprioceptors
response execution
response selection
retention
schema
segmentation

sensation
simplification
specificity of practice
speed–accuracy trade-off
synergy
task-oriented approach
transfer
transfer paradigm
variability hypothesis
variant features

RESOURCES

Textbooks

Magill, R. A. (1993). *Motor Learning: Concepts and Applications* (4th ed.). Dubuque, IA: Brown & Benchmark.

Schmidt, R. A. (1988). *Motor Control and Learning: A Behavioral Emphasis*. Champaign, IL: Human Kinetics.

Schmidt, R. A. (1991). *Motor Learning and Performance: From Principles to Practice*. Champaign, IL: Human Kinetics.

Shea, C. H., Shebilske, W. L., & Worchel, S. (1993). *Motor Learning and Control*. Englewood Cliffs, NJ: Prentice-Hall.

Journals

Acta Psychologica
Human Movement Science
Journal of Motor Behavior
Research Quarterly for Exercise and Sport

Professional Organizations

American Alliance for Health, Physical Education, Recreation, and Dance
North American Society for the Psychology of Sport and Physical Activity
Psychonomics Society
Society for Neuroscience

Internet

World Wide Web
http://sasuke.shinshu-u.ac.jp/psych/
http://nmrc.bu.edu/default.htm
http://ivory.lm.com:80/~nab/

Listservers
Biomechanics and Movement Science
send: subscribe biomch-L <your name>
to: listserv@nic.surfnet.nl

Dynamical Systems
send: subscribe dynsys-L <your name>
to: listserv@uncvm1.bitnet

REFERENCES

Adams, J. A. (1971). A closed loop theory of motor learning. *Journal of Motor Behavior,* 3, 111–150.

Adams, J. A. (1976). Issues for closed-loop theory of motor learning. In G. E. Stelmach (Ed.), *Motor Control: Issues and Trends* (pp. 87–107). New York: Academic Press.

Adams, J. A. (1987). Historical review and appraisal of research on the learning, retention, and transfer of human motor skills. *Psychological Bulletin,* 101, 41–74.

Baddeley, A. D., & Longman, D. J. A. (1978). The influence of length and frequency of training session on the rate of learning to type. *Ergonomics,* 21, 627–635.

Barnett, M. L., Ross, D., Schmidt, R. A., & Todd, B. (1973). Motor skill learning and the specificity of training principle. *Research Quarterly,* 44, 440–447.

Bernstein, N. (1967). *The Co-ordination and Regulation of Movements.* Oxford: Pergamon Press.

Briggs, G. E., & Waters, L. K. (1958). Training and transfer as a function of component interaction. *Journal of Experimental Psychology,* 56, 492–500.

Chamberlin, C. J., & Lee, T. D. (1993). Arranging practice conditions and designing instruction. In R. N. Singer, M. Murphey, & L. K. Tennant (Eds.), *Handbook on Research in Sport Psychology* (pp. 213–241). New York: Macmillan.

Ebbinghaus, H. (1885). *Über das Gedachtnis.* Leipzig: Dunker.

Fitts, P. M. (1954). The information capacity of the human motor system in controlling the amplitude of movement. *Journal of Experimental Psychology,* 47, 381–391.

Fitts, P. M. (1964). Perceptual-motor skills learning. In A. W. Melton (Ed.), *Categories of Learning.* New York: Academic Press.

Gentile, A. M., Higgins, J. R., Miller, E. A., & Rosen, B. M. (1975). The structure of motor tasks. *Movement,* 7, 11–28.

Henry, F. M. (1960). Increased response latency for complicated movements and a "memory-drum" theory of neuromotor reaction. *Research Quarterly,* 31, 448–458.

Keele, S. W. (1968). Motor control. In K. R. Boff, L. Kaufman, & J. P. Thomas (Eds.), *Handbook of Perception and Human Performance: Cognitive Processes and Performance.* New York: Wiley and Sons.

Keele, S. W., & Posner, M. I. (1968). Processing of visual feedback in rapid movements. *Journal of Experimental Psychology,* 77, 155–158.

Kelso, J. A. S. (1984). Phase transitions and critical behavior in human bimanual co-ordination. *American Journal of Physiology: Regulatory, Integrative & Comparative Physiology,* 15, R1000–R1004.

Kelso, J. A. S., Southard, D. L., & Goodman, D. (1979). On the nature of human interlimb coordination. *Science,* 203, 1029–1031.

Kohl, R. M., & Roenker, D. L. (1980). Bilateral transfer as a function of mental imagery. *Journal of Motor Behavior,* 12, 197–206.

Lee, T. D., & Genovese, E. D. (1988). Distribution of practice in motor skill acquisition: Learning and performance effects reconsidered. *Research Quarterly for Exercise and Sport,* 59, 277–287.

Mane, A. M., Adams, J. A., & Donchin, E. (1989). Adaptive and part-whole training in the acquisition of a complex perceptual-motor skill. *Acta Psychologica,* 71, 179–196.

Martens, R., Burwitz, L., & Zuckerman, J. (1976). Modeling effects on motor performance. *Research Quarterly,* 47, 277–291.

Martiniuk, R. G. (1976). *Information Processing in Motor Skills.* New York: Holt, Rinehart, and Winston.

Naylor, J., & Briggs, G. (1963). Effects of task complexity and task organization on the relative efficiency of part and whole training methods. *Journal of Experimental Psychology,* 65, 217–244.

Newell, K. M., Morris, L. R., & Scully, D. M. (1985). Augmented information and the acquisition of skill in physical activity. In R. L. Terjung (Ed.), *Exercise and Sport Science Reviews* (pp. 235–261). New York: Macmillan.

Poulton, E. C. (1957). On prediction of skilled movement. *Psychological Bulletin,* 54, 467–478.

Roland, P. E., Larsen, B., Lassen, N. A., & Shinhoj, E. (1980). Supplementary motor area and other cortical areas in organization of voluntary movements. *Journal of Neurophysiology,* 43, 118–136.

Salmoni, A. W., Schmidt, R. A., & Walters, C. B. (1984). Knowledge of results and motor learning: A review and critical reappraisal. *Psychological Bulletin,* 95, 355–386.

Schmidt, R. A. (1975). A schema theory of discrete motor skill learning. *Psychological Review,* 82, 225–260.

Schmidt, R. A. (1976). Control processes in motor skills. *Exercise and Sport Sciences Reviews,* 4, 229–261.

Scully, D. M., & Newell, K. M. (1985). Observational learning and the acquisition of motor skills: Toward a visual perception perspective. *Journal of Human Movement Studies,* 11, 169–186.

Shaffer, L. H. (1975). Multiple attention in continuous verbal tasks. In P.M.A. Rabbitt & S. Dornic (Eds.), *Attention and Performance* (pp. 157–167). London: Academic Press.

Shea, J. B., & Morgan, R. L. (1979). Contextual interference effects on the acquisition, retention, and transfer of a motor skill. *Journal of Experimental Psychology: Human Learning and Memory,* 5, 179–187.

Shea, J. B., Shebilske, W. L., & Worchel, S. (1993). *Motor Learning and Control*. Englewood Cliffs, NJ: Prentice-Hall.

Shebilske, W. L., Reagin, J. W., Arthur, W., & Jordan, J. (1992). A dyadic protocol for training complex skills. *Human Factors, 34* (3), 369–374.

Thorndike, E. L., & Woodworth, R. S. (1901). The influence of improvement in one mental function upon the efficiency of other functions: (I). Functions involving attention, observation and discrimination. *Psychological Review,* 8, 247–261.

Tuller, B., Turvey, M. T. & Fitch, H. (1982). The Berstein perspective: II. The concept of muscle linkages or coordinative structures. In J. A. S. Kelso (Ed.), *Human Motor Behavior: An Introduction* (pp. 253–270). Hillsdale, NJ: Erlbaum.

Turvey, M. T. (1977). Preliminaries to a theory of action with reference to vision. In R. Shaw & J. Bransford (Eds.), *Perceiving, Acting, and Knowing*. Hillsdale, NJ: Erlbaum.

Turvey, M. T. (1990). Coordination. *American Psychologist, 45*, 938–953.

Wightman, D.C., & Lintern, G. (1985). Part-task training for tracking and manual control. *Human Factors, 27*, 267–283.

Woodworth, R. S. (1989). The accuracy of voluntary movement. *Psychological Review,* 3, supplement 2.

CHAPTER **9**

Sport Psychology

CHAPTER OBJECTIVES

- To examine the influence of personality on participation in physical activity and the impact of participating in physical activity on personality development
- To discuss the positive and negative aspects of stress on human performance
- To examine extrinsic and intrinsic motivation and their relationship to physical activity
- To examine the influence of selected social factors on physical activity

INTRODUCTION

Almost everyone is familiar with the infamous techniques used by Knute Rockne to "psyche up" his football players. Contrast this to the "cool" attitude Pete Sampras displays on the tennis court. These examples, and the many others you can probably think of, highlight the important interaction between the mind and body for optimum human performance. Examination of the mind and body "at play" is central to the field of sport psychology.

Sport psychology as it is known today is probably best considered a double-edged sword. On one side, a sport psychologist examines the influence of participating in sport on an individual's psychological make-up. For example, one might examine the relationship between being exposed to reg-

ular competition in a contact sport and the affinity to exhibit aggressive behavior in other everyday activities. On the other side of the coin, the sport
psychologist is interested in the effect certain psychological factors have on
behavior during or as a result of physical activity. This approach attempts to
gain insight into the role of anxiety, personality, and self-efficacy on a performer's capability to deal with the rigors of a variety of sporting activities.
Imagine for a moment the difference between being a freshman playing in
the Rose Bowl in front of a crowd of 100,000 people and having to sink a
short putt for your personal best score when playing a round of golf alone.
Are both these situations anxiety provoking? What is the effect of the spectators at the football game or the isolation of the golf experience? What
about the effect of playing as part of a team or performing for oneself? These
and similar questions are central to the interests of the sport psychologist.

Sport psychology has gained the attention of many people in recent
years because elite athletes have garnered the service of sport psychologists
to help enhance their performance. For example, Payne Stewart, the 1990
U.S. Open golf champion, hired a sport psychologist to help him improve
his preshot routines. In 1991 the San Diego Chargers spent $90,000 for the

PICTURE 9.1   *The role of physical activity and sport for
women has changed dramatically over the years.* (Photo
credits: left, Archive Photos; right, Will Hart)

services of sport psychologists to help their athletes with a number of different psychological issues.

Sport psychology is not really a new field of study. As early as 1895 an improvement of psychological well-being through engaging in physical activity was being advocated. The Reverend William Augustus Stearn, presi-

---

 HIGHLIGHT

Coleman Griffith—The Father of Sport Psychology

Coleman R. Griffith is considered to be the "father" of sport psychology in North America. He directed a laboratory at the University of Illinois, thought to be one of the earliest laboratories devoted to the study of sport psychology. This laboratory was established in 1925. Griffith's research interests included the study of personality and performance. In 1926 he wrote a book called *Psychology of Coaching.* Another book, entitled *Psychology of Athletics,* followed in 1928. Both are now considered to be classics in the field of sport psychology.

Griffith did not limit his examination of psychological influences on sport performance to studies conducted in the laboratory. He used field observations and personal interviews to support some of his experimental findings from the more controlled confines of his laboratory. For example, he once corresponded with Knute Rockne in order to gather information regarding the role of motivation in sport (Kroll & Lewis, 1970). Furthermore, Griffith's "applied" sport psychology work did not end when his laboratory at the University of Illinois dissolved in 1932. In

1938 Griffith was hired by Philip Wrigley of the Chicago Cubs baseball organization to conduct extensive psychological examinations of each of the Chicago Cub baseball players. This included a psychological profile of baseball legend Dizzy Dean. Thus Coleman Griffith may well have been the first sport psychologist to consult professional athletes.

HIGHLIGHT 9.1   *Coleman Griffith, the father of sport psychology.* (Photo credit: The University of Illinois Archives)

dent of Amherst College, suggested that intellectual functioning would be improved if a student was exposed to a moderate amount of physical activity each day (Leonard & Affleck, 1947). In 1898 Frances A. Kellor suggested that women should forego the formal gymnastics that was central to their physical education class and spend more time with other sports and games. According to Kellor (1898), being exposed to a variety of activities encouraged the students to direct their minds to new mental activity that was not necessary during apparatus work.

One of the earliest sport psychology experiments was conducted by Norman Triplett (1897), who was interested in enhancing the cyclist's performance. In one form of competition, cyclists race alone attempting to "beat the clock." In a quite different race format the cyclists ride with other individuals while trying to beat them and the clock. Triplett examined the cyclists' performance in each of these situations: cycling alone and in the presence of others. What he discovered was rather interesting. Cyclists who raced in the presence of others had approximately 20 percent faster times than cycling alone. Triplett concluded that the presence of another cyclist in a race served to "liberate latent energy in the cyclists not ordinarily available" (Triplett, 1897, p. 533).

Two important events occurred in the 1960s that solidified the importance of the scientific study of sport psychology. In 1965 several hundred individuals from all over the world gathered in Rome, Italy, to discuss their findings on a wide variety of psychological issues related to sport. This was the first International Congress of Sport Psychology. The need to conduct and disseminate research in sport psychology was further underscored by the development of the North American Society for the Psychology of Sport and Physical Activity (NASPSPA) in 1967.

The second major advancement for sport psychology was the emergence of physical educators interested in sport psychology. This is reflected in the magnitude of research publications that appeared in the journal *Research Quarterly* during this period. Studies examined attitudes towards sport and athletes (Kenyon, 1970), personality and sport (Kroll, 1970), the role of mental practice (Corbin, 1967), and the influence of an audience on motor performance (Martens & Landers, 1969). At last Griffith's influence was beginning to take hold.

A specific outlet for research on sport psychology appeared in 1970, the *International Journal of Sport Psychology*. This was followed in 1979 by the *Journal of Sport Psychology*. The emergence of journals specific to the field gave an immediate visibility and recognition to research in this area. In addition, a number of influential texts appeared on the market including *Sport Psy-*

chology: An Analysis of Athlete Behavior (Straub, 1978), *Psychological Behavior in Sport* (Alderman, 1974), *In Pursuit of Excellence* (Orlick, 1980), and *Psychology in Sport: Methods and Applications* (Suinn, 1980).

A couple of additional events that occurred in the mid-1980s changed the face of sport psychology. In 1985 the Association for the Advancement of Applied Sport Psychology was formed. This organization's primary goal is to "promote the development of psychological theory, research, and intervention strategies in sport psychology." Secondly, sport psychology received a tremendous boost in 1986 when it was finally accepted by the psychology community, when division 47 of the American Psychological Association was developed to focus specifically on exercise and sport psychology. Sport psychology had arrived!

PERSONALITY

One of the most popular areas of study in sport psychology is the relationship of personality with participation in various sports and other physical activities. This statement is supported by Fisher's discovery (1984) that over one thousand studies have addressed personality and sport behavior. **Personality** is best described as an individual's characteristic patterns of behavior that contribute to his or her uniqueness (Baron, Byrne, & Kantowitz, 1980). There are a number of approaches to examine the role of personality in sport, including the psychodynamic, trait, and state perspectives. In the following section we will examine each of these in a little more detail by considering the key ingredients of each approach. We will also describe the methods that are central to each approach as well as investigate the research that has surfaced using each of these approaches.

Psychodynamical Perspective

The **psychodynamical perspective** has also been termed the deterministic approach (Silva, 1984). Essentially, this viewpoint suggests that behavior is determined "for" an individual rather than "by" an individual. Much of the psychodynamical perspective is based on work by Freud, who suggested that personality is heavily influenced by events that occur early in life and that behavior is governed by unconscious processes. The psychologist sitting at the end of a couch trying to assess the thought processes of a patient is a common picture of the early days of this approach.

PICTURE 9.2   *The work of Sigmund Freud was very influential in the development of the psychodynamic perspective.* (Photo credit: National Library of Medicine)

Assessing Personality within the Psychodynamical Perspective.
A problem when assessing personality from the psychodynamical perspective is the assumption that much of our behavior is determined by unconscious processes. If this is indeed the case, you can imagine that it is extremely difficult to gather data on something that the subject cannot tell you about. Common methods used by experimenters adhering to this approach are termed projective techniques. These techniques assume that an experimenter can provide insight into the personality through interpretation of a variety of diagram or sentence completion tasks. Probably the most famous projective technique is the Rorschach Inkblot Test (Figure 9.1). This test requires the subject to "tell what they see" in different inkblot "pictures" that are displayed on a card.

Unfortunately, this approach has done little to clarify the relationship between personality and participation in sport. However, the gravitational model did have its origin in psychodymanic thinking. The **gravitational**

FIGURE 9.1   The most famous projective test is the Rorschach Inkblot Test.

model suggests that individuals with certain personality characteristics are drawn to participate in certain sports (Kroll, 1970; Morgan, 1972). When a person has many of the personality qualities that are considered desirable for a particular sport they presumably have a greater chance for success and longevity in that sport.

Trait and State Perspective

The trait perspective has been responsible for a vast amount of research on personality and sport. **Traits** are defined as relatively enduring intrapersonal characteristics that account for unique yet stable behaviors to events in the environment (Vealey, 1992). This approach places special emphasis on the person as opposed to the situation (compare to the interactional perspective).

The Trait Perspective.   In the sporting domain, the trait approach is used to try to identify the "ideal" personality profile of the elite athlete or an athlete for a particular sport. For example, what personality characteristics are necessary to be a Wimbledon tennis champion? Would these individuals be introverts or extroverts? Can they be sensitive and tough-minded? Do you think Pete Sampras and Andre Agassi have similar and "ideal" personality profiles? Some researchers feel that a clear personality package has

PICTURE 9.3   *It is unlikely that Pete Sampras and Andre Agassi have the same personality profile.* (Photo credit: Reuters/Corbis-Bettmann)

emerged especially for some activities at the elite levels (Ogilvie & Tutko, 1972). Others, however, are not so convinced and think a much more conservative approach should be adopted when incorporating personality assessment as part of the athlete selection (Singer, Harris, Kroll, Martens, & Sechrest, 1977).

Assessing Personality within the Trait Perspective.   The most common method used to assess an athlete's personality trait profile is to administer an objective personality inventory. Most popular inventories are paper-and-pencil tests. The most frequently administered trait inventories are the Minnesota Multiphasic Personality Inventory (MMPI), the 16 Personality Factor Questionnaire (16PF), and the Eysenck Personality Inventory (EPI).

The 16PF was a particularly popular test used in the initial stages of sport personality research. Designed by Raymond B. Cattell in 1965, it is composed of 16 primary personality attributes. These factors could be categorized into four personality components: anxiety, introversion/extroversion, tough-minded/tender-minded, and independence/subduedness. A number of sport-specific personality inventories have also been developed. For example, Tutko, Lyon, and Ogilvie (1969) introduced the Athletic Motivation Inventory (AMI), which assesses 11 personality traits assumed to be associated with athletic success: aggressiveness, coachability, conscientiousness, determination, drive, emotional control, guilt proneness, leadership, mental toughness, self-confidence, and trust.

The State Perspective.   It became apparent rather quickly, however, that merely looking at predispositions to certain behavioral tendencies was not sufficient to describe an individual's actions in all situations. Incorporating situational factors and the trait perspective to examine the role of personality has been termed the interactional standpoint. The **interactional approach** suggests that an understanding of personality can only be understood by examining how traits and situation-specific behaviors complement each other. What is important from this perspective is that it gives equal involvement to both dimensions of personality. It still considers an individual's predisposition as a major determinant of behavior but also considers the mediating role of the environment.

Assessment of Personality within the State Perspective.   Probably the best-known state measures used in the sporting domain are the State-Trait Anxiety Inventory (STAI) and the Profile of Mood States (POMS). The STAI will be discussed in a later section on arousal and anxiety. The POMS has been particularly useful in that it has been used to assess populations from at least 18 different sports (Daiss & LeUnes, 1986). The POMS is made up of 65 phrases reported to assess six transient mood states: tension-anxiety, depression-dejection, anger-hostility, vigor-activity, fatigue-inertia, and confusion-bewilderment. The experimenter or clinician can get an overall assessment of mood called Total Mood Disturbance by subtracting the vigor scores from the sum of all the other scores.

Personality Trait-State and Performance.   While a vast amount of research has addressed personality and sport preference, the development of theoretical frameworks from which to base subsequent research efforts has been small at best. Two frameworks have emerged from this work and deserve some attention.

Kroll's Pyramid.   Kroll (1970) proposed a rather simple but feasible conceptualization of the relationship between personality and performance. This proposal is captured in the diagram presented by Silva (1984), shown in Figure 9.2. Essentially, **Kroll's Pyramid** predicts that at the entry level, a great many people will be participating, which results in a great variety of personality characteristics evident at this level. However, as the athlete progresses up the pyramid, the personalities that are encountered are much more homogenous. This is due to what Kroll called modification and attrition. Simply put, you adapt inappropriate characteristics (modification) to move to subsequent levels or you no longer survive (attrition). The system therefore perpetuated the homogeneity of personalities at the elite levels.

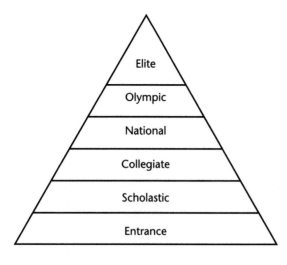

FIGURE 9.2 Kroll's Pyramid model attempts to capture the extent to which personality characteristics are similar at different stages of athletic participation. (From Kroll, 1970)

The Iceberg Profile.   Probably the most significant contribution to the personality-performance relationship was provided by Morgan and Pollack (Morgan, 1980a; Morgan & Pollack, 1977). They conducted a number of studies in which they administered the POMS to elite athletes competing for spots on Olympic teams. A remarkably similar profile was evident for the successful athletes. The profile depicted in Figure 9.3 is reminiscent of an iceberg, which was a function of a high score on vigor and lower scores on tension, depression, anger, fatigue, and confusion. The **iceberg profile** has now been identified with elite athletes in wrestling, rowing, distance running, and cycling.

Exercise and Sport as Mediators of Personality

We have focused primarily on the personality characteristics that might constitute a profile that results in successful performance in a particular sport. This is only one side of the double-edged sword we discussed at the start of this chapter. Another important consideration is the effect participating in

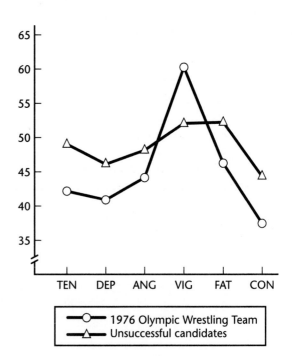

FIGURE 9.3   The iceberg profile has been identified as a consistent personality profile associated with elite athletics in a variety of sports. (From Morgan, W. P. Test of champions. The iceberg profile. *Psychology Today,* 13, 2, 92–102, 108, 1980a.)

regular activity might have on personality development. The slogan that accompanied the fitness "boom" of the 1980s, which included the emergence of aerobics and jogging as part of the daily routine for many people, was "healthy body, healthy mind." Another related issue has captured the attention of parents who feel their children need to participate in structured physical activity programs such as Little League because it will facilitate character development. Let's examine these issues.

There does appear to be some evidence to support the common assumption that "fitness training" can lead to improvements in self-esteem and self-concept. What is particularly interesting is that the improvements in these personality dimensions do not require actual physical fitness improvements to occur. In the case of children, there only needs to be a perception that change is occurring for the child to feel better. In addition, recall the earlier discussion of the iceberg profile reported by Morgan (1980a). Part of the iceberg profile is a reduction in tension, depression, and anger for elite athletes. This type of change in personality would be attractive to most people.

There is some controversy as to the role of physical activity as it pertains to moral or character development. This discussion was sparked by a paper written in 1971 by Ogilvie and Tutko (1971) entitled "Sport: If you want to build character, try something else." Given this title very little elaboration is really needed to identify Ogilvie and Tutko's opinion on this topic. They suggest that many of our personality characteristics are already well established before participation in sport ever occurs. However, given our discussion in previous sections of this chapter, it doesn't appear that there is much evidence to support this contention.

While we might not want to believe the underlying message of Ogilvie and Tutko—that sport does not develop character—there is some evidence to support this conclusion. Kleiber and Roberts (1981) examined the influence of sport competition on the exhibition of subsequent prosocial behaviors of cooperation and altruism. Unfortunately, they found that sport competition reduces prosocial behavior. Vealey (1992, p. 49) concludes that "the literature indicates that sport participation increases rivalrous, antisocial behavior and does not build 'character' or socially valued personality attributes."

What can be concluded from all of this? For sure, the influence of personality on performance and the influence of performance on personality is a complicated story. To help us resolve this dilemma, let's return to a recent article by Vealey (1992) for some guidelines. She proposes six general statements that can be drawn from the current status of the literature. The first two are related. That is, there does not appear to be an individual "athletic profile" or one that differentiates between athletic subgroups. Third, success in sport is enhanced by positive self-esteem and the use of appropriate cognitive strategies. Next, cognitive interventions have not been successful at changing personality traits. Fifth, participating in sport does not develop character. Finally, exercise and fitness can positively impact self-concept.

STRESS AND PERFORMANCE

If you were asked whether "stress" is good for performance, what would your answer be? Most people consider stress to be quite detrimental to successful athletic endeavors. Selye (1973) defined stress as "the non-specific response of the body to any demand made upon it." More importantly, he made a distinction between "good stress" called eustress and "bad stress" called distress. This suggests that performance can benefit from establishing a certain degree of psychological (and of course physiological; see Chapter 5) readiness before an activity begins. Getting "psyched-up" is a term often used to describe psychological preparation. What is the athlete attempting to accomplish by psyching-up? The next section will attempt to answer this question by examining the concept of arousal.

Arousal

The degree of psychological activation or alertness that varies along a continuum from deep sleep (low arousal) to extreme excitement (high arousal) is known as **arousal.** There are a number of neural substrates that work together to maintain an appropriate level of arousal. Let's briefly take at look at these areas in the brain.

Neurological Basis of Arousal.   In Chapter 3, we spent some time discussing areas of the brain that contributed to executing and controlling movements. However, we did not consider the area in the brain that has primary responsibility for controlling arousal. The **reticular formation** is a mass of interwoven neurons extending from the brainstem to the thalamus. Lesions of the reticular formation cause a dramatic decrease in the level of arousal experienced by an individual. Furthermore, sensory information that reaches the cortical regions is difficult to process without background activation provided by the reticular formation. The limbic system also plays an important role. This system is made up of subcortical structures located in

PICTURE 9.4   *Exercise might be one method an individual employs to reduce anxiety.* (Photo credit: Tony Neste)

the medial and ventral parts of the forebrain. The primary influence of these structures is with the formation of emotions.

Anxiety

One of the major factors that contributes to changes in arousal is anxiety. We have all experienced some form of anxiety at some stage in our life. For example, do you remember your feelings on your first date, waiting to take the SAT, playing the cross-town rivals at football, or performing your initial solo violin piece? **Anxiety** can be described as a negatively charged emotional state that is characterized by internal discomfort and nervousness (LeUnes & Nation, 1989). It is difficult to consider arousal and anxiety as absolutely independent. For the most part we might consider that anxiety contributes to the overall arousal displayed by an individual.

At this point it is important to distinguish between two forms of anxiety. **Trait anxiety** is a personality characteristic that implies that an individual is predisposed to experiencing anxiety when faced with a wide range of everyday situations. In contrast, **state anxiety** refers to an individual experiencing a temporary elevation in anxiety when exposed to specific situations. For example, a top-class tennis player may rarely feel anxious when playing even the most challenging of opponents. However, when requested to give a speech, the person may become very nervous.

Assessing Anxiety.   One of the earliest tools designed to examine anxiety was introduced by Janet Taylor Spence in the early 1950s. What has become known as the Taylor Manifest Anxiety Scale is a questionnaire type procedure that purports to measure general anxiety (i.e., trait). Another more commonly used method to assess trait anxiety is called the State-Trait Anxiety Inventory. This inventory was designed by Spielberger and associates (Spielberger, Gorsuch, & Lushene, 1970) and has been used in more than two thousand publications. In addition to responding to statements that refer to trait anxiety, this inventory also contains twenty statements that address state anxiety.

In the 1970s trait and state anxiety inventories were devised specifically for the sport setting. The Sport Competitive Anxiety Test (SCAT) is shown in Figure 9.4. This test introduced by Martens (1977) examines whether an individual generally feels threatened by competitive sport situations (trait). The state anxiety counterpart of the SCAT is called the Competitive State Anxiety Inventory (CSAI), which was also constructed by Martens (1977).

Arousal, Anxiety, and Performance

It is not unusual to hear comments such as "I wasn't psyched up" or "I just couldn't relax" following a performance that was substandard. Such statements might be viewed as anecdotal evidence for the notion that some level of arousal is needed for successful performance. Two important theoretical perspectives called drive theory and the inverted-U hypothesis have been

1. Competing against others is socially enjoyable.
2. Before I compete I feel uneasy.
3. Before I compete I worry about not performing well.
4. I am a good sportsman when I compete.
5. When I compete I worry about making mistakes.
6. Before I compete I am calm.
7. Setting a goal is important when competing.
8. Before I compete I get a queasy feeling in my stomach.
9. Just before competing I notice my heart beats faster than usual.
10. I like to compete in games that demand considerable physical energy.
11. Before I compete I feel relaxed.
12. Before I compete I am nervous.
13. Team sports are more exciting than individual sports.
14. I get nervous wanting to start the game.
15. Before I compete I usually get uptight.

FIGURE 9.4   Sport Competition Anxiety Test (SCAT) items. (Reprinted by permission from R. Martens, 1990, *Competitive Anxiety in Sport,* Champaign, IL: Human Kinetics Publishers, p. 53.)

used to examine the influence of arousal on motor performance. It is to these we now turn our attention.

Drive Theory.   Drive theory was introduced by a psychologist at Yale University named Clark Hull (1943). **Drive theory** suggests that the dominant response for a given stimulus will be elicited when an individual is highly aroused. For highly skilled athletes, we might assume that the dominant response is the correct one because of their extensive practice and experience. If this is the case, drive theory predicts that increasing the level of drive (or arousal) will serve to enhance the production of the appropriate motor performance for a skilled athlete. The relationship between arousal and performance is shown in Figure 9.5. If this relationship is indeed correct you can probably understand why a coach makes use of a pregame "psych-up" talk. It is important to keep in mind, however, that such a method would only be appropriate if the athletes being "aroused" were skilled.

The Inverted-U Hypothesis.   An alternative perspective to the drive theory was championed by Yerkes and Dodson (1908). Their work led to the proposal that the relationship between arousal and performance was curvilinear, or more specifically, an inverted-U. This means that as arousal increases so too does performance (this is similar to drive theory). However, this position also indicates that an optimum level of arousal exists and

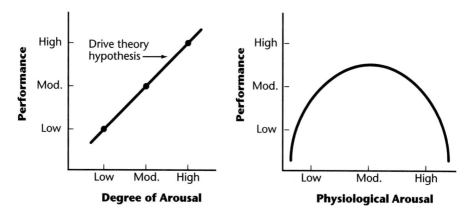

FIGURE 9.5   Drive Theory (left graph) and the Inverted-U Hypothesis (right graph) have been the two most commonly adopted theoretical perspectives for examining the role of arousal and performance.

should the performer exceed this level, he or she would exhibit a detriment in performance.

Fenz and colleagues have provided indirect support for the **inverted-U hypothesis** (Fenz & Epstein, 1967; Fenz & Jones, 1972). They measured the level of arousal of parachutists as they prepared to make their jumps. Arousal was assessed using measures of skin conductance, heart rate, and respiration rate at various times after arrival at the airport to just prior to the actual jump. Fenz and Jones (1972) revealed that the novice parachutists displayed a gradual increase in arousal right up until the time of the jump. In contrast, the more skilled parachutists began to decrease their arousal levels as the jump approached to more moderate levels. This is in keeping with the inverted-U hypothesis.

Another compelling piece of evidence in support of the inverted-U hypothesis was offered by Weinberg and Ragan (1978). College students threw tennis balls at a 5-centimeter target approximately 6 meters away from them. After some practice throws, the students completed a questionnaire. Following this, the students were given feedback that was intended to adjust their arousal levels. In the low arousal condition, the students were told that 30 percent of the population were better throwers than they were. In a moderate arousal condition, the subjects were informed that 60 percent of the population exhibit better throwing performance. Finally, the high arousal condition were told that 90 percent of the population could perform this task better than them. Subsequent throwing performance after the subjects received feedback are shown in Figure 9.6. Individuals in the moderate arousal condition outperformed both the low and high arousal conditions. These data are consistent with the predictions of the inverted-U hypothesis.

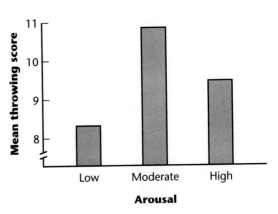

FIGURE 9.6 Throwing proficiency as a function of experiencing low, moderate, or high arousal (Reprinted by permission from R.A. Schmidt, 1988, *Motor Control and Learning,* Champaign, IL: Human Kinetics Publishers, p. 132.)

Factors Mediating the Inverted-U Hypothesis.   Skill level is one factor that is considered to mediate the amount of arousal that is appropriate to successfully perform a task (Figure 9.7). For example, novice athletes may divert the focus of their attention away from pertinent task cues should they experience too much arousal. However, as they become more skilled the additional arousal may channel attention to facilitate the search for critical stimuli that will enhance their performance.

It is also important to note that different sporting activities will also require a different level of arousal to optimize performance. For example, the

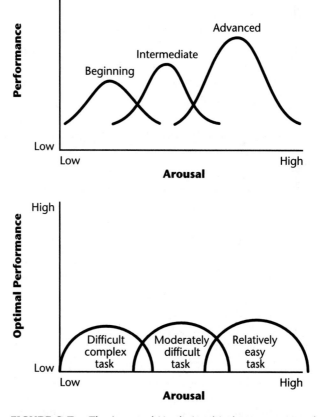

FIGURE 9.7   The inverted-U relationship between arousal and performance will be mediated by (top) the skill level of the performer and (bottom) the activity being performed. (From LeUnes & Nation, *Sport Psychology: An Introduction,* Nelson-Hall Publishers, 1989. Reprinted by permission.)

ideal arousal level necessary to facilitate performance during rifle shooting will obviously be different than that required for powerlifting. This does not mean the inverted-U relationship between arousal and performance no longer exists for powerlifting. What does occur, however, is that the absolute level of arousal (or activation) necessary to optimize performance in rifle shooting and powerlifting will be quite different. What amount of arousal do you think would be needed for a 3-foot golf putt or getting out of the blocks in a 100-meter sprint event?

Intervention Strategies

Most people would agree that being able to control the influence of anxiety is extremely important to the maintenance of appropriate arousal. Imagine for a moment that you are standing on the 10-meter platform before making your last dive in the Olympic finals. You need a good score. What can you do to control the anxiety that might accompany this situation? The following section briefly examines some of the common procedures that can be used to alleviate anxiety.

Classical Conditioning Techniques.   The **classical conditioning** approach works on the premise that an association exists between a unconditioned stimulus (US) and conditioned stimulus (CS). More specifically, a CS is paired with an anxiety-provoking US, which ultimately leads to the display of a fear-oriented response called the conditioned response (CR). That is, a threatening event such as a 100-meter final (US) is accompanied by a fear-eliciting cue such as apprehension (CS), which leads to an increase in anxiety (CR). A procedure called extinction is often used to reduce the UC-CS association and the subsequent production of the CR.

One method that has been used to cause extinction is called flooding. Flooding involves exposing the athlete to extremely high levels of anxiety in the initial stages of treatment. Often these anxiety provoking situations (e.g., serving for the match in tennis) are re-created through the use of mental imagery. However, these threatening situations are being re-created in the safety of the clinician's office. The intention of this procedure is to begin to pair fewer fear-oriented stimuli (CS) with the situation (US) that leads to the anxiety attack (CR) experienced by the patient.

A second method based on classical conditioning principles is called implosive therapy. This is quite similar to flooding in that the subject is exposed to the threatening stimuli that cause anxiety. However, **implosive therapy** uses a hierarchy of fear-eliciting images that the patient has ranked in terms of anxiety provocation. The clinician may systematically work through each image in order to reduce its impact or randomly select appropriate images that need more immediate attention.

Counterconditioning Model.   In contrast to extinguishing a counterproductive source of stimuli (see classical conditioning procedures), the focus of the **counterconditioning model** is to condition a response, that does not elicit anxiety, to the fear-producing stimuli. Probably the most widely used procedure in this area is called **systematic desensitization,** which is designed to countercondition anxiety gradually using relaxation as the incompatible response. Systematic desensitization requires the patient to become proficient in establishing a relaxed state often by using a progressive relaxation procedure (Jacobson, 1938). When using this method, the patient creates an image that is typically accompanied by a feeling of anxiety. At this point the patient is required to try to immediately block out the fear-provoking stimulus and concentrate on achieving a relaxed state. According

PICTURE 9.5   *Relaxation is a vital component of systematic desensitization procedures.* (Photo credit: Tony Neste)

to the basic principle of counterconditioning, the relaxation response will ultimately become associated with the stimulus that previously led to the display of anxiety.

Both the classical conditioning and the counterconditioning methods place the greatest emphasis on the role of the clinician. The patient in each of these cases is quite passive while the fear-evoking stimuli are "destroyed" by the clinician. We will now turn our attention to a number of procedures that involve a much more active role of the patient in coping with anxiety. These procedures might all be considered under the rubric of a **cognitive strategy.** This approach attempts to alter the thought processing of the performers and subsequently influence their responding.

There are four important stages for the methods that use a cognitive strategy. The exploratory phase involves making the athlete aware of the cognitions (perceptions, assumptions, thoughts) that lead to particular emotional and physical states. During the next stage, the educational phase, the athlete discovers the thoughts they evoke are self-defeating and irrational. The treatment phase introduces the athlete to different techniques (relaxation, positive self-talk, imagery) that can be used to help cope or change their cognitions. Finally, the clinician and the athlete work together to implement the newly developed strategies for dealing with anxiety. To reduce anxiety, the athlete uses some of the strategies that are associated with images that are created in the "friendly" confines of the clinic. Then the athlete must take full responsibility for using these procedures in the "real world." Let's take a closer look at a few examples from situations that used procedures similar to those just described.

Cognitive Restructuring and Coping Skills.   Smith (1984) suggests that this approach is "likely to be the most helpful to athletes who are fairly insightful and psychologically minded." In this situation, the clinician seeks to reorganize the thought processes that are engaged by the athlete. In many of these situations, the fear response of the athlete is not removed entirely; however, their reaction to the fear-eliciting stimuli is diminished. The anxiety response is maintained at a manageable level by incorporating coping skills at critical times. The actual coping skills are important tools that ultimately lead to restructuring of the athlete's cognitions.

One particular cognitive strategy that is quite comprehensive is called stress inoculation training (Meichenbaum, 1977). This procedure uses a wide variety of coping skills that the athlete masters that might be used in situations of need. Important coping skills include muscle relaxation and adaptive self-statements. The latter component involves the athlete developing statements that help refocus thoughts when dealing with stress experienced prior to and during a competitive episode. For example, to aid their preparation athletes might remind themselves, "Remain calm, stay relaxed, there is no need to get anxious." To cope with imminent stress, statements such as "You can handle this situation, you have done it before" might be used. Finally, if the stress is too great, "Relax, take a deep breath, stay calm" might be a common diversion to avoid becoming overwhelmed.

Stress inoculation training is seen as a method that might help deal with low to moderate sources of stress often experienced by athletes or other individuals in everyday life. It helps keep the level of anxiety within manageable boundaries. Can you recall the feelings you experience when the instructor first hands you your final exam? It is often good to take a deep breath, tell yourself you have prepared well, and then proceed with a better frame of mind. Unfortunately, mastery of these skills may not help if you have not studied the material very thoroughly!

Cognitive Strategies and Athletic Performance.   Smith (1984) reports one example of using a cognitive approach to treat a 15-year-old figure skater who experienced growing self-doubt and expectations of "choking." Remember, the first goal was to make sure the figure skater understood that her thoughts were self-defeating. The next step was to educate the athlete on the source of this problem. During the initial stages of practicing her relaxation technique, the figure skater also tried to isolate the thoughts that she was having while experiencing anxiety during competition. It was evident that the athlete had a fear of failure and was concerned with disgracing her significant others (family, coach, and so on) with a bad performance. In addition, the figure skater had established perfectionist standards that were unrealistic and therefore counterproductive. The training phase consisted of developing a set of self-statements concentrating on effort rather than outcome in order to counteract the perfectionist tendencies of the figure skater. For example, the skater would remind herself, "I can give no more that 100 percent effort." Using the developed statements, the relaxation was then incorporated into anxiety-producing imagery sessions such as falling during a routine. After considerable practice, the skater found it quite easy to initiate the coping skills during actual performances, especially during precompetition preparation.

Another example of cognitive intervention strategies facilitating athletic performance was offered by Silva (1982). A particular icehockey player was continually in foul trouble, spending as much as five minutes per game in the penalty box. The athlete wanted to reduce the time out of the game for punishment reasons in order to contribute to the team in a more productive manner. After consulting with the athlete, the clinician identified that many of the foul problems occurred as this player skated into a corner following an opposing player. The player found it very difficult not to foul the opposing players in this situation, especially in situations in which he didn't initially obtain the puck.

The intervention program consisted of using the cue phrase "stick-on-ice" whenever, during treatment, the player imaged himself venturing into a corner after another player. This was used to focus the player's attention away from thinking about fouling the opposition. The treatment continued for 6 weeks, for 3 hours a week, and included imagery of successful outcomes when using the cue words. After the intervention, the player's penalty time was reduced 57 percent, his goal scoring and assist rate increased, and he received postseason honors.

We function in an environment that continually causes us to confront anxiety (sporting competitions, new work environments, examinations). This, in turn, has the potential to disrupt our level of arousal, which in some cases may cause a detriment in our performance. It is important to understand and to educate our athletes that there are many procedures that can be implemented to reduce the negative effect of anxiety. However, it is essential that we remember that some stress is useful in order to establish moderate levels of arousal in order to optimize performance.

MOTIVATION

Why does one individual like to participate in team sports and another shy away from this situation? Why might one person diligently get up at 6 A.M. every morning and jog four miles? What causes some people to adhere strictly to an exercise regime and others to quit after the first two weeks? These questions, and many more, are asked by the sport psychologist interested in understanding why people are motivated to participate and "drop out" of a variety of physical endeavors. **Motivation** has been described as "the direction and intensity of effort" (Gill, 1986) and can be characterized by the type of choice, effort, and persistence of behaviors (Weiss & Chaumeton, 1992). In the following pages we will examine some of the most recent findings that address motivation and physical activity.

Participation and Attrition

This section will investigate the factors that motivate people to participate or "drop out" of sport and exercise activities. According to Cratty (1989), the important variables that influence an individual's desire to participate in sport are parental influences, societal pressure, and genetic qualities. Weiss and Chaumeton (1992) summarized the factors that have been identified in recent research efforts as critical to continued participation in sport. These include improvement of skills and fitness, establishing affiliation, experiencing competition, and having fun.

Alderman and Wood (1976) provided some of the initial evidence on participation motives in a study that included information from several thousand athletes. Their data indicated that young athletes consider being accepted by their peers (i.e., affiliation) as the major motive for staying active in athletics. Other factors that were also considered important were achieving excellence, experiencing some stress, and achieving some success. The notion of stress being a motive for participation might, at first, seem quite odd. However, the pursuit of stress and in particular vertigo is not uncommon. For example, do you like to ride the fastest and most daring rides at the amusement park? Why? Have you tried physical activities like sky diving, hang gliding, or driving a speedboat or a Formula One racing car?

In addition to trying to understand why particular individuals like to participate in certain physical endeavors it is also important to understand the antecedents to "drop out." Have you stopped taking part in any sporting activities recently? Are there specific reasons why this occurred? Orlick (1973, 1974) offered some insight into this process. These studies involved interviewing 7- to 18-year-old sport participants in Canada. Some of the findings are not particularly surprising. Many of the athletes who indicated they would discontinue their involvement with sport cited negative experiences. For example, common complaints were too much competition, lack of playing time, and dislike of the coach.

A rather interesting finding from Orlick's work was the role played by age. More specifically, the reasons for dropping out were different for the individuals who were under 10 years and those older than 10 years. The younger athletes were more concerned with lack of playing time and success. In contrast, the older athletes identified other extracurricular activities, including other sport activities, that were more appealing. In fact subsequent work by Sapp and Haubenstricker (1978) indicated that changing interests on the part of the participants accounted for a sizable portion of those who "dropped out."

Attrition sometimes occurs in athletics because of "burnout." According to Cratty (1989), **burnout** is "a reaction to chronic stress and to situations in which the potential rewards are inferior to the emotional and physical costs encountered by the athlete." Smith (1986) suggested that burnout can be reduced by providing the athlete with some coping skills and a good social support structure (e.g., parents and coaches).

Extrinsic and Intrinsic Motivation

Many individuals follow a strict exercise program because of the exhilaration and pleasure they get from rigorous physical activity. This is an example of participation being driven by high intrinsic motivation on the part of the person for that activity. In contrast, those who participate for some external reward such as money, trophies, or peer recognition are considered to be extrinsically motivated. It is still quite common for 10K races to offer T-shirts for those who compete. Do you think all the participants run the 10K because they love to jog or compete? Or do you think some individuals like to collect T-shirts from these road races? It is generally believed that the people who are intrinsically motivated are more likely to adhere to a program even in the face of adversity.

One theoretical position that has provided a framework for much of the work on the influence of intrinsic and extrinsic motivation is called cognitive evaluation theory. We will briefly review this perspective before considering some of the ways of fostering intrinsic motivation.

Cognitive Evaluation Theory.   The central premise of **cognitive evaluation theory** is that rewards can have a dual function (Deci & Ryan, 1985). Rewards can be considered to control behavior or provide information. If rewards are viewed as having some control over an individual's behavior, this is likely to reduce intrinsic motivation. For example, it is not surprising that some professional and college athletes lose their desire to compete when they begin to feel that they are controlled by the wants of significant others such as peers, coaches, owners, or alumni.

In contrast, rewards that are considered to provide information pertinent to performance can increase intrinsic motivation and indirectly affect adherence. The informational aspect of reward relates to an individual's perceived competency for a particular activity. If the reward is received for achieving a goal for which that person was primarily responsible, this carries important information concerning the individual's ability. This results in greater effort and persistence for this activity. One important form of reward with informational significance is feedback. More specifically, positive feedback in the form of praise to a performer is an effective means of increasing a player's feeling of self-worth (Weinberg, 1984).

It is important to note that the controlling and informational dimensions of rewards are not mutually exclusive. For example, Ryan (1980) suggested that certain rewards might be viewed quite differently by female or male athletes. Ryan reported that football players viewed their scholarships as "clubs over their heads," while female athletes often considered the receipt of a scholarship an indicator of excellence.

Methods for Improving Intrinsic Motivation

As already mentioned, establishing or encouraging participation due to intrinsic motivation appears to foster adherence to a sport. It is important, therefore, that some consideration is given to some of the methods that have been used to motivate individuals to take part in regular exercise or sport activity. Weinberg (1984) identified five issues that need to be considered in order to facilitate intrinsic motivation in an athletic setting: using verbal and nonverbal feedback, ensuring some success, increasing individual responsibility, providing a variety of practice experiences, and using goal-setting appropriately.

Most of us feel good after being told that we have just completed an activity that is considered worthwhile. The compliment does not have to be verbalized in many cases because the performer can often assess nonverbal communication that provides the same message. For example, the player leaving the field may not speak to the coach but may interpret the coach's smile (or maybe a scowl) as evidence of approval (or disapproval) for the execution of an action.

Horn (1985) warns that the idea that positive feedback as opposed to negative feedback will always lead to greater intrinsic motivation may be a dangerous overgeneralization. For example, she demonstrated that in some cases when a liberal use of positive feedback is provided to athletes, a perception of performing at an upper limit with no room for improvement is fostered. This ultimately results in a lowering of perceived competence. In contrast, providing feedback that is error-correcting in nature provides the message that performance can improve and the player can move to another level of achievement. The work of Horn (1985) suggests that close attention needs to be paid to the quality of the feedback in addition to the type of feedback. It is interesting to note that feedback emerges as an important factor for movement acquisition and performance throughout several chapters in this book (see also Chapters 8 and 10).

It would seem rather obvious that experiencing some success during the early stages of engaging in a new activity encourages future participation. Of course, people are not always successful at everything they do. This is certainly true in the sport world. However, some attempt should be made to create the opportunity for some success. For example, one can imagine that young children when first introduced to baseball might have limited success hitting a pitched ball from an adult or even a pitching machine. T-ball is an ideal way of reducing the requirements of the task to ensure that the young athlete has moderate success at a fundamental component of the sport, hitting.

Remember, one reward dimension within cognitive evaluation theory was informational. In order to nurture intrinsic motivation, it is important that performers feel they can control their behavior rather than being controlled by significant others. One means of allocating control to performers is to encourage participation in the decision-making mechanism for the activity in which they are involved.

Boredom is a dreaded curse for those in the business of promoting intrinsic motivation. Who wants to participate in something that is not fun or is very repetitive? By varying the content and order of practice or work responsibilities, boredom can be avoided or at least diminished. Practices do not have to be something that players dread. The best practices are often those that incorporate something different or novel. LeUnes and Nation (1989) report the example of a successful central Texas high school football team who went on team fishing trips to develop team camaraderie and togetherness. The idea of introducing novelty or variation into practice is a theme that was also prevalent in the chapter on motor learning (see Chapter 8).

Probably the most researched and important method for maintaining intrinsic motivation is goal setting. According to Locke, Shaw, Saari, and Latham (1981), using this procedure enables performers to focus their attention, mobilize effort, increase persistence, and aid in the formulation of appropriate strategies for meeting performance expectations. A classic experiment in the area of goal setting was conducted by Locke and Bryan (1966). They had subjects use foot and hand movements to control a set of display lights. Some subjects were simply told to do their best to learn the task as quickly as possible. A second group was given a specific goal to strive for. As can be seen from the results in Figure 9.8, the group with the specific goal achieved better performance on the task more quickly.

It has also been suggested that effective goal setting is achieved when goals are relatively precise, challenging but realistic. The Locke and Bryan (1966) study that was just discussed clearly demonstrates that "do your best" instructions are not sufficient. Furthermore, goal setting cannot be effective

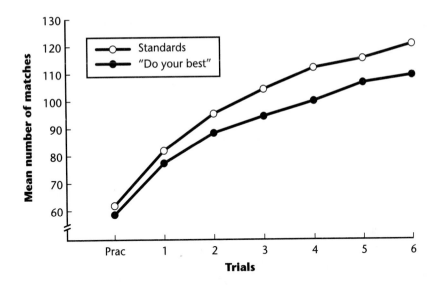

FIGURE 9.8 Asking individuals merely to do "their best" is not sufficient to optimize performance. (From *Journal of Applied Psychology,* 1966. The American Psychological Association.)

if achievement of the goals that are set cannot be evaluated. Therefore, it is essential that the learner is provided with frequent knowledge of results. The dramatic influence goal setting can have on performance and learning is captured in a narration by Olympic swimming champion John Naber, reported by Locke and Latham (1985, see highlight box).

Attribution Theory

After a great performance, an athletic event, or a bad day at work, it is not uncommon for the individual to reflect on the reasons for success or failure during the activity. The subsequent assessment, while seemingly trivial to some, can have a great impact on an individual's motivation to participate in this activity at a later date. You can probably recall trying to draw inferences as to why something happened. For example, why did I lose the racquetball match today? There may be many reasons. The reasons reported by performers provide important insight into their causal attributions for particular events.

The primary approach that has tried systematically to address how and why people make judgments about everyday experiences is called **attribution theory.** Heider (1958) was instrumental in providing an initial frame-

The Long and Short of Goal Setting

Locke and Latham (1985) provide a compelling account of the importance of short-term goal setting to achieve long-term goals. John Naber was a swimmer on the U.S. national team and he describes how he set goals prior to the Olympics. He writes:

In 1972 Mark Spitz won seven gold medals, breaking seven world records. I was at home watching him on my living room floor. And I said to myself at that time, "Wouldn't it be nice to be able to win a gold medal, to be able to be a world champion in Olympic competition." So right then I had this dream of being an Olympic champion. But right about then it became a goal. That dream to goal transition is the biggest thing I learned prior to Olympic competition—how important it is to set a goal. Certainly, motivation is important. A lot of kids have motivation. "Gee, I'd love to be great. . . ."

My personal best in the 100 back was 59.5. Roland Matthes, winning the same event for the second consecutive Olympics (1972), went 56.3. I extrapolated his, you know, three Olympic performances and I figured in 1976, 55.5 would have been the order of the day. That's what I figured I would have to do. So I am four seconds off the shortest backstroke event on the

Olympic program. It's the equivalent of dropping four seconds in the 440-yard dash.

It's a substantial chunk. But because it's a goal, now I can decisively figure out how I can attack that. I have four years to do it in. I'm watching TV in 1972. I've got four years to train. So it's only one second a year. That is still a substantial chunk. Swimmers train ten or eleven months a year so it's about a tenth of a second a month, giving time off for missed workouts. And you figure we train six days a week so it's only about 1/300th of a second a day. We train from six to eight in the morning and four to six at night so it's really only 1/1200th of a second every hour. Do you know how short a 1200th of a second is? Look at my hand and blink when I snap, would you please? OK, from the time when your eyelids started to close to the time they touched, 5/1200th of a second elapsed. For me to stand on a pool deck and say, "During the next sixty minutes I'm going to improve that much," that's a believable dream. I can believe myself. I can't believe that I am going to drop four seconds by the next Olympics. But I can believe I can get that much faster. Couldn't you? Sure. So all of a sudden I'm moving.

Did this work for John Naber? Well, the record books for the 1976 Olympics provide the answer!

work within which to study attribution processes. His work suggested that personal forces such as ability and trying (i.e., effort) were primary contributors to performance outcome. In addition, external forces—namely, task difficulty and luck—were also thought to mediate outcome.

Wiener (1972) added an additional dimension—stability—to the original notions of Heider. Weiner felt that some of the aspects identified by Heider might be more stable and less likely to change over time. More specifically, ability and task difficulty were considered to be relatively stable, whereas effort and luck were viewed as very transient and could be quite different from performance to performance. Taking Heider's original conceptualization and incorporating his own, Weiner presented the model depicted in Figure 9.9. This model was quite successful in capturing attributions made in many educational settings.

Unfortunately, Roberts and Pascuzzi (1979) revealed that Weiner's model was less successful at accounting for the multitude of attributions that seemed specific to the athletic arena. Using 346 male and female students at the University of Illinois, they revealed that only 45 percent of the student responses to simulated situations as players or spectators fell within the boundaries identified by Weiner. They recommended a number of changes to the original model, as presented in Figure 9.10.

It is clear that identifying and understanding the underlying causes and motivational consequences of attributions are very complex. Brawley (1984)

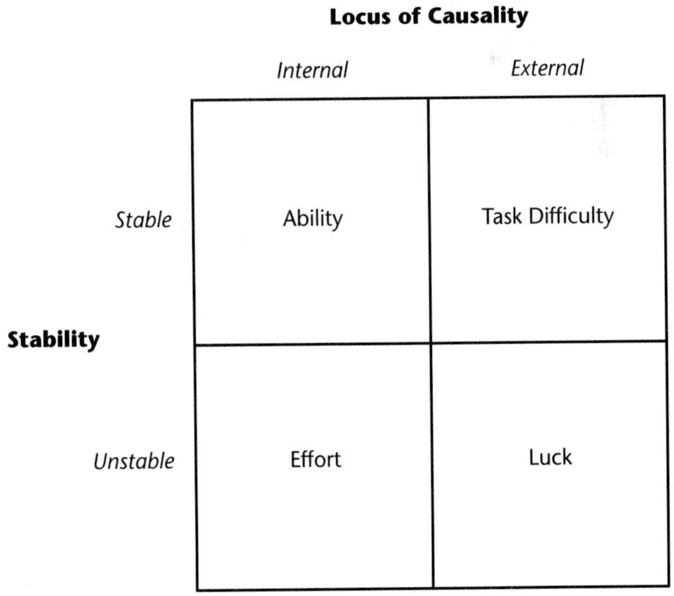

Locus of Causality

	Internal	*External*
Stable	Ability	Task Difficulty
Unstable	Effort	Luck

Stability

FIGURE 9.9   Dimensions and elements of Weiner's two-dimensional taxonomy for causal attributions. (Reprinted by permission from L. R. Brawley & G. C. Roberts, 1984, Attribution in sport: Research foundations, characteristics, and limitations. In *Psychological Foundations of Sport*, edited by J. M. Silva III & R. S. Weinbert, Champaign, IL: Human Kinetics Publishers, p. 201.)

Locus of Control

	Internal	*External*
Stable	Ability	Coaching
Unstable	Effort Psychological Factors Unstable Ability Practice	Luck Task Difficulty Teamwork Officials

Stability

FIGURE 9.10   Dimensions of sport-related attributions according to the work of Roberts and Pascuzzi (1979). (From Roberts & Pascuzzi, *Journal of Sports Psychology,* Champaign, IL: Human Kinetics Publishers, 1979.).

contributed to this complexity by suggesting that situational factors mediate the type of attributions made about outcomes in the sports domain.

SOCIAL ISSUES AND SPORT

It is generally accepted that the socialization process has a major impact on an individual's behavior. However, this issue has received only a cursory examination by sport psychologists. Greendorfer (1992) suggests that investigations addressing a number of issues in the areas of sport psychology and motor behavior (including motor development, learning, and control) would benefit from applying a "social" perspective. For example, research focusing on modeling, observational learning, audience effects, social facilitation or inhibition, competition, and motivation is impacted by social factors. Nonetheless, some sport psychologists have embraced topics that either address how individuals are socialized *into* sport or socialized *through* sport. Let's take a look at some of these topics: group cohesion, audience effects, aggression, and gender issues.

Group Cohesion

It is not uncommon in many sport, industrial, or military settings that people are required to work as a unit or group to achieve a goal. In some cases, different individuals bring to the group a different set of resources (e.g., cognitive, affective, and psychomotor). However, it is very important that whatever resources are available, they should be mobilized in an efficient manner in order to secure success. The following section examines some of the factors that impact the functioning of individuals in group settings.

Almost everyone has been involved with a group activity. It might have been in the workplace or in a recreational setting. It is also likely that each of us has experienced some situations in which the group we were part of functioned in a smooth, coordinated fashion. On the other hand, we have probably been part of a unit that was totally dysfunctional in which no movement toward the intended goal ever seemed to occur. What were some of the differences in the two units of which you were a part? Which group did you enjoy being with the most? Why? Before we can provide some answer to these questions, it seems appropriate that we define what we consider a group to be. According to Shaw (1976), a **group** is an entity in which "two or more persons . . . are interacting with one another in such a manner that each person influences and is influenced by each other person."

One area of research on which sport psychologists have concentrated to try to get a handle on group performance is the notion of **group cohesion,** which describes a group's ability to stick together in the face of adversity. In the eyes of coaches and other types of team leaders, this is an important group attribute and is usually very desirable.

Models of Group Cohesion. Carron (1984) has outlined three models that capture how cohesion fluctuates during the development and in some cases the disbandment of particular groups. The **linear model** suggests that team cohesion continues to increase as a group of individuals progress through each stage of group development. For example, little cohesion is evident when the group is initially formed. After resolving any early polarization, the individuals begin to cooperate to enhance team performance. During the progression from meeting to finally playing together, the team progressively becomes more cohesive according to the linear model.

An alternative model known as the **pendular model** suggests that cohesion is in a continual state of oscillation. For example, when athletes try out for a local soccer team, they come to the group as a set of individuals. At this point, this group is obviously far from cohesive. The pendulum swings as the athletes start to mingle and establish an initial camaraderie, improving the unit's togetherness. However, the pendulum swings back in the opposite direction when the group is segregated into smaller units to practice (e.g., goalkeepers, defensive players, midfielders in soccer). Finally, the group has the opportunity once again to cultivate cohesion because those selected for the team now have a common bond.

The final model revealed by Carron portrays a more complete picture since it examines cohesion from the creation of the group to the time it dissolves. This is termed the **life-cycle model.** This model has many of the attributes of the two previous models, highlighting the range of levels of cohesion that occur as the group is formed, as it matures, and then as an antecedent to separation. It is clear that these models are not mutually exclusive. In fact, there are many similarities between the three perspectives. While no one model has been universally adopted, it is clear to say that group cohesion must be considered a dynamic process, not one that is static.

Group size has been reported as a particularly important factor that mediates group performance. In general, it is believed that as the number of individuals making up the group is increased, there is an increased potential for problems to arise. This can ultimately lead to a reduction in team cohesion. There have been numerous suggestions as to why this problem emerges. For example, communication is more difficult when the group is larger. Moreover, there is a greater chance for information or feedback to be interpreted differently by different performers. Another obstacle to avoid as the group gets larger is the development of smaller cliques or subgroups. This can have a very disruptive effect on the performance of the group as a whole. Obviously, as group size increases, the coach or instructor should be acutely aware that group cohesion could suffer.

Audience Effect

Recall the example from the beginning of this chapter that referred to the freshman quarterback who enters the Rose Bowl in front of 100,000 spectators. Most of us would predict that this would be an overwhelming experience for this player that could influence the outcome of the game. What about a quite different situation such as hitting golf balls at the driving range among many other people participating in the same activity? What is the effect that this type of "spectator" might have on the golfer's performance? The questions are central to understanding the role of audiences on performance. A primary theoretical perspective that has tackled this issue is called social facilitation and inhibition.

Social Facilitation and Inhibition.   In order to understand **social facilitation** and **social inhibition,** let's return to Norman Triplett's (1897) experiment. Remember, he was interested in how people perform, alone and in groups. More specifically, he was interested in helping cyclists obtain their best performance (i.e., fastest time). Cycle racing took two forms at that time. In one case, a cyclist would race around the track alone, trying to get the fastest time. A second method involved cyclists competing together on the track for the fastest time. When Triplett examined the records associated with these two methods, he found that cyclists who raced in the presence of others had approximately 20 percent faster times than cyclists who raced alone. While this effect may have been due to the presence of others, it is also possible that it was caused by drafting (riding behind another cyclist to avoid wind resistance) or some other physical effect. So Triplett devised a rather simple experiment. He asked children to wind up a fishing reel as quickly as possible. Children performed this task either alone or in the presence of other children working on the same task. Once again, Triplett found that the fastest times occurred when the children worked in the presence of others.

A flurry of studies followed Triplett's work; in general this research found that people performed better when they were in the presence of others. The results were found when the others were competing, co-acting, or serving as an audience (Travis, 1925; Allport, 1924). One researcher (Chen, 1937) even found that ants worked harder (removed more balls of dirt from the tunnel) when in the presence of other ants than when they worked alone! From these data, we might conclude that there is a social facilitation effect such that the presence of others aids learning and performance.

Aggression

One personality characteristic that has captured the attention of many sport psychologists is that of aggression. It is interesting to note that actions that many of us consider aggressive are not defined this way in the literature. **Aggression** is defined as "any behavior directed toward the goal of harming or injuring another living being who is motivated to avoid such treatment" (Baron, 1977, p. 7). Aggressive behavior needs to be distinguished from **assertive behavior,** which consists of those actions that have no intent to harm or injure another person, nor do they violate constitutionally agreed-upon rules for the sport being played. These behaviors are very common occurrences of such sports as basketball, football, hockey, rugby, and soccer.

It is important to distinguish between two types of aggression. **Hostile aggression** has as its focus the intent to harm an individual physically or psychologically. On the other hand, **instrumental aggression** is exhibited to achieve some nonaggressive goal. For example, a linebacker in football might hit a quarterback hard to knock the ball from his grasp. If the linebacker purposefully landed on the quarterback's arm as they hit the ground and could have avoided it, this would be classified as hostile aggression. The obvious next question that comes to mind is, Why do some people have a more aggressive personality than others?

There are three different theoretical positions focusing on aggressive behavior: instinct theory, frustration-aggression theory, and social learning theory. We will consider each of these in a little more detail. Instinct theory proposes that individuals are generally predisposed to being aggressive. In essence, aggression builds up over time and at some point must be expressed (Gill, 1986). However, the expression of the aggression can be directly aimed at another individual or displaced through catharsis in a sporting pursuit. From this perspective, sport serves an important societal function in that it provides an avenue through which hostile behaviors can be channeled.

An alternative explanation is termed the frustration-aggression theory. This position suggests that aggressive behavior occurs as a result of experiencing frustration because a goal action is blocked. In basketball, for instance, a player may not get an expected call from the referee. In this situation the player vents frustration in the form of an aggressive act against an opposing player. The third explanation that has been forwarded as an explanation for the use of aggressive actions is social learning theory. The basic premise of this perspective is that aggressive tendencies are developed through observation of others who exhibit this type of behavior (Bandura, 1973). For example, it is not uncommon to see young athletes emulating their heroes' actions in their pee-wee football games or Little League baseball games. Moreover, "trash talking" is becoming all too prevalent in professional sports. This is also becoming a problem with younger athletes. Remember, this is a subtle form of aggression if the talking imparts psychological harm to the opposing player.

Gender Issues

For many years broaching the topic of women in sport and athletics was considered taboo. This is certainly not the case in the present day. A landmark that made an important contribution to beginning a movement to resolve the inequalities in sport was Title IX of the Higher Education Act of 1972. Essentially, this instigated efforts to provide equal opportunities in sport.

A great deal of research effort concerning women in sport has addressed the role of menstrual functioning or other physiological issues that are not the focus of this section. However, one psychological variable that has mustered interest among sport psychologists is that of psychological androgyny. Androgyny is most often described as "a mixture of both male and female tendencies combining assertiveness and competence with compassion, warmth, and emotional expressiveness" (Anastasi, 1982, p. 557). Essentially, one might think of masculinity and femininity as ends of a continuum with androgyny somewhere in between.

Research that has focused on the gender role orientation of the female athlete has led to a number of rather controversial conclusions. First, the female athlete does not express a feminine sex role orientation. This seems to be the case for athletes who participate in a wide variety of activities including badminton and field hockey. However, females participating in individual sports tend to be more feminine in orientation (Wrisberg, Draper, & Everett, 1988). Second, a masculine sex role orientation is prevalent in female participation in sport. For example, female collegiate swimmers often view themselves as more masculine in sex role orientation than do nonathletes. Finally, there is also evidence that a large number of female athletes exhibit an androgynous orientation. However, the range of responses that fall within this category vary greatly from study to study.

Another issue that has attracted both psychologists and sociologists is the manner in which females are socialized into the sport setting (this is also a current issue in the area of sport pedagogy; see Chapter 10). One fallout of the socialization process through sport participation for the female athlete is the emergence of role conflict. For example, Allison (1991) notes that a conflict has been reported between the traditional view of a female—graceful, beautiful, and passive—and the requirements in sport—aggressiveness, strength, and toughness. So female athletes find themselves in an awkward situation in that achieving success in athletics may make them appear less feminine.

The important question is whether the female athletes actually experience this conflict. Sage and Loudermilk (1979) report that only 20 percent of sampled athletes felt this type of conflict. A similar finding was documented by Anthrop and Allison (1983). In light of these findings it is difficult to understand why sport psychologists and sociologists are so preoccupied with role conflict and the female athlete. It would appear that the traditional view of the female personality make-up is and will continue to be difficult to dispel.

FINAL COMMENT

We began this chapter by suggesting that sport psychology can be considered a double-edged sword. From one side, a sport psychologist is interested in how sport participation influences the psychological make-up of an individual. For example, does sport participation lead an individual to be more anxiety-prone? Alternatively, the sport psychologist examines the role of particular psychological factors on behavior in sport. For instance, one might observe that increasing an individual's level of anxiety results in severe detriments in his or her tennis game.

It is clear from the first section on personality that definitive answers to psychological issues may not be simple matters to resolve. For example, the research addressing personality has indicated that it is not sufficient merely to examine the predisposition of the performer to elicit particular psychological characteristics (i.e., generally anxious). The researcher must also take into account how an individual responds in particular circumstances (i.e., on the playing field compared to the classroom). It does appear however, that elite sport participants exhibit a similar iceberg profile when administered the Profile of Mood States.

Another important relationship, the inverted-U, has also been described to account for the influence of arousal on performance. More specifically, if the individual is either underaroused or overaroused, performance will suffer. In cases in which athletes are prone to experience arousal levels that are inhibiting their capabilities, numerous intervention strategies can be used to help them cope and ultimately reduce their arousal levels. Many of these intervention strategies involve a combination of relaxation and imagery techniques.

In Chapters 5 and 6 the physiological benefits of participating in regular exercise were discussed. In addition to these benefits, there also appears to be some psychological gains. For example, some evidence indicates that improvements in self-esteem and self-concept can occur. If this is true, it would seem important to try to motivate the individual to continue to participate in sport or exercise over an extended time period. It turns out that adherence to exercise programs and sporting activities can be enhanced by increasing the participants' intrinsic motivation. While there are a number of methods that have been successful in improving intrinsic motivation, incorporating both short- term and long-term goals into the activity plan turns out to be particularly effective.

In recent history, sport psychologists have not paid a great deal of attention to the role of sport in and on society. While this has typically been considered the domain of sport sociologists, there are numerous issues associated with sport psychology and motor behavior that involve the socialization process. It is important to note, however, that not all topics related to sport socialization have been ignored by sport psychologists. For example, there is a wealth of literature addressing group dynamics, social faciliation and inhibition, and the role of aggression in sport. Moreover since the introduction of Title IX of the Higher Education Act of 1972, the role of gender has surfaced as a popular research topic. Recent research efforts have focused on the female athlete's tendency to display an androgenous psychological make-up. This occurrence may be associated with the role conflict some female athletes experience as they are socialized into the sport or exercise setting. This issue surfaces once again in the next chapter, where we will examine socialization processes that exist in the movement education setting.

QUESTIONS FOR THOUGHT

- Personality can be examined from both a state and trait perspective. Discuss the similarities and differences between these approaches.
- The physiological benefits of exercise were discussed in Chapter 5. What are some of the psychological benefits of exercise?
- The acquisition of motor skills was an important part of the chapter that addressed motor learning and control. How do changes in arousal affect skilled performance?
- The chapter on motor development paid close attention to the influence of growth and maturation on motor behavior. How can sport and exericse contribute to the psychological well-being of a child? Or can it?
- Goal-setting techniques were identified in this chapter as critical for improvements in skilled performance. Can these techniques be modified to facilitate improvements in mechanical or physiological components of the human performer?
- What are the major agents of socialization in the sporting domain? Do they have a positive or negative effect on exercise or sport adherence?

KEY TERMS

aggression

anxiety

arousal

assertive behavior

attribution theory

burnout

classical conditioning

cognitive evaluation theory

cognitive strategy

counterconditioning model

drive theory

gravitational model

group

group cohesion

hostile aggression

iceberg profile

implosive therapy

instrumental aggression

interactional approach

inverted-U hypothesis

Kroll's Pyramid

life-cycle model

linear model

motivation

pendular model

personality

psychodynamic perspective

reticular formation

social facilitation

social inhibition

state anxiety

systematic desensitization

trait anxiety

traits

RESOURCES

Textbooks

Horn, T. S. *Advances in Sport Psychology.* Champaign, IL: Human Kinetics.

LeUnes, A. D., & Nation, J. R. (1989). *Sport Psychology: An Introduction.* Chicago: Nelson-Hall.

Weinberg, R. S., & Gould, D. (1994). *Foundations of Sport and Exercise Psychology.* Champaign, IL: Human Kinetics.

Journals

Journal of Applied Sport Psychology
Journal of Sport and Exercise Psychology
Research Quarterly for Exercise and Sport
Sport Psychologist
Women in Sport and Physical Activity Journal

Professional Societies

Association for the Advancement of Applied Sport Psychology
North American Society for the Psychology of Sport and Physical Activity
American Alliance for Health, Physical Education, Recreation, and Dance
American Psychological Association

Internet

World Wide Web (WWW)
http://www.cdc.noaa.gov/~jac/sportpsy/
http://fiat.gslis.utexas.edu/~lewisa/womsprt.html
http://sasuke.shinshu-u.ac.jp/psych/

Listservers
Sport Psychology
send: subscribe sportpsy <your name>
to: listserv@vm.temple.edu

REFERENCES

Alderman, R. B. (1974). *Psychological Behavior in Sport.* Toronto: Saunders.

Alderman, R. B., & Wood, N. L. (1976). An analysis of incentive motivation in young Canadian athletes. *Canadian Journal of Applied Sport Sciences,* 1, 169–176.

Allison, M. T. (1991). Role conflict and the female athlete: Preoccupations with little groundings. *Journal of Applied Sport Psychology,* 3, 49–60.

Allport, F. H. (1924). *Social Psychology.* Cambridge, MA: Riverside Press.

Anastasi, A. (1982). *Psychological Testing* (5th ed.). New York: Macmillan.

Antrop, J., & Allison, M. T. (1983). Role conflict and the high school female athlete. *Research Quarterly for Exercise & Sport,* 54(2), 104–111.

Bandura, A. (1973). *Aggression: A Social Learning Analysis.* Englewood Cliffs, NJ: Prentice-Hall.

Baron, R. A. (1977). *Human Aggression.* New York: Plenum.

Baron, R. A., Byrne, D., & Kantowitz, B. (1980). *Psychology: Understanding Behavior* (2nd ed.). New York: Holt, Reinhart, & Winston.

Brawley, L. R. (1984). Attributions as social cognitions: Contemporary perspectives in sport. In W. F. Straub & J. M. Williams (Eds.), *Cognitive Sport Psychology* (pp. 212–230). Lansing, NY: Sport Science Associates.

Brawley, L. R., & Roberts, G. C. (1984). Attribution in sport: Research foundations, characteristics, and limitations. In J. M. Silva & R. S. Weinberg (Eds.), *Psychological Foundations of Sport* (pp. 197–213). Champaign, IL: Human Kinetics.

Carron, A. V. (1984). Cohesion in sport teams. In J. M. Silva & R. S. Weinberg (Eds.), *Psychological Foundations of Sport* (pp. 340–352). Champaign, IL: Human Kinetics.

Chen, S. C. (1937). Social modification of the activity of ants in nest-building. *Physiological Zoology,* 10, 420–436.

Corbin, C. (1967). Effects of mental practice on skill development after controlled practice. *Research Quarterly,* 38, 534–538.

Cratty, B. J. (1989). *Psychology in Contemporary Sport* (3rd ed.). Englewood Cliffs, NJ: Prentice-Hall.

Daiss, S., & LeUnes, A. (1986). The utility of the profile of mood states in sport research: An annotated biliography. *Journal of Applied Research in Coaching and Athletics,* 1, 148–169.

Deci, E. L., & Ryan, R. M. (1985). *Intrinsic Motivation and Self-Determination in Human Behavior.* New York: Plenum.

Fenz, W. D., & Epstein, S. (1967). Changes in gradients of skin conductance, heart rate, and respiration rate as a function of experience. *Psychosomatic Medicine,* 29, 33–51.

Fenz, W. D., & Jones, G. B. (1972). Individual differences in psychological arousal and performance in sport parachutists. *Psychosomatic Medicine,* 34, 1–8.

Fisher, A. C. (1984). New directions in sport personality research. In J. M. Silva & R. S. Weinberg (Eds.), *Psychological Foundations of Sport* (pp. 70–80). Champaign, IL: Human Kinetics.

Gill, D. (1986). Psychological dynamics of sport. Champaign, IL: Human Kinetics.

Greendorfer, S. L. (1992). Sport socialization. In T. Horn (Ed.), *Advances in Sport Psychology* (pp. 201–218). Champaign, IL: Human Kinetics.

Heider, F. (1958). *The Psychology of Interpersonal Relations.* New York: John Wiley & Sons.

Horn, T. S. (1985). Coaches' feedback and changes in children's perceptions of their physical competence. *Journal of Educational Psychology, 77,* 174–186.

Hull, C. E. (1943). *Principles of Behavior.* New York: Appleton-Century-Crofts.

Jacobson, E. (1938). *Progressive Relaxation.* Chicago: University of Chicago Press.

Kellor, F. A. (1898). A psychological basis for physical culture. *Education, 19,* 100–104.

Kenyon, G. (Ed.) (1970). *Contemporary Psychology of Sport.* Chicago: Athletic Institute.

Kleiber, D. A., & Roberts, G. C. (1981). The effects of sport experience in the development of social character: An exploratory study. *Journal of Sport Psychology, 3,* 114–122.

Kroll, W. (1970). Current strategies and problems in personality assessment of athletes. In L. E. Smith (Ed.), *Psychology of Motor Learning* (pp. 349–367). Chicago: American Academy of Physical Education.

Kroll, W., & Lewis, G. (1970). America's first sport psychologist. *Quest 13,* 1–4.

Leonard, F. E., & Affect, G. B. (1947). *A Guide to the History of Physical Education.* Philadelphia: Lea & Febiger.

LeUnes, A., & Nation, J. (1989). *Sport Psychology: An Introduction.* Chicago: Nelson-Hall.

Locke, E. A., & Bryan, J. F. (1966). Cognitive aspects of psychomotor performance: The effects of performance goals on level of performance. *Journal of Applied Psychology, 50,* 286–291.

Locke, E. A., & Latham, G. P. (1985). The application of goal setting to sports. *Journal of Sport Psychology, 7,* 205–222.

Locke, E. A., Shaw, K. N., Saari, L. M., & Latham, G. P. (1981). Goal setting and task performance: 1969–1980. *Psychological Bulletin, 90,* 125–152.

Martens, R. (1977). *Sport Competition Anxiety Test.* Champaign, IL: Human Kinetics.

Martens, R., & Landers, D. (1969). Coaction effects on a muscular endurance task. *Research Quarterly, 40,* 733–737.

Meichenbaum, D. M. (1977). *Cognitive Behavior Modification: An Integrative Approach.* New York: Plenum.

Morgan, W. P. (1972). Sport psychology. In R. N. Singer (Ed.), *The Psychomotor Domain: Movement Behavior* (pp. 193–228). Philadelphia: Lea & Febiger.

Morgan, W. P. (1980a). Test of champions: The iceberg profile. *Psychology Today, 14*(2), 92–102.

Morgan, W. P. (1980b). The trait psychology controversy. *Research Quarterly for Exercise and Sport, 51,* 50–76.

Morgan, W. P., & Pollack, M. L. (1977). Psychologic characterization of the elite distance runner. *Annals of the New York Academy of Science, 301,* 382–403.

Ogilvie, B. C., & Tutko, T. A. (1971). Sport: If you want to build character, try something else. *Psychology Today, 5,* 60–63.

Ogilvie, B. C., & Tutko, T. A. (1972). Motivation and psychometric approach in coaching. In J. E. Kane (Ed.), *Psychological Aspects of Physical Education and Sport.* London: Routledge & Kegan Paul.

Orlick, T. D. (1973). Children's sports—A revolution is coming. *Canadian Association for Health, Physical Education, and Recreation Journal,* (Jan.–Feb.), 12–14.

Orlick, T. D. (1974). The athletic dropout—A high price of inefficiency. *Canadian Association for Health, Physical Education, and Recreation Journal,* (Nov.–Dec.), 21–27.

Orlick, T. D. (1980). *In Pursuit of Excellence.* Champaign, IL: Human Kinetics.

Roberts, G. C., & Pascuzzi, D. (1979). Causal attributions in sport: Some theoretical implications. *Journal of Sport Psychology, 1,* 203–211.

Ryan, R. M. (1980). Attribution, intrinsic motivation, and athletics: A replication and extension. In C. H. Nadeau, W. R. Halliwell, K. M. Newell, & G. C. Roberts (Eds.), *Psychology of Motor Behavior and Sport–1979* (pp. 19–26). Champaign, IL: Human Kinetics.

Sage, G. H., & Loudermilk, S. (1979). The female athlete and role conflict. *Research Quarterly, 50,* 88–96.

Sapp, M., & Haubenstricker, L. (1978). Motivation for joining and reasons for not continuing in youth sports programs in Michigan. Paper presented at AAHPER conference, Kansas City, MO.

Schmidt, R. A. (1988). *Motor Control and Learning: A Behavioral Approach* (2nd ed.). Champaign, IL: Human Kinetics.

Selye, H. (1973). The evolution of the stress concept. *American Scientist, 61,* 692–699.

Shaw, M. E. (1976). *Groupdynamics: The Psychology of Small Group Behavior* (2nd ed.). New York: McGraw Hill.

Silva, J. M. (1982). Competitive sport environments: Performance enhancement through cognitive intervention. *Behavior Modification, 6,* 443–464.

Silva, J. M. (1984). Personality and sport performance. In J. M. Silva & R. S. Weinberg (Eds.), *Psychological Foundations of Sport* (pp. 59–69). Champaign, IL: Human Kinetics.

Singer, R. N., Harris, D. V., Kroll, W., Martens, R., & Sechrest, L. J. (1977). Psychological testing of athletes. *Journal of Physical Education and Recreation, 48,* 30–32.

Smith, R. E. (1984). Theoretical and treatment approaches to anxiety reduction. In J. M. Silva & R. S. Weinberg (Eds.), *Psychological Foundations of Sport* (pp. 157–170). Champaign, IL: Human Kinetics.

Smith, R. E. (1986). Toward a cognitive-affective model of athletic burnout. *Journal of Sport Psychology, 8,* 36–50.

Spielberger, C., Gorsuch, R., & Lushene, R. (1970). *Manual for the State-Trait Anxiety Inventory.* Palo Alto, CA: Consulting Psychological Press.

Straub, W. F. (Ed.) (1978). *Sport Psychology: An Analysis of Athlete Behavior.* Ithaca, NY: Mouvement.

Suinn, R. M. (Ed.) (1980). *Psychology in Sports: Methods and Applications.* Minneapolis, MN: Burgess.

Travis, L. E. (1925). The effect of a small audience upon eye-hand coordination. *Journal of Abnormal and Social Psychology, 20,* 142–146.

Triplett, N. (1897). The dynamogenic factors in pacemaking and competition. *American Journal of Psychology, 9,* 507–553.

Tutko, T. A., Lyon, L., & Ogilivie, B. C. (1969). *Athletic Motivation Inventory.* San Jose, CA: Institute for the Study of Athletic Motivation.

Vealey, R. S. (1992). Personality and sport: A comprehensive view. In T. Horn (Ed.), *Advances in Sport Psychology* (pp. 25–59). Champaign, IL: Human Kinetics.

Weinberg, R. S. (1984). The relationship between extrinsic rewards and intrinsic motivation in sport. In J. M. Silva & R. S. Weinberg (Eds.), *Psychological Foundations of Sport* (pp. 177–187). Champaign, IL: Human Kinetics.

Weinberg, R. S., & Ragan, J. (1978). Motor performance under three levels of trait anxiety and stress. *Journal of Motor Behavior, 10,* 169–176.

Weiner, B. (1972). *Theories of Motivation: From Mechanism to Cognition.* Chicago: Rand-McNally.

Weiss, M. R., & Chaumeton, N. (1992). Motivational orientations to sport. In T. Horn (Ed.), *Advances in Sport Psychology* (pp. 61–99). Champaign, IL: Human Kinetics.

Wrisberg, C. A., Draper, M. V., & Everett, J. J. (1988). Sex role orientations of male and female collegiate athletes from selected individual and team sports. *Sex Roles, 19,* 81–90.

Yerkes, R. M., & Dodson, J. D. (1908). The relation of strength and stimulus to rapidity of habit formation. *Journal of Comparative and Neurological Psychology, 18,* 459–482.

CHAPTER 10

Sport Pedagogy

CHAPTER OBJECTIVES

- To develop an appreciation for the field of sport pedagogy and its contribution to the teaching of human movement
- To understand the distinction between research on teacher education and research on teaching in physical education
- To distinguish between the components of teacher education in physical education: the teacher, the student, and the process
- To distinguish between the components of teaching in physical education: class management, instruction, and student supervision

INTRODUCTION

When attempting to identify the ingredients necessary to facilitate our ability to learn how to move most people would not look any further than the teacher as a starting place. Indeed, few people would argue that a good teacher is a critical component in creating an effective learning environment to explore the human's extraordinary capacity for movement. Assuming that good teaching is an important contributor to a student's ability to execute a movement effectively, one might ask, What factors contribute to good teaching? Unfortunately, the answer to this is not as clear cut as one might imagine. In fact, Siedentop (1991) points out that "research on teaching doesn't have a good reputation. It has suffered through a long history of inconclusive results, inappropriately asked questions, and less than useful techniques" (p. 19). However, in recent years some advancement in our knowledge of how the teaching process can be effectively used to acquire movement skills can be attributed to the rapid development of the field called sport pedagogy.

Siedentop (1991) defines **pedagogy** as "the skillful arrangement of an environment in such a way that students acquire specifically intended learnings" (p. 7). In light of this, one might consider the sport pedagogist as someone concerned with how the physical educator effectively organizes the learning environment to facilitate the acquisition of knowledge about movement and how to move. To understand how this is achieved, the sport pedagogists have concentrated on both the preparation of teachers (i.e., teacher education issues) and how teachers implement what they know in the classroom or gymnasium (i.e., teaching behaviors in the physical education domain).

THE DEVELOPMENT OF SPORT PEDAGOGY

The field of sport pedagogy has experienced considerable change in its brief history. Early research efforts addressed very broad questions concerning the profile of the "perfect" teacher and the "perfect" teaching method. In contrast, contemporary efforts reveal that issues in sport pedagogy are multifaceted and require diverse approaches to answer a variety of questions. Moreover the assessment of these issues is based on sound theoretical positions that have emerged from the earlier efforts. In the following sections we will briefly revisit some of the earlier work that helped establish the foundation for the more sophisticated endeavors of current-day sport pedagogists.

Research on teaching in physical education (RT-PE) has been around for approximately 50 years (Silverman, 1991). Silverman suggests that many of the early investigations in the area of sport pedagogy could be construed as applied motor learning research (see Chapter 8). Questions of interest during this period included: How should practice be organized? What forms of practice might best facilitate learning? Should a task be broken into smaller parts to enhance the subsequent acquisition of the task as a whole?

In stark contrast, Dodds and Placek (1991) contend that sport pedagogy did not emerge from research conducted in the area of motor learning. Dodds and Placek feel that a far greater and more important influence on RT-PE stemmed from the work of general education researchers. There seems to be some truth to this statement. For example, many research frameworks validated from educational research have been adopted in the movement domain with some success (Shulman, 1986).

At this point, it is not important to decide whether research in the area of motor learning or general education exerted the greatest influence on the development of sport pedagogy. However, it is useful to develop an appreciation for the different fields of study that have contributed to the shaping of sport pedagogy as it exists today. In fact, you might have noticed that this is a common occurrence in many of the fields of study that are the focus of this book. Despite the disagreement on the origin(s) of sport pedagogy, the general consensus is that two issues attracted a great deal of research attention within the pedagogical domain in the early days. These issues focused on identifying the personality characteristics that were necessary to be a successful teacher and finding the teaching "methods" that resulted in optimal student learning.

Searching for the Best Teacher and Teaching Method

The work of Laminack and Long (1985) captures a contemporary attempt to describe the personality profile of the "expert" teacher. They documented the qualities that undergraduate students felt made their instructors "memorable." A list of the common attributes of many teachers who were rendered exceptional are listed in Table 10.1. Before you examine this list, think about what characteristics you feel are important in order to be a successful teacher. Are the the attributes you identified on the list in Table 10.1?

Unfortunately, the "personality" approach to pedagogy fell from grace for two reasons. First, the judgments of a teacher's success were being made by individuals who were not qualified or well informed to make such judgments (e.g., principals, peer teachers, students). Second, the personality approach requires an implicit assumption that responses on paper-and-pencil personality tests can offer insight into the specific skills a teacher exhibits in the classroom (Siedentop, 1991). Even more damaging to this line of investigation was the finding that effective teachers do not always possess common personality attributes (Graham & Heimerer, 1981). For example, do you think the list of personality traits you identified as important to teacher effectiveness is the same as a list constructed by someone else? Do you believe all "good" teachers would be endowed with each and every one of the attributes that were reported on each list? This is very unlikely.

A second issue that enjoyed intense research scrutiny in the early days is that of the teaching method. For example, numerous teaching strategies were evaluated and compared in the hope that the one particular method would surface as the pedagogist's "elixir." Mariani (1970) investigated the

TABLE 10.1 Commonly identified personality attributes for memorable teachers.

Classroom Management	Personality	Strategies/ Techniques	Appearance
Flexibility	Loving	Variety	Young
Organization	Caring	New ideas	Pretty
Equal	Helpful	Clarity	Well-dressed
Fair	Enthusiastic	Interesting	Jolly
Respect	Encouraging	Inductive	Happy
Firm	Perceptive	Concrete	Attractive
Even-tempered	Warm	Visual aids	
Diplomatic	Vivacious	Centers	
Disciplinarian	Positive	Participation	
	Patient	Individualized	
	Compassionate	Read aloud	
	Cheerful	Involved	
	Understanding	Parents	
	Sensitive	Discussion	
	Honest	Supplements	
	Tactful		
	Genuine		
	Attentive		
	Open-minded		

From Laminack, Lester & Long, Betty, What makes a teacher effective: Insight from preservice teachers. *Clearing House,* 58 (February 1985), 168. Heldref Publications.

effectiveness of the command and task methods of teaching the forehand and backhand tennis strokes. The **command method** is characterized by the teacher dictating how, when, and what is performed in a practice session in order to learn a task as accurately and quickly as possible. In contrast, the **task method** involves encouraging the student to accept more responsibility for the manner in which the task is practiced.

In the study conducted by Mariani, the task method consisted of the students being provided with cards that explained the achievement standards of performance for the forehand and backhand strokes. After an initial explanation and demonstration by the instructor at the beginning of each practice session, the students chose the order and the time spent on any particular task or drill that needed to be practiced. All students were pretested prior to engaging in 12 hours of practice. Students were subsequently tested for forehand and backhand achievement at the conclusion of the 12 hours of practice and again 60 days later. The results revealed that the task method led to significantly better performance of the forehand stroke than did the command method for both the immediate and 60-day tests.

Silverman (1991) points out, however, that much of the research addressing the teaching method was ill fated because of poor research designs. Furthermore, in many cases there was a failure to monitor adequately or verify the instructions that were provided to the students during these studies. For example, Mariani's (1970) study failed to report the exact nature of the 12 hours of practice that occurred for the individuals in the command and task method groups. Did the students using the task method actually select different drills from those practiced by the students in the command method group? Were the drills used in each of the practice methods performed in different order? Did either of the different teaching methods lead to spending more time on any one drill? Did the students experiencing the task method spend more time on the forehand stroke than on the backhand stroke or vice versa? Such questions need to be answered to draw appropriate conclusions about the two teaching methods.

In light of these criticisms, what can be surmised from the literature on teaching methods? It is unlikely that there is a magical teaching method that optimizes learning. Even though Mariani demonstrated that the task method was good for learning the forehand tennis stroke, it would seem foolish to assume that this would be the ideal method to use to teach all other motor skills. In fact, the methods used by a teacher appear to be quite situation-specific, the choice often being dictated by many different components such as the skill level of the student, the content being taught, and the resources available to the teacher.

Observation of Activity in the Gym

Research on teaching in physical education began to flourish in the 1960s with the development of more comprehensive and sophisticated observational tools that allowed the researcher to monitor teacher and student behaviors. This work was pioneered by Dr. William Anderson at Teachers' College, Columbia University. From this work, the classic monograph entitled "Whats Going On In the Gym?" was published (Anderson & Barrette, 1978). This series of papers is essential reading for anyone interested in the discipline of sport pedagogy.

Why is Anderson's work so important to the evolution of sport pedagogy? First, his efforts led to the development of a videotape data bank of teaching scenarios that was made available to researchers to evaluate the activities of

What Should We Teach Our Children about Movement?

In the spring of 1992, the National Association for Physical Education (NASPE) gathered together some of the best minds in physical education and asked them to construct a clear statement describing what students should know and be able to do as a result of experiences in a quality physical education program. The committee was chaired by Dr. Judith Rink, a professor of physical education at the University of South Carolina and a respected sport pedagogist. After a great deal of deliberation the committee offered the following statement of seven broad guidelines.

A physically educated student:

- *Demonstrates competency in many movement forms and proficiency in a few movement forms.*
- *Applies movement concepts and principles to the learning and development of motor skills.*
- *Exhibits a physically active lifestyle.*
- *Achieves and maintains a health-enhancing level of fitness.*
- *Demonstrates responsible personal and social behavior in physical activity settings.*

- *Demonstrates understanding and respect for differences among people in physical activity settings.*
- *Understands that physical activity provides opportunities for enjoyment, challenge, self-expression, and social interaction.*

Not only did this committee offer these general guidelines but they also presented in greater detail specific guidelines for grade levels K–12. In the more detailed version, key points of emphasis for each level are highlighted as are suggested performance benchmarks that indicate that appropriate achievements are documented. Furthermore, the grade-level guidelines provide teachers and educational administrators examples of assessment options that can be used to evaluate the attainment of the specified criteria. Clearly this work will have an important impact on structure of movement education programs in the near future.

Reprinted from Moving into the Future: National Standards for Physical Education *(1985) with permission from the National Association for Sport and Physical Education (NASPE).*

the teacher and student in the gymnasium. Second, initial analyses of this information suggested that the time in the gymnasium was being poorly utilized by both teachers and students. Third, this work provided the impetus for using a more systematic approach to observing and quantifying the time-course of teacher and student behaviors during teaching episodes. Since that time, a number of observation systems have been developed that have facilitated methodical examinations of the pedagogical process. Some examples include the Behavior of Students in Physical Education (BESTPED) system, Cheffers Adaptation of Flanders Interaction Analysis System (CAFIAS), and the Academic Learning Time–Physical Education (ALT–PE) Instrument.

A natural outgrowth of some of the conclusions drawn from Anderson's work on how time was being used during physical education classes was a wealth of research studies examining this issue. In fact, research in the 1980s concentrated heavily on the concept of **academic learning time (ALT)**. Academic learning time is defined as the amount of time a student is engaged in activity or instruction while pursuing class objectives with a success rate of approximately 80 percent. In modifying this definition for physical education, Metzler (1982) conceptualized academic learning time in physical education (ALT–PE) to be the amount of time during class activity that the student is engaged in overt motor responding at a high success rate.

Metzler (1989) provided a comprehensive overview of the research that addressed ALT–PE. Metzler's conclusions are cause for concern for the sport pedagogist. As much as 25–50 percent of both the teacher and student time is spent in noninstructional activities that contribute little to learning. Does this problem sound familiar? This was also one of the primary observations made by Anderson and his colleagues. While it seems important that the instructor strives to increase ALT, it is dangerous to assume that this alone will result in elevated student achievement. Drawing such a conclusion would be much like saying, "If some is good, then more must be better." In other words, the notion of ALT–PE assumes that more time spent on a task will result in greater task acquisition. While there may be some truth to this, Griffey (1983) challenges the notion that more time on a task should always lead to greater achievement. He states that in certain circumstances, spending more time practicing a task can actually be harmful to the learning process. Griffey points out that it is just as important to address the quality of instruction as the quantity of the instruction or practice. He contends that in some circumstances, good teaching can compensate for reduced amounts of time spent learning a task.

DISTINGUISHING RESEARCH IN TEACHER EDUCATION AND TEACHING IN PHYSICAL EDUCATION

The research topics currently entertained by sport pedagogists are quite diverse. To help us navigate through this work, it is helpful to distinguish between **research on teacher education in physical education (RTE-PE)** and **research on teaching in physical education (RT-PE).** Locke and Dodds (1985) suggest that research on RTE-PE concentrates on what and how to teach teachers of motor skills. In contrast, RT-PE concentrates on the factors that influence how we teach motor skills.

An easy way to distinguish between research on RTE-PE and RT-PE is to consider the dependent and independent variables (refer to Chapter 2 for definitions of independent and dependent variables) that are used in experiments conducted in each of these areas. When doing research on RTE-PE, the dependent variable is the change in teaching behavior (e.g., using more positive feedback) and the independent variable would be some aspect of a teacher training program (e.g., student teaching) that is being evaluated. In contrast, for RT-PE, the dependent variable is a change in student behavior (e.g., spends more time on task) and the independent variable would be the type of teacher behavior being investigated (e.g., time spent in management activities). In this example, changes in teacher behavior become the unit of measurement for research on RTE-PE but for RT-PE, teacher behavior is being manipulated by the experimenter (Siedentop, 1991).

At first glance, the distinction between research on RTE-PE and RT-PE may appear trivial. However, many issues currently of interest to the sport pedagogists might not be addressed if RTE-PE was not subjected to research

PICTURE 10.1   *Class management is a topic addressed by* RT-PE. (Photo credit: © Elizabeth Crews/Stock Boston)

scrutiny, such as examination of trainee and teacher characteristics, the role of student teaching, and mentor programs, to name but a few.

THEORETICAL FRAMEWORKS FOR RESEARCH IN TEACHER EDUCATION AND TEACHING IN PHYSICAL EDUCATION

In addition to categorizing research efforts in sport pedagogy within the broad umbrella of RT-PE and RTE-PE, it is also possible to identify distinct theoretical frameworks that have provided the basis for much of this research activity. In fact, current research appears to be motivated by one of two popular theoretical perspectives. The **behavioral approach** attempts to identify lawful behavior on the part of the student or teacher based on systematic manipulations in the learning or teaching environment. For example, different types of class management procedures might be tried in the class setting to assess which procedure results in more orderly behavior on the part of the students. This perspective relies heavily on the idea that for any given teaching intervention, predictable teaching and student behaviors will be evident. Moreover, these behaviors will always surface when the same teaching intervention is used. A strong advocate for this perspective is Dr. Daryl Siedentop at Ohio State University.

An alternative position is the **socialization perspective,** which places a heavy emphasis on the values, beliefs, and attitudes of the teacher and on the factors that impact these characteristics throughout the teacher's career. Teacher socialization is assumed to be influenced by a variety of issues related to society in general or more specifically to sport, athletics, organizations, or bureaucracies. The socialization position argues that it is vital to assess a teacher's personality, perceptions, values, and beliefs as well as their behaviors. In contrast to the behaviorist's assertion that teacher' actions are generalizable and predictable, a socialization position assumes that teaching behavior can be both situation- and person-specific (Lawson, 1983). Dr. Hal Lawson is one of the primary spokespersons for this perspective.

The behaviorist and socialization researchers use very different research strategies and techniques to pursue their research interests. Despite these differences, a new field of study such as sport pedagogy can only benefit from the debate that this division raises. In fact, many people would argue that both perspectives have led to important findings related to both RTE-PE and RT-PE. Let take a look at RTE-PE and RT-PE in more depth.

RESEARCH ON TEACHER EDUCATION
IN PHYSICAL EDUCATION

We will start our overview of the area of research on teacher education in physical education by considering the two most important elements involved in RTE-PE: the student and the teacher. This is an area of sport pedagogy for which researchers using the socialization theoretical framework have provided some important insights. First, let's consider the student.

Teacher Education: The Student

What leads an individual to consider entering the teaching profession? In making this decision the formation of the "subjective warrant" is crucial (Lortie, 1975). According to Dewar and Lawson (1984, p. 15), the **subjective warrant** is "an individual's perceptions of the skills and abilities necessary for entry into, and performance of work in a specific occupation." An important process in constructing one's subjective warrant is observing others already in the profession. Most of us can recall at some point thinking about the merits of a particular occupation by evaluating the individuals who were key figures in that profession. We probably thought about the lifestyle those individuals lead and contemplated whether this was something we might also like to do. If someone concludes that a line of work has potential, that person must consider whether he or she possesses the skills necessary to enter the profession. This process of initially matching interests and current skills has been termed **anticipatory socialization** (Bain, 1990).

What is the attraction to the teaching field in physical education? The answer to this question was obtained from interviews with prospective students of physical education. The responses during these interviews fall into four broad categories (see Dewar & Lawson, 1984). First, the "interpersonal" category is based on the notion that students desire to work with and help other people. Second, a "service" theme suggests that students attracted to teaching in physical education foresee an opportunity to provide a valuable service to society. Third, a great many students gravitate toward teaching physical education because they had very happy and rewarding experiences participating in physical education in elementary and secondary school. Thus, merely having the opportunity for "continuation" in a job that is associated with pleasurable experience is sufficient to recruit some individuals. A large subset of this category have stronger ties to athletic programs than to physical education. In many of these cases, it is the desire to coach, not teach, that is the primary motivation. In fact, many of these students are not committed to teaching but they see this as a convenient route to enter the coaching ranks. For example, Segrave (1980) reported that students who were provided the opportunity to choose between teaching and coaching often choose the latter option. Finally, ease of entrance into physical education programs appears to be an important factor in career selection of many students. For example, Templin, Woodford, and Mulling (1982) revealed that physical education entrants typically demonstrate only average academic performance in high school. It is quite possible that entry into physical education is one of the few routes available to many of these students if they wish to pursue higher education. Clearly, the two latter categories are rather disconcerting for sport pedagogists since they contribute to the negative image many departments of physical education have on college campuses.

Teacher Education: The Teacher

Who is responsible for training the individuals who choose to be the future teachers in physical education? This heavy burden falls on the shoulders of teacher educators. In a recent series of surveys conducted by sport pedagogists, a general picture of the teacher educator was established. Teacher educators are generally experienced teachers who possess little if any advanced training for this role. It is also common that the individuals designated as teacher educators are assigned a disproportionate amount of other administrative and advisement duties within their department. Moreover, in smaller colleges the teacher educator often has a coaching position in addition to these other duties. It is therefore not surprising that most teacher educators have a low research publication rate. Metzler and Freedman (1985) report that only 35 percent of physical education teacher educators have one or more refereed publications. This is quite unusual because research activity is such a high priority in most college settings today. Low research activity on the part of the teacher educators may be a result of time limitations given their other duties or merely a conscious commitment on their part to other tasks such as teaching and student interaction.

It would appear that the findings to date from research on the physical education teacher educator have identified some important shortcomings in the preparation of the individuals serving this role. The lack of specialized training, in addition to the diverse activities that these individuals are required to perform, are issues that will need to be addressed in the near future. Hopefully, the emergence of a growing number of physical education doctoral programs targeting teacher education will revolutionize the preparation of the teacher educator.

Teacher Education: The Process

Our examination of the teacher education process will be made easier by considering three separate stages during the teacher educator's lifespan. More specifically, teacher education can be considered to consist of three phases: preservice, induction, and inservice. **Preservice** includes all activities (e.g., coursework, student teaching, internship, practicum) that are used to prepare an individual to enter the workplace with the necessary skills to be successful. **Induction** refers to the way in which the teacher is socialized into the teaching environment after completion of the preservice phase. Finally, **inservice** refers to continuing education activities that are designed to update the skills of currently certified physical educators.

Locke (1984a) summarized the major findings from research that focused on RTE-PE for the period between 1960 and 1981. During this time, the primary focus of most research endeavors was the preservice component of the teacher's education. More specifically, the topic of student teaching created an avalanche of investigations, accounting for one in three studies that addressed preservice activities. While the preservice component has done little in the way of slowing down since 1981, the induction and inservice phases of RTE-PE have sparked greater interest (Locke, 1984b; Bain, 1990). Let's take at look at each of these phases, starting with the preservice phase.

Preservice: Training to Be a Teacher.   Bain (1990) highlights three important aspects of the preservice phase that have caught the attention of sport pedagogists and that have been subjected to some research scrutiny: program content, program design, and the hidden curriculum. We will examine each of these issues in the following sections.

Program Content.   When constructing the curriculum to train teachers, some consideration needs to be given to the information and skills that will make up the "meat" of the program. These concerns are central to the program content dimension of the preservice phase. It is crucial that any program designed to prepare teachers provides a sound understanding of both content knowledge and pedagogical knowledge.

The subject matter that the teacher will be teaching is referred to as **content knowledge.** In the field of physical education, this is knowledge about movement and the ability to execute movements. With respect to this type of knowledge, three trends have emerged in recent years. First, there is a focus on the science of movement and a deemphasis on sociocultural, philosophical, and historical perspectives. This is consistent with the advent of books much like the one you are now reading. Second, there is still a large portion (as much as 33 percent) of content knowledge obtained through coursework on pedagogy (Murphy, 1980). Finally, obtaining content knowledge pertaining to movement requires performance courses in which individuals actually spend time developing personal skill in the activities they will teach. There is an ongoing debate as to the necessity of performance-based courses. In spite of this, most programs include such courses in some form.

While it is critical that instructors have a solid foundation in the subject matter, they must also be capable of transforming this information into a form that can be understood and used by their students. This issue is the essence of **pedagogical content knowledge,** which involves developing a repertoire of methods for presenting content knowledge. The identification of effective methods to impart content knowledge to the students has been obtained from a number of research investigations focusing on research describing factors that impact skill acquisition (see Chapter 8), research on teacher effectiveness, and interviews with expert teachers (Siedentop, 1989). We will discuss some of these methods when we discuss RT-PE in a subsequent section of this chapter.

Program Design.   To enable the teacher trainee to understand the importance of both content knowledge and pedagogical knowledge, this information must be presented in a coherent and organized fashion. This is often achieved via traditional methods such as classroom instruction. However, there is a growing emphasis on incorporating field experiences and field-based activities that are designed to get the student into a "realistic setting" as soon as possible during training. It is not surprising then that much of the research on program design has focused on early field experiences and student teaching.

A national survey indicated that 86 percent of teacher education programs in physical education require some form of field experience prior to student teaching (Placek & Silverman, 1983). Since such an overwhelming number of programs include early field experiences, one would assume that they must be an effective method for establishing appropriate teacher behaviors. This does not appear to be the case. In fact, little evidence exists to support the usefulness of early teaching experiences (Bain, 1990).

It is possible that early field experience occurs too early in the student's training to be effective. For example, teacher trainees might lack the necessary mastery of content and pedagogical knowledge to be effective in the field setting at this early stage in their training. While this might be true for the early experiences, this should not be the case when they finally enter the student teaching phase. **Student teaching** is the cornerstone of most teacher education programs and consists of approximately 16 weeks of teaching in a school environment while being supervised by a cooperating teacher. It is during this period that the student has primary responsibility for implementing, in the "real world," the knowledge obtained in the classroom. Since this is such an important element of the preservice phase, it is not surprising that a vast amount of research has been directed at student teaching.

What does this research tell us? On the positive side, student teaching provides an opportunity for the trainee to work at the field site with an experienced teacher, called the **cooperating teacher.** It has been shown that the student teachers do copy effective teaching methods used by the cooperating teacher while ignoring teaching behaviors that appear to be ineffec-

PICTURE 10.2 *Most program designs attempt to expose the teacher trainee to field-based experiences early in the training.* (Photo credit: Robert Harbison)

tive. Furthermore, Siedentop (1981) contends that the student teaching environment can be used effectively to teach essential instructional behaviors such as spending less time on gymnasium management problems and increasing ALT–PE. In other words, instead of just viewing student teaching as a chance to see how things work in the real world, it can be used as a testing ground for new or innovative teaching activities. Finally, student teaching offers students the opportunity to confirm or disconfirm their vocational choice and get an initial idea of the complexities and challenges they must be prepared to face.

Some sport pedagogists, however, vehemently question the usefulness of student teaching. They point to evidence suggesting that the student teaching experience results in many negative consequences for the trainee. Locke (1984a) points out that sometimes this process can lead to the trainee's self-image being lowered, the development of poor attitude toward pupils, and an adoption of a more authoritarian approach to the teaching process. Maybe as a consequence of this, some teachers gain job satisfaction from merely being able to control the gymnasium as opposed to enhancing pupil learning.

There are also some problems related to the role of the cooperating teacher. For example, many cooperating teachers have not been trained for this role and lack the skills to direct the activities of the student teacher effectively. Of greater concern is the finding that cooperating teachers often view the appearance of a student teacher as an opportunity to do "other things" while the student teacher "covers" their class. For example, Tannehill and Zakrajsek (1988) had 18 cooperating teachers keep daily and weekly logs of their supervisory activities. Examinations of these logs indicated that these cooperating teachers gave little feedback to the student teachers, held few supervisory conferences, and spent very little time observing the students in "action."

Student teaching is considered a time to refine the skills necessary to impart knowledge about movement. Current empirical evidence suggests that this can be the case. It appears, however, that sport pedagogists will be taking a long, hard look at this requirement in coming years to redefine ways to organize and implement student teaching to optimize the benefits and eliminate the drawbacks of this component of the teacher education program. For this reason, student teaching will probably continue to dominate the research that is conducted on the teacher's preservice training.

Hidden Curriculum.   Few people would have difficulty identifying cooperating teachers and students as influential socializing agents during the preservice phase of a teacher's training. However, there is also another powerful socializing force at work during the teacher education programs that is usually not explicitly or formally recognized, but has a large impact on the trainees' attitudes, values, and beliefs. This is often referred to as the **hidden curriculum** and consists of "tacit messages associated with the rituals and routines of the program" that inform the student what particular knowledge is worth learning and what knowledge is of little value (Bain, 1990). For example, an earlier discussion indicated that teacher educators do not spend a great deal of time conducting research. This could be interpreted by the student to mean that RT-PE has no value for the practice of teaching (Metzler & Freedman, 1985).

Physical education programs also communicate particular messages about other everyday social issues. Two extremely sensitive areas, namely sexism and racism, are sometimes the focus of concern (Bain, 1990). For example, dance and elementary methods have been areas that are historically areas taught by female faculty. However, these areas of physical education are often supplemental and usually play only a minor role in many programs. With respect to racism, it is not uncommon for a large proportion of the varsity athletes on a college campus to be black, yet only a few blacks play a role in the professorial ranks in the academic program. Both situations could be interpreted as evidence that physical education affords only certain roles for particular activities or individuals. This should not be the case. Program administrators have to be continually on the lookout for the influence the hidden curriculum might have on the students to ensure that these individuals enter the teaching field with the appropriate "tools."

Induction: Entering the Teaching Profession.   Imagine you have just completed the preservice phase of your teacher education program after doing a 16-week stint of student teaching. You were lucky enough to secure a position teaching physical education at a local high school. Armed with all the knowledge and skills that were obtained in the preservice phase, you are now ready to begin this exciting new challenge. In the first few days, you realize that there is much more to this job than just organizing and teaching the class units you were hired to teach. The amount of administrative and clerical work for which you are responsible is greater than you imagined it would be. Preparing your classes requires much more time than you originally thought it would. Implementing and maintaining discipline in the gymnasium or on the playing field stretches your emotional and physical strength to the limit. The questions you now ask yourself are: How can I survive? How can I effectively complete all the duties assigned to me?

The transition into the real world of teaching is termed induction. According to Lawson (1983), induction involves the whole process by which the new teacher enters the profession. During this period, as Bain (1990) indicates, teachers learn the norms of their job. Furthermore, the teacher is exposed to a new form of socialization, namely **bureaucratic socialization,** which reveals knowledge about the rules and expectations of the school or organization with which the new teacher is now associated. Another important socializing agent for the teacher in the induction phase is the student. In the early days, it appears that the new teacher places a heavy emphasis on encouraging fun and high student involvement during classes. This is often done at the expense of student achievement (Veal, 1988).

Inservice: Meeting the Demands of a Changing Teaching Environment.   After a few years in the workplace teachers often realize that they require new skills to contend with unique situations that emerge in the teaching environment. For example, computer-aided teaching is becoming routine (Kerns, 1989), innovative activities are continually surfacing (e.g., step aerobics), and having to deal with individuals with special needs (e.g., physical or mental dysfunction) is becoming increasingly more commonplace. During training, teachers may not have been exposed to many of these issues and must therefore reevaluate the tools they need to be successful. Inservice is a form of continuing education designed to provide currently practicing teachers exposure to new information about teaching that will help them contend with the new demands of the teaching environment.

Bain (1990) provided a useful guide to the categories of inservice activities typically used in physical education. One approach, called the **defect approach,** focuses on changing specific teachers' behaviors by using behavioral techniques that focus on encouraging different and more appropriate behaviors (see Siedentop, 1991). The **growth approach** does not assume that the teacher has deficiencies like the defect approach. Rather this method is based on the premise that teachers can learn a great deal by reflecting on past experience. A third category is the **problem-solving approach,** characterized by greater teacher input than the other categories of inservice programs. This method generally addresses problems that have been diagnosed by the teachers. A final procedure is termed the **change approach.** This type of inservice activity has as its focus a means of adapting to changes in society. For example, ensuring gender equality and incorporating handicapped individuals into the mainstream program have been the focus of many recent inservice activities.

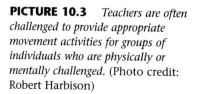

PICTURE 10.3   *Teachers are often challenged to provide appropriate movement activities for groups of individuals who are physically or mentally challenged.* (Photo credit: Robert Harbison)

Given the importance of inservice activities, it is surprising to note that prior to 1981, little research effort focused on this area of RTE-PE. However, since this time, research addressing inservice activities has increased. Locke (1984b) identifies three major reasons for this. First, with the decline in undergraduate enrollment, underused teacher educators focused attention on helping an underutilized resource—the practitioner. Second, funding agencies made relatively large amounts of money available to find ways to prepare individuals to cope with the demands of pupils with special needs. Finally, sport pedagogists realized it was easier to work with experienced teachers when experimenting with a particular intervention. This could be done during inservice-type programs.

What does the research on inservice tell us? Since research efforts are only just surfacing on this topic, it is really too early to draw any conclusions. However, some people feel inservice activities are usually ineffective (Bain, 1990). There does appear to be some hope, however. Recent evidence has surfaced that indicates that teacher-initiated inservice programs can be useful for resolving technical problems faced by the teacher. While most people consider inservice as a crucial part of the teacher's ongoing preparation, future research efforts must help delineate appropriate ways to use inservice activity to maximize its effectiveness.

Greater commitment is being made to understand the preparation of the teacher of physical education. This commitment has concentrated heavily on the preservice facet of teacher education. More specifically, the focus is on student teaching. Future efforts will need to attempt to gain insight into the induction and inservice aspects of teacher training. To facilitate this, these components must be viewed as integral aspects of the teaching process and worthy of study in their own right. These sentiments are echoed in a statement about RTE-PE by Siedentop in an edited text by Vendien and Nixon (1985). He states, "When conceptualized from preservice through the induction period and into inservice training, it [teacher education] no doubt has more power to effect change than any other agency."

RESEARCH ON TEACHING IN PHYSICAL EDUCATION

In the previous sections we focused on research on teacher education in physical education or RTE-PE. The focus now shifts to consider what should and does go on in the classroom, in the gymnasium, and on the field. This is the area known as research on teaching in physical education, or RT-PE. At the heart of this are three broad categories of activities: class management, instruction, and student supervision (Siedentop, 1991). In the following sections, we will explore each of these in some detail. We will begin with class management.

Class Management

A major goal for the teacher is to maximize the time available to the learner to be instructed and engage in appropriate forms of practice. In order for this to occur, the teacher must manage the class setting effectively to minimize the amount of time devoted to readying the learning environment and the learners for activity. **Class management** involves activities that are organizational, transitional, and general non–subject matter tasks that occur during a period of study.

Class management time will depend on the number of management episodes that occur and the length of each of these. According to Siedentop (1991), a **management episode** begins with the teacher initiating a management behavior (e.g., calling role) and continues until the next instructional activity begins. When during the class period do you think the greatest amount of management activity occurs? Usually it is not just the management episode(s) occurring at the beginning or end of class that causes class management time to be inflated (for example, taking attendance, collecting absence slips, and making announcements). Rather, it is an accumulation of small episodes that occur throughout the class period that contribute greatly to increased management time. Such activities include the students being moved in and out of groups, selecting teams, activities or drills being alternated, and equipment being passed out.

Luke (1989) examined the research addressing management behaviors elicited within the physical education setting. The results are quite shocking. Students spend 15 to 22 percent of the classroom time engaged in management activities. This means that in some cases, almost one-quarter of the class period is devoted to activities in which no instruction or practice is provided and presumably little, if any, learning occurs. The amount of time specifically assigned to class management will of course be dependent on the type of activity being taught. Luke's study revealed that management time accounted for only 7 percent of the class period in fitness classes but as much as 32 percent in a gymnastics class. Furthermore, elementary classes appear to demand slightly greater attention to management activities (25 percent) than secondary classes (22 percent).

Management time does not always have to dominate the physical education class. For example, Siedentop, Rife, and Boehm (1974) recorded the number of managerial episodes and the time of each episode exhibited during a 35-minute teaching period by three student teachers. Table 10.2 reveals that class management time, prior to incorporating a management time game (see highlight) into the class, represented as much as 30–37 percent of the class period. Following the introduction of the management time game, the time the student teachers spent focusing on management activities was as little as 4–6 percent—a substantial reduction. Such innovative methods

 HIGHLIGHT

Providing Incentives to Help Manage the Classroom

A rather innovative method to improve class management was used by Siedentop, Rife, and Boehm (1974). They used a "group contingency management game" that consisted of allowing students to accumulate points that could be traded for receiving free time during a class at the end of a week. During the free time students were allowed to choose the activity they preferred. This might be shooting baskets, trampolining, or just sitting in the bleachers talking with friends. Within the structure of the management game, points were awarded for meeting some simple management goals. For example, two points would be awarded for being in the gym at the appropriate station no later than eight minutes after the scheduled start time of the class. A particularly important part of the game used by the researchers was that for any individual to accrue free time the whole class had to meet the managerial goal. This requirement quickly gets the class to conform as a whole.

TABLE 10.2   Class management time prior to and after a management game was used in the classroom.

		Baseline	*Intervention*
ST-1	Total managerial time per class	10:37	1:46
	Average time per managerial episode	1:49	0:23
ST-2	Total managerial time per class	11:36	2:03
	Average time per managerial episode	1:37	0:25
ST-3	Total managerial time per class	13:33	1:23
	Average time per managerial episode	1:38	0:13

From Siedentop, Rife, & Boehm, Modifying the managerial efficiency of student teachers in physical education. From an unpublished paper, School of Health, Phys. Ed., & Recreation, The Ohio State University, Columbus, OH.

are worthy of consideration for physical education teachers as a means of alleviating the management problems typically exhibited in the physical education setting.

Making Parts of the Class "Routine."   A **routine** is a procedure for performing specific behaviors that can occur relatively frequently during the course of a class period (Siedentop, 1991). A number of routines that can be used in the physical education setting are listed in Table 10.3. It is essential that teachers initially view routines as important as teaching the students to spike a volleyball or dribble a soccer ball. This means that appropriate demonstrations, practice, and feedback should be provided for any routine teachers expect the students to adhere to during a class period.

Fink and Siedentop (1989) monitored seven physical education teachers at the beginning of a school year to evaluate how they used and taught routines. After viewing 42 class periods, Fink and Siedentop found that as many as 17 routines for a physical education class were taught. The most frequently used routine was one termed an "attention/quiet" routine that was used to get the students to stop what they were doing and attend to the instructor. Other routines were commonly designed to move students between activities as well as finish the class period promptly.

Using Rules to Reduce Disruptive Behavior.   One of the major problems in the gymnasium and also one of the biggest contributors to increased management time is disruptive behavior on the part of the students. Each time instructors have to divert their attention to reprimand a student, they are executing a management episode. In order to reduce management

TABLE 10.3   Many different routines can be used to make a physical education class run more efficiently.

Routine	Purpose
Entry	What to do when entering the gymnasium. Most often includes an initial practice activity or warm-up and a specific space to go to.
Warm-up	A specific warm-up to engage in without teacher prompting or supervision.
Attention/quiet	A teacher signal for attention and the expected student response to the signal.
Home base	A specific place (spot, number) on the gym floor that the student goes to when instructed.
Gain attention	An appropriate way for the students to gain the attention of the teacher.
Gather	An appropriate way to gather in a central location when directed by the teacher and the formation to gather into.
Disperse	An appropriate way to disperse from a central location to a more scattered practice formation.
Equipment	Appropriate ways to obtain or put away equipment.
Retrieve	An appropriate way to retrieve a ball when it has invaded the space of classmates during a game or drill.
Start	A procedure for initiating activity quickly on a signal.
Boundaries	Specific procedures for staying within defined boundaries, whether inside a gym or outside on a playing field.
Finish	A specific procedure for ending a lesson that typically includes both a cool-down and a closure to the lesson.
Leave	A procedure for leaving the space and returning to the classroom or locker room.
Housekeeping	All procedures for dealing with things like dressing, using the bathroom, getting a drink, or leaving the space.

From *Developing Teaching Skills in Physical Education* by Daryl Siedentop. Copyright © 1991 by Mayfield Publishing Company. Reprinted by permission of the publisher.

episodes, it is important that the instructor establish acceptable behavior for the gymnasium or playing field by implementing a set of rules that are consistently enforced. A **rule** in this case could be described as general expectations for either acceptable or unacceptable behavior for a variety of situations that might arise during the course of the class period.

A recent study by O'Sullivan and Dyson (1994) examined the way in which 11 high school physical education teachers taught the rules and expectations for their class. This evaluation was based on the first four classes taught at the beginning of a semester. One interesting finding from this study was the difference in time it took teachers to explain the rules and expectations of the class to the students. Some teachers took only one day, whereas others took four days. Most of the discussion related to class rules referred to the dress code. One finding that seems particularly troubling is related to the expectations that many of these teachers had for their class. Essentially, students were informed that by dressing appropriately and trying hard, they would achieve a good grade—hardly a great endorsement for the usefulness of engaging in physical activity. In fact, only a few of the teachers observed discussed the benefits of physical education at any time during the first four days of class. One would hope that this will not be a consistent trend in the data obtained from future studies that examine the role of rules and expectations in the physical education setting.

Instruction

Instructional activities, in addition to management activities, involve minimal practice opportunity for the learner. As much as 33 percent of class time is often used for instructional purposes. It is important, therefore, that teachers continually examine how they instruct their students and identify methods to make their instruction more efficient.

Planning to Instruct. Most effective teachers spend time constructing a plan for teaching the content of their course. In some cases these plans merely provide a "rough" guide to the teacher for each lesson they teach. In contrast, other instructors are quite dependent on the plan they have developed and rigidly follow it as they teach each and every lesson. Whether or not the teacher strictly adheres to the plan during each class does not seem to be the critical issue. What appears to be the common denominator among effective teachers is the fact that at some time, a plan is actually constructed.

A good example of this is captured in a study by Byra and Coulon (1994). They looked at the importance of constructing a plan prior to an instructional period for preservice teachers. Remember, the preservice phase is the training stage a teacher experiences prior to entering the teaching field. Twelve preservice teachers taught one planned and one unplanned basketball class. These classes were videotaped and evaluated. The evaluation included an assessment of the student's academic learning time (ALT), the amount of verbal feedback provided by the teacher, and the clarity of different components of the lesson (e.g., introduction and closure). Byra and Coulon revealed that constructing a plan prior to teaching a lesson led to less time spent in noninstructional activities (i.e., management time) and more time spent on task. Furthermore, the presentation of the material in the planned class was consistently clearer, and verbal feedback was more frequently focused on the aspect of the task that was identified as the major emphasis for that class period. These data clearly support the contention that a plan of action for a class can be useful ammunition for the teacher. The next question is, What should these plans look like?

The Big Picture: Unit Plans.   A **unit plan** maps out a group of lessons that revolve around a particular theme (Rink, 1985). It is unlikely that there is any one "perfect" format for a unit plan. More often than not teachers eventually design the most appropriate unit plan based on what they have found to be the most useful procedures to implement in the gymnasium.

When preparing a unit plan, Mager (1968) identifies three questions that the teacher should consider. First, "Where am I going?" This question requires that the instructor specify the cognitive, psychomotor, and affective objectives for the unit. Next the instructor must ask, "How will I get there?" Documenting the activities and experiences the students will require in order to meet the previously stated objectives is central to this question. Finally, "How will I know I have arrived?" Consideration must be given to how the instructor will evaluate whether the students achieved the performance criteria of the stated objectives. Obviously before the questions posed by Mager can be addressed, it is essential that the teacher appraise the potential limitations the learning environment may exert on achieving the proposed objectives. These may include facility and equipment availability, class duration, and the capabilities of the learner.

The Smaller Picture: Lesson Plans.   How does the lesson plan differ from the unit plan? The **lesson plan** is a guide for instruction that will occur in a single lesson and should be based on the objectives stated in the unit plan (Rink, 1985). Siedentop (1991) suggests that many experienced teachers may have sufficiently detailed components within their unit plan to provide an adequate guide to teaching each lesson. However, this will probably not be the case for the beginning teacher. According to Rink (1985), the essential components of a lesson plan are heading material, student *and* teacher objectives, a description of the major tasks that may be used in the class period, the instructional plan, and the mechanism for evaluating the class.

Implementing the Lesson Plan: An Instructional Plan.   A crucial element in Rink's (1985) conceptualization of a lesson plan is the **instructional plan.** This is a detailed step-by-step outline of what tasks the students will do, how they will perform the task, and when they will perform the task.

The instructional plan should provide an adequate description of the anticipated progression of tasks and how each task will be communicated to the learner (verbally, demonstration, handouts). Furthermore, this plan should include the organizational arrangement of students necessary to practice a task and what contribution each activity is making to the objectives stated in the unit plan.

Linking the Teacher and Student: Communication.   In order to provide appropriate instruction, the teacher must be able to communicate to the learner the relevant information necessary to execute a particular action. Typically we consider the primary medium for communicating information to involve verbal description. While this may be true, it is important for teachers to understand that familiarity with the material being taught can sometimes lead to verbal descriptions being overly complex for the learner while appearing relatively simplistic to the teacher. It is here that the pedagogical content knowledge of the teacher is critical. Recall that this form of knowledge provides a repertoire of methods for presenting content knowledge. Presumably this repertoire includes methods that are not entirely dependent on verbal description.

Can you think of any other form of communication that would be useful in the movement domain? One particularly effective method of com-

PICTURE 10.4   *Demonstrations are a useful method to help the student understand the complexities of some movements.* (Photo credit: © Michael Hayman/Stock Boston)

municating during the instruction of movement is a **demonstration,** which can be considered a form of visual communication. Rink (1985) suggests that demonstrations should be performed accurately (i.e., should be error-free), by a student if possible, and should be accompanied by the teacher identifying important landmarks of the action. In a sense, the student's observation of the action is being guided by the teacher.

This is similar to the notion of cueing, which has been shown to be particularly useful when using another communication procedure—presenting feedback on a videotape (see Rothstein & Arnold, 1976). **Cueing** involves telling students to attend to one particular aspect of their action that is being observed on the videotape being played back. Novices, in particular, seem to benefit greatly from the cueing technique when watching videotapes.

Instructional Formats as Delivery Methods.   This refers to the delivery methods used by the teacher to provide the learner with instruction and appropriate forms of practice. There are many different forms of instruction, including task teaching, peer teaching, interactive teaching, reciprocal teaching, cooperative learning, problem solving, and self-instruction.

One might consider instructional format to be similar to the notion of teaching style (see Mosston, 1981). Mosston's perspective considers the teaching style adopted by the instructor to be dependent on who—the teacher or the learner—is responsible for making the majority of decisions within a particular practice format. A spectrum of teaching styles is proposed to exist from a very teacher-directed style (e.g., command method) to the self-teaching method that gives total responsibility to the student to make practice related decisions. Do you recall Mariani's tennis study discussed earlier in this chapter? Siedentop (1991) indicates that it was once thought that student growth and development were enhanced as the teacher progressed from a style focusing on teacher directives to more discovery-oriented styles of teaching. It is now assumed that the teaching style adopted for any particular situation is based on contextual factors that are present (i.e., the nature of the student, subject matter, learning environment, and time constraints) and on the personal preference of the teacher (see Beckett, 1990; Boyce, 1992).

This latter issue is demonstrated in a study by Rupert and Buschner (1989), who examined the instructional behaviors of individuals who had roles as both coach and teacher. Nine coach-teachers were observed while coaching and teaching their respective activities. The results revealed some interesting differences between instructional behaviors in the coaching and teaching setting. In the coaching environment, these individuals spent more

TABLE 10.4   Teaching formats move from very teacher-oriented approaches to student-oriented approaches.

Mosston's Spectrum of Teaching Styles

The Spectrum of Teaching Styles differentiated among various strategies on the basis of who made decisions (teacher or student), how students were grouped, and how learning activities were paced (teacher-paced or self-paced).

- **Command Style**   Instruction and practice controlled directly by teacher.
- **Task Style**   Some instruction and most practice embedded in tasks that can allow for individualization of content and pacing.
- **Reciprocal Teaching**   Students work in pairs with some instructional functions taken over by student, especially feedback and support.
- **Small-Group Teaching**   Student roles in instruction and practice further differentiated as doer, observer, and recorder.
- **Individualized Teaching**   Content individualized based on student abilities.
- **Guided Discover**   Teacher guides students through a series of problems in which students make decisions and explore alternative solutions.
- **Problem Solving**   Teacher poses problems that students must solve on their own with alternative solutions valued.

From Mosston, M., *Teaching Physical Education,* 1981. Columbus, OH: Merrill.

time providing their students with focused preactivity instructions and praise during the activities. However, in the teaching setting, management time accounted for 22 percent of the class period, which was substantially higher than the 7 percent of time spent with management tasks in the coaching situation. These data support the contention that the contexts of teaching and coaching result in very different behaviors on the part of the teacher/coach.

All's Well that Ends Well: Closure.   At the end of any instructional period, it is essential that the instructor brings the individuals in the class together. What function do you think closure serves? It is during this time that the class can be reviewed as a whole and the important components reestablished in the minds of the learners. Allotting time for closure also offers the opportunity for the teacher to receive feedback from the students concerning their feelings toward the class. Furthermore, if recognition of any particular activity or individual is warranted, this is a perfect time to perform this function. Adequate closure is important; to ensure that it is not overlooked, an effective teacher will carefully prepare and plan for this phase of the class.

Aspects of Supervision

Management and instructional activities detract from the time the learner can spend practicing and should therefore be minimized in a class period. In contrast, supervision is the primary activity the teacher uses to ensure that the student spends time-on-task. Supervision activities on the part of the teacher may constitute as much as 45 percent of a class period (Siedentop, 1991). During this time, the teacher usually provides individual or group feedback, actively monitors the student activity, and offers behavioral prompts.

Use Feedback to Mold Behavior.   When the teacher makes a response about an action produced by a student, it is typically referred to as feedback. Can we learn without receiving this type of information? Can you think of any occasions when you were given feedback, but it didn't help you? Most people assume that feedback is essential for skill acquisition to occur (Rink, 1985). Furthermore, many consider the teacher to be the primary resource for provision of this information (Harrison & Blakemore, 1992). The usefulness of feedback to the learner, however, will vary considerably based on its specificity and the extent to which it tells the learner what to do next. More specifically, feedback can be divided into statements that are general or specific and those that are positive, corrective, or negative. Maybe the importance that teachers place on the provision of feedback is reflected in the finding that the feedback presentation rate is sometimes as high as 30–60 statements in a 30-minute class (Fink & Siedentop, 1989). It seems that when feedback is presented quite frequently, it tends to be more general and corrective in nature (Siedentop, 1991).

Up to this point, we have considered feedback as providing a means by which the learner might correct errors they make in movement production. Essentially, the feedback, especially specific-corrective feedback, can act as a prescription for producing an appropriate action. What other role might feedback play? What might happen if a novice tennis player hears the teacher provide feedback such as "good job"? While this does little in the way of telling the student what to do next, it can provide a great deal of motivation to do better or try harder. The astute teacher never underestimates the motivational or energizing power of feedback.

The Importance of Monitoring Behavior.   Monitoring refers to the teacher passively observing the students engage in time-on-task. A primary goal of monitoring activity is to ensure that the activity the students are performing is congruent with the goals and objectives that are stated in the unit and lesson plans. Why is monitoring so important? It is very easy for teachers to assume that, if they effectively plan management, instruction, and other aspects of their supervision requirements, once the students begin to practice a task, the teacher's job has been completed successfully. But this is far from the truth. Students need to be accountable for engaging in appropriate practice, and nothing encourages this more than the instructor closely observing how they perform.

In addition to keeping students actively participating in goal-related activity, monitoring behaviors on the part of the teacher provide an ideal opportunity to facilitate the grading process. In particular, if grades are assigned based on performance throughout a unit as opposed to a final skills test, it is important that a reliable record of each student performance is kept. This can be done using a formal monitoring system. Examples of this might include task checklists, publicly displayed achievement charts, and periodic skills tests. In addition, performance during game situations can be recorded. In tennis, for example, students might play doubles each class period and the total number of games won by each individual during each class period can be recorded. If necessary and appropriate, this can be made more elaborate by noting first and second serve percentages, number of winners, and number of unforced errors for each class period. This offers the opportunity for the teacher to map the progress clearly of each student throughout the entire semester.

Prompting Appropriate Behavior.   It is not unusual for a physical education class to culminate with a scrimmage or game situation. In many cases the game may be modified to focus on the skill or activity the teacher highlighted that particular day. This is not a time for the teacher to take a break! Ormand (1988) suggested that prompts may be the most appropriate teaching device to use during this facet of the learning environment. A **prompt** is information presented to the student that directs behavior in a particular direction that is appropriate for meeting the demands of the task at hand. Prompts can be as diverse as verbal instructions to a hand signal presented during a baseball game.

FINAL COMMENT

The emphasis of this book is on the constraints (e.g., physiological, psychological, and mechanical) that impact the human's capacity for movement. We would be remiss, however, if we ignored the important contribution that the teaching process made to an individual's ability to move. Researchers in the area of sport pedagogy have examined the role of movement education from two distinct perspectives, namely, teacher education and teaching in physical education. One dimension of the work in teacher education has focused on delineating the characteristics of both the student entering the teaching profession and the individuals specifically trained as teacher educators. It would appear at this stage that the reasons for entry into the teaching profession are not necessarily motivated by a desire to be a movement educator. In many cases this educational route is followed as an avenue to other pursuits such as coaching. Another consideration is the training of the teacher educators; there is great concern at this point in the sport pedagogy ranks that specialized preparation of teacher educators is only just beginning to surface.

Probably the largest volume of interest in the teacher education component has focused on particular phases to which the potential teachers are exposed. These include preservice, induction, and inservice phases. Certainly one of the questions that impacts the information presented during these phases concerns the extent of content knowledge about human movement that the teacher needs. The teacher not only has to understand the physiological, mechanical, and psychological limitations of the learner but has to select which aspects of this information will mediate their instructional practices for different activities. One component that the preservice phase offers teacher trainees to assess their content knowledge and pedagogical skills is student teaching. While intuitively most people assume this to be a fruitful component of the teacher's training, research addressing this issue is not so reassuring. It is likely that this aspect, in addition to reviewing the role of inservice activities, will continue to garner the attention of sport pedagogists in the future.

It should be noted that throughout this chapter the role of social influences surfaces on numerous occasions. For example, teachers are socialized during preservice by the boundaries of the program to which they belong, the faculty with which they interact, and the university they attend. Further socialization occurs when they enter the teaching profession. The agents of socialization in these cases and those discussed in the previous chapter on sport psychology are in many situations very similar. They include family, friends, significant others, and mentors such as coaches or faculty.

Even if teachers have a good grasp of the content of this book and have superior pedagogical skills, they are still faced with pragmatic limitations associated with the teaching domain. This problem is clearly demonstrated in the inefficient use of time by many teachers in the training setting. A great deal of research indicates that too much time is spent managing the class as opposed to instructing and supervising specific movement experiences. Assuming that the time spent engaging practice can be increased with innovative activities such as time management games, the quality of instructional activities can become the focus of the sport pedagogist. In this respect, a collaboration between the sport pedagogist and the motor learner to address issues such as feedback and practice would seem to be particularly useful for the future.

QUESTIONS FOR THOUGHT

- Describe the difference between research in teacher education and teaching in physical education.
- Socialization into sport and through sport was a topic considered in Chapter 9, on sport psychology. Do similar social forces impact sport pedagogy? How?
- Differentiate between preservice, induction, and inservice activities for the teacher educator.
- Is it important that the movement educator be exposed to the mechanical, physiological, and psychological aspects of the human performer that are the focus of this book? Why?
- Motor behaviorists espouse the importance of practice. Alternatively, sport pedagogists focus on the notion of ALT-PE. Are these concepts different? How?
- How does knowledge of the areas discussed in this textbook contribute to each of the content standards for physical education as described by NASPE?

KEY TERMS

academic learning time (ALT)
anticipatory socialization
behavioral approach
bureaucratic socialization
change approach
class management
command method
content knowledge
cooperating teacher
cueing

defect approach
demonstration
growth approach
hidden curriculum
induction
inservice
instructional plan
lesson plan
management episode
pedagogical content knowledge

pedagogy
preservice
problem-solving approach
prompt
research on teacher education in
    physical education (RTE-PE)
research on teaching in physical
    education (RT-PE)

routine
rule
socialization perspective
student teaching
subjective warrant
task method
unit plan

RESOURCES

Textbooks

Harrison, J. M., & Blakemore, C. L. (1992). *Instructional Strategies for Secondary School Physical Education* (3rd ed.). Dubuque, IA: W. C. Brown.

Rink, J. (1985). *Teaching for Learning in Physical Education.* St. Louis: C. V. Mosby.

Siedentop, D. (1991). *Developing Teaching Skills in Physical Education* (3rd ed.). Mountain View, CA: Mayfield Publishing Co.

Pangrazi, R. P., & Darst, P. W. (1991). *Dynamic Physical Education for Secondary School Students: Curriculum and Instruction* (2nd ed.). New York: Macmillan.

Journals

Journal of Teaching in Physical Education
Quest
Research Quarterly for Exercise and Sport
The Physical Educator

Professional Organizations

American Alliance for Health, Physical Education, Recreation, and Dance
American College of Teacher Educators
American Educational Research Association: Division B—Curriculum Studies
American Educational Research Association: Division C—Learning and Instruction
American Educational Research Association: Division K—Teaching and Teacher
    Education
National Association for Sport and Physical Activity

Internet

World Wide Web (WWW)
http://www.tahperd.sfasu.edu/aahperd/naspe.html

Usenet/Listservers
American Educational Research Association
send: subscribe AERA
to: listserv@asuacad.bitnet

American Educational Research Association: Division B
send: subscribe AERA-B
to: listserv@asu.edu

American Educational Research Association: Division C
send: subscribe AERA-C
to: listserv@asu.edu

American Educational Research Association: Division K
send: subscribe AERA-K
to: listserv@asu.edu

REFERENCES

Anderson, W., & Barrette, G. (1978). What's going on in the gym. *Motor Skills: Theory into Practice*. Monograph 1.

Bain, L. (1990). Physical education teacher education. *Handbook of Research on Teaching* (4th ed.). New York: Macmillan.

Beckett, K. D. (1991). The effects of two teaching styles on college students' achievement of physical education outcomes. *Journal of Teaching in Physical Education*, 10(2), 153–169.

Boyce, B. A. (1992). The effect of three styles of teaching on university students' motor performance. *Journal of Teaching in Physical Education*, 11, 389–401.

Byra, M., & Coulon, S. C. (1994). The effect of planning on the instructional behaviors of preservice teachers. *Journal of Teaching in Physical Education*, 13, 123–139.

Dewar, A. M., & Lawson, H. A. (1984). The subjective warrant and recruitment into physical education. *Quest*, 36(1), 15–25.

Dodds, P., & Placek, J. H. (1991). Silverman's RT-PE review: Too simple a summary of a complex field. *Research Quarterly for Exercise and Sport*, 62, 365–368.

Fink, J., & Siedentop, D. (1989). The development of routines, rules, and expectations at the start of the school year. *Journal of Teaching in Physical Education*, 8, 198–212.

Graham, G., & Heimerer, E. (1981). Research on teacher effectiveness: A summary with implications for teaching. *Quest*, 33, 14–25.

Griffey, D. (1983). ALT in context: On the nonlinear and interactional characteristics of engaged time. *Journal of Teaching Physical Education*, (Summer), 34–37.

Harrison, J. M., & Blakemore, C. L. (1992). *Instructional Strategies for Secondary School Physical Education* (3rd ed.). Dubuque, IA: W. C. Brown.

Kerns, M. M. (1989). The effectiveness of computer-assisted instruction in teaching tennis rules and strategies. *Journal of Teaching in Physical Education*, 8, 170–176.

Laminack, L. L., & Long, B. M. (1985). What makes a teacher effective: Insight from preservice teachers. *Clearinghouse*, 58, 268.

Lawson, H. A. (1983). Paradigms for research on teaching and teachers. In T. J. Templin & J. K. Olson (Eds.,), *Teaching in Physical Education* (pp. 339–358). Champaign, IL: Human Kinetics.

Lawson, H. A. (1984). Problem-setting for physical education and sport. *Quest,* 36, 48–60.

Locke, L. F. (1984a). Overview of the RTE-PE literature, 1960–1981. *Journal of Teaching in Physical Education,* (Summer), 23–37.

Locke, L. F. (1984b). Overview of the RTE-PE literature, 1981–1984. *Journal of Teaching in Physical Education,* (Summer), 39–44.

Locke, L. F., & Dodds, P. (1985). Research on preservice teacher education for physical education. In C. L. Vendien & J. E. Nixon (eds.), *Physical Education Teacher Education: Guidelines for Sport Pedagogy.* New York: Macmillan.

Lortie, D. (1975). *Schoolteacher: A Sociological Study.* Chicago: University of Chicago Press.

Luke, M. (1989). Research on class management and organization: Review with implications for current practice. *Quest,* 41, 55–67.

Mager, R. F. (1968). *Developing Attitude Toward Teaching.* Palo Alto, CA: Fearon.

Mariani, T. (1970). A comparison of the effectiveness of the command method and the task method of teaching the forehand and backhand tennis strokes. *Research Quarterly,* 41, 171–174.

Metzler, M. (1982). Adapting the academic learning time instructional model to physical education teaching. *Journal of Teaching Physical Education,* 1, 44–55.

Metzler, M. (1989). A review of research on time in sport pedagogy. *Journal of Teaching in Physical Education,* 8, 87–103.

Metzler, M., & Freedman, M. S. (1985). Here's looking at you, PETE: A profile of physical education teacher education faculty. *Journal of Teaching in Physical Education,* 4, 123–133.

Mosston, M. (1981). *Teaching Physical Education.* Columbus, OH: Merrill.

Murphy, R. D. (1980). Professional discipline orientation in undergraduate curriculums for preparation of teachers of physical education, 1978–1980. *Dissertation Abstracts International,* 41, 2499A.

Ormand, T. (1988). An Analysis of Teaching and Coaching Behavior in Invasive Game Activities. Doctoral dissertation, Ohio State University, Columbus.

O'Sullivan, M., & Dyson, B. (1994). Rules, routines, and expectations of eleven high school physical education teachers. *Journal of Teaching in Physical Education,* 13, 361–371.

Placek, J. H., & Silverman, S. (1983). Early field teaching requirements in undergraduate physical education programs. *Journal of Teaching in Physical Education,* 2, 48–54.

Rink, J. (1985). *Teaching for Learning in Physical Education.* St. Louis: C. V. Mosby.

Rothstein, A. L., & Arnold, R. K. (1976). Bridging the gap: Application of research on videotape feedback and bowling. *Motor Skills: Theory into Practice,* 1, 36–61.

Rupert, T., & Buschner, T. (1989). Teaching and coaching: A comparison of instructional behavior. *Journal of Teaching in Physical Education,* 9, 49–57.

Segrave, J. O. (1980). Role preferences among prospective physical education teachers/coaches. In V. Crafts (ed.), *Proceedings, National Association for Physical Education* (Vol. 2, pp. 53–61). Champaign, IL: Human Kinetics.

Shulman, L. S. (1986). Paradigms and research programs in the study of teaching: A contemporary perspective. *Handbook of Research on Teaching* (3rd ed.). New York: Macmillan.

Siedentop, D. (1981). The Ohio State supervision research program: Summary report. *Journal of Teaching in Physical Education,* (Spring), 30–38.

Siedentop, D. (1989). The effective elementary specialist study. *Journal of Teaching in Physical Education Monograph,* 8.

Siedentop, D. (1991). *Developing Teaching Skills in Physical Education* (3rd ed.). Mountain View, CA: Mayfield Publishing Co.

Siedentop, D., Rife, F., & Boehm, J. (1974). *Modifying the Managerial Efficiency of Student Teachers in Physical Education.* Unpublished manuscript.

Silverman, S. (1991). Research on teaching in physical education. *Research Quarterly for Exercise and Sport,* 62, 352–364.

Tannehill, D., & Zakrajsek, D. (1988). What's happening in supervision of student teachers in secondary physical education. *Journal of Teaching in Physical Education,* 8, 1–12.

Templin, T. J., Woodford, R., & Mulling, C. (1982). On becoming a physical educator: Occupational choice and the anticipatory socialization process. *Quest,* 34, 119–133.

Veal, M. L. (1988). Pupil assessment issues: A teacher educator's perspective. *Quest,* 40, 151–161.

Vendien, C. L., & Nixon, J. E. (1985). *Physical Education Teacher Education: Guidelines for Sport Pedagogy.* New York: Macmillan.

The Internet

The **internet** is a word used to describe a complex connection of computing sites that span the entire globe. The individual networks that exist at each of these independent computing sites are connected so that the various sites can communicate with each other. The total sum of all these internetworked computing sites is informally referred to as the internet.

Various entities are connected directly to the internet—individuals, educational institutions, businesses, military installations. There are also commercial entities offering indirect internet connection services to others (such as AmericaOnline and CompuServe) via a modem connection.

The various sites located on the internet provide rich and innumerable resources. Such resources include information and databases on various subjects, downloadable computer software, data transfer from one computing site to another, electronic mail (e-mail) services, graphics archives, search engines to locate information at computing sites around the world, and information about individuals, institutions, and businesses.

PROTOCOLS AND USER INTERFACES FOR ACCESSING THE INTERNET

A **protocol** is the set of rules by which one machine communicates with another. Just as we have rules about spelling, grammar, and punctuation so that we can communicate with each other in an understandable manner, so do computers have such rules, only their rules are concerned with the order in which the data being transferred must be communicated and interpreted.

A user interface is the actual software that you use to access the various servers and resources of the internet. The user interface that you use depends upon the type of access that you need. Since it is on your machine and it accesses a server, it is also known as the client in a client-server relationship. A client requests information, while a server fills (or services) the request.

You may think of a protocol as nothing more than the language a computer needs to use in order to communicate, and a user interface as the software that you use to access the internet services. Various protocols that you will use include what is called the "Big Three" protocols of the internet: **HTTP** (HyperText Transport Protocol), **FTP** (File Transfer Protocol), and **Telenet.**

Now that you have a basic understanding of what the internet is, and that there are various methods used to access the resources of the internet, we can discuss how we use each method of access. We will begin our discussion with the most popular and powerful access method—the World Wide Web, or WWW.

The World Wide Web. The WWW is a collection of **HyperText Markup Language** (HTML) documents that are served up by the web **server** when a request is made by someone using a web **browser**. HTML is a language in which documents are created so that they can contain text, images, and links to other HTML documents or downloadable files. An HTML document that is created for a specific individual, institution, or site, and that acts as the very first document that is accessed by internet users, is also known as a home page. A home page is simply a primary HTML document (or collection of HTML documents). For simplicity, I will refer to HTML documents in general as home pages.

In order to access a home page on the WWW, two things must occur. First, you must be using a web browser such as **Mosaic** or **Netscape** and have access to the internet. Second, you must know the location of the home page you wish to browse. This location is given in the form of a Uniform Resource Locator, or URL, and takes on the following form when dealing with home pages:

http://_home.page.location_

Mosaic and Netscape share much of the same functionality. Both have MS Windows, Macintosh, and UNIX versions of their browsers. For the purpose of describing how to use a web browser to "surf" the internet in this section, I will use terms and actions associated with Mosaic 2.0 for Windows, though you will find that there will be little difference, if any, in performing the same actions in Netscape, and minor differences if you are using a Macintosh or UNIX machine to run Mosaic or Netscape.

How to Use Mosaic. To surf the internet's WWW servers using Mosaic, use your mouse to open the Mosaic icon, usually by double-clicking on the icon image. At the top of the Mosaic window, you will find a menu bar with the following selections:

<u>F</u>ile   <u>E</u>dit   Options   <u>N</u>avigate   Annotate   Hotlists   Help

To open a home page, select **File,** and then select **Open Document** in the submenu that appears. (Here is one of those minor differences between Mosaic and Netscape: Netscape users will select **F**ile, and then select **Open Location** in the submenu that appears). A *location request box* will appear with a blank area that needs to be filled in. In this blank area, type the location of the home page you wish to browse.

For example, if I wanted to browse the home page of Texas A&M University, I would type in

http://www.tamu.edu

If I wanted to browse the home page of the Department of Health and Kinesiology at Texas A&M University, I would type in

http://hlknweb.tamu.edu/

After you type in the name of the location, press the ENTER key and Mosaic will load the requested home page. As you can see, home page locations are very precise and can be cryptic in their naming. A simple rule to remember is to type in the home page location *exactly* as it is given to you.

A list of interesting home page locations is given at the end of this section. At the end of each chapter there is also a list of homepages specifically related to the discipline covered in that chapter. Another home page that you may use frequently is one that lets you search the WWW by topic for other home page locations. The name of this home page is "Yahoo!"

Home pages contain a special kind of text that appears blue on color monitors and is called **HyperText.** When you click on this blue text with your mouse, you will be taken to another home page or some other action will take place, such as downloading a file to your computer. The location to which you are taken may be in the same set of home pages as you were on, or it may be another home page located on the other side of the world. Another way to move around in a browser is to use the "forward" and "backward" arrows located just below the browser file menu to revisit various home pages that you have just browsed.

When you download a file using Mosaic or Netscape, you may either save it to your own hard drive and/or view it on your computer if it is an image, sound, or video file (and your computer is set up to use these files). You may also print out home pages to a printer if your computer is connected to one.

Mosaic and Netscape also provide the added benefits of allowing you to access Gopher servers, Telnet to other machines, FTP files, and to send e-mail to individuals, though there are some limitations to each of these activities. For example, to access the Texas A&M University Gopher, type in the following location in the Mosaic or Netscape location request box mentioned above:

gopher://gopher.tamu.edu

You will find that web browsers are the most useful means with which to access the internet.

Gopher.   **Gopher** is a document delivery service distributed around the world. It is based on a hierarchical menu system that allows users to move around in "Gopher space" in a seamless manner. Gopher enables you to give requests to search engines to find and return documents that contain certain key words in which you are interested. Two of these search engines are known as Veronica and Archie. Veronica allows you to search through the menus of a Gopher server(s) by using a keyword(s). A complete description of the use of Gopher falls outside the scope of this section, but it is simply a matter of starting the Gopher software on your own computer and following the system of structured menus to points of interest.

Telnet.   Telnet is a client software application that allows you to connect your computer to a remote computer (one that is located a distance away) and manipulate resources on the remote computer such as running programs or accessing databases. In order to Telnet to a remote computer you must have a user ID and password to gain access to the remote system. Also, there will be a formal log-in procedure to gain access to the remote computer.

How to Use Telnet.   In order to Telnet to another computer using Mosaic or Netscape, the browsers must first be set up to perform Telnet sessions in the "Preferences" sections of the software. In the Preferences section, simply tell

Mosaic or Netscape where your Telnet software program is located. Once Telnet capabilities have been set up in your browser, you may perform Telnet sessions by entering the remote machine location in the document *location request box* mentioned in the previous section on how to use Mosaic.

For example, to Telnet from within Mosaic to a fictional computer with the host name of bob1.com, enter the following in the location request box:

telnet://bob1.com

To Telnet using a telnet program outside of a web browser, simply start the telnet program, type in the name of the machine you wish to log on to, and follow the commands that you are given by the remote computer. Please remember that normally you must have a user ID and password to access the remote computer.

File Transfer Protocol.   File Transfer Protocol, or FTP, is a method to access the internet in order to transfer files from your own computer to a remote computer. Using FTP you may either send files to the remote computer (if you have the appropriate access rights, or permission), or retrieve files from the remote computer to your own computer. If you have log-on privileges on a remote computer, you may access it using the user ID and password assigned to you when you were given those privileges. Another way you may access a remote machine to transfer files using FTP is Anonymous FTP, when the service provider has allowed the public to have limited access for the purpose of transferring files. Anonymous FTP differs from other FTP sessions in that you will use the user ID "anonymous" to log on to the remote machine, and you will supply your e-mail address as the password. Mosaic and Netscape have a built-in ability to do anonymous FTP sessions.

How to Use FTP.   To start an anonymous FTP session from within Mosaic, enter in the host name of the machine you wish to open an FTP session with by typing the location into the *location request box* that was described earlier in the section on how to use Mosaic. For example, to use FTP anonymously with a fictional machine with the host name bob1.com, type in the following location:

ftp://bob1.com

Follow the directory structure to the location of the file you want to get. Simply click on the HyperText and Mosaic will ask you where on your own computer the retrieved file should be saved to. Enter in a directory/folder and file name and click on the SAVE button.

There are numerous client software applications that will allow you to establish FTP sessions with host machines. The variety is so extensive that it is beyond the scope of this section. To assist you in your FTP efforts we have listed the most frequently used FTP commands along with a short section on anonymous FTP.

Helpful FTP Commands

ftp	Begins an FTP session
open host.name	Tells the session which computer you want to access
ls	Lists all the files and directories of the current directory
cd	directory_name Changes to the requested directory
cd..	Changes back to the previous directory
get filename	Retrieves the specified file from the remote computer
mget file1 file2	Retrieves multiple files at a single request
put filename	Sends a file from your computer to the remote computer
mput file1 file2	Sends multiple files to the remote computer
bye	Ends an FTP session

Anonymous FTP

To FTP anonymously to a remote machine that allows anonymous FTP, follow these general commands:

1. Type **ftp** at the command prompt. (Start FTP session.)
2. Type **open** host.name at the *ftp>* prompt.
   (The remote machine will then ask you to log in; respond with "anonymous" as ID.)
3. Type **anonymous**
   (The remote machine will then ask you to send your e-mail address as a password.)
4. type **my@email.address**

Use the above FTP commands during your FTP session to find files on the remote computer and to transfer files between the two computers.

Usenet.   **Usenet** is a collection of news server sites from all over the world. Each site has a news administrator responsible for maintaining the site. Newsgroups are created by sending out "control messages" to news systems. You can access Usenet by the use of a news reader. Most news readers are free and can be downloaded from various sites around the internet. To participate in a newsgroup discussion, simply subscribe to the newsgroup and respond to postings using your news reader. Unlike list services, you will not receive a copy of every post sent to the group. You have to initiate the contact if you want to read a particular post. You may want to do a search on Yahoo! to find a free version of a news reader that you can download on your own computer if one is not already available to you.

List Services.   **List services** are formed by groups of people who wish to discuss a specific topic of interest—such as politics, art, or computers—by e-mail. You can subscribe to existing list services by sending e-mail to the list requesting that you be subscribed. Once you have successfully subscribed to a list service, you will begin receiving e-mail from the other group members as they post their e-mail to the list service. There are basically two types of list services: **listserv** and **majordomo.**

To subscribe to a majordomo list, do the following:

1. Send e-mail to the majordomo at the host.name
   (example: mail majordomo@host.name)
2. Leave the subject line blank.
3. On the very first line of the e-mail message, type:
   subscribe [listname] [your@e-mail.address]
4. Send the message.

To subscribe to a listserv list, do the following:

1. Send e-mail to the listserv at the host.name
   (example: mail listserv@host.name)
2. Leave the subject line blank.
3. On the very first line of the e-mail message, type:
   subscribe [listname] [your name]
4. Send the message.

You should receive a confirmation letter that you have been subscribed and you should start receiving e-mail from the list. Please be mindful of a few important rules of **netiquette:**

Rule 1: Be nice, and avoid **flaming** others. Make yourself look good.

Rule 2: E-mail that is sent to you in private should never be posted to the list without first obtaining permission from the author.

Rule 3: When you first subscribe, read the posts for a while and catch up on what is being discussed. Get to know the group members before you start to post to the group.

INTERESTING GENERAL HOME PAGES

Yahoo!	http://www.yahoo.com
Internet address book	http://www.addressbook.com
Thomas	http:// thomas.loc.gov
Library of Congress	http://www.loc.gov
U.S. President	http://www.whitehouse.gov
Texas A&M University	http://www.tamu.edu
MIT	http://web.mit.edu
Harvard University	http://www.harvard.edu
c/net	http://cnet.com
ESPN sports net	http://espnet.sportszone.com

Glossary

academic learning time The amount of time a student is engaged in activity or instruction while pursuing class objectives with a success rate of approximately 80 percent. In the physical education setting this translates into the amount of time during class activity that the student is engaged in overt motor responding at a high success rate. (10)

acceleration The change in velocity over time. Since velocity is always displacement divided by time, then acceleration is displacement divided by time, divided by time. For example, acceleration is expressed as feet per sec/per sec, which can also be stated as feet per sec^2. (4)

acclimatization The collective adaptive responses that improve an individual's tolerance to a new environment. Altitude acclimatization may require from days to months, depending on the specific adaptation and the altitude. (5)

acquisition The period of time during which experiences are provided that are thought to enhance learning. (8)

actin A thin protein filament found in the myofibrils that is important to the muscle contraction process. (3)

action plan The step-by-step sequence of events and associated neural commands that comprise a planned movement. (8)

acute injury Injury characterized by sudden onset; typically related to a specific incident. The symptoms of acute injury are localized pain, swelling, and limited ability to use the injured area. Examples of acute injury are sprained ankle or knee, pulled muscle, and stress fractures. (6)

adenosine triphosphate (ATP) The source of energy for shortening of the sarcomeres as the z-lines move closer to each other. This process comes from the breakdown of ATP into adenosine diphosphate (ADP) and phosphate. (3)

adolescence A developmental period that encompass the approximate age range of 12 to 18 years. (7)

adulthood A developmental period that involves both peak performance and regression due to aging. (7)

aerobic glycolysis An aerobic energy system that results in the complete breakdown of glycogen into water and carbon dioxide. (5)

aerobic metabolism The chemical reactions that result in the breakdown of carbohydrates and fats into carbon dioxide, water, and energy. This reaction occurs in the mitochondria and requires the presence of oxygen. (5)

afferent neurons   Neurons that carry signals to the brain or spinal cord; also called sensory neurons. (3)

affordance   a concept used in action-perception theory that is assumed to describe to an individual the available functions (including actions) given the current perceptual array. (7)

age-predicted maximum heart rate   A method of predicting maximal heart rate, determined by subtracting your age from 220. (6)

aggression   A behavior directed toward the goal of harming or injuring another living being who is motivated to avoid such treatment. (9)

agonist   A muscle that moves a joint in a desired direction when it is contracted. (3)

alveoli   The terminal branches of the lungs where gas exchange occurs. (5)

amenorrheic   When a female's body fat drops below 11–13 percent or she ceases to have menstrual periods. It is not unusual for young female gymnasts, distance runners, and dancers to be amenorrheic. (6)

amphetamines   Powerful stimulants that are banned from use in athletics and are controlled by law. These drugs stimulate the central nervous system, resulting in increased heart rate and blood pressure, and play a role in altering the synthesis and metabolism of natural central nervous system stimulants (catecholamines). (5)

amphiarthrodial articulation   A type of articulation that contains fibrocartilaginous discs, allowing some movement between the bones contained in the joint. An example of this type of articulation is the vertebrae in the spinal cord. (3)

anaerobic glycolysis   An anaerobic energy system that results in the production of

ATP but at the expense of producing an unwanted by-product called lactic acid. Glycolysis involves the breakdown of glycogen (carbohydrate) into pyruvic acid in the absence of oxygen. (5)

anaerobic metabolism   A complex series of chemical reactions that partially break down carbohydrates to provide small amounts of energy. This process does not require oxygen. (5)

analysis of variance (ANOVA)   A set of statistical procedures used to test for difference in two or more means that considers not only how far apart the means are but how variable the scores are about the mean. (2)

anatomical kinesiology   The discipline concerned with the study of the anatomical structure of the body and their movement functions. (1, 3)

androgenic-anabolic steroids   Drugs that function in a manner similar to the male hormone testosterone. Androgenic refers to compounds that result in effects associated with the development of secondary male sex characteristics. Anabolic refers to compounds with growth-stimulating characteristics. (5)

angina pectoris   A temporary but often intense pain in the area of the heart that may indicate that the oxygen supply to the heart has reached a critically low level. Angina typically subsides after a few minutes of rest. (6)

angle of attack   The angle of a projectile that maximizes lift while minimizing drag. Ganslen examined the optimal angle of attack for throwing a discus. This study suggested that the optimum lift–drag ratio (best combination of small drag and large lift forces) is at approximately 10 degrees for this track and field event. (4)

angular acceleration   The rate of change of angular velocity; specified as degrees per sec/per sec or degree per sec^2 (could also be stated in terms of revolutions or radians). (4)

angular displacement   The change in location of the rotating body. (4)

angular distance   The angle between the initial and final positions when measured by following the path taken by the body. (4)

angular momentum   The product of the body's moment of inertia and its angular velocity. Just as with linear momentum, angular momentum is initiated by an external force or torque. Once the external torque is exerted, the body continues to rotate until a new torque is applied to the system or another resistive force is experienced. This refers to conservation of angular momentum. (4)

angular motion   Motion where the body rotates around a point called an axis of rotation. (4)

angular velocity   Angular displacement across a fixed period of time. (4)

anorexia nervosa   A serious eating disorder that requires intervention to prevent permanent damage and/or death. Diagnosis and treatment are often difficult, however, because the anorexic is obsessed with self-control and full of denial about the condition. Although anorexia nervosa is most often seen in teenage females, the number of young men with anorexia is increasing. (6)

antagonist   A muscle that opposes the movement of a joint. (3)

anticipatory socialization   The process of initially matching one's interests and current skills against the requirements of a potential profession. (10)

anxiety   A negatively charged emotional state characterized by internal discomfort and nervousness. It is difficult to consider arousal and anxiety as absolutely independent. For the most part we might consider

that anxiety contributes to the overall arousal displayed by an individual. (9)

apparently healthy   A classification of health risk where the individual does not have symptoms suggestive of cardiopulmonary or metabolic disease and is apparently healthy, with no more than one major coronary risk factor. (6)

appendicular skeleton   A subset of the skeleton, consisting of the upper and lower, right and left extremities. (3)

applied research   Research aimed at testing potential solutions (hypotheses) to problems that present themselves in real-world settings. The tasks utilized in applied research are typically real-world tasks and the testing occurs in real-world environments. (2)

arousal   The degree of psychological activation or alertness that varies along a continuum from deep sleep (low arousal) to extreme excitement (high arousal). (9)

arteries   The large vessels that carry blood away from the heart. (5)

articulation   The junction between two bones. The type of articulation dictates the type of joint that exists in an anatomical unit and subsequently the type of movement that joint can support. (3)

assertive behavior   Actions that have no intent to harm or injure another person and do not constitutionally violate agreed-upon rules for the sport being played. (9)

associative stage   The stage of learning (Fitts, 1964) concerned with performing and refining a skill. The important stimuli have been identified and their meaning is known. Conscious decisions about what to do become more automatic. (8)

atherosclerosis   Hardening of the arteries, which appears to be associated with high levels of low density lipoprotein (LDL). (6)

atrioventricular node (A-V node)   A specialized heart tissue that, when stimulated by the S-A node, causes the action potential to move across other specialized tissue that branch into both the right and left ventricles. This conduction system results in a coordinated contraction that efficiently pumps blood. (5)

atrium   The chambers of the heart that collect blood to be passed to the ventricles. (5)

attribution theory   A theory that proposes that personal forces such as ability and trying (i.e., effort) are primary contributors to performance outcome. In addition, external forces—namely, task difficulty and luck—are also thought to mediate outcome. The theory attempts to explain how and why people make judgments about everyday experiences. (9)

autonomous stage   The stage of learning (Fitts, 1964) characterized by a nearly automatic kind of performance. The performer seems to be performing on "autopilot." (8)

axial skeleton   A subset of the skeleton that consists of the skull, thorax, pelvis, and vertebral column. (3)

axon   A single extension of the neuron that carries messages to thousands of terminal branches that reach out to dendrites of other neurons. (3)

balance   An individual's ability to control his or her stability. (4)

basal ganglia   Four masses of gray matter located deep in the forebrain. This center modifies commands from other structures in the brain in ways that are not completely understood. One result of these modifications is to regulate "background" muscle tone. For example, when we write, the basal ganglia prepares the appropriate parts of the body for hand movements by tensing the upper part of our arm. (3)

basic research   Research involved in testing hypotheses in laboratory and field settings using tasks specifically designed to involve/isolate the process(es) and/or environmental demand(s) under study. (2)

behavioral approach   An approach used in sport pedagogy to research that attempts to identify lawful behavior on the part of the student or teacher based on systematic manipulations in the learning or teaching environment. This perspective relies heavily on the idea that for any given teaching intervention, predictable teaching and student behaviors will be evident. (10)

biaxial joint   A joint that allows movement around two perpendicular axes. Typical movements entertained by this joint type are flexion-extension and adduction-abduction. Biaxial joints also support circumduction, which is a combination of the aforementioned movements. Examples of this type of joint include the wrist and thumb. (3)

bioelectric impedance   A method of determining percentage of body fat based on the concept that an electrical current will be conducted better by hydrated fat-free tissue (lean body mass) than by fat. (6)

biomechanics   The study of the structure and functions of biological systems by means of the methods of mechanics; the "physics" of human movement. (1, 4)

blood doping   A practice of infusing red blood cells into the athlete prior to competition. The blood is typically taken from the athletes about 3 weeks prior to competition and stored. Before the competition, the athlete's system restores the lost blood cells by natural processes. Just prior to competition the blood cells are transfused back into the athlete, increasing the total number of red blood cells. (5)

blood pressure   Pressure created in the vascular system by pumping blood out of the heart. (6)

body density The ratio of body mass to body volume. (6)

bottom-up reasoning The development of hypotheses based on observations (facts) and induction. Typically the hypothesis is derived as a result of organizing or contrasting observations and the conditions under which they arise. (2)

brainstem Nerve tissue connecting the rest of the brain to the spinal cord. The brainstem contains four important parts: the medulla, the pons, the cerebellum, and the midbrain. (3)

bronchi The smaller passages of the bronchioles that conduct the air to the alveoli. (5)

browser A client application—such as Mosaic or Netscape—used to surf the WWW. (Appendix)

Bruce protocol (1971) A continuous treadmill exercise test in which the workload increases steadily during the test with no rest between stages. This treadmill protocol is used with a wide variety of subjects/patients ranging from normal risk to high risk. (6)

bulimia An eating disorder in which an individual, usually of normal weight, thinks constantly of food and alternates between starving and binging. After eating too much food the bulimic "purges" the food by forced vomiting. (6)

bureaucratic socialization Refers to the process whereby a teacher is exposed to knowledge about the rules and expectations of the school or organization with which the new teacher is now associated. (10)

burnout A reaction to chronic stress and to situations in which the potential rewards are inferior to the emotional and physical costs encountered by the athlete. (9)

caffeine A stimulant available in many over-the-counter drinks including coffee, tea, and cola products. High or even normal usage of these products results in mild central nervous system stimulation within fifteen minutes. (5)

calorie The amount of heat energy required to raise the temperature of a gram of water 1 degree centigrade. A kilocalorie (KCAL) is equal to 1000 calories. (5)

capillaries The microscopic vessels that connect the arteries to the veins. It is in the capillaries that blood/tissue gas exchange occurs. (5)

carbohydrate A group of chemical compounds, including sugars, starches, and cellulose, containing carbon, hydrogen, and oxygen only. There are simple and complex carbohydrates. (6)

carbohydrate loading A precompetition routine in which long-distance athletes like marathoners or triathletes will go through a succession of exhaustive workouts to deplete the muscle stores of glycogen. The athlete then eats a carbohydrate-free diet for 3 days followed by 3 days of carbohydrate-rich diet. This process actually supersaturates the muscle glycogen stores. (6)

cardiac output The amount of blood pumped from one ventricle of the heart in one minute. The heart will pump about 5 or 6 liters of blood per minute when the individual is at rest and up to 35 liters per minute in a highly trained individual during heavy exercise. Cardiac output is the product of stroke volume and heart rate. Increased cardiac output with training results primarily from increased stroke volume. (5, 7)

cell differentiation Used to describe the further refining of the role and function of particular neurons. Differentiation is also linked with the more general progression of motor control from gross, often ill-defined movements, to very coordinated and intricate control. (7)

cell integration   Used to describe the interweaving of the developing neurons from agonist and antagonist muscle groups to allow the coordinated action of these muscles that is characteristic of mature movers. (7)

cell migration   Used to describe that fact that cells begin to move to the location within the body for which they are designed. In essence, the cells migrate to meet other cells that will have a similar function. Cells become more elaborate when they reach their terminal location within the system. (7)

cell myelination   An important marker of neurological development in which myelin is deposited around the neuron, which speeds up transmission of impulses and offers some resistance to fatigue. The degree of myelination for sites in the body vary considerably. (7)

cell proliferation   The rapid production of neurons that begins around the second prenatal month. This process is virtually complete by the time of birth, with the newborn having approximately 10 to 100 billion neurons. (7)

center of gravity   The point about which a body's weight is equally balanced in all directions; the body's balance or pivot point. In the human body the center of gravity is not fixed because the body is made up of many segments that can move or remain stationary at any moment in time. (4)

central fatigue   Fatigue arising from the central nervous system (brain, brainstem, spinal cord). (5)

central nervous system (CNS)   The "control" center for the human body, composed of two important parts: the brain and the spinal cord. (3)

central processes   Processes conducted within the central nervous system. From the information processing viewpoint, these processes are sensation, perception, response selection, and response execution. (8)

central tendency   Measures used to characterize the average, middle, or "typical" score of the distribution. There are three measures of central tendency: the mean, the median, and the mode. (2)

cephalocaudal   Growth that proceeds longitudinally from the head to the feet. (7)

cerebral cortex   A part of the brain that controls many functions, including abstract reasoning and speech. This part of the brain accounts for about 80 percent of the brain's weight. The cerebral cortex has right and left cerebral hemispheres. (3)

change approach   An approach to inservice that focuses on means of adapting to changes in society. For example, ensuring gender equality and incorporating handicapped individuals into the mainstream program have been the focus of many recent inservice activities. (10)

childhood   A developmental period that involves approximately ages 2 to 12 years and includes many qualitative changes in a child's movement capacity. (7)

chronic injury   An injury that lasts a long time or recurs with some regularity. Usually chronic injury begins gradually and is often difficult to relate to a specific incident. Chronic anatomical injury is often referred to as overuse injury. Examples of chronic injury are shin splints, bursitis (irritation of the bursa in the knees, hips, shoulder, or elbow), low back pain, and tendinitis (inflammation of the tendon). (6)

cinematography   An important technique used to study human kinematics. Cinematography requires camera(s) specifically designed to film actions at very fast rates to allow the researcher to examine the kinematics of a movement. (4)

classical conditioning An intervention technique based on the premise that an association exists between an unconditioned stimulus (US) and a conditioned stimulus (CS). A CS is paired with an anxiety-provoking US, which ultimately leads to the display of a fear-oriented response called the conditioned response (CR). That is, a threatening event such as a 100 m final (US) is accompanied by a fear-eliciting cue such as apprehension (CS), which leads to an increase in anxiety (CR). A procedure called extinction is often used to reduce the UC–CS association and the subsequent production of the CR. (9)

class management Activities that are organizational, transitional, and general non–subject matter tasks that occur during a period of study. Class management time will depend on the number of management episodes that occur and the length of each of these. (10)

closed environments Situations that are relatively stable such that conditions do not change from moment to moment. For example, the environmental conditions you encounter in bowling are relatively fixed. The pins do not move without you displacing them and the conditions of the lane remain fairly constant from frame to frame. (8)

closed-loop control Motor control in which feedback is used to adjust the progress of an ongoing movement. (8)

cognitive evaluation theory A theory whose central premise is that rewards can have a dual function: to control behavior or to provide information. If rewards are viewed as having some control over an individual's behavior, this is likely to reduce intrinsic motivation. (9)

cognitive stage The stage of learning (Fitts, 1964) in which the learner is first introduced to the motor task. The learner must determine the objective of the skill as well as the relational and environmental cues that control and regulate the movements. (8)

cognitive strategy An intervention technique that attempts to alter the cognitive or thought processing of the performer and subsequently influence responding. (9)

command method A teaching method characterized by the teacher dictating how, when, and what is performed in a practice session in order to learn a task as accurately and quickly as possible. (10)

concentric contraction A muscle contraction that results when the active muscle shortens. (3)

concurrent validity The extent to which a measurement or test is related to a criterion measure or test. For example, we could assess the concurrent validity of a skinfold method of determining body fat. (2)

conduction The process of heat transferred from warmer to cooler objects that come in direct contact. Walking on the hot sand transfers heat to the soles of your feet by conduction. (5)

condyle A rounded prominence of the bone that is an important part of an articulation with another bone. (3)

confirmation bias The tendency for judgments based on new ideas to be overly consistent with preliminary hypotheses. (2)

conservation of momentum A principle that is an outgrowth of Newton's third law that states that in a system in which forces act on each other, the momentum in the system remains constant. (4)

construct A concept or characteristic that is difficult to define without first clarifying how the concept or characteristic is measured. Fitness, health, and intelligence are examples of constructs. In order to define these constructs carefully it is necessary to clarify how we measure them. (2)

construct validity The extent to which performance can be partitioned into constructs. If the performance under consideration can be partitioned into a clearly defined set of constructs then the measurement scheme is said to have construct validity. (2)

content knowledge The subject matter that the teacher will be teaching. With respect to physical education, this is knowledge about movement and the ability to execute movements. (10)

content validity A logical validation procedure that assesses the extent to which the measurements consider the content or behavior under consideration. This method implies a close relationship between the task or content under scrutiny and the measurements. A measurement that does not appear to represent the important components of the task under consideration or does not appear to be related to the content that was presented lacks content validity. For this reason content validity is sometimes called face validity or representative validity. (2)

contextual interference Interference created when more than one task is practiced within a single practice session. Blocked practice conditions are thought to promote low contextual interference because the context remains relatively stable from trial to trial. Random schedules, on the other hand, generate high contextual interference because the context within which a given task is executed changes from trial to trial. (8)

continuity Indicates that gradual improvements in performance appear to occur as development progresses.

continuous movements Movements that have no distinct ending. Attempting to catch a parakeet in a cage, running or tackling in football, or guarding an opponent in basketball are examples of continuous motor skills. (8)

control group The group of subjects whose performance is used as a baseline to determine the influence of an experimental manipulation. In an experiment, the control and experimental groups must be treated in exactly the same way except for the one variable under study. (2)

convection Heat transfer from the surface of the skin to the air or water circulating next to the body. Upon entering the water, convection results in the transfer of body heat to the water. (5)

cooperating teacher An experienced teacher at the field site who supervises a student teacher. (10)

coordinative structure A functional grouping of muscles that may be controlled as a group. Also referred to as a synergy. (8)

core temperature Body temperature measured rectally. Normal core body temperature ranges from about 97 to 100 degrees but with strenuous exercise in moderate environments may reach 105 degrees. However, core temperature during exercise in hot and humid environments may exceed 106 degrees, resulting in heat exhaustion or heatstroke. Core temperatures above 108 degrees may result in death. (5)

corpus callosum Nerves that cross the gap between the two hemispheres of the brain. This structure connects the hemispheres so that they can communicate. (3)

correlation A statistical technique that quantifies the extent to which two variables are interrelated. A correlation coefficient can range from +1, meaning that as one variable increases the other increases in a predictable, uniform way, to 0, where the change in one variable does not indicate any predictable change in the other, to –1, such that the increase in one variable indicates a predictable, uniform decrease in the other variable. (2)

counterconditioning model   A technique that focuses on conditioning a response that does not elicit anxiety to the fear-producing stimuli. (9)

crawling   A movement in which infants use their arms to pull themselves forward while at the same time pushing with their legs. An important characteristic of crawling is that the stomach stays in contact with the ground. (7)

creeping   A movement in which infants use their arms to pull themselves forward while at the same time pushing with their legs, keeping the stomach and chest off of the surface on which they are ambulating. (7)

critical period   A period of time during development in which a particular behavior must be acquired if it is to be performed optimally. (7)

cross-bridge cycling   The most commonly accepted model of muscle contraction that proposes that as cross bridges are established when the action potential moves down the muscle, other cross bridges are released and subsequently reattached. (3)

cross extensor reflex   A spinal reflex that responds to a painful foot stimulation by innervating the musculature on the unprovoked limb to cause straightening of the leg which enables weight bearing to occur. (3)

cross-sectional method   A research method used in motor development in which the experimenter collects data on different groups of individuals at the same time, but the subjects differ in age. (7)

cross training   Training that involves alternating between two or more aerobic activities. The most popular forms of aerobic

activity are walking, running, cycling, swimming, and aerobic dance. Cross training helps to prevent boredom and decreases the likelihood of overuse injuries. (6)

cueing   The act of telling the student to attend to one particular aspect of the action that is being observed. (10)

curvilinear motion   Movement when the path is curved. (4)

deduction   The process of reasoning from a general principle or theory to an unknown, from general to specific, or from postulate to testable hypotheses. (2)

defect approach   An approach to inservice that focuses on changing specific teacher behaviors by using behavioral techniques that focus on encouraging different and more appropriate behaviors. (10)

demonstration   A method of visually communication during the instruction of movement. (10)

dendrites   Tiny branchlike fibers extending from the cell body of a nerve that receive messages. (3)

dependent variable   The variable that is measured. In an experiment, the change in the dependent variable is assumed to be a result of the manipulation introduced by the experimenter. (2)

descriptive statistics   Statistical methods used to organize and summarize raw data in order to communicate the important features more effectively. (2)

diarthrodial articulation   Form of articulation supporting free movement. Important elements of this form of articulation is hyaline cartilage and synovial fluid. (3)

diastole   The relaxation phase of the cardiac cycle. During diastole, pressure in the ventricles is low, allowing the chamber to refill with blood from the atrium. (5)

discontinuity   Indicates that dramatic qualitative changes occur during development even though performance measures indicate that gradual improvements are made in motor performance. (7)

discrete movements Movements with a distinct beginning and a distinct end. Motor skills such as serving in tennis, driving in golf, shooting in basketball, or writing your name are discrete motor skills. (8)

displacement The straight-line distance from the initial position of an object to its end location. (4)

distance The length of the path that an object, individual, or limb takes between the origination and target points. (4)

distributed practice Occurs when a practice session is organized such that the practice intervals are shorter than the rest intervals. (8)

drag The fluid force that opposes the forward motion of the body and reduces the body's velocity; often referred to as fluid resistance. (4)

drive theory A theory proposing that the dominant response for a given stimulus will be elicited when an individual is highly aroused. For highly skilled athletes we might assume that the dominant response is the correct one because of their extensive practice and experience. If this is the case, drive theory predicts that increasing the level of drive (or arousal) will serve to enhance the production of the appropriate motor performance for a skilled athlete. (9)

dynamical systems perspective A theoretical perspective that suggests that changes in motor patterns occur as a result of human behavior being inherently complex, self-organizing, dynamic. and influenced by multiple intrinsic and extrinsic factors. (7, 8)

dynamics The study of a system when the system is in a state of acceleration. (4)

eccentric contraction A contraction that results when the active muscle lengthens. (3)

eccentric force A force whose direction is not in line with the center of gravity of a freely moving object or the center of rotation of an object with a fixed axis of rotation. (4)

ecological validity The degree to which the conditions of the experiments are representative of conditions encountered in the real world. Ecological validity increases when the experiment involves performances in real, everyday, and culturally significant situations. The ecological concern is that as the experimenter more carefully controls the experimental conditions and tasks, the results tell us less about how a person performs in everyday situations. (2)

economy The cost of conducting a experiment or utilizing a measurement scheme; considered in terms of time, money, and risk. Often we substitute field tests for laboratory tests because it is felt that the additional costs are not offset by the increase in precision of measurements. (2)

efferent neurons Neurons that carry signals from the brain or spinal cord; also called motor neurons. (3)

electrocardiogram (ECG) A recording of the electrical activity of the heart as sensed by electrodes placed on the surface of the chest. The ECG is an integral component of exercise testing because of its use in diagnosing various heart problems, especially those associated with cardiac rhythm, electrical conduction, oxygen supply to the heart muscle, and actual heart muscle damage. (6)

electromyography (EMG) A technique used to identify the magnitude and timing of activation in muscle groups that contribute to a movement by sensing the electrical signals emitted from the contracting muscle. (4)

empirical   Based on observation and/or literature rather than theory. (2)

endomysium   Connective tissue that separates muscle fibers. (3)

energy   The capacity to perform work. (5)

energy nutrients   Sources of food energy: protein, carbohydrates, and fats. (6)

epimysium   A fibrous connective tissue that surrounds the entire muscle. This connective tissue becomes tapered at the ends of the muscle to form the connective tissue called tendons. (3)

essential fat   The fat within the nerves, brain, liver, and bone marrow. When fat levels drop below the essential level, some physiological functions are altered. Essential fat for males is 3 percent of the total body weight. Essential fat for females is 11 to 13 percent because of additional fat in the female reproductive organs. (6)

evaporation   The transfer of heat to the environment as water is vaporized from the respiratory passages and the surface of the skin. Evaporation provides the major natural defense against overheating in hot, relatively dry environments. Evaporation is assisted by approximately 3 million sweat glands distributed over the surface of the body. (5)

exercise duration   The total time devoted to an exercise at a single session. In strength training, duration is a product of the number of sets and number of repetitions per set. (6)

exercise frequency   The number of exercise sessions performed in a given time period (e.g., a week). (6)

exercise intensity   The physiological stress placed on the body during exercise. (6)

exercise physiology   The discipline concerned with the study of the physiological processes that provide the basis for our capacity to move. (1, 5)

experiment   An investigation in which a researcher manipulates one variable while measuring its effect on some other variable. (2)

experimental group   The group of subjects whose performance is influenced by an experimental manipulation. In an experiment, the control and experimental groups must be treated in exactly the same way except for the one variable under study. (2)

expiratory reserve volume (ERV)   The additional amount of air that can be moved during a maximal expiration above that during a normal expiration. (6)

extension   Movement resulting in an increased joint angle. (3)

external validity   The extent to which the results of the experiment are generalizable. (2)

exteroceptors   Sensory receptors such as vision, audition (hearing), taste, and smell. These sensory receptors provide us with information about the world around us. (3, 8)

extrinsic feedback   Feedback received prior to, during, and/or after the response from some outside source. Coaches, teachers, experimenters, and even some special devices are capable of providing extrinsic feedback to the performer. (8)

fast twitch fibers   A type of muscle fiber that has a limited capacity for aerobic metabolism and is more easily fatigued. These fibers are activated by larger neurons, are generally richer in energy stores, and generally contain more myofibrils. Fast twitch fibers have a large anaerobic capacity because these fibers can very rapidly develop a great deal of force. (3)

fat   A concentrated form of food energy (also known as lipids) that protects and cushions internal organs. One gram of fat provides 9 calories per gram, while protein and carbohydrate each provide 4 calories per gram. Dietary fat is essential for the functioning of each cell in the body. (6)

fatigue   The inability to maintain power output or force during extended or repeated contractions. (5)

File Transfer Protocol (FTP)   One of the "big three" protocols on the internet. It is used to transfer files from one machine to another. (Appendix)

first-class lever   A lever that consists of a fulcrum placed between the resistance and the applied force. (3)

fitness   The capacity to perform the activities required of an individual. (2, 6)

Fitts' Law   A mathematical relationship between movement time and the difficulty of a movement specified by the movement's index of difficulty. Specifically, as the index of difficulty increases, movement time also increases. (8)

flaming   Criticizing or demeaning another person on the internet. (Appendix)

flexibility   The total amount of movement through which the components of the articulation can pass. We also refer to a joint's range of motion as flexibility. (3, 7)

flexion   Movement resulting in a decrease in joint angle. (3)

foramen   A hole in the bone through which nerves pass. (3)

force   A push or pull acting on the body. If the push or pull is sufficient enough, the body will alter its state of motion. (4)

forebrain   An area of the brain that is critical for perception, conscious awareness, cognition, and voluntary actions. The forebrain includes important centers such as the cerebral cortex, hypothalamus, thalamus, and basal ganglia. (3)

force arm   The length of the lever between the fulcrum and the applied force. (3)

force platforms   Devices that allow the movement scientist to measure the forces produced by an individual or object in three dimensions: vertical, mediolateral, and anteroposterior. Such devices are sometimes referred to as force plates. (4)

forced vital capacity (FVC)   The sum of the inspiratory reserve volume and the expiratory reserve volume or the total amount of additional air that can be moved in one maximal breath above that of a normal breath. (6)

force transducer   A mechanical device that offers the biomechanist the opportunity to conduct kinetic movement analyses.

formative measurements   Measurements used to track changes in a variable that are taken during a particular time period, such as an experimental training period. (2)

fossa   A shallow, dishlike area on a bone that is often a space where articulation with another bone occurs or a muscle attaches. (3)

fractionated practice   A form of part-whole practice in which one or more parts of the whole task is practiced. (8)

frontal plane   The plane of the body that cuts the body in half, resulting in a front and back side. (3)

functional aerobic capacity   Measurement taken when a graded exercise test is terminated early. For diagnostic purposes it is recommended that the individual achieve at least 85 percent of age-predicted maximal heart rate because some ECG abnormalities do not appear until the cardiovascular system is stressed to this point (Pollack, Wilmore, & Fox, 1978). (6)

fundamental movement   The basic components of a movement without concern for individualized style or idiosyncrasies. In essence, each movement pattern is examined in isolation from other movements. Examples of fundamental locomotor movements include running, jumping, and leaping. Throwing, catching, and striking are probably the most common nonlocomotor fundamental movements. (7)

general motion Movements that include both linear and angular components. (4)

Golgi tendon organ (GTO) A proprioceptor located in the tendon that monitors tension buildup in the muscle.

graded exercise testing A variety of procedures used to determine an individuals response to standardized exercise workloads. The guidelines for conducting such tests are set by the American College of Sports Medicine. (6)

gravitational model A model that proposes that individuals with certain personality characteristics are drawn to participate in certain sports. (9)

group An entity in which two or more persons interact with one another in such a manner that each person influences and is influenced by each other. (9)

group cohesion A group's ability to stick together in the face of adversity. (9)

growth Often used interchangeably with development and/or maturation. However, growth might be more precisely considered to refer to a quantitative change in body size resulting from an enlargement of a biological unit (e.g., arm). (7)

growth approach An approach to inservice that does not assume that the teacher has deficiencies but is based on the premise that the teacher can learn a great deal by reflecting on past experience. (10)

growth hormone A hormone produced in the pituitary gland; also know as somatotrophic hormone. It is involved in the normal tissue-building process. In the past only natural forms of growth hormones were available for clinical purposes but synthetic forms are now available. (5)

habituation A form of learning that is evident from decreased behavioral response to a repeated stimulus. (7)

health Physical, mental, and social well-being, not just freedom from disease. (1, 6)

health and fitness The discipline concerned with the interaction of exercise, nutrition, and health. (1)

health history Typically a questionnaire used to determine an individual's past and present history on factors that might impact his or her potential risk of cardiovascular disease and/or might limit the utilization of exercise testing as a diagnostic tool. (6)

heart rate Number of cardiac cycles occurring in one minute. Training tends to decrease heart rate both at rest and during exercise. (5, 7)

hemispheric lateralization The specialized function that each side of the brain adopts. Typically music and art appreciation, creativity, emotion, and spatial awareness arise from one hemisphere. In contrast, the other hemisphere is assumed to account for language, logical operations, and other processes requiring analytical processing such as cognitive activities related to science and math problems. (7)

hemoglobin An iron-protein compound found in erythrocytes or red blood cells. For each liter (1000 ml) of blood, hemoglobin is capable of temporarily storing about 200 ml of oxygen. (5)

hidden curriculum Tacit messages associated with the rituals and routines of the program that inform the student about what particular knowledge is worth learning and what knowledge is of little value. (10)

high-density lipoprotein (HDL) A type of lipoprotein that removes cholesterol from the tissue and returns it to the liver for possible degradation. Exercise appears to result in increased levels of HDL. High levels of HDL, the good cholesterol, are associated with protection from cardiovascular disease. (6)

higher risk A classification of health risk where the individual has symptoms of possible cardiopulmonary or metabolic disease and/or two or more major coronary risk factors. An exercise test and medical examination are suggested for higher-risk individuals before engaging in a vigorous exercise program. (6)

hostile aggression Behavior with the intent to harm an individual physically or psychologically. (9)

hydrostatic weighing A method of determining body composition. Hydrostatic weighing is based on Archimedes' principle of water displacement. That is, a body submerged in water will float if its weight is less than the weight of the water that it displaces. Essentially, fat is less dense than water and lean body mass is more dense than water. Thus fat floats and lean body mass sinks. (6)

hyperoxia Higher than normal oxygen concentrations. Research does not support the use of oxygen-enriched gas mixtures as an ergogenic aid prior to a fatiguing event or to enhance the recovery from a fatiguing event. However, breathing an oxygen-enriched gas mixture during exercise, even though impractical in many situations, does appear to enhance performance. The higher than normal oxygen concentrations appear both to decrease the work required for ventilation and to enhance the oxygen available in the muscle cell to support aerobic glycolysis. (5)

hyperplasia The view that progressive resistance exercise promotes an increase in the number of muscle fibers. (6)

hypertension A disease characterized by abnormally elevated blood pressure. Individuals with chronic (prolonged) hypertension have an increased probability of stroke and coronary artery disease.

HyperText Text within HTML documents that appears as blue text when viewed from a web browser and that will connect to another document when selected. (Appendix)

HyperText Markup Language (HTML) The syntax or language used to create documents informally known as home pages on WWW. (Appendix)

HyperText Transport Protocol (HTTP) One of the "big three" protocols on the internet. It is used by web servers to serve HTML documents. (Appendix)

hypertrophy The increase in the size of the muscle fibers due to an increase in the number and size of the myofibrils. (6)

hypothalamus The nerve centers that control body temperature and rate of burning fat and carbohydrates located directly above the brainstem. (3)

hypothesis A tentative prediction of behavior under a specific set of conditions. (2)

iceberg profile A personality profile from the profile of mood states (POMS) in which individuals receive a high score on vigor and lower scores on tension, depression, anger, fatigue, and confusion. This profile has now been identified with elite athletes in wrestling, rowing, distance running, and cycling. (9)

immature movement pattern Movement pattern that is considered to exhibit a minimal level of proficiency. (7)

implosive therapy An intervention technique based on classical conditioning principles. This technique uses a hierarchy of fear-eliciting images that the patient has ranked in terms of anxiety provocation. (9)

impulse The product of force and time. That the change in a body's momentum is equal to the impulse applied to that body can be demonstrated using Newton's second law. A large amount of force applied over a short period or a small amount of force exerted over a greater period can result in an equivalent impulse. (4)

independent variable The manipulated variable in an experiment. The change in the dependent variable is assumed to be a result of the manipulation of the independent variable. (2)

index of difficulty An index of the difficulty of simple aimed movement tasks based on the **a**mplitude (A) to be moved and the **w**idth of the target (W). Fitts proposed the index of difficulty as the following equation (8):

$$\log_2(2A/W)$$

induction The logical reasoning from isolated facts to a more general description. (2)

induction The way in which the teacher is socialized into the teaching environment after completion of the preservice phase; the transition into the real world of teaching. (10)

inertia The resistance of a body to a change in its current state of linear motion. A body's inertia is a function of its mass. (4)

infancy A stage of development from birth to two years of age. (7)

inferential statistics A set of procedures that can be used to make statistical judgments about population characteristics based on the characteristics of the sample. (2)

information processing The various cognitive and sensory processes required to translate a stimulus to move into a movement. Information processing activities are typically classified as those involving sensation-perception, response selection, and response execution. (7, 8)

informed consent Consent for a procedure or participation in an experiment after the individual has been fully informed of the potential risks in all procedures that will be administered. The person should be offered an opportunity to ask questions and be provided with sufficient information to make an informed consent. In the case of a minor or other person legally under the supervision of a guardian, the parent or guardian must provide the consent. (6)

inservice Continuing education activities designed to update the skills of currently certified physical educators. (10)

inspiratory reserve volume (IRV) The additional amount of air that can be moved during a maximal inspiration above that during a normal inspiration. (6)

instantaneous angular velocity Angular displacement assessed over a very short period of time. (4)

instructional plan A teacher's detailed, step-by-step outline of what tasks the students will do, how they will perform the task, and when they will perform the task. (10)

instrumental aggression Aggressive behavior exhibited to achieve some nonaggressive goal. (9)

interactional approach An approach incorporating situational factors and the trait perspective to examine the role of personality. This approach suggests that an understanding of personality can only be understood by examining how traits and situation-specific behaviors complement each other. (9)

intermediate twitch fibers A type of muscle fiber with characteristics somewhere in between the fast twitch and slow twitch fibers. (3)

internal validity The degree to which the manipulation of an independent variable in an experiment truly accounts for the changes observed by the experimenter in the dependent variable. Internal validity increases as the experiment provides a more convincing demonstration that the observed change was a result of the experimental manipulation. (2)

internet   A complex connection of computing sites that span the entire globe. (A)

interneurons   Neurons that originate and terminate in the brain or spinal cord. (3)

intrinsic feedback   Feedback received prior to, during, and/or after the execution of a task from internal sensory receptors. (8)

invariant features   The relative characteristics of a generalizable motor program. These features are thought to be the fundamental characteristics of the movement and include: order of elements, relative force, and relative timing. (8)

inverted-U hypothesis   A hypothesis that proposes that the relationship between arousal and performance is curvilinear, or more specifically, an inverted-U. This means that as arousal increases, so does performance (this is similar to drive theory). However, this position also indicates that an optimum level of arousal exists and should the performer exceed this level, he or she would exhibit a detriment in performance. (9)

isometric contraction   A muscle contraction in which the active muscle produces forces that are insufficient to create overt movement; also called static contractions. (3)

isotonic contraction   A muscle contraction in which the active muscle results in movement; also call dynamic contractions. (3)

kinematics   A method of description of movement with respect to time and space. A kinematic analysis of a movement disregards the forces that produce the movement. Kinematics refers to the geometry of an action. (4)

kinesthetic acuity   The ability to differentiate proprioceptively between two different weights, locations, distances, or forces. (7)

kinesthetic memory   Memory that permits one to reproduce a previously presented movement of particular force, location, or distance. (7)

kinetics   A method of description of movement with respect to the forces that are associated with a movement, including the forces that produce the movement and those that result from the movement. (4)

knowledge of performance (KP)   Information received about the actual performance and execution of the movement goal. (8)

knowledge of results (KR)   Information received concerning the extent to which a response accomplished the intended movement goal. (8)

Krebs Cycle   An aerobic process in which pyruvic acid is metabolized, as are other fuel sources including fats and protein. (5)

Kroll's Pyramid   A conceptualization of the relationship between personality and performance predicts that at the entry level a great many people will be participating, which results in a great variety of personality characteristics evident at this level. As the athlete progresses up the pyramid, the personalities encountered are much more homogenous. The system therefore perpetuates the homogeneity of personalities at the elite levels. (9)

lactic acid   A by-product of anaerobic metabolism. High concentrations of lactic acid in the muscle and blood result in fatigue. (5)

law   A statement describing a sequence of events in nature or human activities that has been observed to occur with unvarying uniformity under the same conditions. (2)

lean body mass   Body mass comprised of muscle, bone, and organs. (6)

lesson plan   A teacher's guide for instruction that will occur in a single lesson and should be based on the objectives stated in the unit plan. (10)

lever A rigid object that revolves around a fixed point called a fulcrum or axis. (3)

life-cycle model A model of team cohesion that implies that cohesion improves throughout early stages of development only to wane as the group eventually dispands. (9)

lift The component of air resistance that is directed at right angles to the drag force. (4)

ligaments Connective tissues that attach bone to bone. (3)

linear model A model of team cohesion that suggests cohesion progresses in a linear fashion as the team develops. (9)

linear motion The motion that occurs when the body moves in such a way that all parts of it travel the same distance in the same time and follow the same directional path. Linear motion can be in a straight line or can follow a curved path. (4)

lipoprotein A compound of cholesterol and protein. Lipoproteins are important because they are the main form of transport for fat in the blood. (6)

list services Services that allow large groups of individuals to communicate with each other across the internet via electronic mail to discuss a topic of interest. Many of these groups that are interested in topics addressed in this text are listed at the end of each chapter. (Appendix)

locomotion The means by which we move about and interact with our environment. While most of us consider walking the primary mode of locomotion, the motor developmentalist also considers creeping and crawling. (7)

locomotor reflex Reflexive responses that resemble later voluntary locomotor responses. The stepping reflex exhibited by a child, for example, is a locomotor reflex. (7)

longitudinal method A research approach in which specific individuals can be selected as the focus of a study and can be followed over a set period of time. Development can be directly observed and recorded and not just inferred. (7)

long-term memory A type of memory that is characterized by an extremely large capacity to hold a variety of types of information including that related to movement. (7)

low-density lipoprotein (LDL) A type of lipoprotein that can carry a large amount of cholesterol. LDL, the bad cholesterol, carries cholesterol from the liver to other body cells. High concentrations of LDL are associated with cardiovascular risk. Diets high in saturated fats will increase LDL. (6)

Magnus Effect A phenomenon that refers to the production of lift due to spin being imparted on an object such as a ball. It is this effect that is primarily responsible for the "curve" in the curveball in baseball. (4)

management episode A period that begins with the teacher initiating a management behavior (e.g., calling role) and continues until the next instructional activity begins. (10)

manual control Controlled movement of the arms and hands in order to manipulate objects. The stages of progression for manual control are usually categorized as reaching, grasping, and releasing behaviors. (7)

mass The amount of matter that makes up a body; a measure of the body's resistance to having its current state of motion, which is called inertia, changed. (4)

massed practice Occurs when practice sessions are organized such that practice intervals are longer than the rest intervals. (8)

maturation Progress toward the optimum integration and functioning of body systems. (7)

maturational theory A theory proposing that a child reaches particular developmental landmarks dictated by heredity. This perspective does not include a role for environmental factors in the development process. (7)

mature movement pattern Movement pattern that is sufficiently developed that it meets sport skill form. (7)

maximum aerobic capacity (VO$_2$max) Estimated as the point at which oxygen uptake plateaus and does not increase with further increases in workload; heart rate increases to age-predicted maximum (220 – age), or volitional exhaustion. Subjects who reach their maximum aerobic capacity cannot continue to work at that intensity for more than a minute or two because their demand for oxygen exceeds their ability to supply oxygen. (6)

mean The arithmetic average obtained by adding up all the scores in the distribution and dividing that sum by the total number of scores. (2)

measurement A value taken to represent a quality or quantity of person, place, or thing. Measurements can be further classified according to their purpose as placement/diagnostic, formative, or summative measurements. (2)

mechanical advantage The ratio of the length of the force arm to the resistance arm. (3)

median The exact middle of the distribution of scores; half the scores fall on one side and half on the other. (2)

membrane potential A chemical imbalance that creates an electric tension across the cell membrane. This process is crucial for the passage of the action potential along the entire length of the cell membrane. (3)

memory Within the information processing framework, a storage location. A number of different storage locations have been inferred including: sensory memory, short-term memory, and long-term memory. Each of the memory systems can be identi-

fied via a number of characteristics including: coding form, duration, and capacity limitations. (7)

mental practice Practice involving mentally rehearsing the performance of a skill in the absence of any overt physical practice. Often mental practice is associated with mental imagery but this is not always the case. (8)

metabolism The sum of chemical reactions that include energy production and energy utilization. (5)

midsagittal plane An anatomical plane of the body that runs through the midline that is perpendicular to the ground. This plane splits the body into right and left halves. (3)

minerals Inorganic substances that perform a wide range of vital functions throughout the body. There are two forms of essential minerals: macrominerals, which are needed in relatively large amounts (greater than 100 milligrams per day), and microminerals, or trace minerals, which are needed in very small amounts (less than 100 milligrams per day). (6)

mobility The amount of movement that can occur before being restricted by surrounding tissue. (3)

mode The most frequently occurring score. (2)

moderate exercise Exercise that elicits a cardiovascular response of between 40 and 60 percent of VO$_2$max. (6)

moment arm The perpendicular distance from the direction of the applied force to the axis or point of rotation. Torque can be increased by lengthening the moment arm. (4)

moment of inertia The combination of the object's mass and distribution of the mass. (4)

momentum The product of the mass of the body and velocity. Essentially, momentum is the quantity of motion a body possesses. (4)

Mosaic A web browser. (Appendix)

motivation   The level of choice, effort, and persistence in direction and intensity of effort. (9)

motoneuronal pool   A group of motor units that can be activated as a group. The force exerted by a muscle usually comes from the combined activity of many motor-units. (3)

motor control   Field of study aimed at understanding the processes that lead to the execution of human movement and the factors that affect the execution of these processes. (1, 8)

motor development   The study of changes in growth and maturation across the life span and the influence of these changes on motor performance. (1, 7)

motor learning   Field of study aimed at understanding the way in which the processes that subserve movement are developed and the factors that facilitate or inhibit this development. (1, 8)

motor-unit   A motor neuron and the muscle fibers it innervates. (3)

movement pattern   The basic functional structure of a fundamental motor skill. This usually entails a description of how a movement unfolds in time and space. This is also referred to as a motor pattern. (7)

muscle fasciculus   A bundle of up to 150 muscle fibers. (3)

muscle fibers   Cylindrical cells that lie in parallel and are separated by a layer of connective tissue. (3)

muscle spindle   Proprioceptive receptor located in the muscle that informs the mover about stretch and the rate of change of stretch in the muscle.

muscular endurance   The ability to sustain a resistance for a period of time. Muscular endurance implies that a given level of muscular work can be continued for a relatively long period of time. (6)

myelinated nerve fibers   Nerve fibers that are surrounded by a myelin sheath that provides insulation from other fibers. Myelin consists of 70–80% lipids and 20–30% protein. (3)

myocardium   The muscle comprising the heart. Heart cells are interconnected such that an action potential spreads throughout the muscle tissue. In this way heart muscle works as a unit. (5)

myofibrils   The threadlike structures in the muscle that contain the proteins essential for contraction. Many myofibrils comprise a muscle cell or fiber. (3)

myosin   A thick protein filament found in the myofibrils that is important to the contraction process. (3)

nature–nuture   An issue in motor development that revolves around whether an individual' genetic make-up or learning experiences dictate development. (7)

Naughton protocol   A discontinuous treadmill exercise test in which the first 15 minutes requires relatively slow walking, the 3-minute stages alternate between rest and walking at increasing speed and elevation. This treadmill protocol is used with cardiac and high-risk patients. (6)

netiquette   Basic informal rules used to measure appropriate behavior on the internet (Appendix).

Netscape   A web browser. (Appendix)

neurons   Cells that receive and send messages throughout the nervous system. Your brain contains 100 to 200 billion neurons, and each one connects with many others. (3)

Newton's first law   A body continues in a state of rest or uniform motion until acted upon by an external force of sufficient magnitude to disturb this state. (4)

Newton's second law   Acceleration of the body is proportional to the force exerted on it and inversely proportional to its mass. (4)

Newton's third law   Every action has an equal and opposite reaction. This law refers to the way in which forces act against each other. (4)

nonaxial joint A joint that does not exhibit angular movement. The movement that this type of joint supports is a gliding motion. (3)

normal curve A normal curve is symmetrical (left half is a mirror image of the right half) so that the mean, median, and mode are identical and the scores cluster about the mean in a very special way such that the distribution has a bell shape. (2)

nutrients The components of food needed by the body. There are six classes of nutrients: protein, carbohydrates, fats, vitamins, minerals, and water. (6)

objectivity The extent to which personal or situational factors influence measurements. (2)

observational practice Practice that involves observing the performance of others. (8)

open environments Situation in which the performance conditions are continually changing. (8)

open-loop control A movement executed from beginning to end by predetermined instructions. Feedback is not used to change these instructions while the movement is being executed. (8)

operations research Research that involves the testing of the impact, control, and management strategies required to optimize the implementation of new techniques into real-world settings. At this level, principles discovered in the laboratory and confirmed in applied experiments may still be found impractical or too costly for implementation. (2)

overload principle The finding that training effects only occur when a physiological system is exercised at an unaccustomed level. A system that experiences overload responds, within some limits, with gradual

adaptations that increase the capacity of the system. (6)

paradigm The plan for an experiment. (2)

part–whole practice Practice in which one or more parts of a task are practiced independently. Wightman and Lintern (1985) identified three methods for constructing part practice; fractionation, simplification, and segmentation. (8)

peak performance A time period in which an individual exhibits peak physiological function that contributes to maximal motor performance. This is generally assumed to occur between 25–30 years of age. (7)

pedagogy The skillful arrangement of an environment in such a way that students acquire specifically intended learnings. (10)

pedagogical-content knowledge A teacher's repertoire of methods for presenting content knowledge. (10)

pendular model A model of team cohesion that suggests that cohesion is in a continual state of oscillation. (9)

perception The act of utilizing long-term memory to organize, classify, and/or interpret sensations. (8)

perimysium Connective tissue that surrounds a bundle of 150 or more muscle fibers. (3)

peripheral fatigue Fatigue arising from the neuromuscular system (motor neuron, neuromuscular junction, muscle). (5)

peripheral nervous system (PNS) The communication network that transmits information to (i.e., sensory) and from (i.e., motor) the CNS. The PNS is made up of sensory nerves that relay messages from the senses back to the CNS. In addition, the PNS also contains motor nerves that take the commands from the CNS to the muscles that will be involved in executing a movement. (3)

peripheral processes Information processing activities that involve the activation of sensory receptors and muscles as well as the transmission to (afferent) and from (efferent) the CNS. (8)

personality   A description of an individual's characteristic patterns of behavior that contribute to his or her uniqueness. (9)

placement and diagnostic measurements   Measurements that are taken for the purpose of classifying individuals. These measurements may be used to place subjects into groups with similar characteristics or to determine the extent to which a subject possesses a particular characteristic. (2)

population   All the persons or experimental units that meet a particular set of conditions (male, female, right-handed, blue-eyed, college student). (2)

postural reflex   Provide the infant the opportunity to respond to gravity and changes in equilibrium. (7)

postulate   Assumption based on theory and not grounded in fact, a basic principle derived without proof. (2)

power   The ability to generate force very rapidly and is calculated as the product of force and velocity (speed). (6)

practice composition   Practice manipulations that vary the number of tasks or task variations intermingled in a practice session or that vary the manner in which a task is practiced (physical, mental, observational, or simulated practice). (8)

practice distribution   Practice manipulations that vary the practice–rest intervals. Generally this involves changing the ratio of practice time to rest time within blocks of trials but also includes manipulations of the time between practice sessions. (8)

practice scheduling   Practice manipulations that cause a change in the conditions under which, or the context within which, a specific task is executed. Manipulating the order with which tasks are learned or manipulating practice–rest intervals are examples of practice scheduling. (8)

predictive validity   The extent to which a measurement or test is capable of predicting performance on another measurement or test. Entrance exams like the SAT (college), MCAT (medical), GMAT (business), or GRE (graduate) are said to have high predictive validity if high scores on the exam are related to future success in the program. (2)

preprogramming   Advanced planning that occurs when an individual organizes and prepares a response prior to the signal to respond. (7)

preservice   All activities (e.g., coursework, student teaching, internship, practicum) that are used to prepare an individual to enter the workplace with the necessary skills to be successful. (10)

primitive reflex   A reflex, exhibited by the fetus, associated with ensuring that the child can obtain nourishment and secure protection. (7)

problem-solving approach   An approach to inservice characterized by teacher input. This method generally addresses problems that have been diagnosed by the teachers. (10)

process-oriented approach   An approach that emphasizes the study of the cognitive and motor processes and mechanisms underlying movement. Researchers who employ this approach feel that these processes and mechanisms can be exposed and ultimately understood by carefully manipulating experimental conditions and observing the changes in behavior. (8)

profile drag   A form of drag created when the flow of air past an object reunites behind the object. This forms a low pressure pocket of air behind the object that actually exerts a "pulling" effect on the object impeding its forward motion. (4)

progressive resistance exercise.   A common method of strength training that involves the practical application of the overload principle. As the exercised muscle group becomes stronger the resistance is increased correspondingly. (6)

prompt Information presented to the student that directs behavior in a particular direction that is appropriate for meeting the demands of the task at hand. Prompts can be as diverse as verbal instructions to a hand signal presented during a baseball game. (10)

proprioceptors Sensory receptors that receive stimuli that provide information about the current state of our body. These include the vestibular apparatus, muscle spindles, and Golgi tendon organs, as well as various pressure and temperature receptors. (3, 8)

protein A compound composed of complex chains of amino acids, the major structural components of all body tissue. Every cell in our body contains protein, which is necessary for tissue growth and repair. Proteins are components of hormones, enzymes, cellular structures, and blood transport systems. (6)

protocol The rules used by computers to communicate with one another. (A)

proximodistal Growth that proceeds from the center of the body to the periphery. (7)

psychodynamic perspective A perspective that suggests that behavior is determined "for" an individual rather than "by" an individual; also called the deterministic perspective. (9)

P-wave A part of a typical ECG that represents the depolarization and subsequent contraction of the atria. (6)

QRS complex A part of a typical ECG, caused by the depolarization and subsequent contraction of the ventricles. (6)

radiation A form of heat transfer through the air from one object to another. For example, heat radiation from the sun is transferred to a person exercising in the sun as well as the ground and other objects. (5)

range A measure of the spread of a set of scores, calculated by subtracting the lowest from the highest score. (2)

range of motion The total amount of movement through which the components of the articulation can pass; also referred to as flexibility. (3)

ratings of perceived exertion (RPE) A subjective judgment of exercise exertion. (6)

rectilinear motion Movement that follows a straight line. (4)

reflex An involuntary movement response elicited by a variety of sensory stimuli including a sound, light, or touch. (7)

regression (a) A set of statistical procedures that use, in a mathematical sense, the correlation between two or more variables to construct an equation that best summarizes the relationship(s). In many cases the relationship is linear or a straight line, but this is not always the case. (2)

regression (b) The fact that cardiorespiratory function, muscle strength, and psychomotor functioning decrease past a certain age. (7)

reliability A measure of consistency with which a variable is recorded under a specific measurement scheme. (2)

research on teacher education in physical education (RTE-PE) Research that concentrates on what and how to teach teachers of motor skills. (10)

research on teaching in physical education (RT-PE) Research that concentrates on the factors that influence how we teach motor skills. (10)

residual volume (RV) The amount of air remaining in the lungs during a maximal inspiration and expiration. Residual volume tends to increase with age. Thus inspiration and expiration reserves become smaller with age. (6)

resistance arm   The length of a lever between the fulcrum and the resistance. (3)

response execution   A phase of information processing concerned with developing and executing a movement plan. (8)

response selection   A phase of information processing concerned with deciding on a plan of action or inaction. (8)

retention   Delayed practice experiences (test or game) on a task that was experienced during acquisition. If we practice a task and then are tested at a later time on that task, the test would be considered a retention test. (8)

reticular formation   A mass of interwoven neurons extending from the brainstem to the thalamus. Lesions of the reticular formation cause a dramatic decrease in the level of arousal experienced by an individual. (9)

routine   A set procedure for performing specific behaviors that can occur relatively frequently during the course of a class period. (10)

rule   General expectations for either acceptable or unacceptable behavior for a variety of situations that might arise during the course of the class period. (10)

sample   A subset of a population. The experimenter desires to use a sample that is representative of the population since it is rarely feasible to test an entire population. (2)

sarcolemma   The cell membrane of a muscle fiber. (3)

sarcomeres   The part of the muscle fiber that actually shortens during contraction. Sarcomeres are separated by a thin disc of protein referred to as a z-line. Within each sarcomere are areas in which the actin and myosin filaments overlap and regions in which they do not overlap. (3)

sarcoplasmic reticulum   A network of membranes in a muscle cell that surrounds and runs parallel with the myofibrils. The sarcoplasmic reticulum is the storage site for calcium. (3)

schema   An abstraction or a set of rules for determining a movement prototype (Schmidt, 1975). (8)

second-class lever   A lever with a fulcrum at one end and the resistance applied closer to it than the force. (3)

segmentation   A form of part–whole practice that involves partitioning the skill along spatial or temporal dimensions. (8)

senile macular degeneration (SMD)   One of the most prevalent causes of loss of visual acuity in the elderly caused by a reduction in the number of photoreceptors, a reduced blood supply to the retina, and loss of ocular reflexes. (7)

sensation   Sensory information detected and/or selected from the continual barrage of transmissions constantly impacting the central nervous system. (8)

sensitive period   A time frame in motor development in which an individual is particularly ready to learn a specific motor skill. (7)

sensory memory   A type of memory characterized by its capacity to hold an incredible amount of information for a very short period of time (~1 s). (7)

sequential method   A research approach that incorporates aspects of both the longitudinal and cross-sectional methods. Another term used for this method is the mixed-longitudinal method. This procedure involves studying several different samples (i.e., cross-sectional) over a number of years (i.e., longitudinal). This design allows subjects differing in age or educational background, for example, to be compared at the same time, in order to identify any current behavioral differences. (7)

set-point theory   A concept introduced by researchers who think that every individual has an internal hypothalamic thermostat regulating weight. The body is comfortable at this point and may even defend that particular weight even if dietary changes begin to invoke weight change. Genetics, body type, body size, gender, and dietary habits all may affect how an individual reacts to energy imbalances. (6)

short-term memory   A type of memory characterized by a limited capacity of about seven pieces of information that can reside in this storage space for 30–60 s. (7)

simplification   A form of part–whole practice that involves reducing the demands of one or more of the task components so as to reduce the overall difficulty or complexity of the skill. (8)

sinoatrial node (S-A node)   A specialized heart tissue that when stimulated, causes the action potential to spread throughout the atria. This causes the atria to contract and in turn stimulates a second specialized tissue called the atrioventricular node (A-V node). (5)

size principle   The most popular theory of how orderly recruitment of motor units is controlled. According to the theory, the sequence depends on the size of the motor neurons. Motor-units with the smallest motor neurons are recruited first and deactivated last. Motor-units with the largest motor neurons are recruited last and deactivated first. (3)

skeleton   The bony structures of the body, which can be divided into two separate subsections, the axial and the appendicular skeleton. (3)

skinfold   A method of determining body fat that utilizes a special pair of calipers to determine the thickness of folds of skin at various sites on the body surface. Depending on the method used, the sites used to take skinfold measurements may be weighted differently for males and females. The skinfold measurements are entered into an equation in order to estimate body density and percent body fat. (6)

skin temperature   Body temperature measured on the surface of the skin. (5)

slow twitch fibers   A type of muscle fiber with the capacity for relatively high aerobic metabolism, resulting in a high resistance to fatigue. The neuron that activates slow twitch fibers is generally smaller and slower conducting than that of fast twitch fibers. Slow twitch fibers are generally smaller than fast twitch fibers. (3)

social facilitation   A phenomenon in which an individual's performance is facilitated when performance occurs in a group setting. (9)

social inhibition   A phenomenon in which an individual's performance is negatively affected when performance occurs in a group setting. (9)

socialization perspective   A perspective that places a heavy emphasis on the values, beliefs, and attitudes of the teacher and on the factors that impact these characteristics throughout the teacher's career. (10)

spatial awareness   An ability to draw inference as to our location in space within the environment in which we are moving. An interaction between visual and kinesthetic information is presumably very important to perform this function successfully. (7)

specific gravity   The ratio of body weight and the weight of an equal volume of water. An individual will float if his or her specific gravity is less than or equal to one but will sink if it is greater than one. (4)

specificity of practice   A hypothesis that proposes that motor skills are specific and only superficially resemble other similar motor skills. This implies that changing the motor task only slightly produces a new motor task for which a new motor program must be developed. (8)

specificity principle The finding that physiological adaptations are specific to the components of a system that are overloaded during exercise. (6)

speed The distance covered divided by the time it takes to cover the distance; average velocity. (4)

speed–accuracy trade-off The findings that when we increase the speed with which we do something, we tend to increase the errors we make. To perform more accurately we must slow down. This basic principle is that performers must trade off speed in order to increase accuracy or trade off accuracy to increase speed. (8)

sphygmomanometer A blood pressure cuff used to estimate the pressure in the arterial system. Systolic blood pressure is measured during systole and diastolic blood pressure is measured during diastole. Normal blood pressure in an adult male is 120/80 (systolic/diastolic) and 110/70 in adult females. (5, 6)

spinal cord A part of the central nervous system composed of nerve tissue running from the brainstem through the backbone to the lower back. It contains a "bent H" of gray matter surrounded by white matter. The gray area is composed of unmyelinated nerve fibers; the white area contains myelinated fibers. The white matter carries information to and from the brain. Ascending nerves carry sensory information up to the brain. Descending nerves carry commands down from the brain to the muscles. (3)

spinal reflex Automatic action by the spinal cord such as the patellar tendon (knee jerk) reflex. (3)

spirometer A device used to measure the volumes and capacities of the lungs. This device and the measurements it provides may be helpful in detecting and quantifying lung disease. (6)

sport pedagogy The discipline concerned with understanding and optimizing the process of teaching movement skills. (1)

sport psychology The discipline concerned with the study of effect of psychological factors on behavior and the effect of participation on those psychological factors. (1)

stability Resistance to a disruption in the equilibrium of the body. (4)

stall angle The point at which lift force is eliminated and drag force increases abruptly. (4)

standard deviation A measure of variability expressed in the same units of measurement as the raw scores. The standard deviation is the square root of the variance. (2)

state anxiety A temporary personality characteristic in which an individual experiences a temporary elevation in anxiety when exposed to specific situations. (9)

statics The study of a system when it is in a state of constant motion, such as when the body is either motionless (at rest) or moving with a constant velocity. (4)

stroboscopy A lighting technique that enables the experimenter to superimpose many images on a single photograph. During the filming of a movement, a flashing light (strobe) turns on or off at a predetermined rate (e.g., 60 Hz). The camera records each image during the lighted period on top of the previously recorded image. (4)

stroke volume The amount of blood pumped by the heart in one beat. Stroke volume increases as a result of training and is related to both the increased contractile capacity of the heart muscle and the increased venous return to the heart. Increased cardiac output with training results primarily from increased stroke volume. (5)

student teaching   Typically the culminating experience in a teacher education program in which a student spends approximately 16 weeks teaching in a school environment while being supervised by a cooperating teacher. (10)

subjective warrant   An individual's perceptions of the skills and abilities necessary for entry into, and performance of, work in a specific occupation. (10)

summation   When the frequency of stimulation is such that the force from one stimulation adds to the force from a previous stimulation. (3)

summative measurements   Measurements taken after a research or training sequence in order to assess the "sum effect" of the treatment, program, or intervention. (2)

surface drag   The resistance experienced by a body that is a result of the fluid rubbing against the surface of that body. (4)

synapse   A junction between two neurons. (3)

synarthrodial articulation   A type of articulation that minimizes movement. The sutures between bones in the skull that allow a minute amount of movement to occur are an example of this type of articulation. (3)

synergy   A functional grouping of muscles that may be controlled as a group. Also referred to as a coordinative structure. (8)

systematic desensitization   A widely used procedure based on the counterconditioning model. This technique is designed to countercondition anxiety gradually using relaxation as the incompatible response. According to the basic principle of counterconditioning, the relaxation response will ultimately become associated with the stimulus that previously led to the display of anxiety. (9)

systole   The contractile phase of the cardiac cycle. During systole the pressures in the respective ventricles increase rapidly until they exceed the pressure in the pulmonary artery and aorta. At this point blood is pumped into both the pulmonary and systemic circulation. (5)

task method   A teaching method that involves encouraging the student to accept more responsibility for the manner in which the task is practiced. (10)

task-oriented approach   An approach that emphasizes the study of the effect of environmental conditions and specific task conditions on performance without regard to the underlying cognitive processes. (8)

Telnet   A means of accessing the resources of a remote computer (Appendix).

tendons   Connective tissue that attaches muscle to bone. (3)

tetanus   The blending together of contractions. (3)

thalamus   Two egg-shaped structures located above the hypothalamus that integrate incoming sensory information from all parts of the body. (3)

theoretical   Based on theory rather than observation and/or literature. (2)

theory   A proposed explanation or statement of the processes that account for the lawful phenomenon. (2)

thermoregulation   The processes that protect an individual from heat stress by regulating core temperature. Body heat can be lost or gained by radiation, conduction, convection, and/or evaporation. (5)

third-class lever   A lever in which the fulcrum is at the end of the lever but the force is applied closer to it than to the resistance. Third-class levers are prevalent in the human body. (3)

tidal volume (TV)   The amount of air moved during inspiration or expiration during normal ventilation. (6)

top-down reasoning The development of hypotheses based on theory and deduction. Typically, the hypothesis is derived as a result of the predictions of a theory. (2)

torque The turning effect that can be exerted on a body; the product of force and the length of the moment arm. (4)

total cholesterol The total amount of cholesterol in blood that can be divided into two classes depending on the compound called lipoprotein that is carrying the cholesterol. (6)

total lung capacity (TLC) The sum of the residual lung volume and vital capacity. (6)

trachea The air passage way from the mouth to the lungs where air is filtered, humidified, and adjusted to body temperature. (5)

training-sensitive zone An exercise intensity that elicits a heart rate between 70 and 90 percent of age-predicted maximum heart rate. Heart rates in this zone assure that the individual is exercising at an intensity sufficient to overload the aerobic system and therefore invoke a training effect. The lower and upper limits should be used only as a guideline for healthy, active individuals. (6)

trait anxiety A personality characteristic that implies that an individual is predisposed to experiencing anxiety when faced with a wide range of everyday situations. (9)

traits Relatively enduring intrapersonal characteristics that account for unique yet stable behaviors to events in the environment. (9)

transfer Delayed practice experiences (test or game) on a variation of the task or on another task that was not experienced during acquisition. (8)

transfer paradigm An experimental protocol that involves experimental groups being tested on a task of interest after a sufficient time delay, usually exceeding short-term memory duration limits, while being exposed to the same level of the independent variable. (8)

translation Movement of the body as a unit without individual parts of the unit moving in relation to one another. Another term often used for translation is linear movement. (4)

transverse plane The plane of the body that divides the human body into a top and bottom half; also referred to as the horizontal plane. (3)

transverse tubules The plumbing extending into the myofibrils for spreading the action potential from the outside to the inner regions of the cell. When a nerve impulse crosses the neuromuscular junction it travels down the transverse tubules. (3)

triaxial joint A joint that permits movement in three planes. A more common name for this type of joint is the ball-and-socket joint. (3)

t-test A statistical procedure used to determine if two means are significantly different from each other or if a mean is significantly different from a population value. This procedure considers not only how far apart the means are but how variable the scores are about the mean. (2)

tuberosity A raised section of a bone that provides an ideal location for tendon, ligament, or muscle to attach to the bone. (3)

T-wave A part of a typical ECG that represents the repolarization of the ventricles. (6)

uniaxial joint A joint that allows movement around a single axis. This type of joint is often referred to as a hinge joint. (3)

unit plan A teacher's map of a group of lessons that revolve around a particular theme. (10)

universality Perspective adopted in motor development that assumes that the development process follows approximately the same path for each individual. (7)

Usenet   A collection of news servers distributed around the internet. Usenet is organized according to subject of interest. (A).

validity   The extent to which a measurement tool measures what it was intended to measure. Validity can be assessed mathematically or determined on logical grounds. (2)

variability   The dispersion or scatter of the scores. Distributions with low variability have scores that are tightly clustered, while high variability indicates a large spread between scores. Measures of variability include range, variance, and standard deviation. (2)

variability   Perspective adopted in motor development that pays close attention to individual differences since the assumption is that each person can develop in a unique fashion. (7)

variability hypothesis   A hypothesis that proposes that variable but related practice experiences enhance the memory states responsible for motor control. This hypothesis was derived from schema theory. (8)

variance   A measure of variability computed as the average of the squared deviations from the mean; the sum of the squared differences from the mean divided by the number of squared deviations. (2)

variant features   The absolute characteristics of a generalizable motor program that must be specified to produce a movement. The variant features are thought to include the specific muscles to be used, the actual force, and actual timing of the movement. (8)

veins   The vessels that return blood to the heart. (5)

velocity   The amount of displacement across time. (4)

ventricle   The heart chambers that pump the blood to the lungs or body. (5)

videography   An emerging technique used to study human kinematics based on video technology. (4)

viewer   A third-party software application (usually shareware) that can be used within a web browser to view graphics, video, or listen to sound. (Appendix)

vigorous exercise   Exercise that elicites a response greater than 60 percent VO_2max. (6)

vitamins   Organic substances that the body needs in small amounts but cannot manufacture itself. Vitamins play a role in proper functioning of nerves and muscles, in releasing energy from foods, and in promoting normal growth of body tissues. Vitamins provide no calories and cannot be used as a fuel. (6)

walking   A movement that shifts weight from one foot to the other, with at least one foot contacting the surface at all times. (7)

wave drag   A form of drag on a performer that is created by the production of waves. (4)

weight   The force with which the earth pulls on the body's mass. (4)

wellness   A term used to capture general health and fitness and includes emotional, intellectual, spiritual, interpersonal, social, and environmental well-being. (6)

with disease   A classification of health risk where the individual has diagnosed cardiac, pulmonary, or metabolic disease. An exercise program for individuals with disease should be initiated only with a physician's approval. (6)

work   Mechanical work is the product of force and distance. Biological work occurs whenever energy is liberated, heat is produced, and forces are applied even though movement may not occur. (5)

Index